T0251440

Second Edition

Cybervetting

Internet Searches for Vetting, Investigations, and Open-Source Intelligence

Second Edition

Cybervetting

Internet Searches for Vetting, Investigations, and Open-Source Intelligence

Edward J. Appel

CRC Press
Taylor & Francis Group
Boca Raton London New York

CRC Press is an imprint of the
Taylor & Francis Group, an **informa** business

CRC Press
Taylor & Francis Group
6000 Broken Sound Parkway NW, Suite 300
Boca Raton, FL 33487-2742

© 2015 by Taylor & Francis Group, LLC
CRC Press is an imprint of Taylor & Francis Group, an Informa business

No claim to original U.S. Government works

Printed on acid-free paper
Version Date: 20140623

International Standard Book Number-13: 978-1-4822-3885-3 (Hardback)

This book contains information obtained from authentic and highly regarded sources. Reasonable efforts have been made to publish reliable data and information, but the author and publisher cannot assume responsibility for the validity of all materials or the consequences of their use. The authors and publishers have attempted to trace the copyright holders of all material reproduced in this publication and apologize to copyright holders if permission to publish in this form has not been obtained. If any copyright material has not been acknowledged please write and let us know so we may rectify in any future reprint.

Library of Congress Cataloging-in-Publication Data

Appel, Edward J.
 [Internet searches for vetting, investigations, and open-source intelligence]
 Cybervetting : Internet searches for vetting, investigations, and open-source intelligence / Edward J. Appel, Sr.
   pages cm
 Completely revised edition of the author's Internet searches for vetting, investigations, and open-source intelligence.
 Includes bibliographical references and index.
 ISBN 978-1-4822-3885-3 (alk. paper)
 1. Employee screening. 2. Criminal investigation. 3. Internet searching. 4. Employee crimes--Prevention. 5. Computer crimes--Prevention. 6. Personnel management--Information technology. 7. Business enterprises--Security measures. I. Title.

HF5549.5.E429A67 2015
363.25′202854678--dc23   2014021634

Visit the Taylor & Francis Web site at
http://www.taylorandfrancis.com

and the CRC Press Web site at
http://www.crcpress.com

To my wife, Kathy, my guide in composing life's final chapters

Contents

Introduction xiii

About the Author xix

SECTION I BEHAVIOR AND TECHNOLOGY

1 The Internet's Potential for Investigators and Intelligence Officers 3
Introduction 3
Growth of Internet Use 4
A Practitioner's Perspective 12
The Search 13
Internet Posts and the People They Profile 16
Finding the Needles 19
The Need for Speed 19
Sufficiency of Searches 20
Notes 20

2 Behavior Online 25
Internet Use Growth 25
Evolution of Internet Uses 29
Physical World, Virtual Activities 34
Connections and Disconnecting 34
Notes 37

3 Use and Abuse: Crime and Misbehavior Online 39
Introduction 39
By the Numbers? 40
Online Venues 41
Digital Delinquency 42
"Free" Intellectual Property 42
The Insider 44
Misbehavior Online 46
Notes 46

4 Internet Search Studies **49**
Introduction 49
Academic Study 50
    Study Summary 51
iNameCheck Cybervetting Case Study...54
Notes 57

5 Implications for the Enterprise...**59**
Introduction 59
The New User: Someone You Would Trust? 60
Employer Liability 61
Vetting, Monitoring, and Accountability.......................................62
The Evolving Personnel Security Model...65
Notes 69

SECTION II LEGAL AND POLICY CONTEXT

6 Liability, Privacy, and Management Issues **75**
Liability for Service Providers 75
Liability for Employers...77
Accountability for Employees 79
Notes 81

7 Laws...**83**
Introduction 83
Constitutional Rights 83
Statutes 85
    Federal Statutes..85
    State Statutes 89
Federal Rules of Evidence and Computer Records..........................91
International Treaties and Standards 93
US Legislative Proposals 94
Notes 95

8 Litigation..**97**
Introduction 97
Internet Search Litigation 97
Anonymity..99
Expectation of Privacy 100
Due Process 103
Libel/Defamation 105
Invasion of Privacy Torts..107
Sanctions for Public Postings 107
Internet Privacy for the Twenty-First Century 108

Admissibility of Electronically Generated and Stored Evidence 111
Trends and Legal Challenges to Investigative Searching 112
Notes 112

9   **International and Domestic Principles** **117**
Us and International Privacy Principles... 117
Government Standards 122
Parallel Guidance: Internet Research Ethics 125
Notes 125

10   **Professional Standards and the Internet** **127**
Introduction 127
ASIS Standards 128
National Association of Professional Background Screeners.................... 131
Association of Internet Researchers... 132
Librarians.. 135
Inside and Outside the Workplace 136
Reputational Risk, Public Affairs... 137
Bottom Line 138
Notes 138

11   **The Insider Threat** **141**
Introduction 141
Benevolent Big Brother 143
Notes 145

SECTION III   FRAMEWORK FOR INTERNET SEARCHING

12   **Internet Vetting and Open-Source Intelligence Policy**....................... **149**
Introduction 149
Legal and Ethical Limitations.. 150
Policy.. 153
Information Assets Protection.. 155
Notes 156

13   **Tools, Techniques, and Training**... **157**
Introduction 157
Training Analysts... 162
Open-Source Intelligence Process 163
Quality Control... 166
Notes 168

14   **Proper Procedures for Internet Searching**... **169**
Introduction 169
Criteria 170

Security 172
Standard Methodology 175
Notes 175

SECTION IV   INTERNET SEARCH METHODOLOGY

15 Preparation and Planning **179**
Introduction 179
The Library 182
Scope Notes 184
Notes 186

16 Search Techniques **189**
Introduction 189
Internet Content 189
The Browser 190
The Search Engine 191
Metasearch Engines 195
Finding Search Engines 195
Search Terms 196
Social and Commercial Searching 197
        Social Networking Sites 197
        E-Commerce Sites 202
        Directories 204
        Blogs 205
        Chat 205
Notes 206

17 Finding Sources **209**
Introduction 209
US Government 210
State, County, and Local Governments 211
Other Government-Related Sources 213
Business-Related Sources 214
News 215
Web 2.0 215
Looking Up Subscribers 219
E-Mail 221
Commercial Database Providers 222
Notes 223

18 Automation of Searching **225**
Introduction 225
Why Automate Searching? 226

Enterprise Search Middleware 227
Best-in-Class Desktop Tool...229
Investigative Search Tool Requirements.....................................229
A Homegrown Solution 231
Reducing Analytical Time Using Automation 231
Caching and Data Mining...232
The Human Interface in Internet Investigations 233
Notes 235

19 Internet Intelligence Reporting...237
Introduction 237
Records..238
Content..238
Analyst's Comments 240
Organization and Formatting..241
Source Citations...243
Attribution...243
Verification 244
Notes 247

20 Illicit Websites and Illegal Behavior Online 249
Introduction 249
Cybercrime 249
    Child Pornography and Internet Porn...................................250
    Unauthorized Use of Computer Systems 251
    Contraband Digital Assets..253
Information (Cyber) Warfare 256
Notes 258

21 Model Cybervetting Investigative Guidelines.......................261
Introduction 261
Enterprise Strategy...261
Model Internet Search Guidelines 263
Authorized Internet Search (Cybervetting) Personnel...............265
Definitions to Consider 266
Notes 267

22 A Model Internet Investigation Policy 269
Introduction 269
Key Considerations...270
Higher-Risk Candidates..270
Application Procedures and Forms 271
Legal Issues..272
Confidentiality...273

Ethics in Investigations 273
Disciplinary Action 274
Model Forms for Candidates 274
Notes 276

23 A Model Internet Posting Policy **277**
Note 279

24 Internet Intelligence Issues **281**
Introduction 281
Privacy 281
Smoking Guns 283
Completeness of Internet Searching 284
Adjudication 285
Conclusion 286
Notes 287

Index **289**

Introduction

At the March 2014 RSA Conference in San Francisco, the usual discussions of the need for robust cryptography and sound computer functions to protect business and government were eclipsed by startling revelations by Edward Snowden, the National Security Agency (NSA) low-level contractor who copied a large quantity of top-secret files and gave them to the media and WikiLeaks, fleeing to Russia.[1] As Booz Allen Hamilton vice chairman Mike McConnell (former NSA director) said, "Snowden has compromised more capability than any spy in U.S. history ... and this will have impact on our ability to do our mission for the next 20 to 30 years."[2] Leading thinkers in cyber security at the conference, including Richard Clarke, Howard Schmidt, Scott Charney, and Bruce Schneier, ruminated about NSA spying revelations, the need to strengthen private-use cryptography, public-private collaboration on computer systems security, alternatives to US surveillance, and the implications that built-in flaws in information technology (IT) both empower and debilitate cyber security.

In the second edition of this book, it has been necessary to rewrite most of the first edition's content, so profound have been the changes since late 2010 in the Internet, cyber war, cyber security, cyber attacks of all kinds, social use of computers, and the World Wide Web—and enterprise inability to defend against or cope with all of these. Ubiquitous wireless connectivity, cheap data storage (both local and "in the cloud"), proliferating online devices, mass social networking, and seemingly ever-receding privacy are among the profound changes. In a way, Snowden's revelations appear to lack the "wow factor," when Anonymous and many other "hacktivists" claim to have penetrated every important government and business network, and major retailers, media outlets, utilities, government agencies, and Internet service providers admit almost daily to breaches jeopardizing millions of users. For public and private enterprises, IT has enabled improved efficiencies but has introduced increased levels of complexity and vulnerability that—at least 25 years into widely networked computing—still present a daunting challenge for enterprise and personal security.

Some of the more evident observations about the current phase of the Internet age are the growing dependence of Western society on networked systems for all of our critical infrastructures and our inability to protect them. While our military attempts to prepare for cyber war, its inability to defend us against cyber attacks by virtually anonymous state actors presents a striking contrast with the physically strongest armed forces on the planet. To paraphrase Lenin, we have fashioned the rope with which we can be hung. Black-hat hackers, cyber espionage, and cyber-crime appear to be able to overwhelm our private, business, and public systems. Ironically, while governments develop cyber weapons to enable them to wage and defend against cyber war, they are contributing to the cyber attackers' arsenals of hacking tools, which in their increasing sophistication enable growing groups of "script kiddies"—those with intent but few programming skills—to carry out attacks online. As we approach 25 years of widespread Internet use, we have yet to master how to plug the holes we created.

Individuals have also swallowed the same pills of technology that were adopted for government and business use and are nearly all connected 24-7 via the Internet on wireless, search-enabled devices by which they are constantly distracted, informed, empowered, and debilitated. Host networks and institutions are conflicted, needing to adopt the latest systems, but unable to fully defend them against error and mali-cious attacks. As the Great Recession of 2008 recedes slowly behind us, employers are in a strong position to demand accountability from employees and candidates, yet appear largely unable to do so if the use of computers is concerned. Human resources, legal, IT, and security functions have not yet fully grasped and integrated the implications of personal computing habits into enterprise systems architecture. Instead, each stage in the evolution of networked workers is a crisis to be addressed: bring your own device, connect at work, store personal data and contraband in work servers, use employers' Internet portals for personal web surfing, copy enterprise applications and data for personal purposes, freely express anti-employer sentiments on both intranet and Internet channels, and post impulsively for humor, harass-ment, or any private reason at all. Online activities at most employers are expected to include at least some personal Internet time in every workday. All of these examples can create nightmares for enterprise IT security and management.

As Stewart Baker, former NSA general counsel and assistant secretary of the Department of Homeland Security has noted, privacy will become a luxury avail-able to the privileged and rich as we balance privacy rights with security concerns. He does not worry so much about government surveillance, after 60 years of IT growth, as he does about private-sector and black-hat hacker (e.g., Anonymous) abuse and cyber warfare.[3] Protecting society as emerging technology presents increased risks and vulnerabilities will demand the sacrifice of privacy, as we struggle to adopt effective security measures. Similarly, Richard Clarke, antiterror-ism and cyber security coordinator for several US presidents, predicted that cyber attacks, both by nation-states and criminals, will result in additional billions of dol-lars in losses and could even become outright cyber war, waged by such nations as China and Iran.[4] Clarke noted that we cannot defend ourselves successfully against a cyber attack, especially when we cannot prove who conducted it.

As we confront the dangers, as well as the great opportunities presented by nearly ubiquitous all-the-time computing, it seems that privacy will remain a key unresolved (perhaps unresolvable) US Internet issue. However, even with the increased emphasis on individual control over personal data, Americans (particularly the young) appear prone to expose more of themselves online than ever before. Perhaps the desire for free online services (such as the collection by Google and Yahoo of user information to facilitate marketing) outweighs discretion. Like its employees, contractors, and customers, the American enterprise appears to believe that more exposure is better, and both businesses and governments have embraced social networking and websites as necessary means of interaction and transactions. The competing philosophies of exposure and protection of information only seem to tilt toward more security when disaster strikes, and then the expense and complexity of assurance—for a time—are accepted as costs of doing business. Because an estimated average of 10 million Americans face identity theft issues yearly,[5] it is time that they understood that institutions face similar challenges of balancing security with freedom.

A key concept of critical infrastructure protection, which appears to lack acceptance even after years of learning, from President Reagan's time to the present, is the need to ensure that each individual meets the standards of the agency or business and is held accountable for carrying out his or her role in security. If the words *human resource* (HR) or *human capital* have meaning beyond mere "personnel," it is that the right people, carefully chosen and fully supported, make a successful enterprise. However, paralysis and low budgets among the key actors in HR, legal, security, and IT departments often cause insufficient vetting (both before and after hiring); overreliance on technical measures to protect systems, networks, and data; and insufficient investment in employee orientation, training, supervision, mentoring, and monitoring to ensure information assurance. Because nearly every organization is dependent for its existence, operations, and progress on its information systems, even one malicious insider constitutes an unacceptable risk. At a time when corporations hoard cash and ignore the critical value of the individual insider, it is not surprising that catastrophic failures occur.

Annual reports by a range of public and private institutions chronicle the state of cyber security and the trends in motion. A large number of such reports were reviewed in the preparation of this book, some of which are end-noted. While I remain skeptical of the reliability and specific value of the statistics in cyber security reports, like the river flowing green in Chicago on St. Patrick's Day, one does not need to know how many gallons of coloring, by whom, or where the green dye was injected to observe that the river is now green. The state of our cyber security is unacceptably low. Unless we address the human factor, it will remain so.

This book is dedicated to intelligence, investigative, and research professionals who utilize the Internet in their duties, are of varying ages and technical capabilities, and may be constantly online or only search the Internet sporadically. Technology and societal changes require that all investigators adapt rapidly, and continually learn what is available, to collect online. Some institutions, businesses, and other organizations adapt more slowly than others. The law (statute, litigation, regulation) is also deliberate in addressing technological and social change. Because this book is about Internet intelligence methodology and legal frameworks, it is also about how to approach changes. Every effort has been made to keep this text forward looking, timely, useful, and adaptable to likely outcomes.

Open-source intelligence increasingly relies on fusion of data from all-source collection and analysis, with Internet data included. Such intelligence is a vital part of national security, competitive intelligence, brand protection, marketing research, benchmarking, and background vetting. Without items posted online, an investigative report on any topic may not be timely or complete or include the basis for reliable predictions and trends, visualization, geolocation, and statistical analysis.

To enable collection of data documented on the Internet, it is important to understand the legal and privacy principles necessary to keep Internet searches lawful, fair, equitable, and transparent, especially for cybervetting (background investigations incorporating online information).

This book was written to advocate improved security measures and establish guidelines for adopting Internet searches, including cybervetting, conducted as part of investigations and intelligence collection, with legal, policy, and procedural principles and methods suitable to the purpose. The guidance here should help both the government and private sectors, lawyers, and investigators of all kinds to apply the right techniques and thereby significantly improve their practices. Likewise, this book is meant to help investigative professionals develop the core skills and techniques to exploit the many, quickly growing resources available on the web on every topic imaginable and to integrate them into analytical processes that are useful in academic, professional, and personal life.

It is hoped this second edition can be used to learn or review cybervetting methods, explore legal frameworks for Internet searching as part of investigations, assist in integrating cybervetting into existing screening procedures, or find resources on these topics.

Notes

1. See https://search.wikileaks.org/search?q=snowden; Gellman, Barton, Edward Snowden, after months of NSA revelations, says his mission's accomplished, *Washington Post*, December 23, 2013 (accessed April 29, 2014); and NPR summary, http://www.npr.org/search/index.php?searchinput=%22edward+snowden%22.
2. King, Rachael, Ex-NSA Chief Details Snowden's Hiring at Agency, Booz Allen, *Wall Street Journal*, February 4, 2014.

3. Baker, Stewart, Why Privacy Will Become a Luxury, video interview, http://live.wsj.com/video/stewart-baker-why-privacy-will-become-a-luxury/10DB86DC-26F3–4634-A665–76419E9D06D4.html#!10DB86DC-26F3–4634-A665–76419E9D06D4 (accessed April 29, 2014).
4. Clarke, Richard, *Economist* interview, http://www.youtube.com/watch?v=6_ek8mugOUc (accessed April 29, 2014).
5. FTC Consumer Sentinel annual fraud and identity theft reports, http://www.ftc.gov/enforcement/consumer-sentinel-network/reports (accessed April 29, 2014).

About the Author

Edward J. (Ed) Appel, Sr., is owner-principal of iNameCheck, a boutique private investigative, consulting, and training firm. Ed is a retired FBI special agent and executive, specializing in counterintelligence and terrorism, and served as director, Counterintelligence and Security Programs, National Security Council, the White House. Besides consulting for private industry and government, Ed served as vice president, CertCo (digital security); security director, Level 3 Communications (fiber-optic telecommunications); and president, Joint Council on Information Age Crime (a public-private nonprofit). He previously volunteered on the ASIS (formerly American Society of Industrial Security) International Law Enforcement Liaison Council and founded the International Association of Chiefs of Police Computer Crime and Digital Evidence Committee. He co-authored the (IACP)-Defense Personnel Security Research Center (PERSEREC) study *Developing a Cybervetting Strategy for Law Enforcement* and its companion for National Security; edited the *Guide for Preventing and Responding to Information Age Crime*, 2001; authored *Insider Threat Mitigation through Improved Information Systems Security in DOD Environments*, PERSEREC, 2005; authored *Computer-Related Crime Impact: Measuring the Incidence and Cost*, 2003; was author/lecturer, Executive Security Management Course, Northeastern University, 2005, The New World of Digital Evidence, Northeastern University, 2007, and Computer Crime and Digital Evidence; edited and co-authored *Report on the Digital Evidence Needs Survey of State, Local and Tribal Law Enforcement*, National Institute of Justice, Department of Justice, 2005; *Mitigating the Insider Threat*, Department of Homeland Security, 2005; a Digital Evidence Awareness, Search and Seizure course for law enforcement, 2004; and wrote numerous unpublished government-sponsored classified and unclassified counterintelligence and counterterrorism studies, lectures, and papers. Ed is a graduate of Georgetown University, the Defense Language Institute, and the National Cryptologic School, and taught at the FBI Academy and as visiting lecturer at such institutions as Carnegie-Mellon, MIT Lincoln Labs, Georgetown University, and Johns Hopkins University.

BEHAVIOR AND TECHNOLOGY

1

> When I took office, only high energy physicists had ever heard of what
> is called the World Wide Web. ... Now even my cat has its own page.[1]

Since the early 1990s, profound changes have taken place in Internet use, patterns of behavior involving information systems, and the quantity and availability of data online. Meanwhile, an increasingly serious challenge to enterprise and information security in agencies and businesses and for individuals is posed by these changes. Among the personnel security and counterintelligence implications of these changes is the need to prevent, detect, and respond to illegal behavior on an employer's system and on personal systems that implicate an employer; pose a threat to people, assets, or information; or threaten an institution's reputation. Along with the threat comes an opportunity, as the Internet provides increasingly rich resources to address risks online.

Evidence of illicit and illegal behavior on the public Internet by employees could expose an employer to significant and unforeseen liabilities and damages.[2] Although the world seems to agree that the employer has the right to monitor and control enterprise systems, which are, after all, the employer's property, users are able to compromise enterprises through misuse of not only their employer's computers but also their personal devices and have been known to do so on the public Internet. Failure to consider online behavior by employees, candidates, and others connected with an enterprise (e.g., contractors, partners, and customers) can result in serious vulnerabilities. Similar implications apply to any person or entity of concern to decision makers, such as executives, competitors, products, and the latest developments.[3] For investigators, intelligence analysts, and researchers, the Internet has reached the stage at which it is more likely than not to provide valuable information on any topic.

In this section, the need for Internet searching for investigations, including vetting and intelligence, is explored.

Notes

1. Clinton, Bill, Excerpts from Transcribed Remarks by the President and the Vice President to the People of Knoxville on Internet for Schools, The White House, Office of the Press Secretary, October 10, 1996, http://govinfo.library.unt.edu/npr/library/speeches/101096.html (accessed August 6, 2010).
2. SANS on Internet security, http://www.sans.org/reading_room/; NIST Computer Security Resource Center, http://csrc.nist.gov/; US Department of Justice, Computer Crime and Intellectual Property Section Internet Security resource list, http://www.cybercrime.gov/links1.htm#ISSRb.
3. Dam, Kenneth W., and Lin, Herbert S., editors, *Cryptography's Role in Securing the Information Society*, National Research Council (Washington, DC: National Academy Press, 1996); Schneider, Fred B., editor, *Trust in Cyberspace*, National Research Council (Washington, DC: National Academy Press, 1999); Lewis, James A., project director, *Securing Cyberspace for the 44th Presidency, a Report of the CSIS Commission on Cybersecurity for the 44th Presidency* (Washington, DC: Center for Strategic and International Studies, December 2008); O'Harrow, Robert, Jr., *No Place to Hide* (New York: Free Press, 2005).

Chapter 1

The Internet's Potential for Investigators and Intelligence Officers

Introduction

The Internet is a global electronic communications system that connects computer networks and all types of organizations' computer facilities around the world.[1] Standard Internet protocols (IPs) are used for electronic, optic, wired, and wireless connections for several billion users of telecommunications services. Hypertext documents, music, and videos, for example, are exchanged on the World Wide Web, which has made the words *web* and *net* more or less synonymous with the Internet.

By design, the Internet is "public." Incredible quantities of data on the Internet are available to anyone with a computer and a browser. Some websites limit access to hosted data in various ways, and some allow the individual posting information to invoke privacy restrictions on unauthorized access. If no limitations apply, posted information is open to the public. Some websites require users to register to gain access to data, but registered users are not restricted in their use of the site's data, within its authorized use policy (AUP) and applicable copyright and trademark law. Therefore, on a great number of sites, the posted information could be deemed public even with access limitations. AUPs on some sites prohibit certain uses of hosted information, such as for commercial purposes or marketing (e.g., spam, unsolicited commercial e-mail). Advanced computer users ("hackers") might be able to bypass programs restricting access and illicitly view, copy, delete or alter data, or reprogram servers online. Users often must agree to abide by AUPs

3

to gain access to websites, but enforcement of AUP violations is predominantly rare and ineffectual.

Growth of Internet Use

The Internet and World Wide Web were created to facilitate communications and exchange of government and private-sector research information. Starting in the early 1990s, the Internet began a process of rapid expansion, in terms of linked computers, users, types of devices, data accessibility, and activities taking place online. The global network of networks has continued to grow, and with the addition of wireless connectivity and processing power in cell phones, tablets, and other portable devices, the Internet has permeated every facet of society—the "information society" in global parlance.[2] Studies of American Internet usage by the Pew Internet and American Life Project chronicle the fact that living life online has rapidly become a habit for about 85% of the US population, with younger, better-educated, and more well-to-do individuals more likely to be Internet users.[3] About 2.4 billion people of 7 billion worldwide are online, meaning that global Internet use has grown by 566% since 2000 (as of June 3, 2012).[4]

Diversity of Internet use has fueled growth, as has addition of IP-connected devices. Marketing and news reporting, social networking, entertainment (music, video), government services, and research have helped spur rapid expansion. Bandwidth provided by fiber-optic, cable, satellite, and wireless networks has enabled enhancements to the capabilities of public safety, communications, and data-sharing services that are viewed as vital to society. Both paid services (e.g., Internet-TV-phone, films, games online) and free access (e.g., Internet search, news, music, videos, tax returns, county records) supported by advertising, fees, and agency budgets have expanded industries' and governments' automated services. Services "in the cloud" (i.e., on servers accessible online) are in a steep growth curve, spurred by the need for access from multiple devices and locations to voluminous data, applications, and computing power offered by providers to industry, governments, and individuals. As a result of this growth, Cisco reported that "Global IP traffic has increased fourfold over the past 5 years, and will increase threefold over the next 5 years. Overall, IP traffic will grow at a compound annual growth rate (CAGR) of 23 percent from 2012 to 2017."[5] Cisco said that expansion of mobile devices, data centers "in the cloud," and bandwidth-intensive, multidevice Internet use will accelerate IP traffic volume over the next 5 years.[6] Website host growth also reflects net expansion.[7]

The charts in Figures 1.1 to 1.4, which should be interpreted as high-level estimates, show recent and projected Internet growth.

Pew's 2008 study of networked workers[8] revealed some interesting trends in American workplaces and homes; among these are that government workers are more likely to use the Internet or e-mail daily at work (72%), and 62% of

World Internet Usage and Population Statistics June 30, 2012						
World Regions	Population (2012 Est.)	Internet Users Dec. 31, 2000	Internet Users Latest Data	Penetration (% Population)	Growth 2000–2012	Uers % of Table
Africa	1,073,380,925	4,514,400	167,335,676	15.6%	3,606.7%	7.0%
Asia	3,922,066,987	114,304,000	1,076,681,059	27.5%	841.9%	44.8%
Europe	820,918,446	105,096,093	518,512,109	63.2%	393.4%	21.5%
Middle East	223,608,203	3,284,800	90,000,455	40.2%	2,639.9%	3.7%
North America	348,280,154	108,096,800	273,785,413	78.6%	153.3%	11.4%
Latin America/Caribbean	593,688,638	18,068,919	254,915,745	42.9%	1,310.8%	10.6%
Oceania/Australia	35,903,569	7,620,480	24,287,919	67.6%	218.7%	1.0%
WORLD TOTAL	7,017,846,922	360,985,492	2,405,518,376	34.3%	566.4%	100.0%

Figure 1.1 According to data collected by Internet World Stats, global Internet use has grown more than 566% since 2000 (see Note 4).

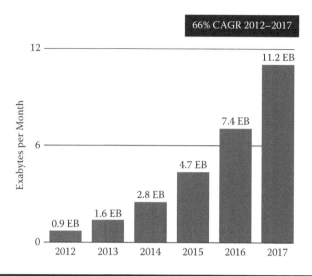

Figure 1.2 Cisco's forecast of the rapid compound annual growth rate (CAGR) of mobile Internet traffic is testimony to the popularity of handheld, wireless, always-online devices (see Notes 5 and 6).

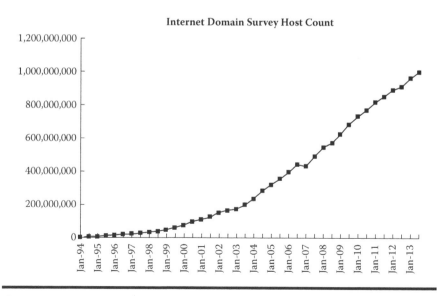

Figure 1.3 The number of website hosts keeps growing as Internet uses expand (see Note 7).

Demographics of Internet Users

% of adults in each group who use the Internet (the number of respondents in each group listed as "n" for the group)

		Use the Internet
All adults (n = 2,252)		**85%**
a	Men (n = 1,029)	85
b	Women (n = 1,223)	84
Race/ethnicity		
a	White, Non-Hispanic (n = 1,571)	86[c]
b	Black, Non-Hispanic (n = 252)	85[c]
c	Hispanic (n = 249)	76
Age		
a	18–29 (n = 404)	98[bcd]
b	30–49 (n = 577)	92[cd]
c	50–64 (n = 641)	83[d]
d	65+ (n = 570)	56
Education attainment		
a	Less than high school (n = 168)	59
b	High school grad (n = 630)	78[a]
c	Some college (n = 588)	92[ab]
d	College + (n = 834)	96[abc]
Household income		
a	Less than $30,000/yr (n = 580)	76
b	$30,000–$49,999 (n = 374)	88[a]
c	$50,000–$74,999 (n = 298)	94[ab]
d	$75,000 (n = 582)	96[ab]
Urbanity		
a	Urban (n = 763)	86[c]
b	Suburban (n = 1,037)	86[c]
c	Rural (n = 450)	80

Source: Pew Research Center's Internet & American Life Project Spring Tracking Survey, April 17–May 19, 2013. n = 2,252 adults. Interviews were conducted in English and Spanish and on landline and cell phones. Margin of error is ±2.3 percentage points for results based on Internet users.

Note: Percentages marked with a superscript letter (e.g., [a]) indicate a statistically significant difference between that row and the row designated by that superscript letter, among categories of each demographic characteristics (e.g., age).

Figure 1.4 Pew Research consistently provides the most useful profiles of American Internet use. As this profile shows, nearly everyone is online (see Note 3).

all workers do. About 42% of workers do some work at home, but 56% of networked workers do some work at home. This poses obvious security concerns as data moves between workplace and home. The mobility of employees in the workforce and the proclivity of some to keep copies of proprietary information to which they gain access on the job are only two of many data protection issues.

It appears that the vast majority of Internet users (Figures 1.5 and 1.6) enjoy many types of nonbusiness activities, from e-mail and texting to games, dating,

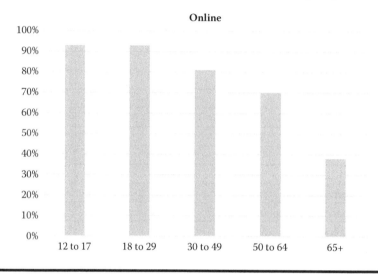

Figure 1.5 Pew's 2009 studies showed that almost all young people are online; most older people are as well.

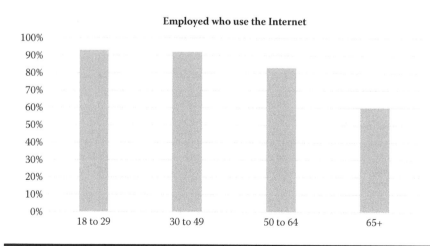

Figure 1.6 Pew's 2008 study of networked workers showed that most employees go online (see Note 8).

news, and blogging. Increasingly, people are looking to the Internet for entertainment, including films, videos, music, TV, and applications that they can access for free or at low cost. Declining revenues at television networks, newspapers, and publishing houses testify to the shift from TV and print to online media. But, enjoyment of the virtual world has brought about a large-scale change in society's views about intellectual property rights. Copyrighted movies, music, publications, and software are traded openly over Internet sites specifically designed to deter criminal investigations and to facilitate transfer of goods without royalty to producers, such as by peer-to-peer networks.[9] Departing employees often take proprietary data from employers, as 50% of those surveyed admitted to a Ponemon Institute-Symantec survey.[10] Are users of fee-free films, music, and software more likely to misappropriate their employer's digital intellectual property for their own use?

One of the more fascinating aspects of computers and the Internet from a behavioral point of view is whether the use of such technology has changed how people act, and if so, the implications. In just two areas, child exploitation and fantasy games, disturbing trends have become visible (if not yet fully understood). For almost 25 years, child pornography, solicitation of minors by predators, and illicit group activities centered on sexual exploitation of children have dominated the computer crime and digital evidence efforts of federal, state, and local US law enforcement.[11] "Massively multiplayer online role-playing games" and other fantasy games, like *Second Life*, allow players to live an alternate existence, complete with the option to commit virtual and actual criminal acts with no real-world consequences. Not surprisingly, crimes like money laundering have already invaded virtual reality games. Even some video games focused on crime (*Grand Theft Auto*) and warfare (*Fantasy Wars*, the *Halo* series) may encourage players to act out violently or criminally. The wide popularity of child porn and even wider popularity of fantasy may or may not portend new neuroses or inclinations to commit physical criminal acts, but some psychologists and psychiatrists have expressed concerns. One of the world's oldest professions, prostitution, occupies its place in e-commerce,[12] alongside drug distribution facilitated by "anonymous" payments online.[13]

Some concerns raised about online habits do not relate to crime or misbehavior but rather to such topics as users' cognitive ability and attention span. A recent Pew study[14] suggested, among other things, that "there will be some teens and young adults who will suffer cognitive difficulties from unhealthy use of the internet, Web, social media, games, and mobile technology." The point of including this speculative prediction is that many purposes for cybervetting exist beyond finding evidence of illicit or illegal behaviors online. Failure to address users' online habits avoids consideration of training and orientation to overcome the users' undiscovered handicaps when they are hired.

While federal agencies have created, expanded, and reorganized units to deal with crime online and digital evidence, state, local, and tribal police have struggled and are inundated with cases. The volume and variety of digital evidence—often including terabytes of documents, texts, photos, and videos in various formats from many different types of devices—has become daunting to forensic specialists and street investigators alike. Yet, the opportunity presented by ubiquitous digital evidence and intelligence, from cell phones to computers to tablets to memory devices to social networking, can be wonderful for law enforcement and intelligence. The investments required in expertise and technology appear to lag behind, while crime, including external attacks to computer systems and online frauds, threatens the safety and security of the systems themselves.[15]

Digital evidence is not confined to the devices used in criminal acts (which are instruments of the crime) but often can be found in the network logs of Internet service providers (ISPs), telecommunications companies, and computer systems hosts. Internet-based digital evidence can be transient and remote, including data stored abroad, where records' unavailability to US law enforcement may protect foreign cybercriminals. International cybercrime agreements have recently been strengthened to attack such problems. Sadly, it appears that today only a small minority of Internet criminals are being identified and prosecuted. Cybercriminals also appear to pose a new threat to society in the form of potential insiders, working in government, business, or academia while committing crimes anonymously on intranets and the Internet.

Although most Internet users stay well within legal bounds, recent expansion of Internet use and the quantity and types of systems and data available have created an opportunity and a necessity for cyber background vetting, investigations, and open-source intelligence of all types. An interesting phenomenon accelerating the popularity of the Internet is the evolution of search engines, with Google dominating the field over rivals, including Yahoo, Microsoft's search engine Bing, AOL, and Ask. Consolidation of search engines is inevitable and is ongoing, as Google and Bing (essentially the tool used by Yahoo) divide the search function for most US users, and a Chinese search engine that is popular in the People's Republic of China. The usefulness of Internet searches is aptly measured in the billions of dollars of Google stock value, as well as Google's expansion into offering applications, online storage, e-mail, computers, and more. "The ultimate search engine would basically understand everything in the world, and it would always give you the right thing. And we're a long, long ways from that," said Google co-founder Larry Page.[16]

Yet, searching has become essential to those online. Internet users, including investigators, human resources staff, attorneys, and everyone else involved in assessing people in the workplace, are apt to conduct searches when they believe it is potentially useful. Today, that includes googling applicants, co-workers, superiors, subordinates, and just about anyone else deemed interesting. Although most organizations wait to consider the right (ethical, fair, effective) way to include Internet vetting in personnel processes, the staff has already adopted their own policies, procedures, and methods for inquiring into individuals' online presence.[17] Many employers use the Internet as a part of the application process, requiring candidates to fill in online application forms and communicate at least in part online during preemployment processing. Automation not only makes the process potentially more efficient, accurate, and timely but also can allow candidates a greater measure of control and understanding of the various stages (e.g., declaration of interest, formal request to be considered, presentation of credentials, competitive evaluation, interview, conditional offer of employment, background investigation, adjudication).[18]

The personally identifying information exchanged in the background review process is sensitive and should be protected to ensure applicants' privacy. Employers conduct background investigations to verify the applicant's background and determine the candidate's eligibility, suitability, qualifications, and trustworthiness and compare the competitive attributes of prospective employees, existing employees, and candidates for clearance or promotion. Traditionally, within federal and state laws, employers verify the facts on a résumé and application, including checks of identity, residences, education, prior employment, arrests, convictions, civil suits, bankruptcies, legal sanctions, and similar indicators of past behavior, either in-house or through background investigation firms. Because past behavior is the single most reliable indicator of future behavior, a candidate's track record often provides the most convincing evidence of the likelihood of success in his or her new position. Likewise, a record of past misbehavior may indicate that the candidate would be likely to fail; to cause a loss to the new employer; to pose a threat to people, assets, and information in the workplace—or simply be less qualified than rival candidates.

Internet activities have become a new "neighborhood," where people are likely to have posted information, to be recorded in directories and other online databases, and to have been the subject of postings by other people. Scores of federal, state, and local records are available online, including criminal and civil court records, residence and telephone directories, employer websites, business directories, professional associations, and similar files accessible from the Internet. Some of the data available on the public Internet include text, photographs, video, audio, and media records that chronicle serious misbehavior by individuals.[19] Past investigations for government clearances often included "neighborhood investigations," where those living near a candidate were canvassed for information about the candidate. Government hiring standards specify the factors used to determine eligibility and establish knowledge, skills, and abilities, providing the evidence needed to offer employment, grant clearances, and document suitability for the job. All investigative steps may uncover derogatory information that could disqualify a candidate or make candidacy less competitive than others. Over the past several decades, the neighborhood investigation (although still carried out) has produced less information of value than previously.[20] Not only are neighbors less likely to share derogatory observations about the candidate, but fewer neighbors are likely these days to even know the person. This is particularly true because many people move frequently and reside in multifamily structures or neighborhoods where social contact is minimal.

One concern raised by those with objections to cybervetting is that factors that could be used to discriminate against a prospective candidate might be discovered or documented online (e.g., Title VII attributes like sex, race, nationality, religion, etc.). Many such factors are perceptible to those processing applicants from sources other than the Internet. There is no valid inference that mere knowledge of such a factor resulted in discrimination. However, the process of documenting results of cybervetting may be critical to remove doubt that discrimination may be present in the adjudication of background investigation results, regardless of the sources used.

Today, an individual's social circle may not be defined as much by geography as it is by electronic connectivity. Using social networking websites, instant messaging, and similar connectivity, people are likely to exchange information about themselves by posting it online or sending it (illustrated with photos, video, and sound) to a list of friends and acquaintances located nearby or far away—or to any of several billion Internet users who care to look. The profiles created often include peccadilloes, problems, and misbehavior unlikely to have been communicated or documented electronically in a previous era.[21] To address publicly posted evidence of misbehavior, about 45% of employers (up 20% from the previous year) told a 2009 CareerBuilder.com survey that they search the Internet for social postings by applicants to see if what they find may have an impact on a hiring decision. About 35% reported that social website postings and similar online data resulted in "no-hire" decisions. Among the reasons cited in the CareerBuilder survey for no-hire decisions were provocative/inappropriate photos or information; drinking or drug use; bad-mouthing previous employers, co-workers, or clients; poor communications skills; discriminatory comments; misrepresentation of qualifications; and shared confidential information from a previous employer.[22]

A Practitioner's Perspective

In over 8 years of systematic Internet searches on individuals under investigation, my company has found a wide variety of types of derogatory information, some exclusively seen online and some collected both on the Internet and from other sources. The vast majority of the information found supports subjects' candidacies, verifies their background, shows the subjects in a good light, or is otherwise positive in nature. In our experience, about 10% of those being screened for employment have had references online significant enough to warrant concern about their eligibility or suitability. Results of two studies supporting the 10% derogatory ratio of cybervetting results appear further along in this book. During investigations and collection of open-source information about suspected individuals (those likely to have committed wrongdoing), we have found online documentation of illegal, illicit, or socially unacceptable behavior considerably more often than not. The bottom line is that the Internet is a valuable source of information on individuals.

Beyond people who often appear in Internet files, we found that businesses, organizations of all kinds, groups, entities, brands, and topics are profiled more efficiently when Internet sources are used, in addition to any other investigative and research methods. By experimenting with the timing and nature of the searches used, we found that often, descriptive information can be found and a "dossier" started literally within a few minutes on virtually any topic. This can enable more rapid, accurate, complete, and sophisticated planning of the range of sources to be used and steps to be taken in collecting and analyzing required information. Among the uses for these kinds of searches are due diligence; mergers and acquisitions; litigation support; marketing; brand protection; competitive intelligence; counterintelligence; counterterrorism; identifying groups for and against an issue; scoping out the extent of a particular illegal or illicit activity online; following comments and postings about a current topic (e.g., a trial or dispute, as in litigation support); and contractor surveys prior to a request for proposals. Marketers today rely heavily on the Internet to find indicators of consumer tastes and trends and to distribute all kinds of ads.[23] We found an astonishing array of different types of data, which can enable a much better analysis of available information on any topic, when Internet search results are included.

Besides intelligence, investigator, and security exploitation of the Internet, professionals in many different areas have come to rely on information available over the Internet. Two examples are clinicians and librarians, based on recent articles and books illustrating how important reference materials online have become to efficiency in their practices.[24] Another example is social media monitoring for marketing and sales purposes, with over 400 different tools providing corporations instant feedback on customer perceptions.[25]

The Search

Creation and innovation in Internet search tools have provided the opportunity for Internet research to grow quickly. Finding open-source information on virtually any topic has been made easier, and all types of data available on the public Internet continuously expand. The quantity of data itself has become an issue, as expansion of information, storage capacity, and online availability (e.g., through "cloud storage") has occurred at a previously unimaginable pace.[26] For example, the Internet itself is estimated to contain 71 billion web pages,[27] the human genome mapping project and astronomical data online contain many terabytes of information, and more than 500 million Facebook users spend 8 billion minutes daily uploading photos (1.2 million per second).[28] The International Data Corporation reported that the amount of global data created and replicated during 2012 was 2.7 zettabytes.[29] Cisco estimated that by 2017 the amount of global IP traffic will reach 1.4 zettabytes a year.[30] Because most humans are still struggling to understand that 20 gigabytes of data constitute a pile of 8.5 by 11 inch, single-spaced, printed pages the height of the Empire State Building, the transition from gigabytes to terabytes to petabytes to exabytes to zettabytes has come all too quickly. The prefix *zetta* indicates the seventh power of 1,000 and means 10 to the 21st power in the

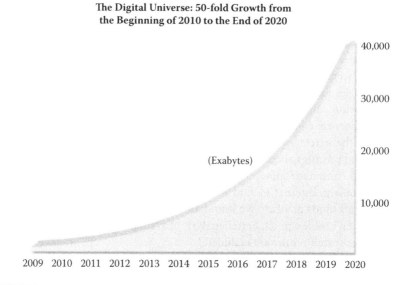

The Digital Universe: 50-fold Growth from
the Beginning of 2010 to the End of 2020

(Exabytes)

40,000

30,000

20,000

10,000

2009 2010 2011 2012 2013 2014 2015 2016 2017 2018 2019 2020

Figure 1.7 Growth in stored data available online has been staggering and forced a change in the scales of measurement used from gigabytes and beyond to exabytes and zettabytes (see Note 26).

International System of Units. (See Figure 1.7, which shows the trend in exabytes of online data storage.)

Based on recent statistics, it appears that hundreds of billions of queries are made through search engines monthly, and Google searches alone have climbed to over 5 billion searches daily (almost 2 trillion annually; see Figure 1.8).[31] In 2008, Google said its search engine had "crawled" (collected and indexed material) from 1 trillion unique URLs (uniform resource locators), or web addresses,[32] and as of 2013, claimed its index contains over 100 million gigabytes.[33] Although these statistics are provided to give a sense of the volume of Internet searches conducted and data cached, their most important meaning is that Internet searches are popular with users and even more popular with advertisers and e-commerce sites that depend on search engines for much of their revenue. Just as we should be a bit skeptical about the statistics' precision, we should also understand that search engines exist primarily to sell, and as Google's multibillion-dollar income illustrates, the audience is huge and continuing to expand. Both data growth and data mining are related to the uses made of the Internet and its usefulness to researchers. Both are forecast to continue.

One conclusion haunting security and counterintelligence officers is that finding the information needed (on or off the Internet) and information assurance will become more challenging and important with time. Investigators, security officers, adjudicators, intelligence personnel, and other authorities all use the Internet to

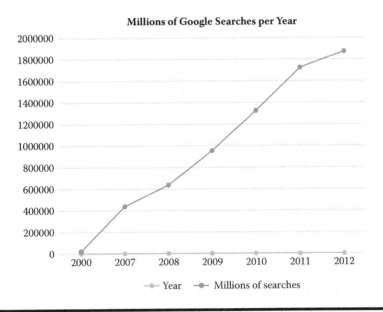

Figure 1.8   Google annual search statistics show steady growth in the number of Internet searches per day and per year (see Note 31).

find facts quickly. Because they utilize common search engines like Google (along with perhaps more than 66% of the population, depending on which market share statistics you believe),[34] they often find references that are instructive, informative, and useful about people, organizations, and topics of interest. There are few regulations or guidelines for random Internet searches conducted out of curiosity, for a business purpose, or for research. Many people have adopted their own approach to searching, with more or less skill depending on their level of interest, training, or experience. The ubiquity of Internet searching and lack of guidelines can create issues. When is it appropriate or inappropriate to use Internet searching to collect information about an individual? The answer depends on interpretation of a variety of current laws, regulations, and standards, among which are the Fair Credit Reporting Act (as amended), Privacy Act (as amended), and state employment laws. Several laws, including the Health Insurance Portability and Accountability Act, Gramm-Leach-Bliley, and Sarbanes-Oxley Act, control the protection of personally identifying information in certain industries. In a nutshell, information collected for an investigative purpose that creates a record containing personally identifying information may be subject to privacy and security requirements in US laws and regulations. It is potentially problematic if casually searched, individual-specific information is handled inappropriately. US government laws and regulations require that if a federal employee acquires Internet search data to be used or retained, it must be placed in an authorized records repository. Although it is not forbidden to look for, find, and record such data, possession of Internet search results imposes both declared and implied responsibilities on persons, depending on what they do with the data.

The ethics of Internet searching and use of the results thereof are another challenge. Is it appropriate (legal and ethical) to use a highly personal item posted on a social site to share with friends and family in an employment adjudication? Some argue that the intent of the one posting personal information should be respected by others, yet anything posted publicly is by its nature made available to anyone and everyone. In the absence of policies or procedures (or adherence to them), a person in authority may selectively conduct Internet searches on some, but not all, individuals of interest. Search methods may vary. Analysis of search results may be disciplined and effective or not. Depending on the searcher, the search itself and analysis of the results may be incomplete, ineffective, and inaccurate. Information gleaned may be correct or incorrect. The subject of the search may be aware of it or not. Casual searching can therefore raise issues of fairness, competence, proper handling and analysis of data, secure storage, privacy protection, redress, and perhaps other questions.

There is nothing wrong with using the Internet as a telephone directory, method of connecting with someone else, or reminder of facts about an individual of interest. Profiles with photos online make it easy for two new acquaintances to meet in a crowded public place because each recognizes the other from their online pictures. It is when an inquiry begins to delve into the personal profiles of others with potentially adverse consequences that questions arise. After all, the information is posted on the Internet in a manner that makes it available to anyone inquiring—so it hardly can be said to enjoy privacy protection. However, depending on the role and intentions of the searcher, Internet data that may have an impact on a decision assumes another character and must be approached according to some basic principles. The alternative could result in unfair, arbitrary, or prejudicial treatment.

Internet Posts and the People They Profile

"On the Internet, nobody knows you're a dog," said a famous *New Yorker* cartoon, in which a dog at a keyboard was speaking to another dog.[35] Even when the name, nickname, "handle," or other identifiers of the person of interest appear on a web page, one may not know who actually posted it. Essentially, there are many ways to post material anonymously or falsely in another's name, with or without skilled hacking or knowledge of another person's password. Current social norms include the use of nicknames for many types of social networking profiles, as well as game sites, interest group pages, sales sites like eBay and craigslist, blogs, Internet Relay Chat (IRC), and free e-mail accounts. Such nicknames are in fact aliases, and some would suggest that it is proper to conceal the true (or full) identity of the person by use of the nickname. This may help protect the individual against unwelcome contacts from strangers and sales pitches. Protocols of e-mail address naming have evolved to recognize the uncomfortable fact that executives and public figures should not employ a straightforward e-mail address lest they subject themselves to a deluge of unwelcome spam. Ironically, these evolving naming conventions create a situation in which almost everyone fails to list all their "virtual identities" (i.e., those used on the Internet) as aliases when filling out application forms. In addition, it is common for users to have both a formal e-mail address (e.g., John.Doe@gmail.com, John.Doe@bigbusiness.net) and a recreational, more personal e-mail address (e.g., BigJD123@yahoo.com). Identifying individuals online is rendered more difficult when they use multiple identities for different Internet activities and communications. However, if one can find out all or most such nicknames, each one can be used as a search term to find instances where the individual appears online. Analysis of the results must always include the caveat that the individual found may not really be identifiable with the person of interest because multiple individuals can use the same nickname, people can pretend to be someone else, and users can share the same computer with the same virtual identities (e.g., spouses using the same e-mail address).

While those who post information can provide a treasure trove of useful facts about themselves, it is true that people often upload items about other individuals as well. Many personal profiles carry a fairly large body of information, including blogs, messages posted (e.g., Facebook friends' comments), photos, and links to the personal profiles of a social circle. By reading not only the postings of one individual but also those of his or her connections, it is often possible to develop a more complete impression of the subject's behavior, characteristics, and suitability. As indicated, most often a person's online profile results in a positive impression of the subject because most people behave well in the virtual presence of others, including their social circle. However, it also occurs relatively frequently that misbehavior can be seen where the person has that proclivity. Even though more mature people all should know that postings without privacy controls can be seen by anyone, it is not unusual to find postings that are scandalous, embarrassing, and likely to result in denial of employment by any employer made aware of them.

There are many examples of notorious conduct emblazoned for history on the public Internet by persons of whom one could only ask, "What were they thinking?" Among such examples are two New York Congressmen, Chris Lee and Anthony Weiner, who respectively sent flirtatious notes and shirtless photos to a woman via craigslist using a Facebook e-mail in his own name and sent lewd photos of himself to a college student via his Twitter account. Lee resigned from office in February 2011. Weiner first denied what he did, claiming hacking, then admitted it shortly thereafter, and in June 2011 resigned.[36] Weiner attempted a comeback as a candidate for New York City mayor but was decisively defeated. Although it may not be shocking that many people post or send embarrassing things about themselves, it is remarkable how thoughtless of the consequences ostensibly intelligent and responsible individuals can be in online misbehavior.

As with caveats about postings ostensibly attributable to a known individual, postings by a person about someone else may suffer from several defects, including lack of attribution (i.e., an anonymous poster, perhaps a hacker attempting "social networking" to infect computers with malware), untrue or unverifiable allegations, and practical jokes or slander. The questions that must be asked about such postings include the following: Who said what about whom? Are there any other indications of similar allegations verifying the information? Are the statements, photos, videos, audio recordings, and so on believable? Despite the care that must be exercised with postings by one person about another, examples abound of useful information found online. A son revealed his father's illegal activities and hatred for his employer. A man's social profile contained a link to his ex-wife's blog, which detailed his many years of misbehavior, including domestic abuse. A woman and her friends posted stories and photos of their drunken partying, complete with sexual content and ample examples of faulty judgment. Another woman recounted her history of drug abuse and sales in postings on a friend's blog. A skilled computer security employee spent hours at work playing a commander in an online war game, and his bragging was quoted in posted interviews and news stories.

A category of postings that should not be forgotten is false social networking profiles that are used to lurk and observe, deceive, harass, bully, slander, or otherwise victimize others. Two notorious examples are worth mentioning. Lori Drew, the mother of a 13-year-old girl with a rival, Megan Meier, the same age, created a false MySpace profile with the picture of a fictitious 16-year-old boy named "Josh Evans." Drew used this fake profile to torment Meier, who "had a history of depression and suicidal impulses," flirting with Meier for a time, then suddenly telling Meier that Evans "no longer liked her," and that "the world would be a better place without her in it." Shortly thereafter, Meier killed herself. Drew then deleted the fake account.[37] She was federally prosecuted. Latisha Monique Frazier disappeared in August 2010, shortly after leaving work, and her family frantically searched for her, distributing posters and using the media. A Facebook profile appeared, harassing and threatening Frazier's family. An investigation resulted in the arrest and prosecution of six people for Frazier's disappearance and murder.[38]

A key example of third-party postings is the ever-widening variety of records that appear online. All records may include errors. However, records are especially useful because they are kept in the normal course of business and are apt to be accurate on the whole. That is why records are an exception to the hearsay rule and are admissible in court. Online records include not only public government databases but also media reports, directories, and cross-references such as telephone numbers and web identifiers like IP addresses, profiles, and lists of links. All of these provide information by one person or entity about another, and although each should be viewed as requiring verification, they are an excellent way to amass facts, leads and perhaps suspicions for an investigation about a subject.

Finding the Needles

Those familiar with database administration will no doubt understand that the "data density" and unstructured formatting of Internet data add complex problems to the task of thorough searching. Because society has gotten used to using Google as its overwhelming choice for most Internet searching, it may come as a shock that Google provides neither complete nor unbiased results. Although the results page may show millions of "hits," Google will most likely provide only up to 1,000 results, 1 page of 10 at a time, unless you adjust the settings. Google (and similar search engines) use elegantly designed algorithms to find and rank references to the search term entered. Rather than searching the Internet that exists at the moment the search is launched, search engines refer to mammoth databases of information collected ("cached") and indexed by "spiders" that systematically record website content continuously, month by month. Not all websites, and not all pages or website-accessible databases, allow spiders to record their contents. Therefore, even in the best of circumstances, a search engine can only deliver a small portion of available information to the searcher.[39]

A key challenge is finding information identifiable with a person, entity, or topic of interest. The volume of data available on the Internet is such that there will most likely be many references to any search term, and filtering out the irrelevant information is necessary. Further, finding references and links that lead to more useful, detailed, or relevant information (based on the purpose of the search) is at times a difficult task. Many researchers become so bogged down in "hits" from search engines that they fail to utilize the wide variety of sites where databases with more useful information reside, such as professional associations and publications, social networking, business or organizational websites, and activity group sites like blogs, calendars, and chat. Mining data that could more likely provide accurate, detailed results requires insightful analysis of the subject of inquiry, based on his or her known profile, and exploiting Internet sites likely to provide nonindexed (but richer) information. In short, nothing can substitute for knowledge of and experience on the Internet (not even Google).

The Need for Speed

Because of the large volumes of data available on the Internet, the rapidity of collection, filtering, and analysis is an important aspect of searching. If they take too long, Internet searching and analysis become counterproductive as investigative methods. Fortunately, search and analysis tools enable much greater efficiencies. A 40-hour search and analysis project can be reduced to less than 2 hours for experienced analysts, provided that they have the right systems, processes, training, and experience. Over 8 years' experience with my group of skilled web searchers have proved two insights: The human analyst remains a key processor in Internet searches, and two or more competent analysts will most often come up with better results if they work as a team. This phenomenon is related to the facts that individuality causes online profiles to differ, no one analyst knows (or thinks of) all the possible Internet sources to use, and two or more heads are inevitably better than one. A corollary is that by pursuing linked people and terms, a fuller profile of the subject may emerge than if one confines the search to the first set of references that are presented by a search engine. When appropriate technology and methodology are applied, Internet searching can be a great equalizer, producing a relatively complete profile of a subject in a short time.

Sufficiency of Searches

Because the oceans of data available on the Internet contain valuable facts on many topics, structured and thorough searching has become necessary for complete investigations and intelligence production. For individuals, businesses, and government agencies, an Internet presence is critical for networking, information dissemination, marketing, recruiting, and customer fulfillment. Large-scale efforts to make data of all kinds accessible online are paying off, as reference materials, government records, media reports, books, and profiles of people have been added. Along with records, social, fantasy, recreational, and gaming data have been added for hundreds of millions of users. Both the benign and the derogatory appear in large quantities of references on people, enterprises, and topics. It follows that business and government should require searching for numerous purposes to ensure that one has the facts needed to make timely, valid decisions. Over the past several years, extensive Internet research has demonstrated that unique and valuable information can be found on the Internet, benefitting investigations, open-source intelligence, and vetting. Unfortunately, many firms, agencies, and organizations lack a policy, procedures, or a thoughtful approach to Internet searching. This does not mean that searches are not conducted. Quite the contrary: Searches are done in great numbers, many incompletely or poorly, and results are not always used as they should be. If the approach outlined in the following chapters is used, an enterprise can structure its approach to Internet searching so that results are not only useful but also lawful, fair, and fully within national and international standards.

Notes

1. Merriam-Webster, Internet definition, http://www.merriam-webster.com/netdict/internet; Wikipedia, http://en.wikipedia.org/wiki/Internet (accessed October 24, 2013).
2. Organization for Economic Cooperation and Development (OECD) resources on policy issues related to Internet governance, Information Society studies, http://www.oecd.org/document/56/0,3343,en_21571361_34590630_34647416_1_1_1_1,00.html (accessed June 1, 2010).

3. Pew Internet and American Life Project statistics, http://www.pewinternet.org/Static-Pages/Trend-Data-(Adults)/Whos-Online.aspx (accessed October 25, 2013).

4. Internet World Stats, http://www.internetworldstats.com/stats.htm (accessed October 25, 2013).

5. The Zettabyte Era, Trends and Analysis, Cisco estimate of Internet traffic growth, http://www.cisco.com/en/US/solutions/collateral/ns341/ns525/ns537/ns705/ns827/VNI_Hyperconnectivity_WP.pdf (accessed October 25, 2013).

6. Cisco Visual Networking Index: Global Mobile Data Traffic Forecast Update, 2012–2017, http://www.cisco.com/en/US/solutions/collateral/ns341/ns525/ns537/ns705/ns827/white_paper_c11-520862.html; http://tools.cisco.com/search/results/en/us/get#q=total+Global+IP+traffic&pr=enushomesppublished&basepr=enushomesppublished&prevq=&sort=cdcdevfour&start=0&hits=10&qid=4&websessionid=w0P5nGl6i9LDUz5_ei-dMZ_&navexp=&navlist=&navsel=&navop=&to=0&fr=7&un=true&aus=false&ec=0&pf=& (accessed October 25, 2013).

7. Internet Systems Consortium host count survey, http://www.isc.org/services/survey/ (accessed October 25, 2013).

8. Madden, Mary, and Jones, Sydney, Networked Workers, September 2008, http://www.pewinternet.org/Reports/2008/Networked-Workers.aspx (accessed November 3, 2013).

9. Meetings of Computer Crime and Digital Evidence Ad-Hoc Committee, International Association of Chiefs of Police, 2005–2012, in which briefings were received from law enforcement on computer crime and digital evidence trends seen by law enforcement and private sector investigators.

10. King, Rachael, Departing Employees Are Security Horror, *Wall Street Journal*, October 21, 2013, http://online.wsj.com/news/articles/SB10001424052702303442004579123412020578896 (accessed October 25, 2013), reporting results of a survey by Ponemon Institute and Symantec.

11. See Note 9.

12. Halpin, James, Prostitution Moving from Street Corners to Online Ads, Experts Said, *Scranton Times-Tribune*, October 13, 2013, http://thetimes-tribune.com/news/prostitution-moving-from-street-corners-to-online-ads-experts-said-1.1568034 (accessed October 25, 2013).

13. Reed, Brad, Bitcoin Bust: Feds Break Up Country's Largest Bitcoin Drug Ring, *Yahoo News*, October 2, 2013, reporting FBI breakup of the drug-organized crime ring known as Silk Road, http://news.yahoo.com/bitcoin-bust-feds-break-country-largest-bitcoin-drug-034516881.html (accessed October 25, 2013).

14. Anderson, Janna Q., Elon University, and Rainie, Lee, Pew Research Center's Internet and American Life Project Millennials Will Benefit *and* Suffer Due to Their Hyperconnected Lives, February 29, 2012, http://www.pewinternet.org/~/media/Files/Reports/2012/PIP_Future_of_Internet_2012_Young_brains_PDF.pdf (accessed November 5, 2013).

15. Meetings of Computer Crime and Digital Evidence Ad-Hoc Committee, International Association of Chiefs of Police, 2005–2012.

16. Page, Larry, Google's Goal: "Understand Everything," *Business Week*, May 3, 2004, http://www.businessweek.com/magazine/content/04_18/b3881010_mz001.htm (accessed August 6, 2010).

17. American Management Association, 2007 Electronic Monitoring and Surveillance Survey, http://press.amanet.org/press-releases/177/2007-electronic-monitoring-surveillance-survey/ (accessed May 5, 2010).

18. Nixon, W. Barry, and Kerr, Kim M., *Background Screening and Investigations, Managing Risk from HR and Security Perspectives* (New York: Elsevier, 2008).

19. Studies and investigations I conducted of thousands of individuals have found that a significant percentage have serious derogatory references online. More on this subject appears in subsequent chapters.

20. Security Policy Reviews, Intelligence Office, National Security Council, The White House, Washington DC, January 1995–May 1997, by the author as director, Security and Counterintelligence Programs, Personnel Security Working Group, et al., *Evaluation of DCID 1/14 Investigative Requirements* (Washington, DC: Director of Central Intelligence, April 1991): "The least productive sources include neighborhood interviews, which are also the most expensive and time consuming." PERSEREC, SSBI Source Yield: An Examination of Sources Contacted during the SSBI, TR 96-01, March 1996, explored the net value of sources used in background investigations; see http://www.dhra.mil/perserec/index.html.

21. Madden, Mary, Fox, Susannah, Smith, Aaron, and Vitak, Jessica, Digital Footprints, Online Identity Management and Search in the Age of Transparency, Pew Internet and American Life Project, December 16, 2007, http://pewresearch.org/pubs/663/digital-footprints (accessed June 24, 2010).

22. CareerBuilder.com survey, August 20, 2009, http://thehiringsite.careerbuilder.com/2009/08/20/nearly-half-of-employers-use-social-networkingsites-to-screen-job-candidates/ (accessed March 30, 2010); Kwoh, Leslie, Beware: Potential Employers Are Watching You, *Wall Street Journal*, October 29, 2012, http://online.wsj.com/news/articles/SB10000872396390443759504577631410093879278#printMode (accessed October 25, 2013).

23. DeMers, Jayson, The Top 7 Online Marketing Trends that Will Dominate 2014, *Forbes*, September 17, 2013, http://www.forbes.com/sites/jaysondemers/2013/09/17/the-top-7-online-marketing-trends-that-will-dominate-2014/ (accessed November 4, 2013).

24. Beyea, Suzanne, Finding Internet Resources to Support Evidence-Based Practice, *AORN Journal*, September 2000; Cassell, Kay Ann, and Hiremath, Uma, *Reference and Information Services in the 21st Century, An Introduction*, 2nd ed. (Chicago: Neal-Schuman, 2009), http://www.neal-schuman.com/reference21st2nd.

25. Brynley-Jones, Luke, What to Look for in a Social Media Monitoring Tool, November 2012, http://socialmediatoday.com/lbrynleyjones/993011/what-look-social-media-monitoring-tool?utm_source=dlvr.it&utm_medium=linkedin#! (accessed January 22, 2014).

26. IDC Digital Universe Study—Data Growth, http://gigaom.com/2013/10/02/how-the-industrial-internet-will-help-you-to-stop-worrying-and-love-the-data/screen-shot-2013-09-24-at-4-11-40-pm/ (accessed November 4, 2013).

27. Ohio State University Internet guide, http://liblearn.osu.edu/guides/week1/pg6.html (accessed November 4, 2013).

28. Barbara, John J., Data Storage Issues, *DFI News*, September 17, 2013, http://www.dfinews.com/articles/2013/09/data-storage-issues (accessed July 15, 2004) et_cid=3555443&et_rid=454846245&type=cta#.Um7KDM3D_IU.

29. IDC Predicts 2012 Will Be the Year of Mobile and Cloud Platform Wars as IT Vendors Vie for Leadership While the Industry Redefines Itself, December 1, 2011, http://www.reuters.com/article/2011/12/01/idUS150958+01-Dec-2011+BW20111201 (accessed November 4, 2013).

30. Cisco Global Cloud Index Forecast and Methodology, October 2013, http://www.cisco.com/en/US/solutions/collateral/ns341/ns525/ns537/ns705/ns1175/Cloud_Index_White_Paper.html (accessed November 4, 2013).
31. Based on published statistics from comScore, http://www.comscore.com, http://www.searchengineland.com, http://www.searchenginewatch.com, Google, http://www.google.com/trends/explore#cmpt=q, and IDC, Google daily, and annual search statistics, per Statistic Brain, http://www.statisticbrain.com/google-searches/ (accessed November 4, 2013).
32. Lardinois, Frederic, Google Now Knows about 1 Trillion Pages, ReadWriteWeb, July 25, 2008, http://www.readwriteweb.com/archives/google_hits_one_trillion_pages.php (accessed August 6, 2010).
33. http://www.google.com/insidesearch/howsearchworks/crawling-indexing.html (accessed November 4, 2013).
34. comScore search engine rankings, September 2013, http://www.comscore.com/Insights/Press_Releases/2013/10/comScore_Releases_September_2013_US_Search_Engine_Rankings (accessed November 4, 2013).
35. Steiner, Peter, On the Internet, Nobody Knows You're a Dog, *The New Yorker*, 69(20), July 5, 1993, p. 61.
36. Robbins, Ira P., Writings on the Wall: The Need for an Authorship-Centric Approach to the Authentication of Social-Networking Evidence, *Minnesota Journal of Law, Science and Technology*, Winter 2013, http://conservancy.umn.edu/bitstream/147600/1/Authentication-of-Social-Networking-Evidence-by-Ira-Robbins-MN-Journal-of-Law-Science-Tech-Issue-13-1.pdf (accessed January 22, 2014).
37. Robbins, Writings on the Wall; United States v. Drew, 259 F.R.D. 449, 452 (C.D. Cal. 2009).
38. Robbins, Writings on the Wall.
39. Google, http://www.googleguide.com/google_works.html (accessed November 4, 2013).

Chapter 2

Behavior Online

Internet Use Growth

Over 2.4 billion people worldwide, 34% of the world's population, including nearly 85% of adult Americans, frequently use the Internet.[1] Higher percentages of those who are younger, more affluent, and better educated use the Internet for all types of purposes, including communications, social, recreational, and commercial exchanges.[2] The Internet has become an essential element of life for government, industry, organizations, and individuals. Telecommunications ride the Internet protocol (IP) backbone. Retailers and government agency services depend on their presence online for services, marketing, billing, and communications.

As constructive Internet uses have enriched American life dramatically, an equally destructive increase has occurred in the use of the Internet for illegal, illicit, and inappropriate purposes. Susannah Fox of Pew's Internet and American Life Project said in 2008:

> Our research finds that many Americans are jumping into the participatory Web without considering all the implications. If nothing really bad has happened to someone, they tend neither to worry about their personal information nor to take steps to limit the amount of information that can be found about them online. On the other hand, if someone has had a bad experience with embarrassing or inaccurate information being posted online, they are more likely to take steps to limit the availability of personal information.[3]

The phenomenon of Americans revealing a little too much about themselves, including documenting their own misbehavior, suggests that employers should be concerned about what is online. If no "bad news" about a candidate or employee can be found on the Internet, so much the better—that will be the case for the vast majority of individuals. If there is derogatory information, it will either have a bearing on the job or not and will either be of sufficient seriousness (e.g., an arrest or conviction) or not (e.g., party photos). As with all other aspects of a person's background, when handled correctly, online postings can help determine eligibility and qualifications and can be strong indicators of an individual's trustworthiness in using an employer's information technology (IT) systems.

Adoption of Internet services delivered over high-speed Internet connections at work and at home has spurred massive Internet usage both during and after work hours. For example, recent statistics showed that over 1.1 billion users subscribe to Facebook, and half are daily users, with an overall average of 20 minutes per visit per user.[4] The top 15 social networking websites as of November 2013 present quite a change from 2010, as usage has surged and the leading sites, including Facebook, Twitter, LinkedIn, Pinterest, MySpace, Google+, and more (see Figure 2.1),[5] claim increasing time from users. Over 61% of US adults use social network websites (see Figure 2.2).[6]

Social networking sites facilitate information sharing in many different ways. Millions of people use such sites for both work and personal networking over both mobile and computer networks. Sites like LinkedIn facilitate work contacts and often interlink with social sites. Of course, these are only a few of many similar

Rank	Name	Est. Unique Monthly Visitors	URL
1	Facebook	800 million	facebook.com
2	Twitter	250 million	twitter.com
3	LinkedIn	200 million	linkedin.com
4	Pinterest	120 million	pinterest.com
5	MySpace	70.5 million	myspace.com
6	Google+	65 million	google+.com
7	Instagram	50 million	instagram.com
8	DeviantArt	25.5 million	deviantart.com
9	LiveJournal	20.5 million	livejournal.com
10	Tagged	19.5 million	tagged.com
11	Orkut	17.5 million	orkut.com
12	CafeMom	12.5 million	cafemom.com
13	Ning	12 million	ning.com
14	Meetup	7.5 million	meetup.com
15	myLife	5.4 million	mylife.com

Figure 2.1 Fifteen most popular social networking websites in the United States, according to eBiz MBA (see Note 5).

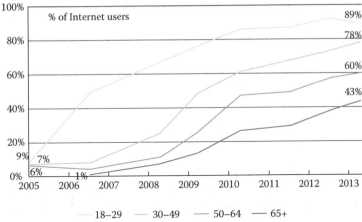

Figure 2.2   Pew's Lee Rainie used this slide in a November 7, 2013 presentation, Networked Worlds and Networked Enterprises, at the Knowledge Management and Enterprise Solutions Conference (see Note 6).

networking sites, and instant messaging through wireless telephone networks and hosts like Yahoo, Windows Live, Google, and AOL share traffic in addition to Twitter. Diversion by "tweet," daily social site profile updates, and scanning friends' sites by themselves represent a challenge to an organization's systems security, productivity, bandwidth use, and authorized use policy (AUP) and creates opportunities for inadvertent disclosures of sensitive information.

Searching for information, for professional or purely personal purposes, occupies a place at the center of Internet activities, as illustrated by the top 10 websites in America, 3 of which, including first-ranked Google, fourth-ranked Yahoo, and tenth-place Bing, have a focus on search.[7] Yahoo, a web portal, shares search engine functionality with Bing, Microsoft's entry (see Figure 2.3).

Browsing, playing games, stock trading, shopping, gambling, and other personal online activities at work are common. Many employers, including military bases abroad, have responded by limiting employees' ability to use devices and applications on enterprise systems and block access to certain websites and online activities. Among concerns are exposure to malicious code, intellectual property theft, and diversion from duties.[8] However, at a higher level, a variety of security vulnerabilities have been introduced by online capabilities, among which are industrial espionage, competitive intelligence, infiltration, social engineering, fraud, and misuse of IT systems, including unauthorized "parking" of illicit data or applications on enterprise systems. A malicious outsider now has many more ways to survey, case, and penetrate a targeted business, agency, or organization. Recruiting the assistance of a complicit or unwitting insider accomplice just became much

Rank	Name	Type of Site	URL
1	Google	Search, web portal	google.com
2	Facebook	Social networking	facebook.com
3	YouTube	Video sharing	youtube.com
4	Yahoo	Web portal	yahoo.com
5	Amazon	Marketplace	amazon.com
6	LinkedIn	Professional networking	linkedin.com
7	Wikipedia	Open-source encyclopedia	wikipedia.org
8	eBay	Marketplace	ebay.com
9	Twitter	Instant messaging	twitter.com
10	Bing	Search, web portal	bing.com

Figure 2.3   Ten most popular websites in the United States per Alexa (see Note 7).

easier. A core vulnerability in a time of greater Internet exposure by an enterprise's employees is that it only takes one compromised insider account to do grave damage because of the very IT infrastructure created to make the enterprise more efficient.

Although innocent Internet uses have exploded, a wide variety of serious crimes and misbehaviors are being committed on the Internet, as many people and sites dedicated to illegal and illicit activities have appeared.[9] Surprisingly, many individuals take part in illegal and illicit activities using the virtual identities (e-mail addresses, user identities) issued by their business and government employers. Many others use virtual identities freely available through Internet service and e-mail providers like Hotmail, Google, Yahoo, AOL, cable and telecom Internet services, and others. Because a user can create a virtual identity that contains no reference to a true name or other validated contact information, a high degree of anonymity can be employed in Internet activities. Given the amount of commercial e-mail (spam), phishing (fraudulent spam), and other threats based on a user's virtual identity, it is normal to use an e-mail address or nickname that does not include one's true name online.

As the types of Internet sites appealing to all types of users have expanded, naturally more websites with a criminal purpose have also come online. Some illicit Internet activities are readily found on public sites that anyone can encounter; others take place on sites that have a degree of exclusivity, such as requiring a user to sign in with a password. Even on such password-protected sites (e.g., Facebook, MySpace), it may be possible to find misuse by searching on true names and e-mail addresses on the public Internet because the websites themselves facilitate search engine indexing of names (so that one can find one's friends). Many popular websites employing user passwords, with tens of millions of simultaneous users, are therefore quite "public" because the only practical function of the sign-on is to facilitate counting, data mining, and contacting users for advertising and not to prevent widespread exposure of postings. Note that sites' AUPs may forbid certain uses of information (e.g., collecting users' identifying data for commercial advertising purposes), but having an account allows a user to see other users' public profiles. Although users can invoke privacy controls, a large number do not choose to do so.[10] This results in a large number of postings of a potentially offensive nature, such as self-admitted drug and alcohol abuse and postings offering pornography. Employees using ostensibly innocent sites can expose the workplace to those offensive postings. Internet use habits thus bring a certain amount of unwelcome content into the workplace. Unfortunately, improper computer use occurs both outside and inside the workplace.

Increasingly, businesses monitor or block employees' Internet surfing, personal e-mail, blogging, social networking, shopping, and other online activities on company machines. A substantial percentage of monitored employees are caught and disciplined or fired for improper systems use. Most employers told an American Management Association survey[11] that although they notify employees of the monitoring, there is an increasing incidence of disciplinary action. Clearly, this indicates that the temptation to abuse employers' systems overcomes the threat of disciplinary action, up to termination. Reportedly, 28% of employers surveyed fired workers for e-mail misuse. At the root of concern is accountability for online actions. As far as we know, no correlation was measured between employers who check candidates' Internet habits before hiring and employers who monitor employees' work computers on the job. As yet, *formal* Internet vetting appears not to be a common practice, at least not so common that it was included in the survey.

The incidence of employee criminal activities detected has grown, according to recent surveys, including studies of identity theft, retail industry losses, data breaches by insiders and outsiders, and intellectual property loss.[12] An additional concern for industry is that employers continue to lose 73% of negligent hiring cases that go to jury trials, as cited by Barry Nixon and Kim Kerr in their excellent book on background investigations.[13] Therefore, available information about trends suggests that employers have reason for concern about the potential incidence, impact, and security implications of illicit computer use by both candidates and employees.

Evolution of Internet Uses

Online activities' popularity and participation reflect the massive surge of individuals of all ages and nationalities embracing the Internet, some allowing migration to automated versions of physical activities (e-mail for postal mail) and some for the new forms of Internet social interaction, entertainment, education, e-commerce, news, games, fantasy, pornography, and communications offered. Increased bandwidth has allowed films, music, video, and TV to stream into computers, handheld devices, and television sets, disrupting traditional sources, while adoption of 4G wireless (and beyond) allows all types of computing to travel. New hardware and software have supported services through low-cost, high-bandwidth, wireless telecommunications, including search, geo-location and networking, building large-scale business, government, academic, and organizational structures to provide online functions.

Frequently updated demographic data from Pew Internet and American Life surveys,[14] as set out in Figures 1.4 and 1.5, suggest that Internet use is much higher for those with more education, higher income, and dwelling in urban areas. For example, 96% or more of college graduates with income over $75,000 annually are Internet users. From the standpoint of a personnel security specialist, virtually all applicants and employees are probably engaged in frequent Internet use.

The highest percentages[15] of those online use the Internet for searching, e-mail, directions, a hobby or interest, weather, shopping, news, web surfing, video, buying, government, social networking, travel arrangements, and so on. Social networking is a highly popular Internet activity (see Figures 2.1 to 2.5),[16] driving many

Online Activity	% of Users	Survey Date
Use a search engine	91	2/1/2012
Send or read e-mail	88	12/1/2012
Find a map or directions	84	8/1/2011
Pursue a hobby or interest	84	8/1/2011
Check the weather	81	5/1/2010
Shop for a product/service	78	9/1/2010
Get news	78	8/1/2012
Web surf for fun	74	8/1/2011
Watch a video	71	5/1/2011
Buy a product	71	5/1/2011
Use a government site	67	5/1/2011
Social networking	67	12/1/2012
Arrange for travel	65	5/1/2011
Look for political news	61	12/1/2012
Bank online	61	5/1/2011
Look for a job	56	5/1/2011
Use online classified ads	53	5/1/2010
Look at Wikipedia	53	5/1/2010
Find "how-to" info	53	12/1/2012
Take a virtual tour	52	8/1/2011
Get sports news	52	1/1/2010
Find info about someone	51	8/1/2012

Figure 2.4   Pew Internet and American Life Surveys have shown the most popular online activities in the past few years (see Note 15).

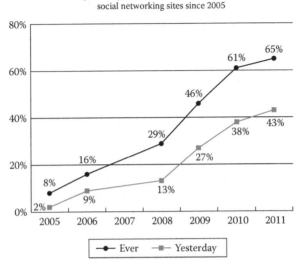

Social networking site use by online adults, 2005–2011
The percentage of all adult Internet users who use
social networking sites since 2005

Figure 2.5 Pew's tracking of social networking growth illustrates the rapid changes in online behaviors in recent years (see Note 16).

adults (not just teens) to use sites like Facebook and Twitter daily. For example, taking and sharing photos with multiple devices, along with brief text messages, have become popular, particularly with younger (age 40 and under) users. As the impact on society of daily Internet use has progressed, so has the "power user" group, that is, those who devote large portions of their days to activities online, using multiple types of devices, applications, and networks.[17] Power users should not be viewed in the same category as ordinary users because they can be a valuable resource for any employer or group, but they can also pose a danger if they are inclined to misuse computing devices (see Figure 2.6).

For well over half of the adult population,[18] mobile and wire line access tools have a symbiotic relationship, largely because of the explosion in the use of wireless broadband networking and handheld devices, at home, in the workplace, and in commercial establishments. Laptops, tablets, and "smart" cell phones increasingly mirror each other's capabilities, often differentiated by such terms as *work* and *home*. Mobile users typically have ready access to high-speed connections at home, often using wireless local-area networks, which results in frequent, if not constant, home Internet use. The digital content on the mobile device often prompts more activity on their broadband-enabled big screen at home. At the same time, the desktop Internet experience easily switches to "on the go" as the handheld becomes a complementary access point to connect with people and digital content wherever a wireless network reaches. Examples include continuously updated sports and news,

---

Profile of a Power User

- Has multiple Internet-connected devices (desktop, laptop, tablet, cell phone, game console, music player, portable gaming devices, e-book reader)
- Uses wireless connections
- Goes online often, daily, everywhere (home, work, outside)
- Has online profiles (e.g., Facebook, Twitter) used often
- Values and protects online reputation and privacy
- Creates and posts content online often

Figure 2.6   Attributes of a power user were derived from studies by Pew Internet and American Life Project.

music, and location-based applications to find destinations and friends who are nearby. Those tied primarily to wired devices may exhibit decidedly less devotion to technology, but their daily use nevertheless consumes substantial portions of their day. By inference from the Pew data, one can discern that a high percentage of job applicants in the 21- to 64-year-old age group spend a significant part of their day online.

A 2007 Pew study[19] of types of online activities that may be unacceptable in the workplace found the following percentage of users who frequently engage in them:

Read online journals and blogs (39%)
Download computer programs (39%)
Download music files (37%)
Upload photos (37%)

So, the question every employer with employees online must consider is whether to accept the kinds of risks posed by Internet diversions (e.g., time to read blogs of personal interest), unauthorized software introduced into workplace systems, music and videos legally or illegally downloaded, occupying storage meant for business data with personal files, and usurping bandwidth for transmittal of large personal payloads. Activities increasingly more popular since 2007 include watching online videos and playing games, which can divert workers from work, can be bandwidth intensive, and may even damage an employer's reputation. More recent trends include "BYOD," that is, bring your own device, which challenges employers worried about mixing business and personal computing, loss of intellectual property, unauthorized network connections, and inappropriate online behaviors. Some recent examples are useful to illustrate the kinds of threats posed:

A foreign-born engineer downloaded hardware and software designs and took them with him to a new employer months before his economic espionage was detected. He had a long history of unauthorized access to his employers' data not necessary for his work, and an examination of his computer use habits would have shown several red flags. He was convicted of economic espionage.[20]

A computer security employee acted as the principal manager of a massively multiplayer online role-playing game (MMORPG) involving thousands of people under his direction in a fantasy space war. He held a live online strategy meeting in which he used racist, sexist, and other inflammatory language contrary to his employer's policies and posted a recording of the offensive remarks online. Because of his prolific postings and newspaper interviews, the true name and employment of the person were widely known. On investigation, it was shown that on numerous occasions he used company time to engage in his Internet fantasy role. Especially in view of his computer security role and his cavalier behavior in violation of his employer's code of conduct, he posed a significant security risk and probably committed felonious theft of salary for services he did not perform while playing at work.

A US soldier deployed to Iraq posted numerous photographs of his deployment on his social network site profile, with no privacy protections, using his military e-mail address as his profile name. Among the photos were sensitive fortifications and an obscene photo of a fellow soldier. Not only could the enemy see the soldier's postings, but also the postings blatantly violated the Military Code of Conduct.

An employee of a defense facility posted a detailed biography, numerous photographs (including military bases and aircraft), travel itineraries of extensive global tourism, dozens of friends and acquaintances (including many from abroad), and indiscreet descriptions of herself as "an adventure junkie." The description included birth in a former Soviet bloc country, friends in nations unfriendly to the United States, plans to travel abroad in the future, and contact information, including true name, work e-mail address, phone numbers, and other personal data—all available for anyone to see. This is a classic case of a blatant security risk, an attractive candidate for hostile intelligence or terrorist interest, and a possible indicator of naïve lack of security awareness by the individual.

Because Internet usage has changed, employers should pay attention to the risks that may be added by employees' online habits and by new employees whose IT system habits are not yet known. The nature of added risks can be significant with even a small number of authorized users whose computer and portable device activities include illegal and illicit behaviors, such as copyright infringement, fraud, and harassment. Ironically, automation provides capabilities that convey what Chinese military leaders like to call a great equalizer because it is the enemy's dependence on computers that allows an external or internal attack to have immediate, disproportionate impact. The US attacks on Iraq and Afghanistan illustrate the impact of cyber warfare, based on media reports of communications and utility outages caused by a combination of physical and cyber assaults. Insider attacks are particularly difficult to prevent and to detect. Even when detected, insider attacks may be so destructive that it is all but impossible to recover.

Physical World, Virtual Activities

Among the activities moving online are several that can cause unanticipated problems in a virtual world because of distinct characteristics that are different from the physical versions that they replace. For example, stolen property was previously offered for sale to pawn shops, flea markets, and in classified newspaper ads. Today, eBay and craigslist (to name just two of many websites) offer the capability of selling to millions of prospective customers while maintaining anonymity in a forest of similar ads. Information can be taken not by photocopying documents but by searching for sensitive and valuable data, downloading and copying, printing, burning to a thumb drive or CD, or simply e-mailing or uploading it out of the enterprise. One example of a physical norm that for most employers does not translate into the virtual world is the request that an applicant provide aliases on preemployment forms. Few employers require a listing of e-mail addresses and other virtual identities, ignoring the widespread behavior of Internet users who have several online personas, including some without any indicator of their true name; several user IDs, also unlike their name; and several nicknames used for specific websites. It is not unusual for today's Internet user to have different user IDs for e-commerce, banking, social sites, e-mail, music, videos, photos, games, hobbies, and so on. Recorded online are activities that in most cases are, like their physical counterparts, legal and proper. However, in the minority of individuals inclined to engage in illegal, antisocial, or offensive behavior, it is likely that they have left evidence online. When this assertion is made to some employers and even investigators, they express skepticism because using anonymous virtual identities is so easy. Nevertheless, there will always be a substantial number of people who blatantly post evidence of their offensive conduct, either inadvertently or purposefully sprinkling the Internet with examples.

Connections and Disconnecting

An observer of the Internet scene remarked that when past generations graduated from college, they maintained contact with their eight best friends, losing track of the dozens of others whom they now only meet at reunions or by chance. Today's graduates often retain contact with "eighty best friends," who link to each other in a variety of ways, including social sites, alumni groups, and mutual interest websites. Today, it is harder to avoid the one or two in every group who have taken a bad turn, such as substance abuse, criminal activities, and association with shady characters. Striving to be one of the "good guys" can expose an individual to people and activities that perhaps could easily have been avoided when our electronic personas did not allow us to be tracked wherever we go. Small indiscretions can become widespread news in a flash. It would seem that discreet behavior would help protect the wired crowd from exposure through today's social networking. However, the opposite appears to be the case. Even in groups that have learned to turn on their Facebook privacy protections, it appears that blatant examples of misbehavior are posted often, if not by an individual about himself or herself, then by a friend, family member, or associate who considers the story, photos, videos, or other items amusing. Almost everyone has something in his or her background that he or she would rather not talk about. Today, it is likely that that something will appear online. Extricating oneself from damning postings can be difficult (although not impossible). A cottage industry has grown up around removal of embarrassing materials from websites, either by those who regret having placed it there in the first place or by those who feel slandered or at least "outed" by others' postings. Two unfortunate factors may impede removal of such postings: The websites may not respond positively in a timely manner, and the cached images of the prior postings could remain available through several search engines and archive sites for some time (years). The only way to be certain that derogatory information is not online is avoiding having it posted in the first place.

Ironically, Pew's research in recent years showed that from 2006 to 2009, the percentage of Internet users in each age group that took steps to limit the amount of information about them available online decreased in all age categories (see Figure 2.7). In a 2012 study,[21] Pew found that teens aged 12–17 were more likely to

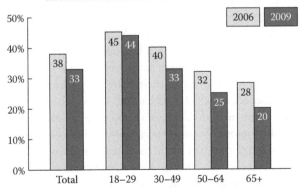

Figure 2.7 In this 3-year period, efforts to limit online information diminished for all age categories.

post their photo, school, city of residence, e-mail address, and cell phone number than before. While these percentages are apt to change as people learn how best to connect electronically, the phenomenon of openness online appears to be here for the indefinite future. When users later have regrets about the impressions given by their postings, they may be unable to purge them.

In fact, it may be easier said than done to keep the Internet free of material about anyone. In doing background investigations on numerous people at all levels of business and government, I have found extensive data even on those with little or no inclination to use the Internet. Among the types of data are directories (addresses, phone numbers), neighborhood maps and satellite photos, even ground-level photos of homes, employers' websites, trade publications, associations, schools, genealogical records, court records, media reports, and more. Besides the free data available on the Internet, services like LexisNexis; Acurint (a Lexis service providing private and public data mined from multiple government, business, and directory sources); Intelius (which provides background data for a fee to anyone with a credit card); and other data providers can be found online that profile virtually anyone for a fee.[22]

Business and government leaders, those who are subjects of news stories, and many others find themselves "available" to anyone willing to inquire: Who are they? What is their background? What have they been accused of? At first blush, it does not seem fair that even those who do not use the Internet would find themselves profiled there for almost anyone to see. Yet, it is precisely this attribute of the information society, as the Europeans would say, that makes the Internet so interesting: You can probably find out about almost anyone. Of course, in Europe, Canada, and Asia, privacy regulations keep much personal information off the Web if the subject of interest is not a public figure and does not "opt in." In the United States, one must "opt out" to protect personal data. More about privacy appears in Section II.

In several cases, executives have sought to find every Internet reference to them and tried to expunge references that reveal too much. Whether they are subject to the chants of demonstrators outside their Manhattan condominiums, kidnapping attempts on their wives and children in Bogota, e-mail extortion threats, letter bombs, or other attacks in San Jose, some well-known individuals have found that Internet publicity has worked to their detriment. Celebrities and politicians are frequently threatened, attacked, and hacked online. Those subjected to attacks by interest groups begin to feel that it is all too easy to learn about their private lives by googling their names. Some corporate efforts have been focused on finding and erasing the postings that can facilitate threats, stalking, harassment, and in some cases, physical attacks. Yet, millions of young people continue to build a rich, multifaceted online record of their life's trivia.

Notes

1. Internet World Stats as of June 2012, http://www.internetworldstats.com/stats.htm (accessed November 12, 2013). Pew Internet and American Life Project, May 2013 survey, http://www.pewinternet.org/Commentary/2011/November/Pew-Internet-Health.aspx (accessed November 12, 2013).

2. Pew Internet and American Life Project, http://www.pewinternet.org.

3. Fox, Susannah, Privacy Implications of Fast, Mobile Internet Access, Pew Internet and American Life Project, February 13, 2008, http://www.pewinternet.org/~/media/Files/Reports/2008/Privacy_Fast_Mobile_Access.pdf.pdf (accessed November 12, /2013).

4. Statistic Brain, Facebook statistics, June 23, 2013, http://www.statisticbrain.com/facebook-statistics/ (accessed November 12, /2013).

5. eBiz MBA, Internet statistics updated monthly, November 1, 2013, http://www.ebizmba.com/articles/social-networking-websites (accessed November 12, 2013).

6. Rainie, Lee, Pew Internet and American Life, Networked Worlds and Networked Enterprises, November 7, 2013, at the Knowledge Management and Enterprise Solutions Conference, Washington, DC.

7. Alexa, Top Sites in the United States, http://www.alexa.com/topsites/countries/US (accessed November 12, 2013).

8. Madden, Mary, and Jones, Sydney, Networked Workers, Pew Internet and American Life Project, September 24, 2008, http://www.pewinternet.org/Reports/2008/Networked-Workers.aspx.

9. Presentations and discussions at semiannual conferences of the International Association of Chiefs of Police (the Computer Crime and Digital Evidence Committee that I founded) and annual presentations at the ASIS International Conference since 1995.

10. Fox, Susannah, Pew Internet and American Life Project, February 2008, based on Pew Digital Footprints Internet Project, December 2007; Symantec cybercrime summary, http://www.symantec.com/norton/cybercrime/index.jsp (accessed August 8, 2010); Paget, Francois, Cybercrime and Hacktivism, McAfee Labs, March 2010, http://www.mcafee.com/us/local_content/white_papers/cybercrime_20100315_en.pdf (accessed August 8, 2010).

11. Bourke, James, Curbing and Battling Employee Misuse of Technology, March 24, 2008. An American Management Association survey found that approximately 75% of respondents monitor their employees' website visits to prevent inappropriate surfing. In addition, 65% of those surveyed used software to block or filter connections to websites deemed off limits to employees, while about one-third (33%) tracked keystrokes and time spent online. Over 50% reviewed and retained e-mail messages sent to and from their employees. http://www.cpa2biz.com/Content/media/PRODUCER_CONTENT/Newsletters/Articles_2008/CPA/Mar/Misuse_of_Technology.jsp (viewed March 30, 2010).

12. Greenemeier, Larry, Information Week Research—Accenture 10th Annual Information Security Survey, July 2007, http://www.informationweek.com/story/showArticle.jhtml?articleID=201001203 (accessed May 5, 2010); The Post Breach Boom, Ponemon Institute, February 26, 2013, http://www.ponemon.org/blog/the-post-breach-boom (accessed November 14, 2013); Insider Threat Study: Illicit Cyber Activity Involving Fraud in the US Financial Services Sector, Software Engineering Institute, Carnegie Mellon University, July 2012, http://resources.sei.cmu.edu/library/asset-view.cfm?assetID=27971 (accessed November 14, 2013).

13. Nixon, W. Barry, and Kerr, Kim M., *Background Screening and Investigations, Managing Risk from HR and Security Perspectives* (New York: Elsevier, 2008).

14. See http://www.pewinternet.org/Static-Pages/Trend-Data-(Adults)/Whos-Online.aspx (accessed November 14, 2013).

15. Catalogued and updated Pew Internet and American Life Surveys, http://www.pewinternet.org/Trend-Data-(Adults)/Online-Activites-Total.aspx (accessed November 14, 2013).

16. Pew Internet and American Life Project statistics, http://www.pewinternet.org/Reports/2011/Social-Networking-Sites/Report.aspx?view=all (accessed November 14, 2013).

17. Pew Internet and American Life studies indicate multiple dimensions in which a person may be called a "power user," http://www.pewinternet.org/Search.aspx?q=power%20users&i=20, including Madden, Mary, Four or More, *The New Demographic*, June 2010, http://www.pewinternet.org/Presentations/2010/Jun/Four-or-More—The-New-Demographic.aspx (accessed November 14, 2013).

18. Horrigan, John, The Mobile Difference, Pew Internet and American Life, http://www.pewinternet.org/Reports/2009/5-The-Mobile-Difference—Typology.aspx, http://www.pewinternet.org/Search.aspx?q=wireless%20use, and http://www.pewinternet.org/Search.aspx?q=home%20wireless (accessed November 14, 2013).

19. Horrigan, John B., A Typology of Information and Communication Technology Users, Pew Internet and American Life Project, May 7, 2007, http://www.pewinternet.org/~/media//Files/Reports/2007/PIP_ICT_Typology.pdf.pdf (accessed June 24, 2010).

20. US Department of Justice, press release, August 2, 2007. On August 1, 2007, Xiaodong Sheldon Meng, 42, formerly a resident of Beijing, China, and resident of Cupertino, California, pleaded guilty to violating the Economic Espionage Act (EAA), the Arms Export Control Act (AECA) and the International Traffic in Arms Regulations (ITAR), http://www.usdoj.gov/criminal/cybercrime/mengPlea.htm (accessed May 5, 2009).

21. Teens, Social Media, and Privacy, Pew Internet and American Life Project, http://www.pewinternet.org/Reports/2013/Teens-Social-Media-And-Privacy/Main-Report/Part-2.aspx (accessed January 25, 2014).

22. O'Harrow, Robert, Jr., *No Place to Hide* (New York: Free Press, 2005).

Chapter 3

Use and Abuse: Crime and Misbehavior Online

Introduction

In 2011, at least 2.3 billion people, the equivalent of more than one-third of the world's total population, had access to the Internet. Over 60% of all Internet users are in developing countries, with 45% of all Internet users below the age of 25 years. By the year 2017, it is estimated that mobile broadband subscriptions will approach 70% of the world's total population. By the year 2020, the number of networked devices (the "Internet of things") will outnumber people by six to one, transforming current conceptions of the Internet. In the hyperconnected world of tomorrow, it will become hard to imagine a "computer crime," and perhaps any crime, that does not involve electronic evidence linked with Internet protocol (IP) connectivity.[1]

Computer-based crime (i.e., criminal acts committed using computers or where computers hold evidence of a crime) is poorly measured. Unfortunately, few if any solid metrics are available on the incidence, proportion, or impact of illegal Internet uses. Regional computer forensic laboratories run by the Federal Bureau of Investigation (FBI) in 15 different US regions have experienced rapid, sustained increases in the types, numbers, and quantities of data involved in all criminal activities involving computers.[2] FBI Director James B. Comey testified before Congress[3] that

> The diverse threats we face are increasingly cyber-based. Much of America's most sensitive data is stored on computers. We are losing data, money, and ideas through cyber intrusions. This threatens innovation and, as citizens, we are also increasingly vulnerable to losing

our personal information. That is why we anticipate that in the future, resources devoted to cyber-based threats will equal or even eclipse the resources devoted to non-cyber based terrorist threats.

The Internet Crime Complaint Center (IC3) reported[4] that in 2012, after double-digit increases since 2008, the IC3 received 289,874 consumer complaints representing over $525 million in losses, an 8.3% increase in reported losses since 2011. A 2013 UN cybercrime study said, "At the global level, law enforcement respondents to the study perceive increasing levels of cybercrime, as both individuals and organized criminal groups exploit new criminal opportunities, driven by profit and personal gain."[5] The UN study found that the victimization rate for cybercrime is significantly higher than that for "conventional crime," particularly in developing countries. The 2013 PriceWaterhouseCoopers (PWC) US State of Cybercrime Survey[6] revealed, among other things:

> The cybercrime threat environment has become increasingly pervasive and hostile—and actions to stem the tide of attacks have had limited effect. We must accept that cyberattacks are now a routine part of doing business in today's uncertain world, and they likely will be a part of doing business going forward. ...
>
> Leaders do not know who is responsible for their organization's cybersecurity. ...
>
> Many leaders underestimate their cyber-adversaries' capabilities and the strategic financial, reputational, and regulatory risks they pose. ...
>
> Leaders are unknowingly increasing their digital attack vulnerabilities by adopting social collaboration, expanding the use of mobile devices, moving the storage of information to the cloud, digitizing sensitive information, moving to smart grid technologies, and embracing workforce mobility alternatives—without first considering the impact these technological innovations have on their cybersecurity profiles.

By the Numbers?

Casing, communications, and planning are fundamental parts of many types of criminal conspiracies, which these days often take place online. Many types of criminal investigations, including Internet child exploitation; sex slavery and prostitution; identity thefts; sale of stolen property; frauds; trafficking in pirated goods such as films, music, software, and hardware; counterfeiting; radical/terrorist activities; intellectual property theft; malicious code use; and denial-of-service attacks, have experienced substantial increases in the past few years. Despite various efforts, including an FBI–Computer Security Institute annual computer crime survey[7] and a US Department of Justice, Bureau of Justice Statistics survey a few years ago,[8] solid cybercrime statistics are still elusive. Increasing numbers reported in the press—including losses claimed at over $100 billion to $1 trillion annually—may be an indication of better Internet crime reporting or may signal rises in crime online (and certainly signal sensational media reporting). After 35 years of association with computer crime investigators and computer forensic examiners, I have no doubt that Internet crime has increased steadily and now has reached prodigious levels. The proof of this proposition is that wherever populations have grown, crime rates have increased—and it appears that the Internet is no exception.

Sadly, Internet crime is rarely reported, rarely investigated, and rarely results in arrests and convictions. The most notorious cybercriminals are comparatively few in number. Federal, state, and local law enforcement have taken tens of millions of reports of identity crimes (mostly frauds), yet can address only a handful of them. Many reported thefts of databases containing private, personally identifying information go unsolved or unprosecuted. Frauds using stolen identities estimated in the tens of millions (dollars and incidents) are unsolved for the most part. Undercover operations on the Internet pitting cops against child molesters and porn traders consistently show large volumes of activity and historically comprised half of anti-cybercrime efforts. Police chiefs have said that they have to limit their officers' involvement in Internet crimes against children. Many chiefs describe these cases as a "bottomless pit" of relentless crimes that are not diminished by high-profile enforcement, such as NBC's "To Catch a Predator" (where, ironically, repeat offenders were encountered because of the insatiable drive in molesters who knew or certainly should have suspected that the "children" encountered online could easily be undercover police—again). Although law enforcement is making strides against cybercrime, it appears that the volume, seriousness, impact, and international reach all continue to grow. This means that for those entrusted with ensuring a trustworthy workforce, conducting investigations, and gathering intelligence, there are more challenges every day, and ignoring the Internet's threats and opportunities is simply naïve and ignorant, as PWC's 2013 survey suggested.

Online Venues

Websites, Internet Relay Chat (IRC), blogs, and hosted group sites have become online clubhouses for gangs and organized criminal groups. For example, there are over 1,000 sites offering/hosting pirated movies, TV shows, music, and software globally. Websites involved in criminal activities like piracy are run, supplied, and patronized by millions of persons who are not being arrested or charged.[9] Perpetrators' identities might be ascertained by Internet investigations. In some cases, their names and virtual identities are widely known, yet they are not brought to justice for many reasons, including locations abroad, where cybercrime laws are weak, nonexistent, or not enforced. Given the current cybercrime situation, employers must confront their responsibilities to protect people, assets, and information against candidates for employment whose online misbehavior may be discoverable. Unfortunately, most cybercriminals have no arrest record. As with all types of criminal activities, Internet crime runs the gamut from high-impact, violent activities like drug trafficking to annoying spam and pop-up ads. Like legitimate businesses, criminal enterprises have discovered that automation, networking, e-commerce, and Internet anonymity can facilitate efficiency, rapidly scaled marketing, quick sales growth, and customer satisfaction.[10]

A good example of organized Internet crime is illicit online pharmaceutical sales. Large numbers of online pharmacies offer discounted brand-name and generic drugs, ostensibly from Canada and Europe, but predominantly from China, India, Russia, East Europe, the Caribbean, and the South Pacific. The average US consumer, facing high drug prices, cannot easily determine the legitimacy of the discount products or websites. US, Canadian, Russian, Chinese, and Indian organized criminals offer prescription drugs without a prescription and ship or mail medicines to customers who will not know if the pills are poison, counterfeit, generic, or the real thing. Even repackaged, diverted products appear in Internet pharmaceutical channels. It is a classic case of the web's ability to host black, gray, and legitimate markets, often indistinguishable from each other to customers.[11]

Digital Delinquency

By its nature, the Internet has spawned illegal activities that are digital. For example, sales and bartering of misappropriated content such as films, videos, music, audio, software, designs, and other intellectual property have become lucrative businesses. Like a criminal form of eBay or craigslist, websites host auctions and sales of stolen credit card data and purloined personal identities. New software and networking systems have been created to facilitate transfer of large digital files, such as Napster and BitTorrent (described as "Download big files fast. Publish and sync files of any size.").[12]

Old-fashioned fencing and duplication of stolen DVDs have been joined by high-speed transfer of films' data files from multiple sites distributed globally. In some cases, individual sites host no technically illegal content (e.g., by hosting only a part of a pirated film), and only a central controller's permission allows users to access, download, verify, and reassemble the whole thing. Some criminal sites' sophisticated uses of authentication, encryption, compression, and high-bandwidth transmission at times exceed the norm of commercial Internet services.

"Free" Intellectual Property

Although copyright violations are illegal, especially for commercial rather than personal use, Internet file sharing has given rise to a quasi-religious belief that information should be free. Large groups of people think that they have a God-given right to all the information accessible to them. Profound changes in music, film, TV, and software production have been necessitated by technological challenges to digital property rights protection (known as digital rights management, DRM). The blogosphere resounds with philosophical wars—some of which have resulted in retrenchment by entertainment companies—when digital rights are asserted and enforced using new technologies. Ironically, it is not the American National Security Agency (NSA), British Government Communications Headquarters (GCHQ), or Russian FSB (Federal Security Service; KGB) cryptographers who are most energized when new commercial encryption is deployed to protect movies, tunes, and software. An entirely new class of "amateur" cryptographers has learned how to attack copyright protections, cooperating internationally and overcoming language, mathematical, and technical barriers to break controls on digital goods.[13] In this context, it becomes clear that intellectual property protections and well-established legal principles are at considerable risk.

Large numbers of Internet users have been quickly mobilized to denounce DRM controls, resulting in entertainment companies like Sony choosing to rescind built-in protections.[14] While dwelling on the reasons for the failure of technology to solve the digital rights conundrum is not necessary here, to be fair, one must allocate some blame to the inadequacy of the technical solutions themselves. The subclass of attackers with large-scale, commercialized criminal operations has benefitted from the anticontrol feelings. This subclass threatens both government and business employers, as well as the companies whose goods they misappropriate. Not only do Internet-facilitated illegal acts create risks for enterprises, but also the cybercrimes themselves skew society's ability to detect, measure, assess, and respond to the types of crime problems that arise. Cybercrime is a category of security risk requiring in-depth study in its own right. For purposes of this review, it is necessary to recognize these key attributes:

- Law enforcement struggles with prevention and enforcement of Internet crimes because international, federal, state, regional, and local police jurisdictions are physical, not virtual, and "Internet patrol" has not yet arrived.
- Rapid evolution of Internet crimes (e.g., phishing, which is the use of spam to entice victims online) often defeats enforcement by the speed, scale, geographic dispersal, and anonymity of the crimes.
- Because the Internet is global, anti-cybercrime enforcers are often unable to bring perpetrators to prosecution. When prosecutions occur, the scale of violations documented (e.g., in seized computer hardware and records) often results in identified perpetrators who are not prosecuted because they are abroad, too numerous, or deemed not to be leaders or for other reasons.
- Prosecutorial choices (e.g., concentrating resources on child exploitation crimes instead of identity frauds) may result in relatively large numbers of cybercriminals who are not prosecuted and crimes not investigated or not

fully investigated. "White-collar" crimes online at times are prioritized lower than violent crimes and so receive fewer criminal justice resources.

- Criminal and civil cases' digital records often contain evidence of wrongdoing not ultimately resulting in recorded sanctions, such as arrests and convictions.
- Corporate security investigations are an essential part of Internet criminal enforcement and vital to law enforcement success in many types of cybercrime, such as external computer system attacks. Corporations therefore are stakeholders and decision makers in many types of online crime. Only a minority of crimes detected by corporate security staffs are reported to law enforcement.
- Personnel security—heretofore relying on the criminal justice system to record prior criminal activity—faces the probability that cybercriminals have no prior criminal record. Further, private databases are more likely than public ones to hold evidence of prior misbehavior, on- or offline.

It is important to recognize the role of hackers and crackers in cybercrime. Hackers are people who have made themselves familiar with the way computers and related devices work. Hackers can therefore use digital devices in more expert ways than the rest of us. Sometimes, you will hear the terms *white-hat hacker, gray-hat hacker*, or *black-hat hacker*, imitating the gray and black market concepts. Like the term *hacker*, these terms are used loosely but may refer to those who dabble in risky but not illegal (gray) activities and those who engage in illegal (black) acts online. Hacking is not illegal per se and in fact is critical to IT security. The federal Computer Fraud and Abuse Act (among others) forbids unauthorized access to computers for an illegal purpose or with damaging impact over a certain dollar amount. Crackers are those who use computers and code to commit criminal acts—something hackers could choose to do, but for the most part do not. It is necessary to understand that, among the cultural groups that have arisen in the Internet age, hackers are the group most likely to offer society the solutions needed to protect computing going forward—thus the term *white-hat hacker*. They are also the ones with the skills to subvert systems without anyone knowing it. Sometimes, we refer to hackers by the more common terms *IT staff* and *programmers*.

The Insider

The place of automation in an enterprise raises profound questions with regard to criminal insiders. Only one malicious employee with access to enterprise IT systems can compromise the most valuable assets, especially with privileged access such as that enjoyed by the IT systems administrators. As business and government systems over the past two decades have increasingly housed vital intellectual resources, the risk of loss from insiders has increased. Yet, few agencies and firms ask detailed questions of applicants about prior Internet activities and confirm their answers by systematic checking. Most employers grant employees full IT systems access from their first day on the job, which increases the risk that people with prior online criminal behavior may threaten the enterprise. Monitoring of computer systems, networks, and data often has the fatal flaw of assuming authorized users are not engaged in illicit activities, even though statistics often show that employee crime, errors, and account takeovers from external attacks are costly to enterprises.[15] Leaving the risk of insider computer crime unaddressed is no longer acceptable, especially if high-value data reside online.

As use of digital evidence and electronic records in investigations has grown, most large employers have faced the realization that their own data may become damaging evidence against them. An employee engaged in cybercrimes while "on duty" puts the employer in jeopardy of criminal or civil charges, and e-mails, true or untrue, can become powerful evidence of misbehavior attributable to the enterprise. Yet, only a small percentage of employers have made a connection between the factors that correlate users' on-the-job and personal computer habits. For example, several trends are well known but not considered in the context of risk to the enterprise:

- Indiscreet, blatant documentation of inappropriate behavior is common on social sites like Facebook and MySpace. Can someone so indiscreet maintain professional discretion at work?
- Exchanges of copyrighted works in digital form—especially films, music, video, and software—without paying for them are rampant. Will workers with such habits choose to protect their employers' digital intellectual property?
- As Internet advertising and marketing illustrate (and the decline of print media reflects), networking through large numbers of professional contacts is key to enterprise reputation and market rank. As today's highly mobile workforce shuttles to their next employer, will they bring these connections with them digitally or leave them with their former employer (to whom they may literally belong, if they are on a customer list)?

These are only a few of many possible examples. When enterprises are dependent (as most are) on IT systems, networks, and data, the individual user's online choices assume greater importance. "Humorous" e-mails can turn into damning evidence in court. Digital evidence is long lived, searchable, retrievable, often available to a legal adversary, and dependent on the input of every employee (even the ones with the worst sense of humor).

Despite the trend toward indiscreet (potentially self-damaging) online revelations and misbehavior, most employers do not address candidates' online habits directly. Screening, orientation, training, and monitoring can mitigate these risks, but strategic changes in personnel security are necessary to address them.

Misbehavior Online

It appears that, like cybercrime, misbehavior (illicit, socially unacceptable acts) online are rising. People in a position of heavy responsibility, high visibility, power, or authority, such as law enforcement and intelligence officers, politicians, celebrities, chief executives, or tax collectors, should carefully consider any public Internet posting. Any posting must meet the "grandmother test" (i.e., be suitable for display to grandma). However, permanently damaging revelations about such incredibly stupid misbehavior abound. For example[16]:

> An Albuquerque police officer shot and killed a suspect during a traffic stop in 2011. He had listed his job description on his Facebook page as "human waste disposal." An attorney sought to obtain access to 57 officers' Facebook pages to see if they had discussed the shooting. The officer involved later said that his Facebook posting was "extremely inappropriate and a lapse in judgment on my part."

> A Peoria, Arizona, police officer was disciplined after posting a photograph on his Facebook page of a President Barak Obama tee shirt riddled with bullet holes with a line of seven men displaying handguns and assault rifles. The Secret Service and the officer's department launched inquiries after the photo was posted. The officer was demoted and suspended by the department because of his violation of its social media policy and because he discredited the department.
> The discipline was upheld following the officer's appeal of the demotion.

> A Chandler, Arizona, police officer was terminated by the department for maintaining a sexually explicit website featuring himself and his wife; the site was operated for money—without any kind of message or social/political commentary—thereby bringing discredit to the city service. A federal appeals court ruled that the officer "may have the constitutional right to run his sex oriented business, but he has no constitutional right to be a policeman for the City at the same time."

Like the other examples of notorious conduct online (e.g., the reference in Chapter 1 to Congressmen Lee and Weiner in 2011), it appears that people with authority must be especially careful about the possibility of exposure. Their employers also have reason to be concerned because no matter how responsible a person's job may be, there is still a possibility that a seriously damaging online incident can occur.

Notes

1. UN Comprehensive Study on Cybercrime, Draft—February 2013, http://www.google. com/url?sa=t&rct=j&q=&esrc=s&frm=1&source=web&cd=1&cad=rja&ved=0CC kQFjAA&url=http%3A%2F%2Fwww.unodc.org%2Fdocuments%2Forganized-crime%2FUNODC_CCPCJ_EG.4_2013%2FCYBERCRIME_STUDY_210213. pdf&ei=lLSTUomMBYvjoATe_YDADQ&usg=AFQjCNFoJTRP-PIsyx__ BHuRMx7J-JPBvQ&bvm=bv.57127890,d.b2I (accessed November 25, 2013).

2. Motta, Thomas G., FBI Digital Evidence section chief, address to Law Enforcement Information Management, International Association of Chiefs of Police (IACP) Conference, Nashville, TN, May 8, 2008, and briefings to subsequent meetings of the IACP Computer Crime and Digital Evidence Ad Hoc Committee.

3. Comey, James B., director, FBI, Statement Before the Senate Committee on Homeland Security and Governmental Affairs, Washington, DC, November 14, 2013, http://www.fbi.gov/news/testimony/homeland-threats-and-the-fbis-response (accessed November 25, 2013).

4. 2012 Internet Crime Report, Internet Crime Complaint Center, FBI and National White Collar Crime Center, May 2013, http://www.ic3.gov/media/annualreport/2012_IC3Report.pdf (accessed November 15, 2013).

5. UN Comprehensive Study on Cybercrime, Draft—February 2013.

6. 2013 US State of Cybercrime Survey, PWC, June 2013, http://www.pwc.com/us/en/increasing-it-effectiveness/publications/us-state-of-cybercrime.jhtml (accessed November 25, 2013).

7. Computer Security Institute–FBI Annual Computer Crime Survey, http://gocsi.com/survey (accessed August 8, 2010).

8. Bureau of Justice Statistics, National Computer Security Survey, 2005, http://bjs.ojp.usdoj.gov/index.cfm?ty=dcdetail&iid=260 (accessed August 8, 2010).

9. Stahl, Lesley, Video Pirates, the Bane of Hollywood, *60 Minutes*, CBS, November 1, 2009, http://www.cbsnews.com/stories/2009/10/30/60minutes/main5464994.shtml (accessed June 1, 2010).

10. Sarno, David, The Internet Sure Loves Its Outlaws, *Los Angeles Times*, April 29, 2007.

11. My Internet investigations over the past 8 years have included online pharmacies' illegal sale of brand-name and generic drugs to US customers, with and without requiring prescriptions, mailing/shipping prescription drugs and controlled substances directly to consumers in contravention of federal and state laws and ethical medical practice.

12. BitTorrent self-description, http://www.bittorrent.com/ (accessed November 25, 2013).

13. Based on 28 years of my experience with cryptography and news media reports.

14. Holahan, Catherine, Sony BMG Plans to Drop DRM, *Business Week*, January 4, 2008, describes the decision by Sony BMG Music Entertainment to drop DRM software included with music to prevent its download over the Internet and compete with Apple's iTunes for sale of downloaded music. Sony was the last of the top four music labels to drop DRM. A 2005 version of Sony's DRM software included in each CD automatically installed controls on users' personal computers that reportedly created vulnerabilities to viruses, which prompted a boycott and lawsuits (BusinessWeek.com, November 29, 2005).

15. Bolshaw, Liz, Personal Devices Pose Biggest Threat to Corporate Security, *Financial Times*, November 15, 2013, http://www.ft.com/intl/cms/s/0/e4b53190-4b82-11e3-a02f-00144feabdc0.html#axzz2kipWPkM2 (accessed November 16, 2013). Checkpoint's survey showed that 93% of US and UK companies use mobile devices to connect to corporate networks, while 67% allow employees to connect personal devices. Detwiler, Bill, Field Guide: Types of People Behind Today's Corporate Security Threats, ZDNet, December 2013, http://www.zdnet.com/field-guide-types-of-people-behind-todays-corporate-security-threats-7000023802/ (accessed December 4, 2013). ZDNet's field guide to help corporations identify and defend against security threats noted that employees are often a company's greatest security threat, through deliberate or accidental acts.

16. Pettry, Michael T, supervisory special agent, FBI, presentation to International Association of Chiefs of Police, Legal Officers' Section, September 29, 2012, San Diego, CA.

Chapter 4

Internet Search Studies

Introduction

Important questions about cybervetting have remained unanswered for several years, and until recently, compelling evidence has been lacking about the necessity and value of cybervetting to an enterprise. A key question is what kind of results Internet searches will produce when they are added to the evaluative process for background investigations and other personnel security measures. Two recent studies—published here for the first time—shed light on the answers needed to make valid risk management decisions.

Until now, research has not produced much evidence about the pros and cons of cybervetting. Articles pointing out that employers' cybervetting risks discrimination, erroneous judgment, and possibly putting off good potential candidates provide little but speculation about the practice and its possible results. To protect the privacy of social networkers and the rapidly developing new media through which their online networking is occurring, some academics, legal scholars, and journalists even go so far as to suggest that publicly posted information should not be used by potential employers.[1] Fortunately, several recent legal articles have outlined best practices for employers to avoid legal, ethical, privacy, and policy pitfalls. Best practices are treated in detail later in this book.

To determine whether cybervetting is necessary and desirable, it would be good to determine answers to the following questions:

1. Can Internet searches be thorough and accurate enough to provide useful intelligence about the subjects most of the time?
2. Are substantive issues found frequently enough to justify cybervetting?

3. Does cybervetting often provide leads or indicators that can help identify and assess issues, or provide investigative sources, for information relating to candidates?
4. Is cybervetting cost-effective (efficient)?

Two studies are presented here in an attempt to shed light on the possible answers to these questions (and some others, including where online most substantive issues may be found). The first is an academic exercise conducted with about 300 volunteers, and the second is a review of over 700 cases in which online investigations were conducted by my firm, iNameCheck. Although it is early in the history of cybervetting to suggest that the results presented here are dispositive, the studies provide valuable indicators of the need for, and prospects for success of, routine cybervetting of candidates and employees. The efficiency of cybervetting was not addressed by the two studies.

Academic Study

The discussion that follows summarizes the results of a study[2] conducted to ascertain how many volunteers from a population of university students would be found to have issues identified by Internet searching that could preclude their employment or a clearance under the federal Adjudicative Guidelines for Determining Eligibility for Access to Classified Information (Guidelines).[3] In summary, the preclusive items in the guidelines are as follows[4]:

Lack of allegiance to the United States: treason, sabotage, anti-US acts, extremism
Foreign influence: foreign relatives, relationships, sympathies, or coercion
Foreign preference: dual citizenship, loyalty to another nation or anti-US group
Sexual behavior: illegal or unbalanced behavior, coercible (not sexual preference)
Personal conduct: dishonesty, bad judgment, unreliability, rule violations
Financial considerations: financially overextended, dishonesty, unexplained affluence
Alcohol consumption: driving under the influence (DUI), drunk and disorderly, frequently drunk, binge drinking
Drug involvement: illegal drug use/dealing, dependency, drug abuse
Psychological conditions: emotional disorders, mentally ill, unreliable or unstable
Criminal conduct: a serious or multiple minor crimes, whether or not charged/convicted
Handling protected information: disclosure of or failure to protect classified/ sensitive information properly
Outside activities: conflicts in employment (foreign), loyalty, or protecting classified data
Use of information technology (IT) systems: illegal/noncompliant acts, unauthorized use

For each of these issues, the guidelines take into account factors surrounding the conduct observed, including its seriousness, frequency, recency, nature of participation by the subject, and the likelihood of recurrence. A recent or recurring pattern of questionable judgment, irresponsibility, or emotionally unstable behavior can itself be disqualifying. Evidence is to be collected and considered both on possible misbehavior and on all mitigating circumstances, so that a balanced judgment can be made. In my experience, adolescent misjudgments, minor drug experimentation, drinking while partying, and similar incidents, provided they took place some time ago, were not repeated and do not represent a pattern of continued behavior, are not normally disqualifying for federal clearances. Also in my experience, the federal government's guidelines provide the most comprehensive and fair framework by which candidates for highly responsible positions can be evaluated.[5]

Study Summary

Student volunteers from across the Michigan State University (MSU) campus participated in a cybervetting study sponsored by the Defense Personnel Security Research Center (PERSEREC) and managed by Dr. Thomas J. Holt of MSU and iNameCheck (my firm). Information provided by volunteers (who received nothing for participation) was used to generate Internet searches to ascertain whether the types of concerns in the Adjudicative Guidelines could be identified with participants in public postings online. Of the 298 participants who responded to the solicitation, 28, or 9.4%, were identified whose postings online raised substantive issues for a background investigation. Fifty-three percent, or 158 of the participants, failed to provide complete or accurate information on their study forms.

The participants were asked to provide their name, nicknames, sex, home mailing address, e-mail addresses, user names (not passwords), websites where they have accounts, and school. Most of the volunteers came from classroom solicitations by instructors using handwritten forms, with about 20% filling out electronic forms in response to e-mail solicitations.

All participants' information was researched online, and a report was compiled only on each individual about whom significant issues of potential concern were found (i.e., reports of findings deemed derogatory). A copy of the report was sent via e-mail to each volunteer with such Internet search findings. Redacted copies of the reports on findings deemed derogatory were provided to MSU's principal investigator and to PERSEREC (i.e., the redacted reports did not identify the individuals or provide information that would lead to their identification). Documents on individuals about whom derogatory information was developed were not disseminated, and the participants' identities will be protected. Those about whom no substantial derogatory information was found were sent an e-mail advising them of that fact.

Within the 28 reports containing derogatory findings, half (14) contained comments related to alcohol abuse, although other issues were identified. Following is a list of issues found and the number of participants with that issue:

Alcohol abuse: 14

 Drinking was depicted in photos, text, and videos.

Profanity, biased and vulgar postings: 10

 Text containing offensive language was repeated multiple times.

Illegal drug use: 8

 Marijuana use, "liking" illegal drugs, and references to being stoned were
  considered.

Mental health issues: 2

 Two individuals posted about their mental health problems.

Overdosed prescribed drugs, suicidal: 1

 Two overdoses led to suicidal thoughts several months before.

Software piracy: 2

 References to misusing copyrighted materials were present.

Possible misuse of IT skills: 2

 Advanced IT skills accompanied by other misbehavior occurred.

Possible academic cheating: 2

 Contents of an MSU test were posted and a test and notes website recommended.

Arrest: 1

 An individual posted that his arrest was due to "self-defense."

Use of malware: 1

 A "how-to" on using malicious code was posted.

Foreign affiliation: 1

 A student's link to a foreign embassy was posted on the embassy website.

E-mail used for online scams: 1

 A student's e-mail address was apparently hijacked and used in scams.

Refused to stop offensive postings: 1

A female with multiple offensive postings refused her family's advice to stop and
  cut off their access to her postings, which remained publicly accessible.

(More than 1 of the 46 issues identified in some instances applied to an individual.)

Among the 28 respondents with issues, 10 were female (7.3% of females participating) and 18 were male (11.2% of males participating). Twitter and Facebook were the websites where most of the issues were found, with a variety of others, including photo and video posting sites such as Flikr, Photobucket, and YouTube, in more than one case. A white paper was furnished to all participants, "Safeguarding Your Reputation Online," with links to resources about the topic.

The results appear to support the proposition that cybervetting can be productive in identifying issues that could disqualify a candidate from a clearance or employment, or require customized orientation and training to ensure that a new employee understands the employer's standards for online behavior on work and personal computer systems. Although all the volunteers knew that an Internet search would be conducted, 9.4% had postings of concern that could readily be found online. The 28 individuals identified did not include persons whose postings contained only vulgar or profane language, gay or lesbian sexual preference, or juvenile pranks except when accompanied by other factors specified in the guidelines. A few of the 28 were identified because of issues that, although not indicative of misbehavior, apparently would need to be resolved during background investigations. Note that contents of the 28 cybervetting reports would be included with other investigative results (e.g., verification of education and employment), possibly could result in additional leads in background investigations, and might not necessarily result in disqualification of a candidate after vetting was completed.

A majority (53%) or 158 of the volunteers failed to furnish complete and accurate information about their online activities, making it more difficult to determine their questionable behaviors online. Missing on their forms were such items as websites and user names, and a few failed to provide their complete names and other identifiers. However, all participants were identified through online research. This lack of candor could inhibit the efficiency and effectiveness of a cybervetting program or raise issues about the honesty of individuals who fail to provide complete and accurate information as required on application forms. It is unclear if the respondents simply did not provide such information because of the voluntary nature of the study, as compared to a job application, for which certain information must be given. Some simply may have forgotten to list websites that they no longer used. Because fair and ethical cybervetting should include notice, acceptance, and some information collection from the candidate, forms that are likely to elicit the information required for Internet searches from all candidates should be used.

The most frequented websites, according to the participants themselves, who ranged from 18 to 43 years old (but were mostly closer to 18), were Facebook, Twitter, MySpace, Yahoo, Google, YouTube, StumbleUpon, LinkedIn, Tumblr, Pinterest, and Amazon. In view of this relatively limited number of frequented websites, it should be possible to automate Internet searches to capture a high percentage of postings while limiting the cost of adding cybervetting to background investigations. Note that to date, analysts are needed in conjunction with automated collection to ensure that references included in cybervetting reports are not false positives.

The study results suggest that background investigations of people within a comparatively modest, yet demonstrably well-educated, group of young people (ostensibly intelligent, serious, and well motivated) that do not include cybervetting may miss substantive issues in an applicant's background. MSU graduates would seem to be among those considered ideal potential candidates for government jobs. In addition, elicitation of candid responses from applicants to questions about their user names and online activities to fully investigate an individual's background online could pose a challenge.

iNameCheck Cybervetting Case Study

I conducted a second study by reviewing all of the investigations of my firm, iNameCheck. The goal was to find those background investigations conducted on individuals who were not suspected of misbehavior, illegal activities, or the like. The group of inquiries selected comprised applicants or candidates for positions and subjects of due diligence and legal support investigations. Each investigation included reviews of information found online that could have an impact on a judgment about the person's suitability for employment, reliability, trustworthiness, or the like (i.e., cybervetting). To provide an objective means of determining that results were either derogatory or not, the Adjudicative Guidelines outlined were adopted as an assessment tool. In each case reviewed, minor issues (e.g., old traffic citations, single instances of posting crude language, common debt problems, and the like) were deemed insufficient grounds for a negative finding. However, for purposes of this study, a large number of such minor issues or aggravated instances (e.g., DUIs, repeated use of racist or profane postings, bankruptcy, multiple civil lawsuits, liens or judgments, and flagrant, repeated recent misbehavior) were deemed derogatory, as were substantial issues needing resolution through further inquiry.

Over 1,900 iNameCheck cases were reviewed, and 736 cases on people (70% male, 30% female) were found for which cybervetting was used in the subjects' background investigations, which were done without prior suspicion of wrongdoing or derogatory information. Subjects who were suspected of wrongdoing or who were investigated for a purpose unrelated to an assessment of suitability (e.g., attempts to locate an individual) were not included in the study. Reports of findings in the 736 investigations were reviewed, and 232 (31.5%) contained substantial derogatory information concerning the subject. Derogatory findings were present in the cases of 66 females (28.4% of negative findings, 30% of females investigated, and 8.96% of all 736 reports) and 166 males (71.6% of negative findings, 32.2% of males investigated, and 22.6% of all 736 reports). Note that the percentage of cases with findings of derogatory information in this batch of cases was substantially higher than one might expect, as 6% to 10% of reports from a presumably innocent population would normally be expected to have substantially derogatory findings. One implication of these results is that including cybervetting in background investigations could uncover substantial issues for about 30% of a group of candidates—three times the rate for the college students.

Tables 4.1 and 4.2 show the nature of the derogatory findings, broken down by male and female subjects, respectively. Financial, foreign influence, and criminal issues formed the most frequent of derogatory findings. Misbehavior and bad judgment, shown by a pattern of civil suits, misdemeanors, and alcohol and drug abuse, were also present, as expected. Because the guidelines were used as a threshold for identifying issues, it is possible that individual cases would be resolved in the subject's favor on review and adjudication. However, cases involving glaring or unresolved substantial issues were identified and categorized as set out previously.

Table 4.1   Male Derogatory Findings

Number	Issue	Other Issues
58	Financial, including unpaid debts or unexplained affluence	8 with criminal issues, 2 judgments
40	Criminal issues, including arrests, convictions, illicit acts	13 financial, 1 sex-drugs, 1 judgment
27	Bad judgment, including lawsuits, misbehavior online	Sexual, criminal, racism issues
18	Foreign allegiance, influence, and preference	
7	Alcohol, 1 with criminal acts and financial mismanagement	
6	Sexual misbehavior with alcohol, drugs, and criminal acts	
5	Misbehavior (e.g., lawsuits) with bad judgment, illegal acts	
3	Drugs, 1 with criminal acts, 1 bad judgment	
2	Mental issues	
166	Total number of derogatory subject reports	

Table 4.2   Female Derogatory Findings

Number	Issue	Other Issues
22	Financial issues, 6 with criminal issues as well	
14	Foreign allegiance, influence, and preference	
11	Criminal issues, 3 also financial issues	1 alcohol issue
6	Misbehavior (2 radical acts, 2 sexual issues)	1 alcohol issue
4	Egregious bad judgment (e.g., sexual postings)	
4	Alcohol issues, 1 also drugs	
3	Sexual issues, 1 pornography	
1	Drugs	
1	Mental issues	
66	Total number of derogatory subject reports	

When one eliminates foreign allegiance, influence, or preference from the negative evaluations (primarily US government issues), 148 males with issues remain (28.7% of the males investigated) and 52 females (22.6% of the females investigated), meaning that 27.2% of all those investigated had derogatory findings.

The implications of this review of iNameCheck cases include a high probability that online evidence will be found of substantial issues to be resolved, prior to hiring, promoting, clearing, or otherwise deciding to trust someone, based on cybervetting. Although cybervetting was used in the findings cited here, sources such as criminal records; court records; acquaintance, employer, and teacher interviews; and similar "traditional" investigative steps would also be expected to yield many of the same findings. Cybervetting was found in many of the cases reviewed to provide leads that could be used to verify or add details to issues identified, such as through physical reviews of records found electronically or interviews with a subject's social networking friends. Although it is not possible to accurately speculate on how many of the issues identified might not be found in a traditional investigation without cybervetting, it is safe to say that the 31.5% negative findings (27.2% without foreign influence issues) are a bright red flag, suggesting that cybervetting is a due diligence necessity.

Based on the results of both studies, here are a few important observations on cybervetting:

- A significant number of issues could go unidentified without cybervetting.
- Some of the issues that might go unidentified, including drug and alcohol abuse, arrests, convictions, civil suits, financial instability, and misbehavior online, could lead to significant problems on the job or in a position of trust.
- Online misbehavior issues identified through cybervetting could be expected to reappear as a person uses an employer's computers, networks, and data. Failure to discover such issues and address them in orientation, training, and on-the-job monitoring of those hired could expose an employer to significant security risks—think of Edward Snowden and Robert Hanssen.
- Intelligence and leads gleaned from a cybervetting program, handled properly, enable an authority to identify and address risks with candidates prior to their appearance later, on the job.
- Failure to look for and find obvious online issues could subject an enterprise to losses, damage, and legal sanctions for neglecting to exercise due care in personnel security, including vetting.

In my view, my company's 8 years of experience in applying cybervetting to the practice of investigations have yielded much stronger results than those investigations would have produced without online searching. Although it is understood that some government agencies, private businesses, universities, and organizations still do not use cybervetting, particularly in background investigations, it appears that they are taking a serious risk by failing to do so. Based on the results of cybervetting outlined here and elsewhere in this book, the evidence for its necessity is overwhelming. Further, it is clear to me that the costs for failing to include cyber-vetting in personnel security and background investigations will be substantially higher than that for incorporating the practice into existing programs.

Notes

1. Jodka, Sara H., The Dos and Don'ts of Conducting a Legal, Yet Helpful, Social Media Background Screen, *Law Practice Today* (American Bar Association monthly magazine), September 2013, http://www.americanbar.org/content/newsletter/publications/law_practice_today_home/lpt-archives/september13/the-dos-and-donts-of-conducting-a-legal-yet-helpful-social-media-background-screen.html, (accessed November 26, 2013). Clark, L., and Roberts, S., Employer's Use of Social Networking Sites: A Socially Irresponsible Practice, *Journal of Business Ethics*, 2010, http://homepages.se.edu/cvonbergen/files/2013/01/Employer%25E2%2580%2599s-Use-of-Social-Networking-Sites_A-Socially-Irresponsible-Practice.pdf (accessed January 20, 2014).
2. Holt, Thomas J., and Appel, Edward J., Sr., Detecting and Assessing Online Misbehavior by Candidates and Employees of DoD: Phase II—Identifying Issues of Concern through Automated Internet Searching, an unpublished study conducted by iNameCheck (author's firm) and Michigan State University College of Criminal Justice, December 2012, for the US Department of Defense Personnel Security Research Center.
3. *Code of Federal Regulations*, Government Printing Office, July 2012, http://www.gpo.gov/fdsys/pkg/CFR-2012-title32-vol1/xml/CFR-2012-title32-vol1-part147.xml (accessed January 28, 2014). See Chapter 9.
4. Terminology is mine, derived from the guidelines (not the official version).
5. When I was assigned to the National Security Council, I led an interagency group that rewrote the guidelines during the Clinton administration, about 1996; these were approved by the president and have withstood the test of time ever since.

Chapter 5

Implications
for the Enterprise

Introduction

Surveys, media reports, and quotations suggest that because of online misbehavior, some employers are adding Internet searches to prehiring background investigations.[1] Although studies of what is often called "social media vetting" vary on the percentage of employers, recent surveys have verified indications over the past several years that many employers do some form of cybervetting:[2]

In 2011, the Society for Human Resource Management found 56% of employers reported using social media in hiring.

A June 2013 nationwide survey by CareerBuilder found 43% of employers who vetted applicants online did not hire an applicant based on information found online, including

- 50%—Posting provocative/inappropriate photos or information;
- 48%—Posting about drinking or using drugs;
- 33%—Badmouthing a prior employer;
- 30%—Bad communication skills;
- 28%—Making discriminatory comments related to race, gender, religion, and so on;
- 24%—Lying about qualifications.

Of employers, 19% found online information that supported hiring candidates.

However, the media reports appear to indicate that most private- and public-sector employers lack several key ingredients necessary for fair, legal, and appropriate use of Internet searching for hiring adjudications, including a written policy, procedures, antidiscrimination measures, search methodology, adjudication methods, notice to applicants, consent (as currently used for background investigation interviews with prior employers or schools), and an opportunity to correct adverse findings.[3] These and certain other procedures would insulate an employer from potential liabilities arising from Internet searching, including possible violations of the Fair Credit Reporting Act and Equal Employment Act. Without proper procedures and safeguards, an employer's human resources and other decision makers might use Internet searches and the results thereof inappropriately.

A related trend is for employers to spend considerable sums on systems to monitor their employees' use of work information technology (IT) systems for online misbehavior, blocking access to certain Internet sites, filtering and archiving e-mail, and even key logging.[4] In recent years, the costs of litigation, losses, and reputational damage to enterprises that failed to control employees' systems misuses have skyrocketed.

The New User: Someone You Would Trust?

Background investigations, combined with resumes, applications, interviews, and a "whole-person" evaluation of eligibility, qualifications, experience, and compatibility with the enterprise, are the current gold standard for hiring the best candidates. Like all investigations, vetting allows an employer to consider facts and observations in making a decision. When the open position has multiple applicants, the goal is choosing among those most competitive and likely to succeed. The applicant's profile—factual, verified, and analyzed—is the basis for adjudicating whether to hire the individual. In this context, analysis of prior computer/Internet use has somehow been omitted by many employers. Most US employees (62% in 2008) use the Internet or e-mail at work, and nearly all of those own personal cell phones and computers, according to a Pew Internet and American Life study. About 45% of employed Americans reported doing at least some work from home in a 2008 Pew survey.[5] In considering the impact of automation on employees, several recent trends are significant:

1. Most US workers come into a job with prior online experience.
2. Most US workers are granted immediate access to their new employer's IT systems.
3. The "networked worker" of today is much more likely to use computers and devices to accomplish a mix of personal and professional tasks throughout the day, whether it is a workday or day off and whether during work hours or in off-hours.
4. Workers carry networked devices, including cell phones, laptops, and tablets, and are likely to bring them to work.

Employers have a variety of issues to address with today's workforce in relation to their computer, network, and data use, among which are the following:

■ Ascertaining and evaluating employees' level of experience and expertise with computers, applications, and processes, especially as those relate to job tasks.
■ Assessing employees' awareness of computer system security, IT hygiene, history of online safety, and potentially threatening habits (e.g., using risky websites or exchanging provocative content).
■ Including candidates' online experiences in the background vetting process, to ascertain and evaluate eligibility for access to the employer's systems (in light of established authorized use policy [AUP]) and potential need for extraordinary orientation and training, should the candidate's history suggest the need for the same. The inclusion of online history in vetting is neither trivial nor simple; hence, it will be treated in depth in later chapters.

In confronting the issues described, the employer must weigh the relative criticality and value of enterprise data, computing and networking infrastructure, as well as the risks inherent in potentially allowing employees to use the employer's systems however they wish. Although today's enterprises, including many small businesses (i.e., those with up to 500 employees), have robust IT security built in, it is not unusual to find that the individual authorized user has a great deal of discretion in using work systems and interconnecting from outside the enterprise.

There is a long list of potential problems and risks associated with enterprise computing. The user poses the single greatest risk because he or she can often defeat even the best security measures. Unless the employer addresses individual users, the security of the enterprise's IT systems, networks, and data, as well as any potential for misuse, will depend on each individual user.

Employer Liability

An area of criminal and civil law still in flux is the question of the due diligence required of an employer for Internet postings by employees using the employer's systems. When a tort arises because of actions of an employee, the courts have generally assessed whether the employee was acting in the capacity of an employee or (perhaps illicitly) on his or her own. The Internet has provided an opportunity for such tortious acts as slander, libel, harassment, cyber bullying, defamation of character, unauthorized access to or release of confidential information, copyright violations, and so on. Whether the employer could be held liable for illicit employee behavior online or not, the risk of criminal or civil charges alone has motivated some firms and agencies to step up monitoring of employees.[6] Clearly, the "deep pockets" of the employer (and perhaps an insurance company) are greater than that of the offending employee. What if the employer has ignored blatant evidence of online misbehavior?

Another motivator for employers is the potential cost in lost bandwidth, work hours, and reputation of employee Internet use for personal purposes, such as social networking, shopping, stock trading, surfing the net, and other non-work-related activities. One case involved a government employee who was caught burning porn videos from the Internet onto DVDs all day at work, then selling the DVDs from home. It turned out that the heavy-duty DVD burner and DVD blanks were purchased through the agency supply office.

Litigation, although limited to date, has focused on personal injury, theft, domestic violence, harassment, and other issues arising from Internet use at work. When a candidate or onboard employee has a past history of misbehavior that can be carried out or facilitated by Internet use, the employer would be well advised to consider the person's prior online behavior. Should the employee act out illegally in the physical world with potential digital evidence, a subsequent investigation would be likely to include both work and personal computers, especially if the employer does not prevent misbehavior online by using stringent controls on IT systems. With computer forensics and e-discovery increasingly involved in all types of criminal and civil investigations, the employer who is not acting to prevent misuse may find that internal security lapses are the least embarrassing and potentially costly aspects of risk incurred.

Introduction of digital forensic evidence is evolving along with the technologies and practices that create, retrieve, verify, and present its content. Among the challenges is to find the fit within a traditional legal context for electronic files that are readily changeable; may require expert interpretation; challenge hearsay, best evidence, and chain-of-custody rules; and often need systems administrators to introduce them in court. "Technospeak" may confuse the court officers, juries, and witnesses. A witness presenting what he or she knows may be hard to distinguish from one providing an opinion about the attribution of documentation. Judges must apply rules with limited precedent and sometimes-questionable expert advice. Nevertheless, the contents of what are essentially electronic documents often are admitted into courts and play a vital and increasing role in both criminal and civil judgments.

Vetting, Monitoring, and Accountability

A somewhat controversial area of best security practices is employers' approach to employee IT systems use, including whether background vetting addresses prior computer use; the degree to which enterprise systems are monitored to prevent, detect, and mitigate potential abuse; and the accountability (or lack thereof) to which authorized users are held. The issue of vetting is handled in depth elsewhere. Monitoring of one's own IT systems has become an imperative today, if only to prevent viruses from bringing down computers vital to production. The question with which most employers struggle is what kind of monitoring is appropriate and cost-effective. Further, what will be done with employees or other authorized users (perhaps including vendors, partners, and customers) who violate the AUP?

Americans' acute sense of privacy and desire to be left alone by authority must be considered in any discussion of vetting, monitoring, and accountability. Because the sociological aspects of Internet use are progressing more rapidly than the law, policy, and established business practice can adapt, every employer must think carefully about not only what security measures to employ, but also what to do with information demonstrating the culpability of an authorized user. Simply because an act is against the rules is not necessarily a reason to take draconian measures, yet failure to address bad behavior is a recipe for further, more damaging delinquency. Sometimes, group behaviors online defeat the impulse to punish one person's misdeeds because the employer cannot afford to fire the entire department. For example, a large employer found that a group of technicians were all enjoying Internet porn sites during the workday but could not afford to fire the whole group. Further, the employer may not make the essential connection between the initial assessment of a new employee's proclivity to misbehave online in the context of the monitoring and controls that are routinely exercised in the enterprise. In any case, an employer needs to analyze security risks and countermeasures as they relate to any potential rogue user or group.

In the social contract that has evolved since automation became so much a part of our lives, new philosophical issues have arisen.[7] Can an enterprise survive and succeed if its people, systems, networks, and data are constantly at risk because of individual users' misbehavior? Will the best-available workers wish to work in a place where ubiquitous surveillance is a constant in enterprise systems and physical space? Can an employer in the information age find the right mix of humanity and authority for the workplace? Cynics may point out that, in the past few years, more Americans have been laid off, downsized, and fired than in many previous decades. Shedding workers, especially in the recession under way at this writing, is merely a way for firms and agencies to survive the lack of sufficient income and the overgrown structure that so many enterprises took on. One could ask whether IT systems monitoring is as big an issue when keeping the job at all is a struggle, even for the best workers.

The social compact between employer and wired worker should have the following foundational elements:

- Enterprise systems, networks, and data confidentiality, integrity, accessibility, and security depend on each and every authorized user.
- Users should expect, and be notified, that all computer systems are monitored.
- There are limits to employers' ability to monitor and enforce all AUP rules.
- When an authorized user is documented abusing AUP rules, discipline will result.

When online misbehavior is involved, both the employer and the employee realize that verification and attribution can be issues. Therefore, the following principles apply: (1) The employee will always be a party to considering the facts involved in misbehavior (usually in the form of an interview), and (2) employees will be held accountable for their behavior. These principles, coupled with those enumerated, are more difficult to apply than it would appear (at least my experience). Often, employers decline to take meaningful action against an employee found to violate the AUP or to commit an illicit act. This is often because, however privately the case is handled, employers fear adverse reactions from other employees and fear lawsuits from those discharged, suspended, or sanctioned for misbehavior. "A good talking to" is often the solution, with an attempt to extract a promise that "I won't do it again." This raises a question about the nature and effectiveness of the accountability an employer demands.

At this writing, achieving precision in attribution for online misbehavior often depends on expensive and challenging enterprise computer forensics that appear to be overkill in the average case of misbehavior. In some business networks, it is reasonable to expect that someday, real-time forensic collection, analysis, and enforcement could literally prevent user error and malicious individuals from violating enterprise AUP rules. If "pop-ups" remind users of the limits of their authorized use, that can be a good thing. However, for most employers today, there is a reliance on the individual user to know and abide by the rules. Such reliance must include user accountability, or the AUP has no impact. Defining user accountability is an art akin to composing the enterprise's AUP. Among the key attributes of a successful user accountability policy are the following:

- Consistently applying rules that are provided to, discussed with, and known to all
- Supporting integrity as a core requirement for success in the workplace
- Relating the accountability required of all employees to success factors of the enterprise (such as teamwork to enable market-leading innovation, protection of intellectual property (IP), discretion, exceeding customer expectations, and maintaining a professional reputation)
- Making every authorized insider a conscious player in enterprise security, for example:
  - Reminders in log-on screens and shared data folders of data protection rules
  - Security updates with real-life examples
  - Required workstation scanning and authentication prior to enterprise connection
  - Adherence to security rules included in performance evaluations
- Interviewing individuals involved in security inquiries, whenever possible, as a normal step in final resolution

The Evolving Personnel Security Model

In the early 1990s, when the Internet was just starting to take off as a massively scaled platform for networking, security strategies for government and business were rethought to

1. Incorporate risk management (rather than risk avoidance)
2. Provide critical infrastructure protection (to mitigate against failure of vital resources)
3. Practice risk assessment (to allow comprehensive review of threats, vulnerabilities, and protection plans)
4. Add practice security in depth (i.e., a layered series of measures designed to help prevent, slow, detect, and mitigate any malicious attack)

At the same time, development of privacy protections matured, with one approach, common in Europe, Canada, and Asia, centered on a strong regime with sanctions for privacy violations, requiring an "opt in" for personal data sharing, and a second approach, in the United States, centering on an "opt-out" choice to protect privacy.[8] After September 11, 2001, new impetus impelled government and industry to adopt stronger critical infrastructure protections, public-private partnerships, proactive measures to prevent terrorist acts, and even more intensive risk assessments. The net result omitted the improvement needed at this time in history in the most critical element of security: bringing personnel security up to date, to address the insider threat and networked information systems as part of workers' lives.[9] Managing the risk from insiders (employees, contractors, vendors, etc.) means achieving the proper balance of oversight and worker autonomy.

The American worker historically has bridled at intense scrutiny. Close supervision is unwelcome. Depending on the nature of the workplace, tasks, teamwork, and review of results, it may behoove an employer to allow minor violations of security rules to promote job satisfaction and possibly productivity. On the opposite side of the coin, employers must judge the extent to which minor security lapses lead to larger ones and inadvertent disclosures of sensitive data lead to deliberate theft of IP. It is people, not information systems, who are responsible for protecting the IP that is the lifeblood of today's businesses and government agencies.[10]

In automating the enterprise, executives have made their business processes considerably more efficient, including the communication, collection, analysis, storage, retrieval, and application of information resources. For trusted IT systems users, these capabilities can create the means to exploit an employer's IP for their own purposes. Digital rights management, access controls, systems logging, and monitoring and blocking of prohibited activities have been introduced. Some IT systems have elaborate control regimes. Where the value, vulnerability, and usage of IP dictate, employers are beginning to invest more resources in IT systems security and information security in general. Yet, where every user can become a serious threat, a personnel security challenge remains.

The history of espionage—both national and corporate—is replete with examples of individuals who entered the enterprise in all respects innocent, as well as a select few who signed up with the intent of betraying their employer and, in some cases, their country. Today's sociological trends are unfortunately leading to more, not less espionage.[11] Examples of those trends, which interact to raise the specter of increased spying, include the following:

- Technology allows easy, undetected search, retrieval, and storage of proprietary data.
- Expanded global gray and black markets for protected information exist.
- Internationalization of science, technology, commerce, networking, and travel place more insiders in contact with peers abroad who are in the market for trade secrets.
- Internet connectivity allows easy, anonymous sale and transfer of large data sets.
- More people are vulnerable to severe financial stress, a prime motive for espionage.
- Gambling, drugs, alcohol, and other expensive vices contribute to financial stress and impulsive illicit acts.
- Employer-employee dynamics today often do not include mutual loyalty and a sense of obligation and respect, and adverse actions, including layoffs, incite acts of revenge by disgruntled employees.
- Ethnic, ideological, and global conflicts and population mixtures are changing, with multiple philosophies motivating mobile actors to commit espionage for what they believe are justifiable reasons.

Government agencies' and high-tech firms' background investigations are aimed at preventing the hiring and clearance of persons whose prior behavior proved that they were untrustworthy. Information age employers have not all confronted the dual challenges of initial clearance and reinvestigation (i.e., verification that the employee still qualifies for a clearance). To establish a candidate's trustworthiness for initial hiring, employers need to consider several factors currently ignored by the vast majority of enterprises, including an applicant's history of

- Computer systems uses
- Internet uses, including social, game, and chat sites
- Penalties for computer abuse (e.g., Internet service provider and employer sanctions)
- Violations of AUPs of employers, schools, or other hosts
- Violations of copyright or other proprietary information use restrictions (e.g., software, films, video, music, IP)

- Cracking, malware creation or use, and other malicious code experiences
- Anonymous Internet activities and avoidance of IT systems controls

Admitting prior misbehavior of some types cited may not be sufficient reason to deny employment to a candidate. As with adjudication of other types of derogatory background investigative results, the employer should consider the seriousness, dates, frequency, repetition, likelihood of recurrence, and willingness to avoid future misbehavior of the same type. Today's employer depends on IT systems and knows (or should know) about the damage that only one malicious insider can do. Therefore, employers should upgrade their hiring processes to include prior IT systems and Internet use in evaluations and investigations. Most employers are unable to answer the questions about the orientation and training needed by new IT systems users, especially those relating to security. For the new employee who is immediately granted IT systems access, the level of employer risk assumed is proportional to the proclivity to misuse systems, networks, and data and the employer's information assurance effort. Unless the individual insider is evaluated for trustworthiness with access to IT systems, the employer could be said to be negligent in IT security practice.

Beyond hiring, the lessons of insider crime suggest that there is always a danger of "good employees going bad." Mitigating this risk is essential but difficult. The individual's online behavior should be reevaluated periodically, and perhaps randomly, in much the same way as employers have required random and prescheduled drug testing. One potentially successful strategy is continuous monitoring of insider actions to prevent, detect, and mitigate IT system abuse. Another is to conduct follow-up vetting.

Because computer misuse at home may have an impact on an employer's systems, data, and reputation (among other things), checking employees' recent online activities (i.e., those that are public) can help find the few insiders who pose a threat to the employer. The employer may discover behavior of concern that can be addressed soon enough to deter the insider from acts that are more damaging. If serious wrongdoing is uncovered, it is better to address such problems sooner rather than later.

Examples of the insider as traitor include the following:

> Robert Hanssen pled guilty to espionage against his employer, the Federal Bureau of Investigation (FBI), and against other agencies of the intelligence community; he conducted this espionage over a period of more than 20 years. Hanssen (a hacker who became a cracker) was adept at programming computers and, over the years, exploited his knowledge of FBI systems to provide the Russian intelligence services with voluminous, highly damaging data. His betrayal contributed to the deaths of 10 or more sources of US intelligence, who risked their lives as agents in place, and his disclosures led to the compromise of top-secret US collection systems worth billions of dollars.[12] As with all highly damaging spies, the

Hanssen case led to personnel security and counterintelligence reforms designed to help prevent such betrayal and to discover moles. One key lesson is that computers helped Hanssen to wreak severe damage on US national security in much greater proportion than would have occurred without automation. A corollary is that monitoring and security assessment of the computer systems Hanssen used for his spying could have prevented or mitigated at least some of the damage. Press reports suggested that not only the FBI but also other intelligence community agencies have strengthened their systems to prevent similar spying in the future.[13]

Former US Army intelligence analyst Pfc. Bradley Manning, 25 (now self-described as "Chelsea Manning"), was convicted on 20 counts in a court martial July 30, 2013, of leaking voluminous, highly classified materials, including video and 700,000 Iraq and Afghanistan war-related documents, to WikiLeaks, a website devoted to publishing information deemed to expose misbehavior by governments and businesses. Manning was acquitted on a charge of aiding the enemy. On August 21, 2013, he was sentenced to 35 years of confinement, reduction to the lowest enlisted rank, dishonorably discharged, and forfeiture of all pay and allowances. Undoubtedly, Manning's ability to accumulate from government computer systems, undetected, digital documents and videos that he believed exposed US military excesses in war, and to convey them to others he knew would most likely publish them, enabled his betrayal. Manning, who may suffer from various types of maladjustment, apologized that he had made a misguided attempt to change government policy. Because of the content of the leaked documents, which included diplomatic cables, grave damage was cited by US government officials.[14]

In June 2013, Edward Snowden, an ex-CIA employee and cleared computer administrator for a National Security Agency (NSA) contractor, declared himself[15] the leaker of highly classified documents to the *Guardian*, the *Washington Post*, the *New York Times*, and several other global press outlets. He fled to Hong Kong from his Hawaiian home and subsequently to Moscow, where he sought asylum. Press reports indicated that Snowden used readily available computer communications and encryption tools to convey voluminous and highly sensitive documents about US intelligence activities to reporters.[16] The leaks inspired public and private debates over NSA's ability to amass information about virtually anyone and created diplomatic tension over allegations of US spying on Americans and allies, as well as terrorists and spies. At this writing, reviews of US intelligence methods and policies continue. Snowden claimed that he did not bring his cache of sensitive data to Russia,[17] but it appeared from press reports that he continued to leak highly classified documents. The press speculated that he possibly stored the stolen documents in a secret place "in the cloud," as a "doomsday" measure, to allow exposure after his arrest or demise. Because the documents appeared to have revealed some of the most sensitive and detailed sources and methods of US intelligence, it is likely that among results will be loss of capabilities, expensive revisions to methodologies, and extensive reorganization at NSA and elsewhere in the US intelligence community. Contemporary incidents of violence in the workplace, including shootings by cleared individuals at US military bases, have provoked reviews of clearance and reinvestigation procedures along with the Manning and Snowden cases.

To be successful, today's personnel security model must incorporate an evaluation of authorized users' past computer system abuse, if any, and include periodic reinvestigations and monitoring to verify that insiders continue to protect the proprietary systems and data with which they are entrusted. If the IP protected is highly valuable or priceless, "trust but verify" must be the mantra.

Notes

1. Rosen, Jeffrey, The Web Means the End of Forgetting, *New York Times Magazine*, July 25, 2010, http://www.nytimes.com/2010/07/25/magazine/25privacyt2. (accessed July 25, 2010); quotes recent Microsoft survey saying 75% of US recruiters and human resource professionals report that their companies require them to do online research about candidates, and many use a range of sites when scrutinizing applicants, including search engines, social networking sites, photo- and video-sharing sites, personal websites and blogs, Twitter, and online gaming sites. Seventy percent of US recruiters report that they have rejected candidates because of information found online, such as photos and discussion board conversations and membership in controversial groups.
2. Jodka, Sara H., The Dos and Don'ts of Conducting a Legal, Yet Helpful, Social Media Background Screen, *Law Practice Today* (American Bar Association monthly magazine), September 2013, http://www.americanbar.org/content/newsletter/publications/law_practice_today_home/lpt-archives/september13/the-dos-and-donts-of-conducting-a-legal-yet-helpful-social-media-background-screen.html (accessed November 26, 2013).
3. Jodka, The Dos and Don'ts; and Ody, Elizabeth, Keeping Your Profile Clean, *Washington Post*, May 18, 2008: "A recent survey by ExecuNet, a networking organization for business leaders, found that 83% of executives and corporate recruiters research job candidates online, and 43% have eliminated a candidate based on search results." Bigam, Kate, Employers May Be Eyeing Students' Facebook Accounts, KentWired.com, 2006, related an October 2006 report by CareerBuilder.com saying that 26% of employers searched candidates online, including 1 in 10 hiring managers, and 63% of employers chose not to hire based on discoveries, key facets of which included lying about job qualifications, poor communications skills, and engaging in criminal behavior. Peacock, Louisa, Social Networking Sites Used to Check Out Job Applicants, March 17, 2009, http://www.personneltoday.com/articles/article.aspx?lia rticleid=49844&printerfriendly=true, said 25% of employers worldwide check social networking sites such as Facebook and MySpace for information about job candidates. A 2009 study by Development Dimension International (DDI) found 52% of those that did look up prospective employee profiles used the information in making hiring decisions. Hechinger, John, College Applicants Beware: Your Facebook Page Is Showing, *Wall Street Journal online*, September 18, 2008, http://online.wsj.com/article/SB122170459104151023.html. Ten percent of admissions officers in a survey of 500 top colleges admitted checking social networking sites to evaluate applicants, and 38% said that what they saw "negatively affected" their views of the applicant.
4. American Management Association, Electronic Monitoring and Surveillance Survey, 2007, http://press.amanet.org/press-releases/177/2007-electronicmonitoring-surveillance-survey/. For an example of monitoring file use and protecting data at work, see Verdasys, http://www.verdasys.com/ (a former client of mine).

5. Madden, Mary, and Jones, Sydney, Networked Workers, Pew Internet and American Life Project, September 24, 2008, http://www.pewinternet.org/~/media/Files/Reports/2008/PIP_Networked_Workers_FINAL.pdf (accessed November 26, 2013).

6. Electronic Monitoring Survey (Note 4).

7. Hall, George M., *The Age of Automation* (New York: Praeger, 1995).

8. Bouckaert, Jan, and Degryse, Hans, Opt In versus Opt Out: A Free-Entry Analysis of Privacy Policies, December 2005, http://weis2006.econinfosec.org/docs/34.pdf (accessed June 1, 2010).

9. Shaw, Eric, Ruby, Keven G., and Post, Jerrold M., The Insider Threat to Information Systems, Political Psychology Associates, 1999, http://www.pol-psych.com/sab.pdf (accessed August 9, 2010).

10. Computer Science and Telecommunications Board, National Research Council, *The Digital Dilemma, Intellectual Property in the Information Age* (Washington, DC: National Academies Press, 2000).

11. Fischer, Lynn F., *Espionage: Why Does It Happen* (Richmond, VA: DoD Security Institute, October 2000); Kramer, L., Heuer, R. J., Jr., and Crawford, K. S., *Technological, Social, and Economic Trends that Are Increasing US Vulnerability to Insider Espionage*, TR 05-10 May 2005, http://www.dhra.mil/perserec/reports/tr05-10.pdf (accessed November 27, 2013).

12. Wise, David, *Spy, The Inside Story of How the FBI's Robert Hanssen Betrayed America* (New York: Random House, 2002).

13. Rowan, J. Patrick, deputy assistant attorney general, U.S. Department of Justice, Enforcement of Federal Espionage Laws, Statement before the Subcommittee on Crime, Terrorism, and Homeland Security, Committee on the Judiciary, US House of Representatives, January 29, 2008. Herbig, Katherine L., and Wiskoff, Martin F., *Espionage against the United States by American Citizens 1947–2001*, Technical Report 02-5 (Defense Personnel Security Research Center [PERSEREC], Monterey, CA, July 2002).

14. Reports of US Department of Defense, including http://www.defense.gov/news/news-article.aspx?id=120556 and http://www.defense.gov/news/newsarticle.aspx?id=120655 (accessed November 27, 2013).

15. Leonnig, C. D., Johnson, J., and Fisher, M., Tracking Edward Snowden, from a Maryland Classroom to a Hong Kong Hotel, *Washington Post*, June 15, 2013, http://articles.washingtonpost.com/2013-06-15/world/39988583_1_anime-hong-kong-world (accessed November 5, 2013).

16. Maas, Peter, How Laura Poitras Helped Snowden Spill His Secrets, *New York Times*, August 13, 2013, http://www.nytimes.com/2013/08/18/magazine/laura-poitras-snowden.html? (accessed November 5, 2013).

17. NPR reports, http://www.npr.org/search/index.php?searchinput=%22edward+snowden%22 (accessed November 5, 2013).

LEGAL AND POLICY CONTEXT

A good illustration of the issues involved in using the Internet for intelligence is the concern that the search engine companies and other Web service providers collect information from users for their own purposes, primarily including marketing.[1] The intentions driving search engine providers such as Google, Bing, Yahoo, and so on are commercial: Advertisers are their first priority because they pay the bills. Searchers, consumers, browsers—users—are not as high a priority. That is not to say that Google et al. do not provide valuable and effective search machines.

As discussed here, in the United States, where opt-out policies are applied, the user must ask that personally identifying information not be collected, opting out by request or by settings on a computer application. Even then, Internet service providers (ISPs), search engines, and websites collect and utilize information about Internet behaviors for business purposes, most frequently depositing cookies or small program fragments in the user's browser memory and logging user activities in their databases. That is why a product from a retailer you have visited online will pop up in an ad when you use your browser—the cookies tell a tale on the user. In many respects, the great benefits of the Internet as an information provider are supported by advertising and market measurement that depend on data mining of online behaviors and enable "free" services. However, there is well-placed concern about whether businesses will regulate themselves when it comes to self-interest over the privacy of the individual. As the US Congress and Americans contemplate the appropriate limits that should be imposed on Internet sites to ensure privacy protection, those contemplating how to exploit Internet information must confront similar issues. Meanwhile, in Europe, strong privacy protections apply to users' data, and users must provide informed consent before a government agency or private company can make use of a person's identifying data.

Network and Internet service providers and commercial websites collect detailed data from users for many valid reasons, including ensuring continuity, security, and quality of service. Most websites generally express their policies in statements about privacy and authorized use that are made available on the site. By tradition, links are often found at the bottom of the home page. The place of the ISP and some commercial websites in the spectrum of network services allows these businesses exceptions to laws forbidding interception of electronic communications and collection and retention of customer-identifiable data—for the limited purposes of quality assurance and service continuity. Many online service providers declare that they do not retain information specifically identifying a person's Internet uses, claiming instead only to aggregate anonymous data. However, it is technically feasible to trace activities online. Many Internet businesses were initiated for marketing purposes and rely on their ability to collect data on large groups of current and prospective customers to carry out their business-to-business activities. Therefore, it behooves customers to understand the privacy and use policies of ISPs, and to make informed decisions about what website services to use, based on the customer's comfort level in sharing private data with service providers.[2] Further, some skepticism is appropriate about the possible gap between the claims made about protecting users' privacy and actual practice.

To be fair, consumers' identifying and transaction information is collected by brick-and-mortar businesses, utilities, government agencies, academic institutions, and organizations with whom accounts are established. The databases of such institutions are often sold or provided to data aggregators and marketing firms, enabling such firms to conduct other businesses, among which are credit bureau services; law enforcement and private investigative support; verification for identity, credit cards, bank checks, employment, rentals, financing, and other purposes. The legal "owner" of the data on a particular consumer or on all the customers in a database is considered to be the business or agency itself. In America, data aggregators conduct a thriving business, regulated by the Federal Trade Commission and various federal and state statutes. Because of errors in the data and mistakes in using the data for decisions such as issuing credit, employment, and conducting investigations, there is increasing pressure to regulate the collection, retention, and use of personally identifying information. In short, excesses by those using consumer data have prompted crackdowns, and Internet businesses are no exception.

Google is an interesting case in point. As of this writing:

> Google admits to collecting[3] information about the device(s) used to contact Google, what you do on Google, where you were (if available through Global Positioning Systems), applications from Google, local storage, and cookies about your interactions with Google and its clients. Google has many clients, some of whom users find with the Google search engine.
>
> Google was fined[4] for violating people's privacy during its Street View mapping project, when it scooped up passwords, email and other personal information

from unsuspecting computer users. In agreeing to settle a case brought by 38 states involving the project, the search company for the first time is required to aggressively police its own employees on privacy issues and to explicitly tell the public how to avoid such privacy violations.

The settlement also included a fine of $7 million. Privacy advocates and Google critics saw the agreement as a breakthrough for a company they claim often violates privacy.

Complaints about Google have led to multiple enforcement actions in recent years, including European agencies' investigations into the mapping project's collection of personal data of private computer users.

A related concern is the strategy of an Internet information collector: Will the collector use a proxy to "anonymize" searching so that it is not possible to know who is asking about whom? Are privacy options of the search engines and browsers used effectively?

Notes

1. Google, Inside Search: How Search Works, http://www.google.com/insidesearch/howsearchworks/ (accessed November 29, 2013); Tsukayama, Hayley, Google Begins Collecting Users' Data Across Its Services, *Washington Post*, March 1, 2012, http://articles.washingtonpost.com/2012-03-01/business/35447283_1_alma-whitten-google-users-google-history (accessed November 29, 2013).
2. Schlein, Alan M., *Find It Online, the Complete Guide to Online Research*, 2nd edition (Tempe, AZ: Facts on Demand Press, 2001).
3. Del Castillo, Michael, Six Kinds of Your Information Google Openly Admits to Collecting, August 15, 2013, http://upstart.bizjournals.com/news/technology/2013/08/15/6-data-categories-google-collects.html?page=all (accessed December 4, 2013).
4. Streitfeld, David, Google Concedes that Drive-By Prying Violated Privacy, *New York Times*, March 12, 2013, http://www.nytimes.com/2013/03/13/technology/google-pays-fine-over-street-view-privacy-breach.html?_r=0 (accessed December 4, 2013).

Chapter 6

Liability, Privacy, and Management Issues

Liability for Service Providers

The wide varieties of activities on the Internet spawned by creative businesses offer many types of social, recreational, hobby, communications, and business functions that work well and scale globally. In the early days of the Internet, it was possible to categorize service providers by the types of online activities offered, but soon "one-stop shopping" firms like America Online (AOL) created services with many types of interactions. Many of those online still use services like AOL, Microsoft's Live, Google+, Yahoo!, and major telecommunications firms' portals for a wide variety of functions, such as Internet access, e-mail, social networking, news, voice-over-IP (Internet protocol) telephony, chat, instant messaging, searching, and others. Social networking sites have become major portals, as have large online retailers like Amazon.

Government agencies depend on the Internet to convey information and services to the public and registered users of all kinds. Mobile devices increasingly provide a widening variety of online activities and applications. Today, the role of the commercial Internet portal in connecting users is to provide multiple, bundled services, often with applications allowing increasingly integrated and interconnected options. Examples include geolocation; finding nearby sites and people; texting a circle of "friends," often with photos and videos; "face time" video telephone calls; interlacing multiple e-mail, instant messaging, and "tweet" contact lists and postings; evaluating retailers and business services; meetings; and updating agendas. Storage of large files such as video, photographs, music, and books is provided free or at low cost "in the cloud." As a facilitator of the human interactions enabled by the multifaceted network, Internet service providers (ISPs), hosts, telecommunications companies, and interconnected service providers must understand the market forces, predominant personal views, laws, and ethical limitations of the activities riding their wavelengths.

Based on historical profiles of crime patterns within communities, it is predictable that a variety of criminals will take advantage of networked services to carry out their acts in a more efficient, anonymous, and (for them) pleasurable manner. Already, major telecommunications providers and ISPs have been forced to deal with many warrants, subpoenas, court orders, and requests requiring production of customer records, legal intercepts, and service details, based on serious criminal activities. No self-respecting drug dealer is without a cellular connection, whether on a "throwaway" cell phone or a Blackberry, iPhone, or Android device allowing multiple connections and messaging options. A classic case in a northeastern state involved a clue found at a murder crime scene, an apparent mob "hit," which was a long-distance calling card from a telephone network that was traced to a man from Florida through his credit card. The man claimed he was in Florida at the time of the murder, but his cell phone records identified precisely where he was and with whom he discussed the murder he committed. He is now serving time for the murder. The records of the cell phone location and calls were vital to the investigation, but even more important was the capability of identifying the calling card customer through the vendor's credit card sales records.

Telecommunications networks, ISPs, and website hosts generally take the position that they are not responsible for their customers' activities because they are providing a virtual venue through which people can carry on legal behaviors. Unfortunately, services like eBay and craigslist have discovered that the sale of stolen, contraband, and misappropriated items is sufficiently rampant that they have felt compelled to field a first-class team of former law enforcement and prosecutorial personnel to prevent, detect, and alert law enforcement to, otherwise respond to, and process data concerning illegal activities. Although the illegal activities may be only a small part of the service provided, it is significant to those victimized, such as an online purchase for which a customer received no goods. Not all Internet firms take the initiative or incur the expense that eBay has to ensure the integrity of a service that is open to virtually everyone. However, large Internet businesses all are compelled to field teams to answer court warrants and subpoenas issued for records relating to online criminal activities.

Criminal and civil courts have so far agreed with the large majority of ISPs, websites, and others online that they are not responsible for the criminal behaviors of their customers, despite pressure brought on web service providers to prevent unlawful activities online.[1] In some instances, courts have recognized the authorized use policy (AUP) as in effect the governing rule on a website and held the customer who violates the AUP (and therefore the site's terms of service) to be engaged in illicit activities by definition. In various communities, counties, and states, there have been occasional cries to shut down or criminally sanction websites that have become a venue where illegal acts take place, including such activities as prostitution, fencing, and drug sales, but in general, it is understood that websites operating properly still may be used in crimes.[2]

Among the special class of services online are those belonging to universities, colleges, other educational institutions, and some nonprofits. Many educational and nonprofit sites have a large amount of storage, a variety of applications, and high bandwidth—just what a cybercriminal may be looking for. Educational sites also operate in a wide-open environment. For example, at the start of each semester, hundreds or thousands of students may "plug in" to the college information technology (IT) network. The educational system may be required for research, study, communications with teachers, class attendance, test taking, cafeteria access, campus access, bill paying, and a variety of other student, faculty, and staff services. Often, the university e-mail system also accommodates alumni, a special target of solicitations for donations and support for the school. The size and openness of the educational IT infrastructure make it a prime target for cybercriminals, spammers, and marketers. As a consequence, many educational sites have found it necessary to adopt robust and inventive security measures that can guarantee system functions, integrity, and continuity, while keeping out malicious code, inadvertent infections, and deliberate attempts at misuse (e.g., changing grades, cheating on tests and papers, bulk spam).

These examples are not limited to ISPs, other network service providers, and educational institutions. Unfortunately, many corporations have found that their employees have placed large quantities of contraband and illicit materials in shared storage (e.g., pirated MP3 music files, videos, and software in violation of copyrights and child pornography laws). For example, an employee of a high-bandwidth company was arrested for running his own business on the side, selling child pornography from his personal website that he had installed on company servers. Like the service providers, businesses are potentially liable for the content of their IT systems and must face the fact that at least a small percentage of their users will misuse their systems. The larger the systems, the greater the likelihood that illicit content and unauthorized behaviors are taking place on them. System owners must decide who, in effect, will be the sheriff in town. In all the instances discussed, it is the people who decide to misbehave on computer systems to which they are granted access that cause the risk to service providers. Like viruses, illicit acts online should be sought out, discovered, and dealt with by Internet-connected hosts, if only for self-preservation and reputation protection.

Liability for Employers

Employers in the private sector are governed by a series of constitutional, federal, state, county, and local statutes and legal standards.[3] This is not the appropriate place to itemize them. However, a key question that must be considered in all legal and policy discussions of Internet searching that applies to persons (individuals and legal persons) is the legal standards that must be applied. Therefore, it is necessary to focus on how one can conduct Internet and open-source information collection without incurring legal liability for violating a statute or standard.

Employers must contemplate the laws that apply, whether they are conducting an internal criminal investigation, vetting potential employees, collecting business/competitive intelligence, assessing market competition, doing due diligence, managing brand protection, or assessing security risks and vulnerabilities, to name some of the main reasons for enterprise intelligence functions. This discussion deliberately omits market studies because the rules governing Internet social research (a very different animal from intelligence collection) should be applied for market research. However, some of the discussion in other chapters bears directly on such operations.

Two key areas of concern are applicant background investigations and protection of people, assets, and information (i.e., corporate security). Although an employer has legal obligations that must be met in assessing candidates for employment, the obligation to provide a safe and secure workplace is also vital. When an employer discriminates in hiring under Title VII of the Civil Rights Act of 1964, liability is created, and lawsuits will probably follow. When an employer fails to anticipate the likelihood of a threat such as an insider victimizing fellow employees, customers, or others, liability may be incurred. It is only a matter of time before the legal theory that an employer should have known and acted on information published and readily available on the Internet finds its way into a courtroom, especially if violence, crime, or serious loss occurs in or outside the workplace. Physical world negligence suits against employers asserting a standard of due care in hiring have succeeded, and it is likely that cyber-world torts will as well.[4]

The federal government, counties, states, and municipalities to varying degrees oversee the application of employment laws. The courts apply the laws for criminal and civil judgments. One aspect of the rapid advances in IT is the lag time between societal changes such as large-scale Internet use and the adaptation of the legal system to new realities.[5] For example, at a time when millions of Internet users illicitly download films, music, and software for personal use in violation of copyright laws, how can an employer judge how much illicit activity of this kind should preclude a person from employment? How many downloads are tolerable? Is it likely that people who misappropriate movies would also commit economic espionage? Can that likelihood be judged by the amount of past illicit downloading done? Business and government are, at this writing, just beginning to contemplate the metrics of adjudications in the Internet era.

Avoiding serious liability will require employers to look carefully at the standards they apply to vetting employees, both for hire and for continued employment, promotion, or clearances. Fortunately, according to court cases reviewed to date, there is no requirement in the United States for an employer to take additional steps to utilize any public information in background investigations, provided that the process includes notice, signed (informed) consent, and a verification process. Should an employer wish to include questions to candidates about their computer use and abuse and verification of their responses using Internet vetting, it would be prudent to include explicit prior notice about those topics in the process. Suggested methods appear in further discussion. At least 12 states, including Nevada and New Jersey, forbid employers from requiring candidates or employees to reveal social networking passwords or providing access to private postings.[6] Therefore, before asking a prospective or current employee to grant access to a private social networking account, an employer should know whether that is legal. At this writing, it is *not* illegal or unethical to access or consider publicly available Internet information for employment purposes.

Most application forms and the government's SF-86 form[7] (among others) ask applicants to list the other names or aliases by which they are known. Because a large percentage of Internet users (at least 30%, based on studies by Pew and others) have multiple virtual identities online, it is important in the background investigation process to collect them. Virtual identities include e-mail addresses, nicknames, "handles," user names, and other pseudonyms used for Internet activities. Asking for these aliases does not exceed the current norm for forms used, but 4 years' study has shown that few employers explicitly ask applicants to include virtual identities on the form. The SF-86, which is used for US government candidates for jobs with clearances, asks for both home and work e-mail addresses and for aliases. Recently added to the SF-86 are questions about prior misbehavior using computers. Yet, almost no agencies at this writing explicitly instruct candidates to include their Internet identities, which may have been used in such misbehavior. Some state statutes forbid an employer from requiring a candidate or employee to provide a user name, but it is common for user names and e-mail names to be identical.

The discussion that follows is designed to help put Internet intelligence gathering in an appropriate legal context. However, statutory and case law are rapidly developing in this area of Internet law.

Accountability for Employees

Automation of the workplace and widespread evolution of social norms for computer use have dramatically changed the landscape in ways that enterprises may not have considered. Habits acquired in personal computer use may invade the business, and business topics are being included in off-hours blogging, social networking, and a variety of other Internet activities both desirable and undesirable from the employer's standpoint. In most workplaces, it is easy to acquire digital goods, including designs, customer lists, marketing plans, information about employees, and other trade secrets and privacy-protected data. Espionage cases over the past 20 years in both government and industry have highlighted how much more damaging just one insider can be because of the volume, quality, and scope of the data stolen, particularly when IT systems are exploited.[8]

It must be acknowledged that most computers, networks, and data are

- Intrinsically not secure and perhaps not absolutely securable in the near term
- A gateway to most enterprises' most sensitive and valuable data
- Accessed by employees as trusted users with little oversight
- Protected more strongly against outsiders than insiders
- A higher risk than most employers understand

Recent experience demonstrated that most enterprises have attempted to strengthen their information security and have sought to improve protection through employee security awareness. Laudable though those efforts are, they may be inadequate for the task. Studies of insider crime have demonstrated since biblical times that there is almost always an insider willing to commit serious crimes within any sizable enterprise. After years of frustration with inadequate metrics, questionable survey statistics, and corporate security experience as a practitioner, colleague, and consultant to business and government, my rule of thumb is that at least 6% of employees will commit a felony crime against their employer yearly. I regret having to report this, just as I regret having participated in the arrest of priests, nuns, and Federal Bureau of Investigation (FBI) agents. One only need look at the high crimes and misdemeanors of the nation's once-respected politicians, law enforcement officers, intelligence officials, clergy, business leaders, and nonprofit executives to demonstrate that there is no sacrosanct group of human beings in any workplace. Aspiring to greatness does not prevent crime in the ranks. So, the logical question for every enterprise is how to approach the virtual goods that are at the disposal of every authorized user through information systems. US military and intelligence agencies take the approach that all online activities involving classified data and systems will be logged, monitored, and serious breaches prevented.[9] Alas, even those systems with the strongest protections have been victimized by clever, malicious users, such as the FBI's Robert Hanssen and Edward Snowden of the National Security Agency (NSA) and Central Intelligence Agency (CIA). It is clear that it is the person, not the machine, that should be the focus of behavioral assessment because it is the person who can make a mistake or commit a crime.

Twentieth-century personnel management can be characterized as evolving from the workplace cruelty of the Industrial Revolution to the civilized protections, led by unions, of the information age. Yet, there are those who would contend that there were more layoffs, outsourcing, and treatment of workers as commodities from 1980 to 2010 than from 1950 to 1980. It was a period when the lifelong aspiration to work for just one employer (other than the government) came to a painful end. The trust and emotional attachment between employer and worker ended. You can hear it in the terms used for employees: human resources and human capital—just another form of currency.

Perhaps it sounds too strident to observe that an employer, viewed even in the press as likely to downsize or outsource, is apt to be looked on by employees with a wary eye. The employer, needing to keep key talent, may engage in strategies to use economic leverage to prevent the exodus of its brain trust. Employees, for their part, may collect as much data as they can from the workplace in anticipation that bringing the data with them will enhance their value in the next job. Several surveys suggested that this is actually happening frequently in the twenty-first century.[10]

Employee accountability in this context can be a sensitive topic, given the atmosphere described previously. However, the compact between the employer whose net worth is largely in data and the employee with access to that data must include a strong element of trust if the enterprise is to succeed. In most agencies and firms, a formula for success is holding each individual user accountable for actions taken, both offline and online. All trusted users should sign a confidentiality agreement. At log-on, workers should be reminded that, as a condition of access, their use of data and online activities are controlled by programs to prevent misuse, as well as to log events. This accountability should start before the applicant is hired, should be stressed during indoctrination and training, and continue with periodic audits, reinvestigations, monitoring, and enforcement of AUPs during employment. Internet investigations are a natural part of preemployment screening and reinvestigations. Like the Internet, intranet behavior can be a prime indicator of danger for the enterprise when users violate the law, policies, and rules. Given the invaluable nature of information assets, today's automated employer owes nothing less to stockholders, customers, and the employees themselves than vigilance and efficiency in protecting its information assets from malicious users.

Notes

1. Center for Democracy and Technology, http://webcache.googleusercontent.com/sea rch?q=cache:I4J3DH5q178J:https://www.cdt.org/files/Intermediary-Liability-6p. doc+&cd=9&hl=en&ct=clnk&gl=us (accessed November 29, 2013).
2. Krasne, Alexandra, What Is Web 2.0, Anyway? *TechSoup*, December location, 2005, http://www.techsoup.org/learningcenter/webbuilding/archives/page9344.cfm (accessed June 1, 2010). Cybercrime information collected in law enforcement briefings of the International Association of Chiefs of Police ad hoc Computer Crime and Digital Evidence Committee (which I chaired 2009–2011).
3. Nixon, W. Barry, and Kerr, Kim M., *Background Screening and Investigations, Managing Risk from HR and Security Perspectives* (New York: Elsevier, 2008).
4. Lawson, Thomas C., Expert witness in several negligent hiring cases in California and Arizona, http://www.apscreenemploymentscreening.com/articles/case_samples.pdf (accessed May 25, 2010).
5. Herritt, Henry H., Jr., dean, Chicago-Kent College of Law, The Internet Is Changing the Public International Legal System, Illinois Institute of Technology, 1999, http://www. kentlaw.edu/cyberlaw/perrittnetchg.html (accessed December 18, 2013); Depoorter,

Ben, Technology and Uncertainty: The Shaping Effect on Copyright Law, *University of Pennsylvania Law Review*, 157: 1831, 2009, https://www.law.upenn.edu/live/files/78-depoorter157upalrev18312009pdf (accessed December 18, 2013); *American Bar Association Journal*, http://www.abajournal.com/ (accessed December 18, 2013); e-commerce law reports, http://www.e-comlaw.com/e-commerce-law-reports/#!.

6. National Conference of State Legislatures, http://www.ncsl.org/research/telecommunications-and-information-technology/employer-access-to-social-media-passwords-2013.aspx (accessed December 18, 2013); DelDuca, M. V., Barrueco, A. L., and Dolinsky, K. A., New Jersey's New Social Media Privacy Law: Balancing Employee Rights and Employer Protections, Pepper Hamilton, September 16, 2013, http://www.mondaq.com/unitedstates/x/262784/employee+rights+labour+relations/New+Jerseys+New+Social+Media+Privacy+Law+Balancing+Employee+Rights+And+Employer+Protections (accessed December 18, 2013).

7. Questionnaire for National Security Positions, SF-86, http://www.opm.gov/forms/pdf_fill/sf86.pdf (accessed May 26, 2010).

8. Shaw, Eric D., Ruby, Keven G., and Post, Jerrold M. The Insider Threat to Information Systems, Political Psychology Associates, 1999, http://www.dm.usda.gov/ocpm/Security%20Guide/Treason/Infosys.htm (accessed December 18, 2013); Kipp, Steven P., Espionage and the Insider, SANS Reading Room, https://www.sans.org/reading-room/whitepapers/basics/espionage-insider-426 (accessed December 18, 2013).

9. For example, DOD Directive 5220.22-M, Chapter 8, Information Systems Security, Section 6, Protection Requirements, US Department of Defense, Washington, DC, February 2001.

10. Moore, Andrew P., Cappelli, Dawn M., Caron, Thomas C., Shaw, Eric, and Trzeciak, Randall F., Insider Theft of Intellectual Property for Business Advantage: A Preliminary Model, Carnegie Mellon Software Engineering Institute and CERT, appearing in the First International Workshop on Managing Insider Security Threats (MIST 2009), Purdue University, West Lafayette, IN, June 15–19, 2009.

Chapter 7

Laws

Introduction

This chapter contains brief reviews of the statutes that may assist those seeking guidance about the legal framework that applies to Internet intelligence and investigations. For the most part, federal and state laws have not contained restrictions on the use of the Internet to collect information—especially public or published information—for use by investigators until recently, beginning about 2009–2010. State laws regarding social networking and privacy, federal and state laws regarding copyrights and intellectual property, and some cybercrime provisions are changing, albeit much more slowly than the Internet and societal norms online. The summaries and views expressed here do not constitute legal opinions or advice, or an attempt to detail every law related to cybervetting, but are conveyed as commonsense interpretations of the meaning of current laws and indications of the intent of Congress, legislatures, and the judiciary, even if the laws themselves do not address Internet investigations directly. Because people have differing views and strong opinions about their privacy rights, some of the interpretations that follow may be controversial.

Constitutional Rights

The US Constitution's amendments[1] enshrine the following rights relevant to Internet searching:

- First: Freedom of speech
- Fourth: Freedom from unreasonable search and seizure
- Fifth: Freedom from being forced to give witness against oneself or to be denied due process of law
- Sixth: Right of an accused to call witnesses and face an accuser in court

None of these rights precludes Internet searching under the appropriate circumstances. Litigation to date concerning constitutional rights has provided no successful challenge to Internet searching. Only a few cases have been brought. Litigation will be considered in further discussion.

Decisions by the Supreme Court and other federal courts in general have upheld the rights of individuals to protection of their information (e.g., postings) if there is a reasonable expectation of privacy. Under the Fourth Amendment, the location where the reasonable expectation of privacy exists is usually interpreted as in one's home, but that has been extended by court decisions to include other places where privacy can be expected (e.g., in a phone booth or hotel room). Although a laptop or handheld device would normally have the same protections as one's information at home, technology changes, border antiterrorist efforts, massive-scale intelligence collection, and the extremely fungible nature of large files on small storage devices are raising new legal questions. On the Internet, a network, or even a person's computer, the privacy of a venue and users' expectation of privacy may often depend on the authorized use policy (AUP) of the website (online servers) and the efficacy of data protection. Where the terms of use call for recognition of individual privacy rights, presumably a collector of information should abide by the AUP or face the possibility that information found may not be legally usable in any court or administrative procedure. Collection itself may even be deemed illegal if it is considered to be for an illegitimate purpose under US federal criminal statutes.

Following are some comments on constitutional rights relating to Internet search:

> The First Amendment right to free speech does not mean that there will be no penalty for expressing views that may be offensive, illegitimate, or destructive. For example, an employee publishing harsh criticism of his employer online may be fired. The exception to such an action might be an employee commenting on the fairness of his employer or about a topic like compensation, which might be protected under National Labor Relations Board (NLRB) laws or regulations pertaining to employee/union rights. The misperception among some people that self-expression is exempt from repercussions because of the First Amendment has muddled understanding of valid privacy rights and the right of an employer to protect its reputation.
>
> Fourth Amendment protection against unreasonable search and seizure has been challenged by modern technologies. The interconnectivity of the World Wide Web, dependent as it is on both private and public connections, exposes communications and postings to view by literally billions of people, sometimes

on purpose and sometimes by accident. When a posting is freely accessible to many Internet users, it is reasonable to expect that law enforcement, an employer, or literally any user may access that posting and react as they are legally entitled. An investigator should be expected to observe that which is obvious (e.g., published online) and to collect as evidence information pertaining to a case that is in plain view. Although a person of interest may not intend for a posting to become visible to the investigator, the person may not enjoy a constitutional protection against its use in court or in an adverse action. Wireless communications may place packets transmitted openly by radio within "hearing" of "listeners" within range—rendering such content accessible to unauthorized parties. Even though interception of data from wireless devices such as cell phones may be illicit, users find themselves vulnerable to electronic surveillance by anyone with the means to do so. Use of illicitly obtained data would be generally inadmissible for any adverse action and might violate federal laws against illegal electronic surveillance.

The Fifth Amendment can raise issues about the use of postings in court, depending on the judge's interpretation of the nature of the postings (e.g., hearsay, private communications, and diaries obtained without process).

The Sixth Amendment's right to face an accuser in court may preclude anonymous postings or those from unavailable witnesses from being used against the accused in court.

Constitutional rights come into play in state courts, as well as federal courts, and state constitutions (which follow the US Constitution in most respects) also apply to court interpretations of evidence obtained online.

Statutes

A review of US laws that may have an impact on Internet searching for information on individuals was conducted. These statutes regulate investigations to varying degrees, depending on the purpose, methods used, and resulting actions. Based on this review, the key issues are the methods used to retrieve the data, the uses to which Internet search results are put, and how decisions are made based on findings. Relatively new state statutes and proposed laws restrict what employers can require candidates and employees to reveal about their online activities and credentials. Following is a summary of those laws deemed most relevant.

Federal Statutes

The Privacy Act of 1971, as amended:[2] Controls government collection, use, and protection of personally identifying information and limits the extent to which federal agencies can disclose records: An individual must consent in writing, a court order must be issued, or the disclosure must fall within one of the statute's exceptions. The Privacy Act does not address personal information collected by private parties, such as data brokers, collection agencies, or consumer credit groups. A privacy impact assessment is required when a government agency establishes a new information system used to store data, including personally identifying information.

The Public Information Act (Freedom of Information Act):[3] Governs disclosure of US Government information, with exemptions for law enforcement and intelligence investigative files. The Disclosure of Confidential Information Act provides criminal penalties for unauthorized disclosure of specified classes of information by government officers and employees.

Health Insurance Portability and Accountability Act of 1996 (HIPAA), Gramm-Leach-Bliley Act of 1999, and Sarbanes-Oxley Act of 2002:[4] Several statutes, including these three, provide for the protection of sensitive, personally identifying information in the hands of the health industry, financial services, and consumer services enterprises.

The USA Patriot Act, Public Law 107-56, 2001:[5] The Patriot Act does not specifically address investigations of candidates for employment or clearances, except for drivers of hazardous cargo vehicles, who must meet federal standards for licensing based on a background investigation. The Patriot Act authorizes government surveillance and information collection activities, including electronic surveillance, designed to prevent terrorism, under appropriate legal authority (e.g., a warrant, subpoena, or national security request). Large-scale government data collection and analysis activities for counter-terrorism purposes were revealed by Edward Snowden, a former National Security Agency (NSA) contractor and Central Intelligence Agency (CIA) employee, who admitted to hacking inside government systems to obtain, and then leak to media outlets, a large quantity of documents about sensitive US Government collection methods. Several types of collection allow governments to amass and exploit large data sets to find indicators of terrorist and criminal behaviors. The Patriot Act's authorizations have been reviewed by Congress and courts and may be amended because of frequent political debates about the proper limits of government surveillance. Snowden's leaks have sparked debates about not only government actions but also those of various service providers who assisted the government in its intelligence functions. Historically, Americans are apt to demand more robust security to prevent attacks like that which occurred 9/11/2001 but to demand less-intrusive security when attacks seem to be contained or are in the past. This debate about sufficiency of intelligence collection is relevant to Internet searches because open-source data, including that of the Internet, have become evermore important to intelligence collection of all types.

The Fair Credit Reporting Act (FCRA), Public Law 91-508 (Title VI § 601):[6] Regulates consumer reports and consumer reporting agencies, establishing standards for the collection and dissemination of credit information and consumer reports, including reports of background investigations conducted by contract firms (but not by employers themselves) establishing eligibility for employment. Key provisions include the ability of the subject of a consumer report to review it and correct information deemed inaccurate. The FCRA protects prospective and onboard employees and must be the basis for policy principles established for Internet vetting by the private sector. The FCRA is examined further in this chapter.

Electronic Communications Privacy Act of 1986 (ECPA):[7] Protects wire, oral, and electronic communications while in transit by requiring warrants for interception and protects communications held in electronic storage (i.e., messages stored on computers). Law enforcement and investigators must obtain warrants or use other specified processes to obtain communications and customer account data. Protects private communications from third-party access, such as Internet service providers (ISPs). ECPA does not restrict collection of data legitimately posted on the public Internet or regulate the personal information that may be made available by users who willingly post such information. ECPA also does not protect employees' communications conducted on employers' systems. Some litigation under ECPA has served to clarify its reach.

Title X, Homeland Security Act of 2002, and Title III E Government Act of 2002, amending the *Federal Information Security Management Act (FISMA) of 2002*:[8] These statutes require that federal programs include information technology training programs and security awareness training for personnel and contractors that include information security risks and responsibilities involved in reducing those risks.

The Computer Fraud and Abuse Act (Title 18, Part I, Chapter 47, § 1030):[9] Forbids, with other federal criminal statutes, criminal activities that occur in the physical world, when they take place in cyberspace, and crimes facilitated by computers. US computer crime is the province of the Computer Crime and Intellectual Property Section of the US Department of Justice (information can be found at http://www.justice.gov/criminal/cybercrime/), which posts much helpful information about computer-related crime and intellectual property protection. Many types of street crimes (e.g., sale of pirated movie DVDs on the streets in Manhattan and Beijing) are also found on the Internet (where millions of users monthly patronize about 1,000 pirate sites offering films, videos, music, and software). This statute and others make it unlawful for an unauthorized person to access computers and data. The unauthorized access provision is controversial among some people, who believe that when information is stored on a system to which they can gain access, its ownership rights have been forfeited by its possessor. As a popular TV show about a master hacker said, "If they didn't want me to see it, why didn't they protect it better?" Most prosecutions under this act are based on demonstrable harm done by intrusions to systems or their owners. Recently, the number and seriousness of intrusions to businesses and institutions have raised alarms about the integrity and security of online systems as a whole.

Although the number of successful black-hat hackers may be small, their impact has increased because of the volume of people affected by breaches. The number of people involved in less-serious illicit acts online, such as copyright violations, remains high. Because millions of people engage in unlawful activities on the Internet, it is unlikely that most of them, given today's enforcement situation, will ever be charged with crimes.

The Computer Security Act of 1987 (Public Law 100-235):[10] This act, subsequent statutes, and appropriations aim to strengthen the security of government computers, networks, and data and assign establishment of computer security standards to the National Institute of Standards and Technology (NIST) and other federal agencies, including training of federal systems users and security measures.

The Children's Online Privacy Protection Act (COPPA):[11] Regulates the information that can be collected about preadult Internet users by websites and other commercial online service providers. COPPA is an example of the concern that the Congress has expressed in statutes, hearings, and studies about the best ways to protect the privacy of all Internet users from collection of personally identifiable transactional data by ISPs, websites, and advertisers. The Federal Trade Commission updated its guidance for business, parents, and small entities in July 2013, emphasizing the goal, which is to put parents in charge of what is publicly available from children 13 years old or younger.[12]

Copyright (Title 17, U.S. Code) and Uruguay Round Agreements Act (implementing international copyright treaties):[13] Protects authors of original works that are fixed in a tangible form of expression, both published and unpublished, giving the author exclusive rights to do and authorize reproduction, distribution, public performance, or display, with fair use and licensing restrictions. Registration and marking of copyrighted material are not necessary for copyright protections to apply. Infringement of copyright can be a federal civil or criminal matter, enforced by the courts, including damages, injunctions, and impoundment. Providing false contact information to a domain name registry creates a rebuttable presumption that the infringement was willful. Criminal infringement includes fines and incarceration for commercial, for-profit misuse, including illicit distribution by computer networks. ISPs are exempt if violations are committed by network users and not the ISPs.

Federal background screening laws: Besides the FCRA, federal statutes controlling background screening and related employer-employee issues include the National Labor Relations Act (NLRA), the Driver's Privacy Protection Act, the Civil Rights Act of 1964, Title VII of the Civil Rights Act 1996 (commonly referred to as Title VII), the Americans with Disabilities Act, the Federal Bankruptcy Act, the Employee Polygraph Protection Act, and the Family Educational Rights and Privacy Act, as well as guidelines set by the Equal Employment Opportunity Commission. None addresses cybervetting. The NLRB has brought actions against employers who have sanctioned employee postings related to unionizing, wages, benefits, or working conditions, which are considered protected under the NLRA. An emerging area of law is defining the limitations on employers whose rules about what employees say online that could potentially harm the enterprise's reputation are considered to limit employees' right to address NLRB-regulated employer-employee relationships. "The National Labor Relations Act protects the rights of employees to act together to address conditions at work, with or without a union. This protection extends to certain work-related conversations conducted on social media, such as Facebook and Twitter."[14]

State Statutes

California statute: Unauthorized Access to Computers, Computer Systems and Computer Data (California Penal Code Section 502-502.08):[15] From the statute:

It is the intent of the Legislature in enacting this section to expand the degree of protection afforded to individuals, businesses, and governmental agencies from tampering, interference, damage, and unauthorized access to lawfully created computer data and computer systems. The Legislature finds and declares that the proliferation of computer technology has resulted in a concomitant proliferation of computer crime and other forms of unauthorized access to computers, computer systems, and computer data. The Legislature further finds and declares that protection of the integrity of all types and forms of lawfully created computers, computer systems, and computer data is vital to the protection of the privacy of individuals as well as to the well-being of financial institutions, business concerns, governmental agencies, and others within this state that lawfully utilize those computers, computer systems, and data.

California Database Protection Act (CDPA), CA Civil Code § 1798.82; Consumer Credit Reporting Agencies Act, CA Civil Code § 1798.16; California Investigative Consumer Reporting Act, CA Civil Code § 1798.83-84; U.S. Comptroller of the Currency guidance to national Banks, OCC Bulletin 2005-13:14:[16] The CDPA, which took effect in July 2003, mandates public disclosure of computer security breaches in which confidential information may have been compromised. The law covers state agencies and all private enterprises doing business in California. Any entity that fails to disclose that a breach has occurred could be liable for civil damages or face class action lawsuits. Personal confidential information includes first and last names in conjunction with the following data: Social Security number, driver's license or California identification card (CID), account number, and credit or debit card number with any required security code, access code, or password that would permit access to an individual's financial account. The US Comptroller of the Currency issued guidance requiring national banks to notify customers of data breaches that include sensitive customer information. California state laws governing background checks include the California Consumer Credit Reporting Agencies Act and the California Investigative Consumer Reporting Act, which expand on the requirements of the federal FCRA. Federal proposals to legislate similar requirements continue.

Examples of other relevant state statutes:[17] California Civil Code § 1798.83-84 and Utah Code §§ 13-37-101, 102, 201, 202, 203 require all nonfinancial businesses to disclose to customers the types of personal information that the businesses sell or share with third parties for marketing purposes or for a fee. Minnesota §§ 325M.01 to .09 prohibit disclosure of an ISP customer's personally identifying information, stored data, and surfing history, except to law enforcement, and provides for civil damages. Nevada § 205.498 requires ISPs to keep confidential all but a customer's e-mail address and requires keeping e-mail addresses confidential if a customer so requests, subject to fines for violations. Delaware § 19-7-705 and Connecticut General Statutes § 31-48d prohibit an employer from collecting e-mail contents and Internet surfing data of employees without written notice, imposing civil penalties for violations. Exceptions are made for criminal investigations. At least 16 states have statutes that require government websites to establish privacy policies and procedures.

A good example of state approaches to guidelines for social media use by state employees and contractors is the state of Oklahoma Social Networking and Social Media Policy and Standards, Revised September 14, 2011 (originally published March 18, 2010). It treats posting policy and security, but not cybervetting. The purpose states, "Office of Management and Enterprise Services (OMES) … and the Oklahoma Office of the Attorney General have been working as a part of a collaborative effort involving the National Association of Attorneys General (NAAG) and the National Association of State Chief Information Officers (NASCIO) working on Terms of Service agreements with a broad range of social media providers who offer free services to users."[18]

In a January 2014 update on Internet privacy statutes, the National Conference of State Legislatures (NCSL) stated:[19]

> Two states, Nevada and Minnesota, require Internet Service Providers to keep private certain information concerning their customers, unless the customer gives permission to disclose the information. Both states prohibit disclosure of personally identifying information, but Minnesota also requires ISPs to get permission from subscribers before disclosing information about the subscribers' online surfing habits and Internet sites visited.

> Minnesota Statutes §§ 325M.01 to.09
> Nevada Revised Statutes § 205.498.

In addition, NCSL reported:

> State lawmakers introduced legislation beginning in 2012 to prevent employers from requesting passwords to personal Internet accounts to get or keep a job. Some states have similar legislation to protect students in public colleges and universities from having to grant access to their social networking accounts. ... As of April 10, 2014, legislation has been introduced or is pending in at least 28 states, and enacted in one state—Wisconsin—so far in 2014.

These proposed statutes appear to focus on keeping social networking user names and passwords private, but some go beyond and forbid employers and other authorities from requiring a person to display or divulge personal social networking profiles.[20] One example of a state statute that has gone into effect is in Nevada, where, as of October 1, 2013, it became illegal for an employer to require, request, or even suggest that an employee or a prospective employee disclose the user name, password, or other access information to his or her personal social media account.[21]

In federal and state laws, both the US Congress and the states have passed statutes aimed at protecting the privacy of computer and Internet users across the board. Many of the statutes restrict government collection and use of data without placing similar restrictions on the private sector. However, no law found prohibits the collection of publicly posted information on the Internet for a lawful purpose.

Federal Rules of Evidence and Computer Records

The most recent (2013) versions of the Federal Rules of Evidence, Federal Rules of Criminal Procedure, and Federal Rules of Civil Procedure[22] contain almost no references to the Internet, except mention of publication online of government information. The Rules of Evidence do not even contain the words *Internet, cyber,* or *digital.* However, they do treat "data stored in a computer or similar device" and state that "a reference to any kind of written material or any other medium includes electronically stored information." The rules apply the same standards for acceptability based on the reliability and trustworthiness of records and information, whether they are computerized or not.[23] They state, "For electronically stored information, 'original' means any printout—or other output readable by sight—if it accurately reflects the information."[24]

To address the issues of admissibility and authenticity of evidence as viewed by a court of law, the Federal Rules of Evidence are considered here, rather than those of each state, selected foreign countries, or some other approach, all of which might fall short of providing consistent and useful guidance. Because the states generally follow the federal approach, and this area of law is evolving with the technologies involved, the federal rules are deemed enlightening and sufficient. They are rooted in the Constitution (e.g., the Sixth Amendment right of an accused to face an accuser).

Federal courts generally consider admitting computer records into evidence under an exception to the hearsay rule, which states (in relevant part): "Hearsay, [which] is a statement, other than one made by the declarant while testifying at the trial or hearing, offered in evidence to prove the truth of the matter asserted … is not admissible except as provided by these rules or by other rules prescribed by the Supreme Court pursuant to statutory authority or by Act of Congress." In lay terms, testimony by John that "Mary said Sam did it" usually would not be admitted in federal court. Exceptions to the hearsay rule include a recorded recollection, or a record of regularly conducted activity, such as a business record. Courts have analyzed the content and circumstances of computer records' creation to determine if they contain hearsay. If a person created the record (e.g., a document, spreadsheet, etc.), then its admissibility may depend on testimony to authenticate the content and assert that it is accurate as recorded (e.g., if it was information that a clerk normally enters in the course of business). If the computer itself created the record by processing data in a programmed fashion, then the record may not contain hearsay but may require someone to authenticate the information to be admitted. Of course, computer records often contain mixed data (i.e., those that are entered by a person, which courts interpret as containing hearsay, and those that result from automated processing). To have computer evidence admitted, then, a party must establish the authenticity of the record and that it falls under the hearsay rule exception.[25]

One reason for considering the Federal Rules of Evidence in connection with cybervetting and Internet intelligence is the reasoning behind the centuries-old court rules, which are based on British Common Law and American practice. The rules point to a central issue: the authenticity and veracity—"trustworthiness"—of the data. Essentially, all intelligence functions must face the same questions as the courts: Is this information real or somehow untrustworthy? Is the information likely to be true or false? Courts apply rules like the hearsay one to keep unreliable information out. As the Justice Department's guidance says:

> The hearsay rules exist to prevent unreliable out-of-court statements by human declarants from improperly influencing the outcomes of trials. Because people can misinterpret or misrepresent their experiences, the hearsay rules express a strong preference for testing human assertions in court, where the declarant can be placed on the stand and subjected to cross-examination.[26]

Among other responses to the challenges of admissibility of electronic evidence, the Maryland District of federal courts issued a Suggested Protocol for Discovery of Electronically Stored Information in the US District Court for the District of Maryland.[27] Because technical and physical norms for identifying and authenticating documentary evidence when it is computerized are a focus of every court case in which such evidence is proffered, it is expected that case law will continue to apply guides like those in the Maryland protocol.

Clearly, computers can be used to create false or misleading records. Internet postings may contain humor, irony, fantasy, exaggeration, deliberate untruth—or factual documents. Because the intelligence analyst often cannot consult the creator of the records, authentication and veracity can be difficult to judge. A key function of open-source intelligence is assembling and analyzing the factors that help determine the trustworthiness of the information found.

International Treaties and Standards

Among the international bodies addressing legal and privacy issues of the information society are the United Nations, the Organization for Economic Cooperation and Development, and the Council of Europe. The European Commission and European Union, as well as constituent nations, have strong privacy protection laws and directives that can be characterized as enforcement of the "opt-in" principle, meaning that for personally identifying information to be collected, the individual must agree to that collection. The 1995 EU Data Privacy Protection Act requires unambiguous consent for information to be gathered online, notice regarding why the information is collected, the ability to correct erroneous data, and the ability to opt out and to be protected against transfer of one's data to countries with lesser privacy protections. Nevertheless, an individual may elect to post personal information online for all to see.

In the Council of Europe Convention on Cybercrime,[28] ratified by the United States in 2001 and in effect since January 1, 2007, convention signatories pledged to criminalize a wide range of computer-related illegal activities and to address electronic evidence, facilitate investigation of cybercrime, and obtain electronic evidence to prosecute all types of criminal investigations and proceedings. The convention reaffirms established principles of free expression and privacy and is the only binding international treaty on the subject to date.

The European Union Data Protection Directive[29] applies to firms operating in the European Union and specifies that "personal data" must have "appropriate security," compliant with either International Organization for Standardization/International Electrotechnical Commission (ISO/IEC) 17799 or BS 7799-2; prohibits an individual's personal information from being accessed and employed for other uses; and requires appropriate measures to protect personal data. The EU directive was strengthened in 2012 to provide further personal data protections. The European Union is in conflict with the United States over privacy and data protection standards and safeguards. The Canadian Personal Information Protection and Electronic Documents Act[30] regulates the use and collection of personal information via the Internet. The act applies not only to Canadian companies but also potentially to any entity that collects personal information in Canada or personal information from Canadian citizens. More sensitive information, such as patient records, should be safeguarded by a higher level of protection. Collection or use of personal information without knowledge and consent appears to be allowed by the act for appropriate, official purposes such as verification of the terms of employment.

Existing laws that may relate to Internet searching can be summarized in a few short points:

- US statutes and legal practice do not forbid the lawful use of public Internet postings for intelligence, investigative, and vetting purposes.
- In Europe, Canada, and Asia, legal privacy protections may limit the types of data that can be collected and used from Internet sources.
- Misuse of personally identifying data, including failure to protect it adequately, can result in legal sanctions in the United States and abroad.
- The law tends to favor the agency or business that provides full disclosure and transparency to consumers, employees, and others, allowing them to see the information about them, correct it if necessary, and provide consent when data about them are used in a manner that may have an impact on their well-being.

Although the US Constitution and statutes do not directly address issues related to Internet investigations, they shed light on the principles that should be adopted for fairness and ethical cybervetting. Additional support for the pillars of Internet search policy for government and private enterprises is found in Chapter 9.

US Legislative Proposals

About 145 bills were introduced in the US Congress in 2013 addressing privacy rights in one way or another,[31] but none treated the entire agenda announced by President Barak Obama. Efforts continued to encourage businesses to adopt privacy principles originally created in the United States but adopted in law in Europe, Canada, and Asia and left to the market in the United States. A primary example is a bill proposed by the Obama administration labeled a Consumer Privacy Bill of Rights,[32] saying American Internet users should have the right to control personal information about themselves collected online, to prevent data collected for one purpose being used for an unrelated purpose, to ensure information is held securely, and to know who is accountable for use or misuse of their personal information. Along with several reportedly more high-profile bills with a longer history of discussion (e.g., strengthening security of data protection), this proposal was not introduced as a separate bill and is not viewed as likely to be enacted into law.

Notes

1. US Constitution, http://www.archives.gov/exhibits/charters/constitution.html (accessed December 19, 2013).
2. For the Privacy Act, see http://www.usdoj.gov/oip/foia_updates/Vol_XVII_4/page2.htm, which contains amendments (accessed August 10, 2010).
3. Freedom of Information Act, http://www.justice.gov/oip/foia_updates/Vol_XVII_4/page2.htm (accessed August 10, 2010).
4. HIPAA, https://www.cms.gov/HIPAAGenInfo/Downloads/HIPAALaw.pdf (accessed August 10, 2010). Gramm-Leach- Bliley Act of 1999, http://banking.senate.gov/conf/ (accessed August 10, 2010). Sarbanes-Oxley Act of 2002, http://fl1.findlaw.com/news.findlaw.com/hdocs/docs/gwbush/sarbanesoxley072302.pdf (accessed August 10, 2010).
5. USA Patriot Act, Public Law 107-56, 2001, http://thomas.loc.gov/cgi-bin/bdquery/z?d107:HR03162:%5D (accessed August 10, 2010).
6. Fair Credit Reporting Act (FCRA), Public Law 91-508, Title VI, § 601, http://www.ftc.gov/os/statutes/031224fcra.pdf (accessed August 10, 2010).
7. Electronic Communications Privacy Act of 1986, http://www.it.ojp.gov/default.aspx?area=privacy&page=1285 (accessed August 10, 2010).
8. Federal Information Security Management Act (FISMA) of 2002, http://thomas.loc.gov/cgi-bin/bdquery/z?d107:h.r.03844: (accessed August 10, 2010).
9. Computer Fraud and Abuse Act, Title 18, Part I, Chapter 47, § 1030, http://www.justice.gov/criminal/cybercrime/1030NEW.htm (accessed August 10, 2010).
10. Computer Security Act of 1987, Public Law 100-235, http://www.nist.gov/cfo/legislation/Public%20Law%20100-235.pdf (accessed August 10, 2010).
11. Children's Online Privacy Protection Act (COPPA), http://www.ftc.gov/ogc/coppa1.htm (accessed August 10, 2010).
12. http://www.business.ftc.gov/documents/Complying-with-COPPA-Frequently-Asked-Questions#General%20Questions (accessed November 29, 2013).
13. Copyright law, http://www.copyright.gov/title17/, http://www.copyright.gov/circs/circ01.pdf, http://www.copyright.gov/title17/92chap5.pdf (accessed August 10, 2010).
14. The NLRB and Social Media, http://www.nlrb.gov/news-outreach/fact-sheets/nlrb-and-social-media (accessed April 27, 2014).
15. California Penal Code, Section 502-502.08, http://www.calpers.ca.gov/eip-docs/utilities/conditions/502-ca-penal-code.pdf (accessed August 10, 2010).
16. California Database Protection Act (CDPA), CA Civil Code § 1798.82, http://www.cybersure.com/documents/seminar/database_protection.pdf and http://www.ffiec.gov/ffiecinfobase/resources/info_sec/2006/occ-bul_2005-13.pdf (accessed August 10, 2010). California Consumer Credit Reporting Agencies Act, CA Civil Code § 1798.16, http://law.onecle.com/california/civil/index.html (accessed August 10, 2010). California Investigative Consumer Reporting Act, CA Civil Code § 1798.83-84, http://www.privacy.ca.gov/icraa.htm (accessed August 10, 2010).
17. For examples of state statutes, see http://www.ncsl.org/research/telecommunications-and-information-technology/state-laws-related-to-internet-privacy.aspx (accessed December 19, 2013).
18. See http://www.ok.gov/cio/Policy_and_Standards/Social_Media/ (accessed April 27, 2014).

19. See http://www.ncsl.org/research/telecommunications-and-information-technology/state-laws-related-to-internet-privacy.aspx (accessed April 27, 2014).
20. See http://www.ncsl.org/research/telecommunications-and-information-technology/employer-access-to-social-media-passwords-2013.aspx (accessed April 27, 2014).
21. See http://www.laborlawyers.com/nevada-inquiring-about-personal-social-media-will-be-illegal (accessed December 19, 2013).
22. US courts: http://www.uscourts.gov/uscourts/rules/rules-evidence.pdf, http://www.uscourts.gov/uscourts/RulesAndPolicies/rules/2010%20Rules/Criminal%20Procedure.pdf, http://www.uscourts.gov/uscourts/rules/civil-procedure.pdf.
23. Federal Rules of Evidence, Rule 803. Exceptions to the Rule Against Hearsay—Regardless of Whether the Declarant Is Available as a Witness (6), http://www.uscourts.gov/uscourts/rules/rules/evidence.pdf (accessed July 16, 2014).
24. Federal Rules of Evidence, Article X. Contents of Writings, Recordings, and Photographs, Rule 1001. Definitions That Apply to This Article, http://www.uscourts.gov/uscourts/rules/rules/evidence.pdf (accessed July 16, 2014).
25. Kerr, Orin S., Computer Records and the Federal Rules of Evidence, *US Attorneys' USA Bulletin*, 49(2), 2001, http://www.cybercrime.gov/ (accessed August 10, 2010).
26. Computer Crime and Intellectual Property Section, Criminal Division, US Department of Justice, Searching and Seizing Computers and Obtaining Electronic Evidence in Criminal Investigations (Manual), July 2002, Appendix F updated December 2006, http://www.cybercrime.gov/s&smanual2002.html (accessed August 10, 2010).
27. See http://www.mdd.uscourts.gov/news/news/ESIProtocol.pdf (accessed April 27, 2014).
28. Text of Council of European Convention on Cybercrime, accessible at http://www.coe.int/t/DGHL/cooperation/economiccrime/cybercrime/default_en.asp.
29. European Union Data Protection Directive and links to individual countries' laws, see http://ec.europa.eu/justice_home/fsj/privacy/law/imple- mentation_en.htm (accessed January 17, 2014).
30. Canadian Personal Information Protection and Electronic Documents Act (S.C. 2000, c. 5), http://laws.justice.gc.ca/eng/acts/P-8.6/ (accessed January 17, 2014).
31. http://thomas.loc.gov/cgi-bin/thomas, accessed January 28, 2014.
32. The White House, Washington, DC, Fact Sheet: Plan to Protect Privacy in the Internet Age by Adopting a Consumer Privacy Bill of Rights, http://www.whitehouse.gov/the-press-office/2012/02/23/fact-sheet-plan-protect-privacy-internet-age-adopting-consumer-privacy-b (accessed January 28, 2014).

Chapter 8

Litigation

Introduction

The intent of this chapter is not to provide a review of all of the relevant court decisions or to argue the privacy issues of cyberspace. It provides no legal advice or analysis but rather describes selected litigation and related information deemed to illuminate key issues regarding Internet searching of persons, legal persons, and entities in law terms. Relatively few court decisions were found that directly concern Internet searching, and few legal reviews of employment disputes, and other sensitive issues, such as privacy, along with cases for which admissibility of electronic evidence issues were adjudicated. Therefore, topical reviews were conducted of decisions that could be used as precedents in a case where an Internet search led to a lawsuit or was used as guidance to professionals seeking to understand the proper way to conduct cybervetting. Commentary is included in an effort to explain potential relevance to this issue.

Internet Search Litigation

A few cases involving claims relating to an employer conducting Internet searching on an employee or applicant were found. In one case, the US Court of Appeals for the Federal Circuit affirmed the firing of a US Government employee on a nonprecedential basis.[1] The employee claimed that "his guaranteed right to fundamental fairness was seriously violated" when his supervisor used Google to search his name and learned and improperly considered that he previously had been removed from a position by the Air Force. However, the court found that the employee himself told his supervisor that he had been subject to employment proceedings before, ruling his due process rights were not infringed in over 100 supported charges of misconduct. A legal comment on this case noted that if an employer "hunts down information on the Internet as a pretext for firing an employee for a truly improper motive, such [as] unlawful discrimination based on race, gender or age, such conduct would not be embraced by the law"; "on the other hand, if an employer learned on the Internet that an employee was engaging in conduct harmful to the employer, such as disclosing company trade secrets or defaming the company, that may be grounds for termination."[2]

Numerous other cases have been filed, but none so far has resulted in decisions against employers where information posted on the public Internet is concerned. Here are some of the more interesting cases:

> In a 2006 New Jersey case, *Pietrylo et al. v. Hillstone Restaurant Group*, bartender Brian Pietrylo and waitress Doreen Marino sued after their termination by Houston's Restaurant (Hillstone) for posting derogatory and obscene comments on a password-protected MySpace profile, claiming that in their restricted group, privacy-protected postings were not meant for public viewing. A third employee was allegedly coerced into providing her log-in information to a manager, who shared the site's contents with other managers, who fired Pietrylo and Marino. A New Jersey court held, and the New Jersey Federal District Court affirmed, that the restaurant's managers violated the Stored Communications Act and the New Jersey Wiretapping and Electronic Surveillance Act by accessing the MySpace page without authorization. However, the court ruled on an invasion-of-privacy claim that the plaintiffs had no reasonable expectation of privacy on MySpace.[3] A federal jury awarded the two a total of $3,400 in back pay and $13,600 in punitive damages.[4]
>
> *Comment*: It is clear that courts will have little sympathy for employers who gain illicit or illegal access to postings and then take adverse action against employee-posters. However, the extent to which a posting is protected has limitations. Coercing someone to provide unauthorized access appears to be a step less acceptable than being given access voluntarily. However, if the site policy clearly restricts access to and use of content, it is unlikely that the employer will have free rein to act solely on what is found in postings. As yet untested are situations in which large numbers of persons have authorized access to defamatory postings, and the courts in the New Jersey case indicated that the employees did not have a valid invasion-of-privacy claim because they had no reasonable expectation of privacy on MySpace. With well over a billion users of Facebook, one could hardly argue that a post available to all Facebook users enjoyed privacy protection, regardless of the website's policy.
>
> In a 2012 case, a 25-year-old Peoria, Arizona, police officer posted a photo on Facebook of several individuals with guns holding up a bullet-hole riddled tee shirt depicting President Barak Obama.[5] Investigations by the Secret Service and the Peoria Police Department led to his demotion and suspension without pay for violation of its social media policy and because he discredited the department. The punishments were upheld on appeal.
>
> *Comment*: First Amendment cases involving public employees' speech have a history long before social media and often hinged on whether the employee made

statements in their official capacity or as a private citizen. Law enforcement officers are considered even more restricted in their speech than other public servants. As the Supreme Court noted in the *Garcetti* case (*Garcetti v. Ceballos*, 547US410 (2006)): "When a citizen enters government service, the citizen by necessity must accept certain limitations on his/her freedom." Government employers have the ability to retain control over speech that "owes its existence to a public employee's professional responsibilities."

In the case titled *City of San Diego v. Roe* (Supreme Court, 2004),[6] a police officer who was terminated after the department learned of his sexually explicit off-duty behavior claimed his firing violated his First Amendment rights. The officer had made a video of himself stripping off his police uniform and masturbating, then sold, on the adults-only section of eBay, the video and other items that connected him to the San Diego Police Department. The Supreme Court, in reversing the 9th Circuit Court, upheld the city's decision to terminate Roe because the police department "demonstrated legitimate and substantial interests of its own that were compromised by Roe's speech," and Roe's sexually explicit conduct "brought the mission of the employer and the professionalism of its officers into serious disrepute." No balancing of interests was necessary as Roe's conduct did not touch on a matter of public concern.

It is safe to say that there will be plenty of litigation exploring the limits of privacy protections on the Internet. However, it is also obvious that public postings have no current, legal privacy protections, and courts have consistently held so.

Anonymity

In 1958, the Supreme Court held Alabama's demand for the identities of all members and agents of the NAACP (National Association for the Advancement of Colored People) unconstitutional, declaring that anonymity was essential to free speech and association, exercise of which would be impaired by disclosure. The court held that forcing the NAACP to disclose its membership lists was "likely to affect adversely the ability of [the NAACP] to pursue their collective effort to foster beliefs which they admittedly have the right to advocate."[7]

Comment: Anonymity enables a wide range of public activities on the Internet, in which those posting information publicly are responsible for deciding whether or not, and in what manner, attribution is included. A number of federal and state courts have held that an enterprise cannot cause a court to require disclosure of the posting individual merely because the material is insulting to the enterprise. A substantial number of businesses have been known to me to investigate illicit and untrue postings to determine who made them. In some cases, it is possible to identify individuals attempting anonymity whose postings include clues to their identity.

In *Griffin v. State of Maryland*, the Maryland Special Court of Appeals upheld the murder conviction of Griffin, approving a Cecil County Court judge's ruling allowing introduction of the MySpace page of Griffin's girlfriend to corroborate testimony of a key eyewitness that he had declined to testify in a first trial with a hung jury because of threats on his life. The judge allowed the MySpace page into evidence because of compelling circumstantial evidence, including the use of the girlfriend's photo with Griffin, her date of birth, number of children, and Griffin's nickname, among other things. Defense counsel objected that the MySpace profile owner "Sistasouljah" had not been conclusively verified as the girlfriend prior to introduction into evidence. The trial and three-judge appeals panel unanimously agreed that despite the use of a pseudonym, she had identified herself by photo and personal background information.[8] On April 28, 2011, the Maryland Court of Appeals reversed the Court of Special Appeals,[9] holding "that the pages allegedly printed from Griffin's girlfriend's (Barber) MySpace profile were not properly authenticated." The appeals court was particularly concerned with the possibility of hacking and suggested that additional forensic evidence to establish the posting's authorship and attribution was necessary and remanded the case for retrial.

Comment: This ruling may suggest that judges will accept good circumstantial grounds for identification of a person with Internet postings, provided that the details are sufficient and clear. In this case, the murderer was included in a photo on the MySpace posting with his girlfriend, whose blatant threat against the eyewitness, her date of birth, boyfriend's nickname, number of children, and other details provided convincing corroboration to support the prosecution's introduction of the MySpace page. A Maryland State policeman testified about the profile outside the jury's hearing, prior to the judge's allowing its introduction into evidence. However, the evidence provided at trial did not include verification from the girlfriend or her computer that she posted the threatening message that caused a witness to change his testimony between a first hung jury trial and the second trial, which resulted in conviction. The lessons from this case for Internet investigators are that every detail that corroborates or may shed doubt on the identification of online content is important and should be assembled to verify the relevance, attribution, and authentication of the facts reported. Otherwise, the information found online may have lead or intelligence value, but it may not be considered probative by the courts.

Expectation of Privacy

In 1967, the Supreme Court established the principle that individual privacy protection (rather than property protection) extends the Fourth Amendment shield to include what a person "seeks to preserve as private"—in this case, a telephone call in a public area. The court used a two-part test to determine when an individual has a "reasonable expectation of privacy": whether government action violated an individual's subjective expectation of privacy and whether that expectation of privacy was reasonable (an objective test).[10] One year later, in 1968, Title III of the Omnibus Crime Control and Safe Streets Act was passed, requiring law enforcement to seek a warrant for electronic surveillance.[11] Subsequent lower federal court decisions have found, under more recent laws, including those recounted previously, that a reasonable expectation of privacy has a variety of nuances, depending on the type of communication and the situation.

Comment: Courts have ruled unanimously that publicly posted information on the Internet carries no reasonable expectation of privacy. More on this topic appears next.

The Supreme Court ruled on a constitutional privacy suit brought by patients and doctors against a New York State statute requiring physicians to report prescriptions for "potentially harmful" drugs to the state. Because the statute included security requirements and use and retention limits for the computer files maintained, the court found the statute constitutional, stating that the privacy arguments were not sufficient to invalidate the law, which was a reasonable exercise of the state's police powers in view of the privacy and security safeguards employed.[12]

Comment: Security protection for personally identifying information on employees, applicants, and other persons ensures that information collected through background investigations, including Internet searching, poses no unreasonable security or privacy threat to candidates and employees. Requiring disclosure of Internet activities that could relate to employment as a condition of a successful background screening is a proper exercise of employer discretion, provided that the information collected is handled and utilized in a lawful, fair, secure manner.

The Supreme Court ruled that a police pen register did not constitute a violation of the Fourth Amendment because the user of a telephone had no reasonable expectation of privacy in the numbers dialed from a home phone.[13] (A pen register is a device that records numbers dialed to and from a telephone, without providing call content.)

Comments: Posting of information by an individual on the public Internet makes that information available to everyone. When users create a public profile, those users have no Fourth Amendment right to protection of that profile because they consented to the terms of the website to gain free access to postings. Most websites have privacy and use policies that spell out what happens to data provided by users. In recent years, Facebook and Google (among others) have been criticized for privacy policy changes, including loopholes in privacy protections that can be invoked by users to keep their data from public view (e.g., making their text and photo postings available only to selected friends and family). When changes to privacy settings exposed postings to unintended viewers, many social networkers loudly complained. Ironically, social networking and Internet service provider (ISP) websites admittedly mine users' data for marketing purposes, which creates another privacy issue. A substantial percentage of social network users, in my experience, place few or no privacy limits on their postings, which is consistent with findings of a 2012 Pew survey of teens' social network privacy settings, which showed that most posted personal details publicly.[14]

The US Court of Appeals for the Armed Forces upheld the conviction of an officer on child pornography and obscenity-related charges, finding that seizure of e-mail and other computer data under a federal warrant was proper, and that after an e-mail was received by the recipient, the sender's privacy interest in its stored content was low, and collection by law enforcement was not subject to the controls relating to interception of an e-mail in transit.[15]

Comment: Some of the data posted to the Internet, such as controversial or offensive blogs, chats, profiles, comments, photos, videos, and message board content, may be regrettable, and individuals involved may wish the data were not online. However, an individual's control and privacy interest may be limited after posting.

In *United States v. Charbonneau*, a federal court ruled that a participant's e-mail and postings in an Internet chat room used to distribute child pornography hold no reasonable expectation of privacy, and the defendant's motion to suppress the evidence was denied. Once the e-mail is sent, the sender loses privacy protections when the e-mail (like a letter) is in the hands of the recipient. A posting in a chat room, where an undercover agent is observing postings, has even less privacy protection, and anything said on the chat is admissible in court.[16]

Comment: This decision appears consistent with findings in all court jurisdictions where open-source public information, such as that posted on the Internet, is concerned. Chat rooms and their logs are worthy of further discussion, which appears in the material that follows.

In *Davis v. Gracey*, the US Court of Appeals for the 10th Circuit dismissed the claimants' assertion that evidence seized on a warrant should be suppressed under the First and Fourth Amendments, the Privacy Protection Act (PPA), 42 U.S.C. 2000aa-2000aa-12, and the Electronic Communications Privacy Act (ECPA), 18 U.S.C. 2510–2711, ruling that a good faith reliance on a court order or warrant is a complete defense to any action brought under the ECPA. To be in good faith, reliance on the warrant or court order must be objectively reasonable. The court ruling enabled a federal district court trial and conviction of the claimants based on the evidence.[17]

Comment: This is an example of defendants' claims of privacy rights that would supersede a warrant (i.e., a finding by a judge that a crime has been committed and evidence of the crime should be seized in the manner specified). It is possible that persons denied employment or a clearance as a result of information found on the public Internet will claim a violation of their privacy rights. Nevertheless, privacy rights clearly do not apply to public data.

The 9th Circuit Court of Appeals held in 2007 in *United States v. Ziegler* that although an employee of a commercial firm had a reasonable expectation of privacy in his locked (nonshared) office space, the employer had the right to monitor his computer use, retrieve copies of his hard drive using a company key, and turn the copies over to the Federal Bureau of Investigation (FBI), resulting in his conviction on Internet access to child pornography charges. The court said that computers are "the type of workplace property that remains within the control of the employer even if the employee has placed personal items in it."[18]

In *Konop v. Hawaiian Airlines*, the Ninth US Circuit Court of Appeals overturned a federal district court, ruling that a personal, restricted website on which Konop, a pilot, posted critical comments about his airline employer and labor concessions sought by the airline were considered protected activity, and unauthorized access could constitute violations of the federal Wiretap Act, 18 USC §§ 2510–2520, and the Stored Communications Act, 18 USC §§ 2701–2710. Airline executives accessed Konop's website using other employees' log-in information and clicked to affirm that they would abide by the site's confidentiality policy—violating that policy against unauthorized access. Hawaiian later placed the pilot on medical suspension, which Konop claimed was in retaliation for his union activity. In court, the airline argued that the pilot's postings were false, defamatory, and outrageous, but the appeals court held that they were within the bounds of labor laws and returned the case to a lower court, reinstating Konop's lawsuit.[19]

In June 2009, the city of Bozeman, Montana, was widely criticized when the AP (Associated Press) and other media outlets published the fact that applicants for city positions were being asked to provide passwords to access social networking and other websites to which candidates belonged. The city quickly rescinded its policy, but for some time, its application form online still requested a listing of all websites that applicants used.[20]

Comment: Bozeman officials conceded that they went too far in requiring applicants to provide passwords, which might provide access not only to social networking sites but also to such protected activities as banking, medical services, and insurance. Nevertheless, Bozeman was at the forefront in asking applicants for their history of Internet use and being in a position to review postings that are public to confirm that applicants meet all the requirements of the position. Guidelines published by the International Association of Chiefs of Police (IACP), "Developing a Cybervetting Strategy for Law Enforcement,"[21] strongly suggest that employers should not ask candidates for passwords. Some police departments ask candidates to log on to sites that they frequent and show their postings to applicant processors to ensure that they only publish content consistent with department policies.

Due Process

The US District Court for the District of Columbia enjoined the US Navy against discharging a US naval officer whose postings on AOL, a major ISP, appeared to embrace a gay lifestyle, and against using information obtained without process by a navy paralegal concerning the officer. The court held the government to a strict interpretation of the ECPA's requirement for obtaining process (warrant or subpoena) to obtain the officer's identity from AOL and opined that the officer's public Internet postings did not constitute proper grounds for the investigation as conducted, in view of the Internet's invitation to fantasy and anonymity.[22]

Comment: A central issue in this case was the Navy paralegal's identification of the naval officer without due process through AOL. The court considered and commented on the public Internet postings that were the basis for the investigation. This decision may be an indication that it is not Internet postings alone that should constitute the basis for adjudications. In addition, the degree of misbehavior in such postings is pivotal in deciding whether they are leads for investigation, grounds for action, or the basis for adjudications that could be adverse to the subject. This is one of only a few cases involving the adverse use of Internet postings to be litigated.

In *Raytheon Company v. John Does 1–21*,[23] Raytheon succeeded in identifying 21 employees who violated company policy and their employment contracts. On February 1, 1999, Raytheon filed suit against 21 employees it alleged had posted or discussed confidential corporate information on a Yahoo message board, in violation of their employment contracts and Raytheon's published employment policy; Raytheon claimed, in addition, that this conduct constituted a misappropriation of Raytheon's trade secrets. To identify the "John Does," Raytheon obtained a court order allowing its counsel to take out-of-state discovery from Yahoo, AOL, EarthLink, and various other ISPs, seeking documents and information identifying the 21.

Analysis: By framing its lawsuit primarily as a breach-of-contract action, Raytheon limited the defendants' ability to rely on a "free speech" defense because typically if an employee has signed a contract that specifically precludes disclosure of trade secrets or other confidential corporate information, the availability of that defense is limited to "whistle-blower" cases. In addition, it is possible that any jurisdictional defenses normally available to defendants outside Massachusetts may have been limited or eliminated by the terms of the employment agreements.

The privacy issue raised by the out-of-state discovery from Yahoo, AOL, and the ISPs—the right of the authors to remain anonymous, if you will—is limited. To access Yahoo's message board and post, the authors each agreed to the terms and conditions set forth in Yahoo's "term-and-conditions" agreement concerning the use of the message board, including providing Yahoo with a valid e-mail address and to the terms and conditions of their ISP. Yahoo's message board disclaimer stated that although Yahoo will take reasonable measures to respect the privacy of users, Yahoo reserves the right to turn over user identification information if Yahoo in good faith believes that disclosure is necessary in certain circumstances, including to comply with legal process or the law. After being served with Raytheon's subpoena, Yahoo apparently provided Raytheon with the authors' e-mail addresses or other information. In May 1999, Raytheon dismissed the lawsuit after several of the identified employees had apparently resigned.

Comment: The contracts used by Raytheon are analogous to the notice and consent that are appropriate for notice to and consent of applicants for jobs and clearances. Such procedures are appropriate not only to add Internet searching to existing background investigative checking but also to send a clear message to candidates and employees that proper use of information systems is a vital requirement of the job. An individual with a history of improper computer use is more likely to misuse an employer's systems or to post items damaging to the employer. In this case, the Raytheon employees made the offending anonymous postings in violation of their confidentiality agreements and employment contracts. Should a prospective candidate have a similar history of postings harmful to his or her employer, the candidate's judgment and integrity (and therefore eligibility for a clearance) would be called into question. Better to deter an applicant before incurring the expense of hiring than to risk suffering a loss because the applicant misuses information systems.

A New Jersey court dismissed an initial and amended claim of violation of privacy by state employees subject to financial disclosure whose disclosure forms were posted on the Internet. The court twice ruled that there was no "difference of constitutional magnitude" between prior publication in hard-copy form and publication on the public Internet, even with employees' names and addresses posted for anyone to see.[24]

Comment: This ruling may have relevance in that Internet postings by other parties about an applicant may be usable in investigation and adjudication processes, even if the applicant claimed that the data were posted without his or her consent.

Courts are still struggling with attribution and authentication where postings, especially those found on social networking websites, are concerned. In a number of criminal and civil cases, courts have accepted into evidence content allegedly downloaded or printed from profiles, communications, and the like. Because of a lack of detailed evidentiary standards for authenticating content, courts have overlooked the possibilities of hacking, falsification of content, inadequate protections against postings by others, and similar issues that arise because of the technologies involved.[25] In reality, authentication of online information as evidence will need to rely on more rigorous standards than mere circumstantial indicators of authenticity. For example, a posting on a website that apparently belongs to an individual may not actually be made by that individual, but by anyone else with authorized or unauthorized access to the profile. Additional forensic evidence, such as an analysis of the computer used by a computer forensic examiner, or an admission of authorship may be needed to verify authorship and the authenticity of online evidence. In such cases as employee or candidate vetting, prior to an adverse action, an employer would be well advised to seek an admission that the online information is what it seems before a final judgment. Online findings are generally intelligence or lead information first and should only be considered definitive after verification through the best-possible means available, including (in the case of a social network profile) account ownership, security, and authorship of a specific post. Otherwise, an individual's due process rights may be violated.

Libel/Defamation

Federal and state courts have had numerous libel (defamation) suits brought against both named and anonymous posters of allegedly libelous materials online. Key findings have included the federal court's decision in *Doe v. 2TheMart.com* in 2001, which held that the First Amendment protects the anonymity of Internet speech, and that use of a civil subpoena to ascertain the identity of those posting allegedly offensive remarks could have a significant chilling effect on Internet speech and thus the exercise of First Amendment rights. The court set out a list of criteria to be met so that a party could not intimidate critics into silence by using civil subpoenas to learn the identity of anonymous posters.[26] Such decisions also track Section 230 of the Communications Decency Act of 1996,[27] which immunizes "providers and users of interactive computer services" from liability for defamatory material posted by third parties.

Although the decisions on libel and disputes over offensive Internet postings do not relate directly to Internet vetting of persons, they indicate that a court is unlikely to empower a party to use the civil court process to discover someone's identity and confront him or her for online behavior unless there is a serious offense and no other method is available. Note that when a person's identity can be deduced from public postings (e.g., when two e-mail addresses or user identities appear in the same posting, attributed to the same individual), the expectation of privacy is not present because the Internet page is publicly accessible.

Comment: Anonymous names were used to mask the true identities of persons in the libel suits reviewed, enabling speech unfettered by the discretion expected from a speaker using a true name. Attribution for offensive postings may not be discoverable unless the poster makes a mistake and allows an "anonymous" identity to be deduced. Availability of legal process (a warrant) may be called into question by the circumstances (e.g., the alleged damage done and the nature of the relationship between the ISP and the user in question). The courts appear to make a distinction between evidence of offensive speech and that of felonious behavior. Even when a valid warrant enables discovery of the user's registration information, investigators sometimes find that the identifying information is incomplete, false, or insufficient to identify the user. For example, large ISPs frequently change the Internet protocol (IP) address of users, and the IP address alone may not be enough to pinpoint a network user. If it is shown that an applicant has a prior history of anonymous postings of defamatory materials, serious questions of judgment, discretion, maturity, and adherence to enterprise standards could indicate ineligibility for employment.

In *Endicott Interconnect Technologies Inc. v. National Labor Relations Board*, the US Court of Appeals for the District of Columbia overruled the National Labor Relations Board (NLRB), concluding that an employee's dismissal for disparaging comments he made to a newspaper reporter and a message the employee posted to the newspaper's website public forum, criticizing the owner's managerial abilities, were so disloyal that they overcame collective bargaining rights enumerated in the National Labor Relations Act.[28]

Comment: The appeals court's ruling took into consideration that First Amendment and labor law protections apply to public communications by employees but said, "We conclude that White's communications were so disloyal to EIT as to remove them from Section 7's protection and that the Board erred in holding otherwise." In my opinion, while the employee had a right to say publicly what he wished, the employer had a right to take appropriate action to protect its reputation and ability to function.

This is consistent with the Supreme Court's decision in *Garcetti v. Ceballos* (2006) that official communications made by public employees are not protected by the First Amendment and that public employers may discipline employees if official communications are deemed improper.

Invasion of Privacy Torts

Common law (tort law) invasion of privacy appears not to apply well on the Internet, based on established law and practice, according to Harvard's Karl Belgum's comparison of three conflicting views of Internet privacy[29] and to Robert Sprague, writing in the *Hofstra Labor and Employment Law Journal*.[30] Four commonly recognized types of invasion of privacy are misappropriation of the name or likeness for another's commercial benefit, public disclosure of private facts, intrusion into seclusion, and "false light," or untrue public attribution of views or circumstances. These "four common law torts are generally considered to be irrelevant when it comes to online privacy issues," according to the review. The essential reason is that such claims have limited applicability because voluntary public posting of information about oneself is the norm, "and no consensus has emerged that time spent on the Internet constitutes time in 'seclusion.'" Further, "on a more general level, the common law privacy torts fail to protect online privacy because they do not protect actions taken in public, and the Internet is arguably a public environment."

Comment: There is clearly room for invasion-of-privacy torts in which false information is posted to damage another's reputation or a person's name or likeness is misappropriated for commercial use. Otherwise, there may be no legal or logical basis for civil privacy claims if data about someone are posted on the public Internet.

In *Oja v. US Army Corps of Engineers*, a complaint that the corps had wrongfully posted personal information about Oja on a government website was dismissed and upheld by the US Ninth Circuit Court of Appeals because it was filed over 2 years after the first posting. Oja had asserted that every day constituted a renewed posting. The court applied the first publication rule, dating the posting when first placed online, relying on state laws on defamation for analogy, saying the ruling would uphold the provisions of the federal Privacy Act to "economiz[e] judicial resources while preserving the plaintiff's ability to bring the claims."[31]

Comment: The Ninth Circuit's application of the 2-year statute of limitations to Oja's claim may raise some questions while answering others. Some claim that Internet postings can "live forever," as cached copies can come back to haunt someone years after original postings, and continued posting increases the likelihood that the web page image will be preserved somewhere. The damage done by the content of an Internet posting can depend in part on the duration of its exposure and the number of people who view, copy, download, and share that content. Because the court dismissed the claim on technical grounds (i.e., that it was filed too late), the court did not address the underlying claim.

Sanctions for Public Postings

Increasingly, individuals are being sanctioned by employers, the courts, or others based on their public postings—which are correctly viewed as publications laid out in plain view of the public. A few examples follow.

In *Stacy Snyder v. Millersville University*, the US District Court for the Eastern District of Pennsylvania upheld denial of an education degree and dismissed her suit demanding monetary damages. A photograph of Snyder with a pirate hat holding a beverage with the caption "drunken pirate" appeared on her MySpace page, on which she also included material regarding her student teaching assignment and otherwise violated university policies. The court found that Millersville University appropriately found her eligible for an English degree rather than a teaching certification, dismissing her claims of First Amendment and other violations and demand for monetary damages.[32]

In 2009, Vaughan Ettienne, a New York police officer with many online postings, including his own body-building profile, testified against Gary Waters, a parolee whom Ettienne arrested after chasing him through Brooklyn, New York, on a stolen motorcycle for felony possession of a handgun and ammunition. Officer Ettienne had undergone a workplace suspension for testing positive for steroids. At trial, the defense attorney confronted Officer Ettienne with excerpts from his MySpace profile, which contained provocative statements such as "Vaughan is watching *Training Day* to brush up on proper police procedure" (a reference to a 2001 movie portraying a corrupt Los Angeles police detective) and comments about how an officer could rough up a cuffed suspect. The defense alleged that Officer Ettienne had gone into a steroid-induced rage, which could have caused him to assault Waters, and in an effort to justify excessive force, Officer Ettienne planted a 9-millimeter Beretta on Waters. The jury acquitted Waters of the felony possession charge but found him guilty of the misdemeanor of resisting arrest. Officer Ettienne was quoted as saying about the acquittal, "I feel it's partially my fault," and about the online profile, "It paints a picture of a person who could be overly aggressive."[33]

In *Cromer v. Lexington-Fayette Urban County Government*, Case No. 20088-CA-000698, 2009 KY App., a Lexington, Kentucky, police officer's dismissal for unacceptable MySpace postings was upheld on appeal. The officer had arrested a well-known singer for driving while intoxicated (DUI), which caused an increase in visitors to the officer's MySpace page. The dismissal noted that Cromer had identified himself on his profile as a Lexington police officer in word and image and posted materials that brought discredit and disrepute to the police, including profane language; disparagement of homosexuals and the mentally disabled, as well as the people and city of Lexington; inappropriate comments on the use of force; a photo of the officer with the singer after the arrest for DUI; an instance in which he did not arrest a friend for DUI; and other derogatory items.[34]

Internet Privacy for the Twenty-First Century

Robert Sprague, an assistant professor at the University of Wyoming's College of Business, contributed an excellent review of the law and the evolution of privacy protection in America in the *Hofstra Labor and Employment Law Journal*.[35] Among the relevant issues treated were the following:

- "Essentially no protection" of applicants' privacy when prospective US employers use the Internet to investigate them, especially when someone self-publishes on the Internet in a blog or social networking profile.
- However, publicity given to private facts (e.g., intimate details of one's private relationships revealed publicly) could be tortious.
- "Certainly no one can complain when publicity is given to information about him which he himself leaves open to the public eye." "Current privacy law suggests that a job applicant who posts embarrassing or personal information on a blog or within a social networking site which can be accessed by anyone with an Internet connection should have no expectation of privacy, and therefore, no recourse, when that publicly-available information is viewed, and potentially used, in an employment decision." Sprague cited cases that, although not specifically about preemployment Internet vetting, nevertheless upheld the principle that postings that are public cannot be held to have privacy protections (citations are included in Note 30).
- Several states protect as private "lawful conduct" that is off duty and does not involve the employer. Litigation generally supports the employer when the employee conduct has an impact on the employer adversely and supports the employee when the employer uses non-job-related off-duty conduct to sanction.

Sprague addressed the conflict between those using the Internet with the intent to share intimate or potentially objectionable materials only with a small group and the millions who can see such materials on the public Internet (i.e., a desire for relative confidentiality vs. wide access). He said: "Even though information published on the Internet is potentially accessible by millions of people, from a practical standpoint, only a few people may actually view the information. And that is often the intent of the publisher of the information." He suggested that protecting confidentiality, if not privacy, is a goal that might be achieved as follows:

> Because current privacy laws will not protect Internet information, perhaps the lawful conduct statutes provide a good start to protect that information. Many of these statutes are incorporated into states' antidiscrimination prohibitions. The Internet provides employers the opportunity to learn a substantial amount of information they would otherwise be prohibited from asking (such as religion, disability, marital status) in a typical employment interview. Even if an employee were to volunteer such information during an interview, the employer is still prohibited from using it in the hiring decision. But, there is no way to know if an employer has used the same information gleaned from an Internet search in deciding whether even to interview an applicant.
>
> One way to protect job applicants from the content of their Internet information would be to amend lawful conduct statutes to prohibit employers from using publicly available personal information that could be obtained through an Internet search in their hiring decisions. As an alternative, or in addition, personal information obtained by employers through an Internet search could be treated as credit reports. Under this model, employers could be prohibited from acquiring

personal information that could be obtained through an Internet search without first informing the applicant in writing and would be required to inform the applicant if this information was used as part of an adverse decision, as well as provide the applicant with a copy of the information found and used. This last requirement would at least inform the applicant there was possibly damaging information on the Internet so steps could be taken to remove, alter, or correct the information.

Comment: Although it is disputable whether publicly posted information deserves some level of privacy based on the intent of the poster, it is a cogent suggestion to address fair treatment of Internet-collected information along with all other information used in hiring and employment decisions. The Fair Credit Reporting Act (FCRA) and nondiscrimination rights exist, even if an employer elects to risk circumventing them. Putting the investigative results of cybervetting into the same category as checking private data repositories seems the right thing to do and probably would not require changes to current law. Explicitly notifying applicants and employees when checks of the Internet will be done, and when adverse decisions are based on Internet search findings, fits neatly within extant, objective, fair FCRA criteria. Creating a right in law that public information must be ignored—even job-related derogatory information—does not seem well founded or likely to gain general support.

In a recent federal criminal prosecution, the legal theory was advanced that the accused adult violated the Computer Fraud and Abuse Act—unauthorized use of a computer system—because she violated the MySpace user agreement by assuming a fictitious teenage identity to harass a teenager, who subsequently committed suicide.[36] The accused woman was convicted for misdemeanors under what was called the first US cyber bullying case.[37] Although the legal theory remains controversial, and this area of Internet law could be described as somewhat fluid, the general practice of users on MySpace and similar social networking sites is to use a "false" pseudonym, and the sites encourage the practice.

Comment: It is common for user agreements to forbid access to a website for an illegal or unauthorized purpose (e.g., misappropriation of other users' identifying data, other site content, or spamming).[38] However, it is doubtful that a claim based on a user agreement between the investigator and the website would prevent an employer from using data posted on a website in an adverse finding about the subject for bad conduct. Where a claim could arise is if an investigator elicited information from or about a subject by fraud (e.g., pretended to be the subject or a friend to see privacy-protected social network postings). However, mere misrepresentation would not be equally actionable (e.g., if the investigator gained access to the subject's privacy-protected postings by misrepresentation as a "new friend" voluntarily admitted by the subject). If a subject could claim a violation of the subject's privacy by the investigator, it could render the adverse use of the information found by the investigator improper. It appears that the investigator can use information that the subject posts openly. However, the investigator must collect posted information by legal means (which could include deception that is not illegal or unethical). A subject might use the argument that a user agreement prevents any investigative use of a social site posting, but because the posting is visible to hundreds of millions of people, the basis for such a claim would be questionable.

Admissibility of Electronically Generated and Stored Evidence

Todd Shipley, an expert in Internet and computer forensic investigations, has written seminal articles[39] on collection of electronic evidence, also known as electronically stored information (ESI), and (in part) noted:

> The procedures outlined in *Lorraine v. Markel American Insurance Co.* [see following discussion]. In that case, the magistrate denied the admission of ESI, but outlined how the evidence should have been properly admitted. Of particular note is his discussion of ESI authentication including the use of hashing (digital fingerprints), ESI metadata, and the collection of data in its "native format." The decision, more than any other existing case, outlines clear guidance for the admission of electronic evidence in a federal civil case. Thus, it can be considered a partial road map for development of a standard methodology for Internet forensics and its successful admission in court.

In the *Lorraine v. Markel* case cited, a thorough discussion of how to authenticate ESI included such common Internet artifacts as e-mail and website images or documents introduced into federal civil courts as evidence. The magistrate outlined ways in which ESI may be accepted into evidence in a 101-page legal memorandum.[40] A summary of the memo's guidance follows:

ESI comes in multiple evidentiary "flavors," including e-mail, website ESI, Internet postings, digital photographs, and computer-generated documents and data files. The following evidence rules must be considered: Is the ESI

1. Relevant as determined by Rule 401 (does it have any tendency to make some fact that is of consequence to the litigation more or less probable than it otherwise would be?);
2. Authentic as required by Rule 901(a) (can the proponent show that the ESI is what it purports to be?)—authentication and identification ensures that evidence is trustworthy;
3. Offered for its substantive truth, thus hearsay as defined by Rule 801, and if so, is it covered by an applicable hearsay rule exception (Rules 803, 804, and 807);
4. An original or duplicate under the original writing rule, or if not, is there admissible secondary evidence to prove the content of the ESI (Rules 1001–1008); and
5. Of probative value and substantially outweighs the danger of unfair prejudice or one of the other factors identified by Rule 403, such that it should be excluded despite its relevance.

The memorandum contains a list of cases in which admissibility of electronic evidence was an issue and the court decisions considered precedents or instructive on the issues involved.

Trends and Legal Challenges to Investigative Searching

In a *Federal Register* notice, the US Department of Homeland Security (DHS) stated that it will routinely monitor the public postings of users on Twitter and Facebook. The agency plans to create fictitious user accounts and scan posts of users for key terms. User data will be stored for 5 years and shared with other government agencies. The Electronic Privacy Information Center (EPIC) filed a Freedom of Information Act lawsuit against DHS on April 12, 2011, and obtained hundreds of pages of documents from DHS about its monitoring of social networks and media organizations. EPIC subsequently campaigned in Congress and the press, claiming that DHS lacks legal authority and primarily wants to detect public criticism of the department. The FBI issued a request for proposals for similar Internet collection.

Comment: Today's criminal and civil courts, investigative dossiers, and files are replete with evidence derived from computer use by persons that relate to the cases, including data from the systems themselves, from postings on websites, and from ISPs and telecommunications firms providing services. It was inevitable that government and private agencies would seek to detect and prevent illegal, illicit, and otherwise-damaging activities by monitoring the web. Although advocates of strengthening terrorism and crime prevention on one side and those campaigning for greater privacy and protection from government intrusion on the other are bound to continue the debate over the balance necessary in a democracy, the legal boundaries of such investigations are as yet indistinct. Meanwhile, massive ("big data") collection is programmed into the Internet, from browsers to websites to social networking applications, for marketing and customer feedback for business. Controversy over users' ability to control commercial collection of their online activities still flares. These debates are likely to find their way into courts and legislatures for years to come.

Although this chapter addressed the legal issues directly and tangentially related to cybervetting and Internet investigations, its main intent was to help establish a framework for principles that can be applied to the policies and practices needed to incorporate life online into the intelligence and security schema of life as we have come to know it.

Notes

1. *Mullins v. Department of Commerce*, U.S. Court of Appeals for the Federal Circuit, 06-3284, appealed from U.S. Merit Systems Protection Board, http://www. ll.georgetown.edu/federal/judicial/fed/opinions/06opinions/06-3284.pdf (accessed August 10, 2010).

2. Sinrod, Eric, Office of Duane Morris LLP, San Francisco, http://technology.findlaw.com/articles/00006/010851.html (accessed August 10, 2010); Sinrod, Eric J., From Googling to Firing? CNETNews.com, May 30, 2007, http:// www.duanemorris.com/articles/article2527.html (accessed August 10, 2010).

3. *Pietrylo et al. v. Hillstone Restaurant Group*, Docket No. 2:06-cv-05754 (D.N.J. 2008), US District Court for New Jersey, Civil Case No. 06-5754 (FSH), July 24, 2008, http://www.dmlp.org/threats/hillstone-restaurant-group-v-pietrylo (accessed January 20, 2014).

4. Searcey, Dionne, Employers Watching Employees Online Stirs Policy Debate, *Wall Street Journal*, April 23, 2009, http://online.wsj.com/article/SB124045009224646091.html (accessed June 1, 2010); Former Bartender and Waitress Sue One-Time Employer over Their MySpace Post, http://3lepiphany.typepad.com/ (accessed August 10, 2010), http://www.lawyersandsettlements.com/settlements/13572/internet-privacy-laws-myspace-forums-forum.html#.Ut7fB_8o7IU (accessed January 21, 2014).

5. Pettry, Michael T, supervisory special agent, FBI, presentation to International Association of Chiefs of Police, Legal Officers' Section, September 29, 2012; http://www.examiner.com/article/cop-demoted-for-posting-a-photo-of-an-obama-t-shirt-riddled-with-bullet-holes (accessed January 19, 2014).

6. Ibid, case cited in presentation in Note 5.

7. *NAACP v. Alabama ex rel. Patterson*, 357 U.S. 449 (1958), http://caselaw.lp.findlaw.com/scripts/getcase.pl?court=US&vol=357&invol=449 (accessed August 10, 2010).

8. *Griffin v. State of Maryland*, Case No. 1132, Lash, Steve, *Baltimore Daily Record*, May 31, 2010, http://findarticles.com/p/articles/mi_qn4183/is_20100531/ai_n53902808/, http://mdcourts.gov/opinions/cosa/2010/1132s08.pdf (accessed September 2, 2010).

9. http://conservancy.umn.edu/bitstream/147600/1/Authentication-of-Social-Networking-Evidence-by-Ira-Robbins-MN-Journal-of-Law-Science-Tech-Issue-13-1.pdf, p. 27 (accessed January 22, 2014).

10. *Katz v. United States*, 389 U.S. 347 (1967), http://caselaw.lp.findlaw.com/scripts/getcase.pl?court=US&vol=389&invol=347 (accessed August 10, 2010).

11. Omnibus Crime Control and Safe Streets Act of 1968, http://www.justice.gov/crt/split/42usc3789d.php (accessed August 10, 2010).

12. *Whalen v. Roe*, 429 U.S. 589 (1977), http://caselaw.lp.findlaw.com/scripts/getcase.pl?navby=search&court=US&case=/us/429/589.html (accessed August 10, 2010).

13. *Smith v. Maryland*, 442 U.S. 735 (1979), http://caselaw.lp.findlaw.com/scripts/getcase.pl?navby=search&court=US&case=/us/442/735.html (accessed August 10, 2010).

14. Madden, Mary, et al., Teens, Social Media, and Privacy, Pew Internet and American Life, May 2013, http://www.pewinternet.org/Reports/2013/Teens-Social-Media-And-Privacy/Main-Report/Part-2.aspx (accessed January 21, 2014).

15. *United States v. Maxwell*, 45 M.J. 406 (1996), http://webcache.googleusercontent.com/search?q=cache:http://www.armfor.uscourts.gov/opinions/1996Term/95_0751.htm (accessed cached copy August 10, 2010).

16. *United States v. Charbonneau*, 979 F. Supp. 1177 (S.D. Ohio 1997), http://www.swlearning.com/blaw/cases/child_porn.html (accessed August 10, 2010).

17. *Davis v. Gracey*, http://scholar.google.com/scholar_case?case=16037774558711975401&q=Davis+v.+Gracey,+111+F.3d+1472&hl=en&as_sdt=10002&as_vis=1 (accessed August 10, 2010).

18. *United States v. Ziegler*, 474 F.3d 1184 (9th Cir., 2007); see the following paper for reviews of similar actions: http://www.howardrice.com/uploads/content/Civil%20 Actions%20For%20Privacy%20Violations%202007%20-%20Where%20 Are%20We.pdf (accessed August 10, 2010).

19. *Konop v. Hawaiian Airlines*, No. 99-55106, D.C. No. CV-96-04898-SJL (JGx), 2002, http://www.internetlibrary.com/pdf/Konop-Hawaiian-Airlines-9th-Cir-Jan-8-01.pdf (accessed September 4, 2010).

20. Frommer, Dan, Montana Town Demands Job Applicants' Facebook Passwords, *Business Insider SAI*, June 19, 2009, http://www.businessinsider.com/montana-town-demands-job-applicants-facebook-pass-words-2009-6 (accessed September 4, 2010); Weinstein, Natalie, Bozeman to Job Seekers: We Won't Seek Passwords, CNET, June 20, 2010, http://news.cnet.com/8301-13578_3-10269770-38.html (accessed September 4, 2010); the posted city of Bozeman, Montana, application for employment asked for "any and all, current personal or business websites, web pages or memberships on any Internet-based chat rooms, social clubs or forums, to include, but not limited to: Facebook, Google, Yahoo, YouTube.com, MySpace, etc." but not for passwords. http://privacy.org/Background_Check_Form_Interview_MASTER.pdf (accessed September 4, 2010).

21. http://www.iacpsocialmedia.org/Portals/1/documents/CybervettingReport.pdf (accessed January 20, 2014). The author co-authored this study.

22. *McVeigh v. Cohen*, 983 F.Supp. 215 (D.D.C. 1998), http://www.netlitigation.com/ netlitigation/cases/mcveigh.htm (accessed August 10, 2010).

23. *Raytheon Company v. John Does 1–21*, Commonwealth of Massachusetts, Middlesex Superior Court, Civil Action 99-816, http://www.netlitigation.com/netlitigation/ cases/raytheon.html (accessed August 10, 2010).

24. *Price v. Corzine*, 2006 WL 2252208 (D.N.J. 2006) and 2007 WL 708879 (D.N.J.).

25. Robbins, Ira P., Writings on the Wall: The Need for an Authorship-Centric Approach to the Authentication of Social-Networking Evidence, *Minnesota Journal of Law, Science & Technology*, Winter 2013, http://conservancy.umn.edu/bitstream/147600/1/ Authentication-of-Social-Networking-Evidence-by-Ira-Robbins-MN-Journal-of-Law-Science-Tech-Issue-13-1.pdf (accessed January 22, 2014).

26. *John Doe v. 2TheMart.com*, USDC C01-453Z, April 26, 2001, http://cyber.law. harvard.edu/stjohns/2themart.html (accessed January 21, 2014).

27. Section 230 of 47 US Code, http://codes.lp.findlaw.com/uscode/47/5/II/I/230 (accessed August 10, 2010); Communications Decency Act of 1996, http://www.fcc. gov/Reports/tcom1996.txt (accessed August 10, 2010).

28. *Endicott Interconnect Technologies v. NLRB*, US District Court of Appeals, No. 05-1371 and 1381, decided July 14, 2006, http://openjurist.org/453/f3d/532/ endicott-interconnect-technologies-inc-v-national-labor-relations-board (accessed September 4, 2010).

29. Belgum, Karl G., Who Leads at Half-time? Three Conflicting Visions of Internet Privacy Policy, 6 Rich. J.L. & Tech. 1 (Symposium 1999), http://www.richmond. edu/jolt/v6i1/belgum.html, found at http://cyber.law.harvard.edu/privacy/ WhoLeadsatHalftime(Belgum).htm (accessed August 10, 2010).

30. Sprague, Robert, Rethinking Information Privacy in an Age of Online Transparency, *Hofstra Labor and Employment Law Journal*, 25: 395, 2009, law.hofstra.edu/pdf/ Academics/Journals/LaborAndEmploymentLawJournal/labor_vol25no2_Sprague.

pdf (accessed March 29, 2010). Excerpts: "Certainly no one can complain when publicity is given to information about him which he himself leaves open to the public eye." "Current privacy law suggests that a job applicant who posts embarrassing or personal information on a blog or within a social networking site which can be accessed by anyone with an Internet connection should have no expectation of privacy, and therefore, no recourse, when that publicly-available information is viewed, and potentially used, in an employment decision." Footnotes: See, for example, *Dexter v. Dexter*, No. 2006-P-0051, 2007 WL 1532084, at *6 & n.4 (Ohio Ct. App. May 25, 2007) (upholding custody for father where mother had posted on her MySpace page, among other online statements considered by the court, that "she was on a hiatus from using illicit drugs [during the trial] but that she planned on using drugs in the future. ... [T]hese writings were open to the public view. Thus, she can hardly claim an expectation of privacy regarding these writings."); Sanchez Abril, Patricia, A (My) Space of One's Own: On Privacy and Online Social Networks, *Northwestern Journal of Technology & Intellectual Property*, 73: 78 (2007) ("Categorically, everyone would agree that those who carelessly post shameful pictures of themselves or incriminating information on profiles that are accessible to everyone on the Internet cannot reasonably claim privacy in their posting."); Crawford, Krysten, Have a Blog, Lose Your Job? CNN Money.com, February 15, 2005, http://money.cnn.com/2005/02/14/news/economy/blogging (citing four cases of employees being fired for what they had posted online, observing that most noncontract employees are at will, meaning they can be fired at any point for any or no reason at all without any recourse and are therefore extremely vulnerable to such employment actions); Simonetti, Ellen, I Was Fired for Blogging, CNET News.com, December 16, 2004, http://www.news.com/2102-1030_3-5490836.html?tag=st.util.print ("The official reason for my suspension [and eventual termination]: 'inappropriate' pictures. The unofficial reason (implied through an intimidating interrogation): blogging.").

31. *Oja v. United States Army Corps of Engineers*, 440 F.3d 1122 (9th Cir. 2006), Privacy Act of 1974 two-year statute of limitations, http://caselaw.findlaw.com/us-9th-circuit/1237864.html (accessed January 21, 2014).

32. *Stacy Snyder v. Millersville University et al.*, U.S. District Court for the Eastern District of Pennsylvania, Case No. 07-1660, decided December 3, 2008.

33. Dwyer, Jim, The Officer Who Posted Too Much on MySpace, *New York Times*, March 11, 2009, http://www.nytimes.com/2009/03/11/nyregion/11about.html?_r=1&pagewanted=print (accessed September 4, 2010).

34. *Cromer v. Lexington-Fayette Urban Co. Gov't.*, #20088-CA-000698, 2009 Ky. App. Unpub. Lexis 71, http://www.aele.org/law/Digests/empl71.html (accessed September 4, 2010).

35. See Note 30.

36. Jesdanun, Anick, Using a Fake Name on the Internet Could Be Illegal, AP, May 2008, http://www.newsfactor.com/story.xhtml?story_id=11100A799HN3&page=1 (accessed November 2009).

37. Steinhauer, Jennifer, Verdict in MySpace Suicide Case, *New York Times*, November 26, 2008, http://www.nytimes.com/2008/11/27/us/27myspace.html (accessed April 20, 2010).

38. Based on review of MySpace, Classmates, Facebook, YouTube, Yahoo, Monster.com, Match.com, and Google privacy policy and user agreements.

39. Shipley, Todd G., Collection of Evidence from the Internet: Parts 1 and 2, *DFI News*, http://www.dfinews.com/articles/2009/12/collection-evidence-internet-part-1 (accessed November 27, 2013).

40. Memorandum Opinion, in the United States District Court for the District of Maryland, Jack R. Lorraine and Beverly Mack, Plaintiffs, v. Markel American Insurance Company, Defendants, Civil Action No. PWG-06-1893, http://www.mdd.uscourts.gov/opinions/opinions/lorraine%20v.%20markel%20-20esiadmissibility%20opinion.pdf (accessed April 27, 2014).

Chapter 9

International and Domestic Principles

US and International Privacy Principles

A large number of discussions, held in academic, government, and private venues over the past two decades, have resulted in generally recognized privacy principles originally incorporated in US statutes in the 1970s. For purposes of this text, the core principles first published in 1981 by the US Department of Commerce,[1] as amended with input from several sources, including the state of California and the Center for Democracy and Technology, deserve mention.[2] Based on considerable legal analysis and debate by privacy advocates, these principles are withstanding the test of time and litigation. It should be noted that US laws generally lack the privacy rights set out in Canadian, European, and Asian laws. Therefore, the principles represent useful guidelines for the proper collection and use of personally identifying information, including Internet information, about individuals. The principles are as follows:

1. Notice to individuals when personally identifiable information is collected (awareness)
2. Limits on use and disclosure of data for purposes other than those for which the data were collected (choice)
3. Limitations on the retention of data
4. Requirements to ensure the accuracy, completeness, and timeliness of information
5. The right of individuals to access information about themselves

6. The opportunity to correct information or challenge decisions made, based on incorrect data (recourse)
7. Appropriate security measures to protect the information against abuse or unauthorized disclosure (data security)
8. Redress mechanisms for individuals wrongly and adversely affected by the use of personally identifiable information (enforcement, verification, and consequences)

A Consumer Privacy Bill of Rights drafted and announced in 2013 by the White House[3] was a nonstarter in Congress, but it illustrated that there is some support for incorporating the principles outlined into US statutes. The US Government (USG) has established presidentially approved Adjudicative Guidelines for Determining Eligibility for Access to Classified Information (latest edition 2006, 32 CFR Part 147),[4] which have existed in substantially the same form since President William Clinton signed them into effect in an executive order (EO) in August 1995. Currently, federal practices include notice, consent, verification, appeal, correction, and confidentiality, which directly conform to the privacy principles cited. In over 45 years of involvement at various levels, from conducting background investigations to overseeing security and counterintelligence in the federal agencies at the National Security Council, I have observed a passionate dedication—in professionals involved in security, investigative, intelligence, clearance, and adjudicative work—to the rule of law, fair play, and the privacy principles listed. Because the adjudicative guidelines contain both behaviors of concern and mitigating factors to be considered in a determination of eligibility for access to classified information, they represent well-established benchmarks for any employer with a need to protect valuable intellectual property in the workplace or ensure the trustworthiness of those hired or cleared.

A brief summary of the federal guidelines for determining eligibility for access to classified information (see Chapter 4) lists types of behavior that might be found by any investigative measure, including Internet searching. They are substantive concerns that could, if verified, lead to denial of a clearance or a position of trust. The guidelines include foreign allegiance, influence, preference, or extremism; illicit or unbalanced sexual behavior; dishonest or insubordinate personal conduct; financial issues (i.e., irresponsibility or unexplained wealth); alcohol or drug abuse; untreated mental or emotional disorders; criminal conduct; mishandling of confidential information; and misuse of information systems. Any conduct demonstrating a recent or recurring pattern of questionable judgment, irresponsibility, or emotionally unstable behavior can itself be disqualifying.

The federal guidelines focus on the reliability factor: An individual exhibiting prior misbehavior described in the guidelines may be a poor choice for a government position that requires loyalty, discretion, and good judgment. The guidelines' preamble includes the following: "The adjudicative process is the careful weighing of a number of variables known as the whole person concept. Available, reliable information about the person, past and present, favorable and unfavorable, should be considered in reaching a determination." The guidelines provide a series of factors to be considered in assessing whether the acts in question should or should not disqualify an individual in a specific case from eligibility for a clearance, including these factors related to the behaviors:

- Seriousness
- Timing, including start, completion, and recency (elapsed time)
- Number of repetitions (frequency)
- Likelihood of recurrence
- Voluntary reporting of the information about the behavior
- Promptness in efforts toward correction
- Truthfulness and completeness in responding to questions
- Willingness to seek assistance and follow professional guidance, if appropriate
- Resolution or likely favorable resolution of the security concern
- Demonstration of positive changes in behavior and employment
- Demonstration of proper motivation by complying promptly
- Unusual circumstances
- Conflict of interest
- Occurrence prior to or during adolescence with no evidence of subsequent conduct of a similar nature
- Potential to serve as a basis for coercion, exploitation, or duress (blackmail)
- Resolution plan with a signed statement of consent
- Successful completion of treatment

Often, assessments addressing the possibility of mitigating factors can help adjudicators understand past mistakes that are unlikely to recur, such as common juvenile misbehavior. In an era when a candidate is as likely to act out online as in the physical world (perhaps more likely), it is important to consider such behavior in assessing the candidate, both for questionable conduct and for mitigation. Further, many enterprises should consider the orientation and training needed if a hiring or clearance decision is made, in the context of established authorized use policies, data sensitivity and value, vulnerability of information systems, and culture of the enterprise.

Today's computer systems misuse issues include a variety of misbehaviors previously seen in a much smaller, physical context, such as cyber bullying; stalking; offensive messaging (e.g., racist, sexually suggestive, vulgar, obscene, or discriminatory texts or images); and other forms of behavior that violate employee behavioral guidelines. Socially irresponsible behavior online can disrupt the workplace and subject the enterprise to accusations of harboring a hostile workplace environment. Although it is important to include these types of misbehavior in employee handbooks to discourage online and offline misbehavior, an employer has an affirmative obligation to prescreen, monitor, and enforce information technology (IT) system norms. When users' actual online habits are unknown to managers because no attempt was made to discover the subgroup guilty of blatant violations of standards, the enterprise is vulnerable to charges of ignoring prehire indicators of unsuitability, or posthire, obvious misuse.

Although not a part of the government clearance criteria, a principle that appears to be emerging in employment standards nationwide is the question of relevance to the duties of the position that past misbehavior may represent. In the case of Internet searching, any kind of prior misdeed could be found, from prior arrests to drug or alcohol abuse to unethical behavior.[5] If an Internet search revealed that the subject had engaged in cybercrime or computer-related illicit acts (e.g., piracy, counterfeiting, malware, spam, harassment), then a candidate whose job would include authorized access to a workstation on the employer's network could be considered ineligible based on computer-related misbehavior. One of the prime reasons to consider Internet vetting as part of background investigations is that it is one of the few ways to ascertain whether the candidate can be trusted to use the employer's information systems properly, and if special training and monitoring are needed, prior to entrusting access to the new hire.

One observation about why more agencies and businesses have not implemented enhanced attempts to address information systems behavior issues in the application, interview, background investigation, orientation, and training processes is that the complexities of employment law, recruitment, and related issues act as deterrents. One aim of this book is to enable any enterprise to address the serious issue of prior computer systems misbehavior legally and ethically. The USG has recently started asking candidates for clearances whether or not they have engaged in forbidden uses of computer systems.[6] Based on legislation, privacy policy, and established personnel practices, it is possible to add appropriate legal measures that are explained further in this book. A review of the relevant statutes and litigation revealed an exception to the privacy safeguards that could potentially limit employers' use of data found on their own systems or elsewhere on the Internet. That exception is proper notice to the employees, contractors, and other users of the employers' information systems, and consent from the same group, to access what legally belongs to the employers: systems, networks, and data owned by the employer. Because of the rapid development of technology and its ever-changing uses, the laws and customs that apply could be described as in a state of flux. However, prior agreement by employees and applicants, as well as others contracting with an enterprise, enables mutual understanding about how the owner intends to protect information and the systems on which it is kept and transmitted.

The proliferation of mobile devices used for both work and personal activities has complicated employees' views about what is private versus open to an employer. For example, an employee may keep online bank, brokerage, and e-mail accounts on a computer, and even on a cell phone, issued by the employer for work. Most employers tolerate a limited amount of time online to conduct personal business during the workday, but the sensitive personal information of the employee is now hosted on the employer's computers and handheld devices. Because many employers issue mobile phones and tablets with which they can contact the employee using instant messaging, e-mail, or paging, obvious issues of employees' sensitive personal data storage arise. When employees use their own cell phones and handhelds to receive personal e-mail and conduct other nonwork communications in the workplace, the data of the employer and employee may again be mixed. The "bring your own device" (BYOD) security issue is currently a hot topic for IT administrators and security staff. Having clear understandings between the employer and employees about the limits of privacy and security for any information, communications, or Internet uses involving the enterprise's computers, network, information, or data storage platforms can help set all parties' expectations and may head off conflicts.

The principle of notice and consent is also often applied to contractual agreements not to compete against an employer (during employment and often for a fixed period of time after leaving) and not to breach the confidentiality of proprietary information without the employer's prior consent. If an employee has copies of an employer's data, such as customer lists, on a portable computing device, the security of that data can be compromised both during and after employment. Anecdotal evidence, including lawsuits by enterprises to prevent ex-employees' use of data collected on the job, suggests that this problem is increasing. If a candidate is in the habit of collecting, storing, using, and sharing files that belong to others (e.g., videos, music, and software obtained without a paid license), then the prospective employer would see in advance that the individual should be made aware of, and agree to, the employer's standards for protection and use of proprietary data before being given unfettered access on the job. Further, just as employees have a right to expect the employer to protect personally identifying information (e.g., bank account data) residing on the employer's systems, so the employer has a right to expect the employees to abide by data use restrictions in the workplace.

An effective way to inform enterprise users and document terms of access to information systems is the notice or reminder posted on computer log-on screens, including the US Department of Defense's banners, such as:

> You are accessing a US Government (USG) information system (IS) that is provided for USG-authorized use only. By using this IS, you consent to the following conditions:
>
> ▪ The USG routinely monitors communications occurring on this IS, and any device attached to this IS, for purposes including, but not limited to, penetration testing, COMSEC [communications security] monitoring, network defense, quality control, and employee misconduct, law enforcement, and counterintelligence investigations.
> ▪ At any time, the USG may inspect and/or seize data stored on this IS and any device attached to this IS.

- Communications occurring on or data stored on this IS, or any device attached to this IS, are not private. They are subject to routine monitoring and search.
- Any communications occurring on or data stored on this IS, or any device attached to this IS, may be disclosed or used for any USG-authorized purpose.
- Security protections may be utilized on this IS to protect certain interests that are important to the USG. For example, passwords, access cards, encryption or biometric access controls provide security for the benefit of the USG. These protections are not provided for your benefit or privacy and may be modified or eliminated at the USG's discretion.[7]

This log-on message clearly is USG centric, but any employer can craft an appropriate warning to users about the rules of systems to which they are granted access. Once users are notified by all appropriate means (e.g., employee handbook, orientation, training, and on-screen notices like the one presented), there is a reasonable expectation that most will follow the rules, and those who do not comply are clearly in the wrong—again, witness Edward Snowden and Robert Hanssen.

Litigation concerning digital forensic evidence taken from computer systems by employers and law enforcement has produced a steady stream of case law that upholds the employer's ownership of the systems, networks, and data and the rights of monitoring of and collection from those systems for any lawful purpose. Courts have almost universally upheld actions based on evidence found on enterprises' computer systems provided for employees' use. Claims centered on the employees' privacy rights, on reasonable expectation of privacy in the workplace, and on personal use of employers' systems have favored the employer and the government over the employee. Rulings to date reportedly have all been in favor of employers who have established policies regulating how employees are to use work systems and who have notified employees that their use of employers' systems constitutes consent to monitoring for security and compliance purposes. In some cases, this has included employees' Internet use. A possible exception might be an employee's use of a personal (nonwork) e-mail system for private communications with an attorney.[8]

Government Standards

The USG has long-established standards for personnel security, based on presidential EOs, cabinet directives, and departmental/agency policies. The nucleus of US standards on classified information includes such documents as EOs on access to classified information, adjudicative guidelines for determining eligibility for access to classified information, personnel and information systems' security policies and procedures, and related directives. In addition, classified information is protected by the espionage statutes. Since September 11, 2001, the Homeland Security Presidential Directive and Patriot Act, among others, has focused on protecting US critical infrastructures. In the private sector, the Economic Espionage Statute of 1996, as amended, prescribes stiff penalties (e.g., 15–30 years of imprisonment) for theft of intellectual property. Trade secrets statutes in many states mirror federal prohibitions against misappropriation of employers' data.

Although further review of USG clearance standards for highly trusted persons is not necessary here, it is worthwhile to note that when protecting valuable and sensitive information, the most rigorous security measures, including in-depth vetting of candidates, are required. Similarly high standards apply for law enforcement and private security personnel. Today's enterprises, in both government and business, including critical infrastructures, often place invaluable information at the disposal of all authorized users of enterprise information systems. Since the early 1990s, security breaches in government and industry have increasingly involved computers, both at work and at home. In truth, the full extent of the security problems that have arisen because of the greater amounts of time spent online at work and at home is as yet unknown. However, anecdotal evidence suggests that, in recent years, agencies and companies have been grappling with computer-related security issues that are more numerous and involve online behaviors previously not seen. As yet, government clearance procedures do not explicitly include Internet vetting or require preemployment disclosure of details of the candidate's life online.[9] Many federal agencies, and some state and local law enforcement agencies, are finding evidence of Internet misbehavior in screening interviews and polygraph examinations and sometimes when background investigators Google candidates. It stands to reason that the established standards for clearances will require enhancements when Internet behavior is added as a focus in government background investigations, as a recent government study based on a notorious act of violence in a government workplace recommended.[10]

Executive Orders 12958, 12968, and 13231 contain the standards by which classified information and critical infrastructures will be protected and by which individuals will be granted access to classified information. These orders do not directly address Internet vetting. EO 13231, Critical Infrastructure Protection in the Information Age (October 16, 2001), includes the following, in part:

(a) The information technology revolution has changed the way business is transacted, government operates, and national defense is conducted. Those three functions now depend on an interdependent network of critical information infrastructures. The protection program authorized by this order shall consist of continuous efforts to secure information systems for critical infrastructure, including emergency preparedness communications, and the physical assets that support such systems. Protection of these systems is essential to the telecommunications, energy, financial services, manufacturing, water, transportation, health care, and emergency services sectors. ...

(d) Recruitment, Retention, and Training Executive Branch Security Professionals. In consultation with executive branch departments and agencies, coordinate programs to ensure that government employees with responsibilities for protecting information systems for critical infrastructure, including emergency preparedness communications, and the physical assets that support such systems, are adequately trained and evaluated. In this function, the Office of Personnel Management shall work in coordination with the Board, as appropriate.

To date, most federal agencies have not included Internet vetting in standards established to evaluate the background of those who will be given access to classified, law-enforcement-sensitive, or critical infrastructure information systems.[11] Efforts to strengthen the critical infrastructures of the United States only rarely have placed special emphasis on personnel security and on the evolution needed in information systems security based on changing vulnerabilities, social behavior, and societal norms. Although observers are concerned about ethics online and the implications of increasing misuse of information systems, as yet there is no consensus that personnel security measures must move more quickly to adapt to evolving computer security vulnerabilities. Increased protection measures for the most essential of our critical infrastructures, the staff, have not been included in enhancements to security, even though they were deemed critical by the Joint Security Commission in its report redefining security to the secretary of defense and director of central intelligence on February 28, 1994, which called for "new strategies for achieving security within our information systems."[12] Unfortunately, most of the new strategies have focused on automated self-protection of computer systems and not on the human element, including digital footprints of human actions online.

The news media reported in the 2008 postelection, preinauguration period that then-President-elect Barack Obama asked potential candidates for high-level appointments to disclose their Internet identities (e-mail addresses, profiles, and nicknames) for their background vetting.[13] This requirement demonstrates the recognition that those selected for responsible positions should not have a history of Internet activities or posted data that indicate they were involved in illegal, illicit, or socially unacceptable behaviors. Public Internet postings were considered too obvious to overlook for cabinet- and subcabinet-level posts. Since the election, equal recognition of the same principle for other federal employees (even highly responsible officials, such as intelligence community and law enforcement members) has not emerged.

A search for explicit authority for the government to use open-source intelligence (including Internet vetting) when investigating candidates for access to classified information turned up little of value. Executive Order 12333, United States Intelligence Activities (December 4, 1981, as amended August 27, 2004), does authorize collection of "information that is publicly available or collected with the consent of the person concerned." This is an exemption from prohibitions against the US intelligence community targeting of US persons (citizens and permanent resident aliens). The Federal Bureau of Investigation (FBI), other law enforcement agencies, and other state and federal agencies would also be authorized to collect information concerning any person suspected of a crime or who applies for employment or access to classified information. The reason why this standard has relevance is that modern norms of intelligence collection and background investigation include legally permissible Internet searching. Even the American Bar Association recommends Internet searching, noting that it can reduce the cost and improve the speed and results of legal research.[14]

Parallel Guidance: Internet Research Ethics

When considering guidance for new types of activities, it is important to consider how ethics are applied in different but parallel endeavors. During the past 20 years, the behaviors of individuals and groups online have become subjects of study by sociologists, linguists, anthropologists, psychologists, and a host of other researchers. Fascination with virtual worlds, new types of communication, and networks of people distributed across the globe, but connected by the power of the Internet, has attracted the attention of both serious and casual students of human behavior. Communities online have developed modes of existence and interaction all their own and created values that have moved researchers to recognize a variety of ethical approaches to their work. Based on published materials, these ethical approaches shed light on the issues, strong beliefs, and alternative approaches that should be considered by intelligence practitioners on the Internet. These ethical norms are covered in Chapter 10.

Notes

1. US Department of Commerce, Elements of Effective Self-Regulation for Protection of Privacy, National Telecommunications and Information Administration Discussion Draft, US Department of Commerce, 1998, http://www.ntia.doc.gov/reports/privacydraft/198dftprin.htm (accessed August 10, 2010).
2. Dempsey, James X., executive director, Center for Democracy and Technology, testimony to U.S. Senate Committee on the Judiciary, April 13, 2005, and California state privacy principles, http://www.cdt.org/privacy/guide/basic/generic.html and http://www.privacyrights.org/ar/princip. htm (accessed March 13, 2010).

3. The White House, Washington, DC, Fact Sheet: Plan to Protect Privacy in the Internet Age by Adopting a Consumer Privacy Bill of Rights, http://www.whitehouse.gov/the-press-office/2012/02/23/fact-sheet-plan-protect-privacy-internet-age-adopting-consumer-privacy-b (accessed January 28, 2014).
4. Adjudicative Guidelines for Eligibility for Access to Classified Information Summary, http://www.state.gov/m/ds/clearances/60321.htm (accessed August 10, 2010).
5. Based on tens of thousands of Internet searches conducted by my firm.
6. *Questionnaire for National Security Positions*, Standard Form-86, Section 27 questions, Use of Information Technology Systems, http://www.opm.gov/forms/pdf_fill/sf86.pdf (accessed August 10, 2010).
7. Copied in April 2008 from a Defense Personnel Security Research Center computer system banner log-on screen.
8. Westmoreland, Jill, Minimizing Employer Liability for Employee Internet Use, *Los Angeles Business Journal*, July 31, 2000, http://www.thefreelibrary.com/Minimizing+Employer+Liability+for+Employee+Internet+Use-a063986324 (accessed August 10, 2010). This article contains good advice about an employer's need to notify and obtain consent from employees regarding monitoring of their online behaviors. *Marina Stengart v. Loving Care Agency, Inc.*, New Jersey Court, A-16-09, ruled that Stengart has a reasonable expectation that personal e-mails to and from her attorney would remain private, although copies were on her workplace computer, http://lawlibrary.rutgers.edu/courts/supreme/a-16-09.opn.html (accessed May 5, 2010).
9. Dinan, Stephen, Rules that Bar Feds from Trolling Facebook, Twitter Could Have Weeded Out Snowden, *The Washington Times*, March 16, 2014, http://p.washingtontimes.com/news/2014/mar/16/ (accessed March 18, 2014).
10. Report to the President, Suitability and Security Processes Review, February 2014, The White House, Washington, DC, http://www.whitehouse.gov/sites/default/files/omb/reports/suitability-and-security-process-review-report.pdf (accessed March 26, 2014).
11. Dinan, Rules (Note 9).
12. Redefining Security, A Report to the Secretary of Defense and the Director of Central Intelligence, February 28, 1994, Joint Security Commission, Washington, D.C.
13. Hurwicz, Macy, Barack Obama Staff to Have Email and Facebook Vetted, *Telegraph*, November 13, 2008, see http://www.telegraph.co.uk/ news/3453916/Barack-Obama-staff-to-have-email-and-Facebook-vetted.html (accessed August 10, 2010).
14. Bliss, Lisa R., Using the Internet to Save on Legal Research Costs, *American Bar Association Litigation News*, July 10, 2009; recommends using Internet searching to reduce legal research costs to ascertain data about cases, background information, media coverage, and blog entries about cases and parties, but verifying findings. See http://www.abanet.org/litigation/litigationnews/top_stories/legal-research-costs-internet.html (accessed August 10, 2010).

Chapter 10

Professional Standards and the Internet

Introduction

Laws are designed to deliver public safety and privacy and ensure human rights. Ethical and behavioral standards are created to carry out laws and regulations and ensure that fairness, openness, and choice (among other values) are employed in professional endeavors. One problem with using relatively new criteria to judge eligibility, capability, and past behavior is that the law is slow to catch up, and the ethical standards and guidelines that normally follow the law are even slower to develop. Internet vetting, when addressed in the few standards and guidelines where it is mentioned, has been discouraged because of the issues that inexpert collection, assessment, reporting, and adjudication of Internet search results can engender. A review of the most important guidance available is revealing and instructive and shows that this emerging area of standards is at an early stage of development. Blogs, chats, discussion forums, networking sites, game sites, mutual interest groups, and massively multiplayer online role-playing games (MMORPGs) present a rich panorama of different types of human interaction; varied "ground rules" in access, privacy, and use; and a challenge for those seeking to impose a definitive set of ethical tenets for those involved.

As difficult as it seems for lawyers and ethicists to address guidance (not really surprising because their focus is steeped in traditional authority, from times long before the Internet), it is strange that those studying the Internet in depth have yet to be consulted for the guidance necessary. If we wait for the lawyers, how much risk will be absorbed by enterprises unable to react in "Internet time"? Authorized use and privacy policies of the websites themselves provide a starting point and are only now being used to enforce requirements for users, over 21 years after the explosion of the use of the Internet. At this time, it is especially important to understand the medium and adopt a practical policy for addressing the legal and ethical issues without waiting for uninitiated legalists to reach final conclusions. After all, they are bound to go to court to litigate unresolved issues (or raise new issues about resolutions found). We should start with the standards that exist.

ASIS Standards

ASIS International, an organization of over 38,000 security management professionals worldwide, provides internationally recognized standards on various security topics. In February 2008, ASIS published its *Preemployment Background Screening Guideline*, which in 2009 was reviewed and updated.[1] The following is a summary (in my words, not the copyrighted ASIS version) of the guidelines' contents on Internet vetting: A new trend is the use by employers of online searches on applicants. Employers should approach online searches with caution because

- Postings may include information not intended for an employer to see, access to which may be controlled by passwords, terms of use, and privacy laws and policies. Although anything on the Internet may be considered public, posted materials may be intended for private use only.
- Employers or recruiters doing background checking on the Internet are not required to abide by the Fair Credit Reporting Act (FCRA), as are contracted investigators, so an applicant may not be notified when Internet data are used in an adverse decision (and will not find out that it was based on what was found online).
- Unlawful discrimination in hiring could occur if an employer used protected status under equal employment laws (e.g., race, religion, age) as the basis for an adverse decision.
- Job requirements should guide an employer's consideration of online content.
- Internet postings may be difficult to attribute to an individual because of shared virtual identities, false postings, unverified name match, or malicious posting of deceptive material.

The ASIS guideline deserves a detailed analysis because it is accepted as a standard by a large number of businesses and some government agencies. Although the volunteers who oversaw the composition of the guidelines (like other ASIS standards and guidelines) worked conscientiously and diligently to create consensus on baseline principles, their conclusions about the Internet, legal questions, and relevant privacy issues did not include mention of dissenting but authoritative views. Even though the ASIS guide adopts a legal approach designed to protect employers against potential lawsuits for using Internet vetting, it eschews adoption of an Internet search methodology adequate to protect employers against online misbehavior by candidates and designed to protect an employer against negligent hiring (which could occur if easily found Internet postings are ignored). The ASIS guideline fails to address the proper, legal manner in which Internet vetting could be accomplished, while discouraging such vetting. Meanwhile, it appears that an increasing number of employers conduct Internet searches on applicants for employment. According to a June 2009 CareerBuilder.com survey of over 2,600 hiring managers,[2] 45% (up from 22% in 2008) checked social networking sites to find out information regarding potential candidates, and 35% reported finding data on social networking sites that caused them not to hire candidates. A 2013 survey by HireRight[3] found that employers using searches of social networking sites in background screening fell from 24% in 2012 to 21% in 2013, and 61% of employers surveyed used social networking sites for recruiting. A June 2013 study by CareerBuilder showed that

> nearly 39 percent of employers use social networking sites to research job candidates, up from 37 percent last year. Of those, 43 percent said they have found information that factored into their decision not to hire a candidate—such as provocative or inappropriate photos and discriminatory comments related to race, gender or religion or the like—while 19 percent said they have found information that influenced their decision to hire a candidate—such as evidence of great communications skills and a professional-looking profile.[4]

The ASIS guidance appropriately says "approach with caution" but does not address appropriate ways to deal with what employers are finding online (i.e., clearly inappropriate behaviors disqualifying to candidates) and the unanswered question of how best to employ cybervetting.

The ASIS guideline expresses concern about the possible risk to someone's privacy if an employer accesses material that "a person did not intend for an employer to view." It is not clear where ASIS found the legal principle that says a person's intent about access to and use of publicly available information supersedes an employer's right to view it and take it into consideration. Public Internet postings are not protected in law, and a right to privacy is not ascribed to someone's publicly visible, illegal, illicit, or offensive behavior. An employer might find it difficult to defend the hiring of someone whose Internet profile notoriously featured illegal, illicit, or offensive behavior. The guideline fails to weigh the possibility that an arrogant or ignorant person boldly can post evidence of his or her ineligibility—and the employer should consider it. Employers include government, law enforcement, and private-sector entities whose staffs must be able to meet the highest levels of scrutiny. Unfortunately, I have seen numerous instances in the past 4 years of illegal, illicit, and antisocial behaviors posted on the public Internet for anyone to see. Fortunately, we found many of them in time to help protect employers against clearly unqualified persons.

It is true, as the ASIS guideline said, that an employer need not abide by the FCRA when the employer (and not a consumer reporting agency) checks the Internet, declines to hire the person, and does not notify the applicant of the reason. Under the FCRA, it is within the employer's legal rights not to notify the person when any investigation is conducted in-house. Although in an ideal world, applicants would be able to find out why they are not hired, there are many legitimate reasons why an employer may choose not to hire someone. Most employers will disclose the reasons if the applicant merely asks. Provisions of the FCRA do not directly address Internet vetting. An employer or contract background investigator can abide by FCRA and still conduct Internet vetting legally and properly using the correct approach.

The ASIS guideline raises the possibility of discrimination under Title VII of the Equal Rights Act of 1964 if Internet vetting is done. Title VII describes the grounds that would be illegal reasons to deny employment, such as racial, sex, or religious discrimination. A decision not to hire based on an Internet search has no relationship with Title VII, which does not address Internet vetting. Only if the employer discriminates as defined in the law would the employer be in violation of Title VII, whether or not an Internet search occurred. Internet vetting itself is not a discriminatory act, but a decision made to hire or not to hire, based on a prohibited factor found in a search, could be discriminatory. Items found in preemployment interviews of a candidate, previous employers, educators or references, records reviewed, or similar screening collection could also include discovery of potentially discriminatory factors. Protected classes should not be identified as such in reports of Internet investigations (or any other type of background screening report, exactly as required for traditional background investigations). Employers should use policies and procedures that ensure candidates fair, nondiscriminatory treatment, regardless of the methods used to collect information about the applicants.

The ASIS guideline raises a valid question about the relevance of Internet search results to job requirements. A candidate's prior misbehavior online can certainly be an indicator of future information systems misuse during employment, as can illegal or illicit behavior that an employer wishes to avoid in selecting applicants for employment. In a recent case, we found that a person had been hired to a senior research position after an extensive and expensive effort by the employer to find the most qualified candidate. The person hired had hidden the fact that he had been sanctioned by the government for scientific misconduct in research, to which he had admitted. Government records, when first checked, contained no reference to the punishment or misconduct. An Internet check revealed government publications saying that the individual had been prohibited from government research contracting for 3 years. In this case, the employer had incurred tens of thousands of dollars in recruitment, hiring, and other expenses, when a simple Internet check prior to finalizing the hire could have revealed the misconduct and the lack of candor by the candidate.

The ASIS guideline raises the issues of identification and attribution but omits the issue of seriousness (because often juvenile postings are humorous and exaggerated). These are key concepts for employers considering Internet searching as part of background investigations. Identifying which references may refer to the subject, may be posted by someone "spoofing" or masquerading as the subject, or may represent a fantasy or an untruth requires careful analysis. A recent contestant on a national TV talent show admitted that photos of her in underwear on the Internet were genuine, but she was slandered by other, pornographic photos that were doctored to include her image and were unscrupulously posted. Producers recognized the difference after a cyber investigation. It is important that investigators and adjudicators exercise great care in using the findings of Internet searching. Like analyses of all investigative results, online data may or may not be factual or relevant. Investigators and employers must make proper use of items collected from the Internet for any finding to play an appropriate role in an application or clearance process, just as they must with any other source of potentially derogatory data. Critical information may be missed without Internet searching. Through cybervetting employing proper procedures, the employer will reap the reward of identifying prior behavior that needs to be addressed, whether the candidate is hired, cleared, retained, or not. It should be noted that based on my experience and two recent studies, 9% to 31.5% of subjects of cybervetting will have potentially derogatory findings, while most results will reflect positively on, or be neutral to, a candidacy.

National Association of Professional Background Screeners

The National Association of Professional Background Screeners (NAPBS), founded in 2003 as a nonprofit trade association, represents the interest of companies offering tenant, employment, and background screening. NAPBS promotes ethical business practices and compliance with the FCRA and fosters awareness of issues related to consumer protection and privacy rights within the background screening industry. Members must abide by the standards and code of conduct and go through an accreditation process. The following standards from the NAPBS Member and Accredited Agency Codes of Conduct call for individual members and agencies to[5]

1. Perform professional duties in accordance with the law and the highest moral principles and the BSAAP (Background Screening Agency Accreditation Program) Accreditation Standard.
2. Observe the precepts of truthfulness, honesty, and integrity.
3. Be faithful, competent, and diligent in discharging professional responsibilities.

4. Be competent in discharging professional responsibilities.
5. Safeguard confidential information and exercise due care to prevent its improper disclosure.
6. Avoid injuring the professional reputation or practice of colleagues, clients, or employers.

However, nothing in this code limits a member from engaging in fair, competitive business practices.

The NAPBS approach depends on the FCRA standards,[6] which are worth a second look:

> The FCRA says that a consumer has the right to be told if information in a consumer report results in an action against him or her (e.g., denial of an application for employment, credit, or insurance); to see the contents of a consumer reporting agency's file concerning the consumer; to dispute and correct inaccurate or incomplete information (which must be corrected if a mistake is verified); and to consent prior to a consumer report being provided to an employer.
>
> NAPBS advocates a highly ethical approach to conducting background investigations and by virtue of its relatively high dues and charges (e.g., for accreditation) is primarily focused on large agencies and their practices.

Association of Internet Researchers

The Association of Internet Researchers (AoIR) thinks of Internet research in terms of observing human behaviors online, for many purposes, most often sociological, psychological, or behavioral studies of human interactions online or of works of art. In this arena, a host of ethical questions arises as researchers interact with individuals in "virtual worlds," social networking sites, blogs, and Internet Relay Chat sites and encounter new types of content (e.g., videos, graphics, photographs) and the like. Questions of disclosure, informed consent, identifying and quoting without permission, and so on have been addressed in rich AoIR discussions from the varied perspectives of the social sciences, the humanities, ethical and legal scholars, and Internet users over the past few years. In confronting national and international laws, ethics, and definitions of privacy, autonomy, and netizens' expectations, AoIR has captured and inspired spirited discussions of many related issues. The AoIR has developed standards titled *Ethical Decision-Making and Internet Research* (2002, and Version 2.0, 2012) to help researchers make ethical decisions in areas that are admittedly fluid and hard to define, particularly in an international context.[7] Among the salient guidelines are the following:

▪ An "ethical pluralism" approach (recognition of different ethical frameworks).
▪ An Aristotle-like attempt "to discern what [doing] the right thing at the right time for the right reason and in the right way may be," through a combination of judgment and the rules that apply in an individual situation.

- Questions to ask, including Internet venue (e.g., home pages, blogs, chat rooms, etc.), with the relevant ethical expectations (e.g., posted site policy) to judge the degree of privacy expected, and who are the subjects (e.g., adults or minors) of research.
- Considerations of timing, communications, and how materials will be used, to protect human subjects' rights to privacy, confidentiality, autonomy, and informed consent.
- Relevant legal requirements and ethical guidelines not only in the country of the researcher but also in those of the subjects (recognizing the international nature of the Internet, e.g., the contrast between EU and US data protection standards).

Additional considerations include the following:

Assumptions (and the validity thereof) of participants/subjects of a study, such as the difference between people observed in private exchanges versus those who view themselves as authors.

The ethically significant risks that the research might pose for a subject, such as intimate content, that could result, if disclosed, in harm to a subject. The principles of "above all, do no harm," and assessing how the benefits to be gained from the research may in some way offset/balance the risks posed, are important benchmarks for ethical decision making. However, a utilitarian approach (as in the United States, where research gains may be viewed as outweighing risk to personal privacy) differs markedly from a deontological approach (as in Europe, where personal privacy almost always outweighs possible research benefits).

The AoIR guide provides other things:

- The AoIR provides case studies that are highly useful in assessing ethical questions online. For example, they examine the question of whether chat rooms are public spaces and how notifications about a researcher's presence may have an impact on those using the chat room.
- AoIR also provides a list of references and outlines of different leaders' processes for ethical decision making and sample consent forms.
- Valuable concepts: AoIR's thoughtful review provides concepts of ethics worth considering in any humanistic endeavor, including obligations of researchers to inform subjects, respect individuals' private lives and families, and keep confidential the information subjects provide; the potential impact of research on a group using a website for its own purposes, that is, when the group must confront the unexpected intrusion of outsiders (possibly even insiders whose role as researchers is suddenly revealed) and the realization that users' customs are not honored. This may come down to recognizing the "human rights" of an avatar or online community of avatars: the changing

nature of Internet activities that themselves attract researchers but can be considered in some senses the province of the users and out of bounds for others.
- ■ The concept of online research itself has become as nuanced as the Internet's wide variety of activities. Virtual lives, MMORPGs, chat, blogs, and list serves (among others) present people in new dimensions. The researchers for science, sociology, and the humanities have considerably different motivations from the researchers for intelligence, criminal investigations, background vetting, and enterprise protection.

As a confessed American (and utilitarian, in the terms of AoIR), I would suggest that where intelligence and investigations are concerned, materials posted for millions to see on the Internet are "fair game." The naïve view that publicly posted content is somehow protected from investigators defies common sense. However, the AoIR's guide and similar thinking must inform the policies applied to unannounced presence in online venues by investigators and the uses to which collected content can be put, which should ideally be influenced by the basic human rights and mutual respect to which we are all entitled. In the end, bad behavior is unworthy of protection in public postings.

Among the Version 2.0 (2012) ethical guidelines, the following are informative:

- ■ Respecting international basic principles of ethical treatment of persons, including the fundamental rights of human dignity, autonomy, protection, safety, maximization of benefits and minimization of harms, or in the most recent accepted phrasing, respect for persons, justice, and beneficence
- ■ Greater protection for those more vulnerable
- ■ Inductive ethical decision making in a specific context, applying the Aristotelian principle of phronesis, that is, practical judgment in the situation
- ■ Considering the rights of persons and the possibility that subjects' rights may supersede the social benefits of the research
- ■ Applying principles and input from all available sources at all steps in the research process, from planning to dissemination of published results

Besides the AoIR standards, a book and journal articles by Heidi A. McKee and James E. Porter provide priceless views from the minds of Internet researchers and their subjects, ethicists, and those overseeing Internet research.[8] For example, the gamers generally feel that their avatars in virtual worlds deserve privacy. Researchers are advised to be intimately familiar with the online community they examine (i.e., they should spend many hours online) because naïve or clumsy intervention can wreck the cyber venue's mode of existence. Even public forum participants have perceived expectations of privacy and are uncomfortable with outsiders capturing content about them. McKee and Porter amply illustrated the fact that, for many millions of people, the Internet is a different dimension of life, where participants' expectations and beliefs about their rights may differ from long-established understandings of behavior in the physical world. Further, the authors' findings help define sensitive situations for both researchers and their subjects, where added care is required because exposure could cause ridicule, embarrassment, or negative publicity pertaining to illegal activity, personal health, sexual activity, religious beliefs, sexual preferences, family background, traumatic or emotionally distressing life experiences (death, injury, abuse), bodily functions, or idiosyncratic behaviors, as well as information that the online community wants kept confidential.

The stock that Internet behavioral researchers place in the feelings and beliefs of the subjects is not as appropriate for investigators and intelligence personnel because it is the feelings and beliefs themselves that are among the facts being collected. The more potentially problematic for the subject that the information may be, the more valuable it is likely to be in understanding the subject's motivations and behaviors. However, the worry that any subject may have about exposure of his or her online activities to investigators should be mitigated by the protections afforded by such laws as FCRA and Title VII, which prohibit misuse and discrimination.

Illegal activity is an appropriate target for investigators, and netizens who engage in it should not be able to shield themselves by their feelings that it should remain ignored. Because of the misprision of a felony law (requiring reporting of apparent crimes to a judge or civil authority such as law enforcement), it could be a problem for Internet researchers to conceal, and not report, felonious behavior they encounter.[9] Researchers focused on computer network protection face similar but different ethical issues in addressing the welfare of the Internet ecosystem.[10] In any case, the ethics of researchers and those of investigators have different purposes and foundations and properly should proceed their separate ways. There appears to be a fundamental dichotomy between academic considerations of ethical treatment of persons in a research context and law enforcement's requirement and need to address illicit behavior that is conducted in public view.

Proposed guidelines for Internet investigations appear in Chapters 11 to 13.

Librarians

The intelligence officer, sociologist, scholarly researcher, and student come together as customers of the librarian, whose services have changed dramatically with the growth of electronic books, publications, and materials and Internet availability of so much data. Indexing and search automation have revolutionized the finding of facts about people, businesses, government, topics, and any academic subject.[11] Not only do librarians provide essential assistance for all types of researchers, but also significant resources are available for free in libraries from subscription services and publications that would otherwise be costly for an Internet researcher. The approach of the librarian is to enable each patron while maintaining his or her confidentiality and privacy. Like the investigator, a librarian looks to the Internet as an additional tool to find all the available, authentic, reliable information on a topic. The Internet is viewed as a pathway to publications. Every intelligence collector, as an informed user, should understand that information placed online joins the world's largest virtual library, made available to the largest collection of readers on the planet.

Inside and Outside the Workplace

Government and business attorneys considering Internet vetting often focus on some courts' concern that background checking should be relevant to the specific position being applied for. In doing so, they often limit the universe of concerns to the workplace tasks and systems to which a newly hired person will be assigned. This is a fundamental mistake in today's society because people use their personal computers for work, for work-related communications, to talk with both insiders and outsiders about work, to look for new work, and to network with many other people in and out of work. In addition, people commit violations of law, ethics, rules, employment standards, and good behavior while on the Internet from home, on their personal devices, and on their employers' systems. In many cases, misbehavior is associated with an employer or with a person whose employment is publicly known. For example, many individuals use their work Internet service for Internet connections from home or elsewhere outside work and use their work e-mail address for all kinds of personal communications, whether from work or home.[12] In some cases, employees use their personal computers to leak or disclose information that is detrimental to their employer, such as complaining about their employer online. Other examples abound. Even those whose workplace systems have stringent controls are not sufficiently scrutinized if the employer ignores what the employee may be doing using a home computer. In the course of 15 years of private-sector investigations, I found many users in online activities tied to their employer, without an authorized purpose. A favorite example is the fact that nearly 1,000 members of one of the armed services used their e-mail addresses issued by the Department of Defense as their identifier in establishing their MySpace profiles, posting voluminous facts about their service for anyone to see. Did they not think that adversaries in every nation on earth could surf the net? Their service likes to use social networking sites to publicize and recruit, but issues users instructions not to reveal military activities improperly.

Monitoring proprietary systems is no longer enough for an employer to conduct due diligence in the pursuit of protecting intellectual property or verifying that employees have not engaged in dangerous breaches of security. While it may not seem rational, many employees mix their roles in and out of work into their Internet activities. By doing so, they involve their employer by necessity in their off-hours online world. Whether in e-mails, social network postings, instant messaging, tweets, or other online communications, at least 30% of today's workers have a prolific presence online.[13] Millennial employers ignore such millennial employees at their peril.

Reputational Risk, Public Affairs

As both business and government have recognized, the instant news and information dissemination taking place online pose an interesting dilemma for today's enterprise. On the one hand, it is possible to get a message across immediately, cheaply, and to a targeted audience. On the other hand, because reports spread virally and are not fact-checked, it is possible for misinformation and damaging information to receive broad exposure. Retraction, correction, and remediation of false reports can take much longer, and be much more difficult, than the originals. Reputational risk has risen for all enterprises, especially because of the online dissemination of all types of information about a business, agency, or organization.[14] Blogs, message boards, social media, and other posting venues are more than a minor matter or distraction to nearly every major corporation. Not only must the public affairs and stockholder services offices work diligently to discover and refute false reports, but also it is normal for large enterprises to have a handful of true but damaging reports online at any one time. Irresponsible employees often post items using "anonymous" identities, usually including a free e-mail account from a major provider such as Yahoo, Google, Microsoft, or AOL. Although it is sometimes possible to trace these anonymous posters, it is nearly impossible to undo the damage.

Reputational risk is a major challenge to every enterprise because everything from stock value to regulators' views of the company rides on what is said about it. Insider revelations can be major violations of Securities and Exchange Commission (SEC) regulations and other rules. When an individual becomes disgruntled in the information age, it is possible for the Internet to magnify the damage done by only a few choice postings, true or not. While the human resources department may still struggle with proper uses of the Internet in vetting, the other departments, including legal, marketing, public relations, security, and investor support, are busy daily with scanning the web for posts about the company. Trade media, now all online, are only one of the types of Internet publications of which they must remain aware. When an employee, contractor, supplier, or partner posts damaging materials about an enterprise, it is in the enterprise's best interests immediately to discover and take appropriate action on the event. In considering any prospective candidate, the enterprise should consider if the applicant has a history of posting damaging material. This is but one of many examples of illicit behaviors that can be trivial or immensely important in the life of a corporation or government agency.

Bottom Line

It is more important to have defensible standards about Internet searching for information collection and intelligence purposes than to count on the specific standards themselves, especially because the legal underpinnings are fluid. The lack of definitive legal rules has resulted in perhaps less Internet vetting than should be done. Uncertainty can be the enemy of sound ethical approaches. Anecdotal evidence suggests that individuals in many companies and government agencies are using the Internet in vetting candidates; looking up fellow employees, superiors, and business associates; and otherwise using web information as a key part of their decision making. Among the issues raised by this behavior is the potential liability of an enterprise without any rules or policies, the possible use of Internet search results in illicit or inappropriate ways, and the mistaken use of incomplete, inaccurate, unreliable, and false data.

The proposed standards in Section III include many of the elements that are informed by the extant legal and ethical approaches provided for guidance to disciplines both inside and outside intelligence and investigations.

Notes

1. ASIS International, *Preemployment Background Screening Guideline*, 2009, http://www. asisonline.org/guidelines/guidelinespreemploy.pdf (accessed August 10, 2010).
2. Haefner, Rosemary, More Employees Screening Candidates via Social Networking Sites, http://www.careerbuilder.com/Article/CB-1337-Getting-Hired-More-Employers-Screening-Candidates-via-Social-Networking-Sites/?ArticleID=1337&cbRecursionCnt= 1&cbsid=ed3b3595c5334cb0b74dab54657de7a4-334768959-RS-4&ns_siteid=ns_ us_g_careerbuilder_survey (accessed August 10, 2010).
3. HireRight, The Evolving Practice of Social Media Background Screening, http:// www.hireright.com/blog/2013/05/the-evolving-practice-of-social-media-background-screening/ (accessed March 30, 2014).
4. Lorenz, Mary, Two in Five Employers Use Social Media to Screen Candidates, July 1, 2013, Survey Results, Talent Factor, http://thehiringsite.careerbuilder. com/2013/07/01/two-in-five-employers-use-social-media-to-screen-candidates/ (accessed April 23, 2014).
5. NAPBS, http://www.napbs.com/media/Factsheet.pdf, http://www.napbs.com/ benefits/code_of_conduct.cfm, and http://www.napbs.com/benefits/BSAA_Code_of_ Conduct.pdf effective as of 2009 (accessed March 30, 2014).
6. Fair Credit Reporting Act, http://www.ftc.gov/sites/default/files/fcra.pdf (accessed March 30, 2014).
7. AoIR Ethics Working Committee, *Ethical Decision-Making and Internet Research: Recommendations from the AoIR Ethics Working Committee*, approved November 27, 2002, by the Association of Internet Researchers (AoIR), an international association

of students and scholars in the field of Internet studies, http://aoir.org/; available online at www.aoir.org/reports/ethics.pdf and Version 2.0, a 2012 report, available at http://aoir.org/reports/ethics2.pdf (both accessed March 30, 2014).

8. McKee, Heidi A., and Porter, James E., Playing a Good Game: Ethical Issues in Researching MMOGs and Virtual Worlds, *International Journal of Internet Research Ethics*, 2, 2009, http://www.ijire.net/issue_2.1/mckee.pdf (accessed September 21, 2010); McKee, Heidi, and Porter, James E., The Ethics of Digital Writing Research: A Rhetorical Approach, *CCC*, 59.4, 2008; McKee, Heidi A., and Porter, James E., *The Ethics of Internet Research, a Rhetorical Case-Based Process* (New York: Peter Lang, 2009).

9. Title 18, US Code, Part I, Chapter 1, Section 4, Misprision of a Felony, http://www.law.cornell.edu/uscode/uscode18/usc_sec_18_00000004----000-.html (accessed August 10, 2010) and similar state statutes.

10. Kenneally, Erin, Bailey, Michael, and Maughan, Douglas, *A Framework for Understanding and Applying Ethical Principles in Network and Security Research*, US Department of Homeland Security Working Group on Ethics, 2010, http://www.caida.org/publications/papers/2010/framework_ethical_research/framework_ethical_research.pdf (accessed August 10, 2010).

11. Cassell, Kay Ann, and Hiremath, Uma, *Reference and Information Services in the 21st Century, An Introduction*, 2nd edition (New York: Neal-Schuman, 2009), which contains excellent pointers for Internet researchers and librarians.

12. Based on my over 15 years of collection and analysis of Internet data.

13. The 30% estimate for those with a prolific presence online is derived from statistics published by the Pew Internet and American Life Project, http://www.pewinternet.org/.

14. Deloitte Insights, *Wall Street Journal*, http://deloitte.wsj.com/riskandcompliance/2013/04/25/three-steps-toward-managing-reputational-risk/ (accessed March 30, 2014).

Chapter 11

The Insider Threat

Introduction

A primary reason for considering Internet vetting is the fundamental changes that have occurred in people's behaviors since the 1970s in the workplace and since the early 1990s on networked computers and computing devices. The insider threat deserves in-depth analysis because it has such a large impact on all types of organizations, but that is left for another day. Studies of industrial crimes, shrinkage, losses ascribed to embezzlement, and espionage have shown increases in the incidence and seriousness of insider crime for the past 20 to 30 years. However, precise metrics are lacking, and the relevance of available survey statistics in a field with so little tangible, public evidence is limited. Are we seeing better reporting, better detection, or a higher incidence of insider crime? We certainly are seeing a higher level of attention paid to the insider threat in government and industry, whether it is leaks, treason, workplace violence, or intellectual property loss that is the focus of concern. Even user errors cause serious losses.

The insider threat is not well understood outside the confines of the individual enterprise because statistical record keeping and reporting are inconsistent at best. Like economic espionage, the problem has been addressed over time much more rarely by law enforcement than by internal investigations and administrative resolutions. Most of the time, in my experience, the perpetrator is laid off, fired, or otherwise moved out. I am aware of some instances when felony crimes were addressed internally, and the employee retained, because of the wishes of high-ranking executives. In any case, insider threat mitigation varies greatly.

As mentioned in previous chapters, an insider with access to information systems, networks, and data is in a position to do great damage to the enterprise with substantially less prospect of detection than in the physical world. After all, the purloined data remain in the possession of the employer, even if the insider copies the data and sells secrets to the highest bidder. The speed with which thefts of massive quantities of information, including designs, plans, personally identifying files, financial accounts, and the like can take place from enterprise computer systems can defeat protective measures. After all, the systems are built to allow rapid searching, collection, copying, and movement of the data to support the enterprise.

From the standpoint of vetting applicants and insiders, employers need to include online behavior, from both intranet and Internet sessions, in evaluations of eligibility. The consequence of omitting online behavior is that insiders will not be evaluated in the one dimension where they can probably do the most damage and cause the greatest losses. As we have learned from studies of espionage and financial services embezzlement, people initially cleared have gone on to commit the crime although their employment background investigations and even updates and periodic polygraphs favored continued clearances.[1] This suggests that, without effective background checks, periodic reinvestigations, and reviews, insiders can commit serious crimes against their employers undetected.

Security, intelligence, and law enforcement practitioners sometimes think too narrowly of venue and territoriality in connection with securing the enterprise. Work computing has moved "off campus" and into hotel rooms, airports, coffee shops, and homes. Symantec and IDC estimated that 73% of the workforce would be mobile by the end of 2011, perhaps a low estimate in retrospect. "Whether inside the employer's space or cyberspace or outside, the vulnerabilities of work-related data are increasing," Symantec's white paper said. "According to industry analysts, 70 percent of security incidents resulting in data loss are perpetrated by insiders. Risk assessment studies by Symantec reveal that an organization with 20,000 employees is likely to suffer up to 400 potential data loss incidents per day." A recent *Wall Street Journal* report showed that half of workers who left or lost their jobs took company confidential information with them.[2] To be perfectly clear, the vulnerability includes vital employer data processed on both work-issued and personal devices, in the cloud, at rest and in transit, at work and outside.

Recent conversations with intelligence, defense, and law enforcement leaders indicated that some cybervetting is under way. Several agencies (which will go unnamed) ask candidates to sit down with a background investigator, log on to Internet services they often use, and take a tour of the content of the candidate's online postings together. Agency leaders believe that this is the best way to review postings (which may be accessible to anyone or to many people) and verify that they are appropriate for an employee of whom the highest behavioral standards will be expected. Asking the candidate to log on also avoids the potentially problematic option of asking for passwords or "friending" applicants. However, not all agencies then follow up with independent searches, designed to ascertain whether the candidate has revealed all the relevant online activities. Concealment or lack of candor is one of the most common potential problems found among applicants.[3] Although it is good to know that the agencies with the highest stakes (i.e., those whose employees hold the highest clearances, carry weapons on duty, and must keep secrets) are beginning to address Internet vetting, it is clear that the process is not uniform or well developed.

As employers contemplate what types of monitoring, if any, to deploy in securing internal information systems, they should also consider whether and how to ascertain what candidates do online, and to verify what candidates provide, by searching the public Internet for signs that insiders may pose a high risk of crimes and misbehavior, leaks, and inadvertent disclosures. It is not unusual for people to post items that are not consistent with their employer's code of conduct or business standards, although this involves only a minority of employees.[4] However, serious crimes or security breaches revealed by Internet searching prior to or during employment would be strong indicators of high risk for insider crime or security lapses. As pointed out previously, it only takes one malicious or negligent insider to do grave damage using an employer's information systems to which he or she is granted full access.

Benevolent Big Brother

To address the insider issue, employers with high-value data, including defense and intelligence contractors, law enforcement, electronics firms, aerospace, biotechnology, nanotechnology, software, leading-edge manufacturers, and market leaders of all kinds, have had to step up monitoring and control over proprietary computer systems, networks, and data.[5] This has been complicated by the need to communicate globally, from workplaces and outside locations, and to access sensitive data from anywhere, anytime. The standard formula until now has been a combination of technical security controls, information assurance activities, user security awareness training, nondisclosure agreements/contracts, and enforcement mechanisms. Included have been new digital data rights management systems, multifactor authentication, and advanced logging solutions. Some of these protections allow an employer to prevent online misbehavior, remind users of rules when they exceed their authority, require supervisory approval for some uses of data, collect real-time forensic evidence of abuse, and enforce standards quickly. Nevertheless, such solutions can only be a part of the insider threat solution because determined insiders can circumvent controls. Again, Edward Snowden and Robert Hanssen should be mentioned because they stole and leaked massive quantities of highly sensitive information from the National Security Agency (NSA) and Federal Bureau of Investigation (FBI) files, two of the best-protected storehouses of data in the world.

Complicating the insider threat issue is the need to influence social media and Internet postings generally in positive ways, benefitting the enterprise. Many companies spend significant sums monitoring the Internet and placing advertising content online. The marketing and sales staff live online, and the investor relations department has a huge stake in image and reputation and ensuring the factual nature of allowable postings about the business, so they look at online content as well. One or a series of postings from an insider can spell legal issues and regulatory investigations and possibly result in loss of market share or stock value. Specialists previously interested in TV time, direct-mail advertising, and Securities and Exchange Commission (SEC) filings now must also focus on Internet image and the posted comments of perhaps thousands of employees, customers, stockholders, and kibitzers. As market reputation has grown in importance, so has the potential for an insider or outsider to have an impact on that reputation.

Every employer also must face the question of how employees view the information systems security controls and enforcement and the potential chilling effects (as well as impediments to efficiency) that security measures can cause. In an era of wild financial swings, layoffs, and restructuring, the written and unwritten compacts between employers and workers are at greater risk today than ever before. Employers exert efforts to treat employees and contractors humanely and structure compensation and benefits, workplace ambience, and atmosphere to make the strongest possible positive impression on insiders. The natural balance and conflict between personnel and security departments figure into the workplace ethos, and both are vital to making the automated enterprise successful in making information technology (IT) a strategic differentiator for success.

Among workers who are most familiar with the information systems they use, such as IT personnel, electronics engineers, programmers, and designers, there is a high recognition of the necessity for good behavior online and the need to monitor and enforce IT discipline. One good reason is the general realization among more sophisticated users that infiltration often occurs when user credentials are acquired by outsiders bent on penetration. Social engineering is a key "cracker" method for intrusions, but password-cracking programs, stolen laptops, inadvertent disclosures, phishing, and shared log-on credentials are also frequent causes. There is a double-edged sword for employers who are successful in online security training and awareness for insiders: They are better prepared to help protect enterprise systems, but they are also more likely to understand the value of the data to which they have access and the potential reward of theft. At the end of the day, the more savvy the user, the greater potential threat posed. Because history tells us that the actual number of malicious users is only a small percentage of the overall population, the risk does not appear unacceptably high. However, the insider is one case for which the potential impact of a security incident is so high that additional preventive methods are needed.

So, the benevolent dictatorship of the enterprise must confront the inevitable balance between big brother and big buddy. A great advantage of knowing each insider through close association with supervisors, mentors, and teammates is that the temptation for abuse and crime is greatly reduced, and the probability of early intervention or detection is greatly enhanced. When information assurance, technical, and human methods are combined, the insider threat is reduced to an acceptable minimum.

Notes

1. Herbig, Katherine L., and Wiskoff, Martin F., Espionage against the United States by American Citizens 1947–2001, Technical Report 02–5, Defense Personnel Security Research Center (PERSEREC), July 2002, http://www.fas.org/sgp/library/spies.pdf (accessed March 30, 2014); Mitre Report (numerous authors), Analysis and Detection of Malicious Insiders, submitted to *2005 International Conference on Intelligence Analysis*, McLean, VA; Shaw, Eric, Ruby, Keven G., and Post, Jerrold M., The Insider Threat to Information Systems, the Psychology of the Dangerous Insider, *Security Awareness Bulletin*, 2–98, June 1998; Randazzo, Cappelli, et al., Insider Threat Study: Illicit Cyber Activity in the Banking and Finance Sector, National Threat Assessment Center, US Secret Service and CERT Coordination Center, Carnegie Mellon University Software Engineering Institute, August 2004; Sulick, Michael J., *American Spies: Espionage against the United States from the Cold War to the Present* (Washington, DC: Georgetown University Press, October 2013), http://press.georgetown.edu/book/georgetown/american-spies (accessed March 30, 2014).
2. Symantec and IDC, Worldwide Mobile Worker Population 2007–2011 Forecast, Symantec White Paper, March 2008; King, Rachael, Departing Employees Are Security Horror: Many Think Nothing of Taking Confidential Company Information With Them When They Leave, *Wall Street Journal*, October 21, 2013.
3. InfoLink Screening Services (Kroll), Applicant Hit Ratio Analysis, 2005 (no longer available online). iNameCheck studies, see Chapter 4. Title 18, Section 1001, US Code, makes it a crime to deliberately falsify or conceal information, including applications for employment, provided to the US Government, with a term of up to 5 years' confinement and fine of up to $10,000 or both. Whether deliberate or accidental, failure to reveal online identities on applications might have the same effect.
4. Based on numerous examples that came to the attention of my firm iNameCheck during the past 8 years.
5. General Accounting Office, Employee Privacy, Computer-Use Monitoring Practices of Selected Companies, report to the ranking minority member, Subcommittee on 21st Century Competitiveness, Committee on Education and the Workforce, House of Representatives, September 2002, http://www.gao.gov/new.items/d02717.pdf (accessed August 21, 2010); Needleman, Sarah E., Monitoring the Monitors: Small Firms Increasingly Are Keeping Tabs on Their Workers, Keystroke by Keystroke, *Wall Street Journal* online, August 16, 2010, http://online.wsj.com/article/NA_WSJ_PUB:SB10001424052748703748904575411983790272268.html (accessed August 21, 2010).

FRAMEWORK FOR INTERNET SEARCHING

The philosophy of open-source intelligence in a world of information dominated by the Internet depends on a foundation and framework designed to address the strategic and ethical issues that confront all organizations. Although an enterprise may expect that every insider using the Internet will abide by the law, regulations, written promises (e.g., confidentiality and noncompete agreements), and enterprise policies, it is unwise to expect that there will be no major problems or misuse. This and subsequent chapters provide a structure by which an organization can exploit Internet information according to generally accepted understandings of risks, benefits, and the needs of individuals and their employers.

Chapter 12

Internet Vetting and Open-Source Intelligence Policy

Introduction

If you are doing research, investigations, or intelligence collection on the Internet, there is not much to worry about in terms of legal restrictions. By its nature, the Internet is a network of networks, designed to facilitate the sharing of information. Certain criminal laws prohibit computer fraud and abuse, including unauthorized access to or use of information that is accessible through the Internet but protected, interception of electronic communications in transit, and misuse of computer systems and data in ways specified in various federal and state laws. Because of the designs of computers, networks, and databases, it is simply not possible beyond a point to secure them. Those who believe that any information that can be accessed is theirs to use as they see fit are sadly mistaken (but this feeling has a rather large following). Abuse is not tolerable—illegal or illicit behaviors are wrong. When we went online, we moved to a virtual neighborhood where most residents only use unlocked screen doors. That does not mean that burglary is no longer illegal.

Before an enterprise embarks on a process to exploit the Internet for open-source information, it is a good idea—in fact, a necessity, according to the best attorneys I know—to have a policy for how to do so.[1] Like other intelligence collection methods, including human intelligence, surveillance, signals intelligence, and so on, open-source intelligence requires a set of standards that both enable success and avoid the pitfalls inherent in the practice. For a business, government agency, nonprofit, or other organization, it is important to recognize that Internet research, which has become indispensable for society, is at a relatively early stage of development, including the legal framework, policy, and procedural foundations that are needed.

Legal and Ethical Limitations

Before using the Internet for open-source intelligence research, it is important to know some of the legal restrictions imposed by law, regardless of the purpose of the search. Normally, it would not be necessary to address this issue because open-source research exploits published materials (free or for a fee) to collect and analyze information and produce reports on topics of interest. However, the Internet differs in several important respects from the county library (although even the county library these days provides computers for information retrieval).[2] Information accessible on the Internet can be categorized into different types, depending on who has it, what is in it, where it is kept, and how it is accessed. Further, retrieving data electronically in a legal manner requires abiding by federal and state laws that, although straightforward, are not necessarily common knowledge. Data from Internet searches also can differ from data sourced from established authority.

A wide variety of hosts on the Internet provides information,[3] such as the following:

1. News media, including newspapers, broadcast news, blogs, news wholesalers, associations, interest groups, educational institutions, and so on publish online. The contents from these providers are often free, but some charge for access to their older, archived stories. The items are generally copyrighted, and permission is needed to reuse reports. Essentially, these sources are considered published information (i.e., data designed to be available to the public). Fair use includes quoting and using facts reported as leads. Businesses, government agencies, and other organizations have websites to provide information to the public, stockholders, citizens, customers, partners, and stakeholders of all kinds. The contents may be copyrighted, but often the intent of postings is to share the information as widely as possible for public relations, awareness, safety, marketing, sales, and networking or to provide public access to periodic updates, such as quarterly and annual reports. As with academic research, the rule of thumb for using these types of published information in open-source intelligence is proper attribution and abiding by copyright law. News generally contains "true facts" (as J. Edgar Hoover reputedly said), that is, accurate, verified information (but like any source, it is not 100% accurate).
2. Most businesses and agencies today have internal applications and databases designed for conducting enterprise functions, and those private systems are connected to the Internet to allow access to authorized individuals (e.g., employees, contractors, partners, and sometimes customers). The degree of

security varies for those allowed access, but internal systems are not intended for public access.

3. Entertainment and social networking sites are optimized for public use and often allow for use by groups that are more private. These websites create networks of individuals so content can be shared, sometimes with access restrictions; connections can be made; and a variety of materials, such as blogs, photos, audio and video files, and other content, can be posted for sharing. Some content may be copyrighted, but much is intended for wide dissemination, and some items are intended for a restricted audience of registered users, friends, and colleagues. Merely requiring membership to see content may not make data posted on these sites private because millions of users have access to postings without privacy protection, and an authorized recipient may reshare content with their own group.

4. Businesses such as Internet retailers, financial firms, service providers, and so on have websites with functions designed to attract and inform customers (completely open to the public); provide data to registered users (restricted use, but relatively open, nontransactional information content); present account information exclusively to account holders (private access); and conduct transactions for registered and authenticated users (closed, limited-access systems designed to prevent fraud and to facilitate online payments). The degree of security afforded to these three or four levels of access (envisioned by the Federal Reserve years ago, in its guidance to the nation's online banks) is greatest at the transactional level. Unfortunately, it is that level of information that black-hat hackers seek to access and exploit.

The first level of control for those setting Internet search standards is to ensure that practitioners understand the difference between public websites and those where restrictions on authorized use of content may have an impact on the decision to collect and utilize posted information. By the time the data collected are reported, it may not be clear to a report reader where the items originated and what limitations, if any, need to be considered for their use. Therefore, the actions (if any) taken on an Internet intelligence report can violate a law, policy, or standard if the method of the search or its product is illicit or improper. One way to address this concern is to require explicit sourcing for each item reported from the Internet, with a notation if the item was retrieved in a manner not authorized by the website hosting the data or not published on the public Internet. Clients of investigative and intelligence reports (e.g., human resources, legal and security departments, policy makers) should establish clear expectations for collectors and analysts so that the enterprise does not inadvertently use reported data in an inappropriate manner, inconsistent with its policy.

The anonymity of users on the Internet can benefit an intelligence officer who might access many websites to find instances of illegal or threatening behavior without revealing his or her role in intelligence. However, the possible uses of the information obtained might be limited by the manner of collection. It is useful to think of stored (not in-transit) information collected by investigators, intelligence, and security personnel in categories:

- Published data intended for use by everyone
- Published data intended for a limited group of people
- Data stored in a limited-access place for authorized users only
- Data stored in a secure place for access by specified users for restricted purposes only

Because of the nature of the Internet, openness of users' postings, and availability of effective search and collection methods, a good investigator will soon find that it is possible to gain access to information that the investigator was never intended to see. Contents of the information may well show the type of behavior or document facts that are most useful for judging the trustworthiness, character, or proclivities of the subject and hence be most useful in assessing the subject. But, because of the method of collection, an item retrieved in this manner may not be admissible as a piece of evidence, usable as a derogatory element in a report, or usable as a question for interviewing the subject directly. The suitability of an item for use in due diligence investigations (e.g., cybervetting) therefore may depend on its method of collection and whether the source can be cited openly. This is not to say that the item cannot be used at all in the evaluation or due diligence process. When a piece of information is found that cannot be used openly in an adverse action, it may still be useful in formulating interview questions; as a lead for further investigation (e.g., interviews of friends, co-workers, or acquaintances of the subject); and as a pointer to other potential sources online or offline, where public variations may be found (e.g., by using the handle or user name found in the private posting to find similar public postings). In addition, it is worth noting that having intelligence about a subject of importance, even if that intelligence cannot be used in a proceeding or report, can be helpful in protecting the security of an enterprise's people, assets, and information. For example, the orientation and training (including indoctrination) of an employee with a history of Internet misbehavior can include material addressing the high standards that apply for workplace computing. Monitoring and mentoring are other possibilities.

Because investigative personnel often operate alone and rarely receive supervisory scrutiny over each step they take, investigators must adhere to the proper ethical standards on their own. At this writing, there are almost no guidelines for Internet searching. Therefore, there is virtually no scrutiny being given to the questions of whether the Internet is used, how cybervetting may be carried out, and the use of results in follow-up investigation. When ethical standards are established for the use of the Internet in investigations, there is a high likelihood that most investigators will follow those standards most of the time. Today, it is up to the individual investigator.

Policy

In any enterprise, government or private, there are four stakeholders with a critical need to address the policy applied to Internet searching for investigative and intelligence purposes: the chief legal officer, the chief security officer, the chief personnel officer, and the chief information officer. Each of these executives has personal operational reasons for needing to address Internet searching, but enterprise strategy and risk management require that the four agree on the following simple principles:

1. Internet searching is a form of open-source intelligence that may, if used properly and ethically, contribute important insights in an investigation.
2. Internet searching should be comprehensive; that is, find a high percentage of available information relevant to the subject.
3. Internet searching results should be screened for accuracy and reliability, that is, verified for credibility and pertinence to the subject of interest.
4. Internet searching, analysis, and reporting should be conducted by experienced, capable analysts using technical tools in an efficient, productive manner.
5. Internet searching should be conducted in a safe manner to avoid causing harm to or increasing the vulnerability of those vetting or vetted.
6. Due diligence decisions should be made on the basis of the quality, quantity, timeliness, and credibility of the intelligence presented; that is, Internet intelligence can add to, but does not fundamentally change, the legacy decision-making process.

Today, no firm or agency would wish to restrict googling by staff, but when results of Internet information collection are to be combined with other intelligence to make corporate decisions, it is important to hold the cyber results to the same standards to which all other sources must adhere. That requirement translates to proper professional methods of online research.

In a large enterprise, it would be interesting to see how many hours daily are spent online in pursuit of strictly business goals.[4] Based on the trends evident in user statistics, it appears that every department in every organization with Internet access on employees' workstations now depends on Internet information for productivity. There is no doubt that Internet searching is already a critical factor in timely information retrieval, assessment of options, and rapid communications, benefitting the enterprise greatly. If the Internet were not a relatively reliable source of information, the productivity gains from its use would not be so evident. However, when the best-available intelligence assessments are critical, it is imperative to require added scrutiny of the Internet information used so that decisions have the best-available basis and misjudgment is less likely.

Legal departments of enterprises have been forced to oversee a growing practice of electronic disclosure, based on the contents of corporate data that may relate to a particular matter under litigation or investigation.[5] E-mail files are especially difficult because their volume, archiving, searching, and applicability to almost any issue are likely to be burdensome on the enterprise and likely to produce evidence against the interests of the enterprise. Several general counsels of major businesses with which I have consulted, and some government agencies, in the past have advocated systematic destruction of e-mails to avoid the "false positives" that are caused when employees include inaccurate, untrue, scurrilous, and defamatory information in their e-mails. Because e-mails occupy that netherworld between the formal business letter and the informal personal note, it is generally up to the user to keep the content true, proper, and civil. However, so much e-mail contains content inconsistent with enterprise policy that it has become a legal issue for almost every organization. Civil litigation nearly always includes a motion for disclosure from enterprise documents and data (e-discovery), including e-mail, imposing procedural and technical issues with ever-growing volumes of documents stored electronically. Recent laws help regulate electronic disclosures in civil cases (e.g., changes to Rule 16, US Federal Rules of Civil Procedure, addressing the timing, scope, and cost of motions for e-discovery), but the law does not do much to mitigate the need to preserve data.

Unfortunately, data on the public Internet may well point to information within corporate walls, and the likelihood that Web references will help investigators to make successful electronic disclosure demands has grown with the volume of data escaping the enterprise and residing on the Internet. In addition, the indiscretion shown in Internet postings could make adversaries even more eager to access corporate data because it is likely to contain some items bolstering legal claims.

In a world of secrets, classified information, and vital intellectual property, the virtue of discretion has suffered a nearly fatal blow. The Internet has become the antisecret. Self-exposure has increased with the changing social norms propelled by the web. Those trained in the protection of classified information (and perhaps coming from an earlier generation) have a natural tendency to be more discreet, say less, and disclose less. Among other things, discretion involves choosing not to tell others something just because one knows it and being careful not to embarrass oneself by exposing something potentially harmful to oneself or one's family, community, or one's employer. The Internet generation appears to be less discreet and more apt to disclose data that should be protected. As indicated previously, even one or a few indiscreet individuals can jeopardize the security and interests of an enterprise. Therefore, a key requirement for protecting classified data and intellectual property is the collective and individual discretion of those with access to it, and the ability of the enterprise to detect instances of disclosure and exert discipline to discourage it.

The rise in attention to social networking as a means of marketing, stockholder relations, and information collection has also given rise to some enterprise policies worth noting, such as the model Social Media Policy posted by the Society for Human Resource Management (SHRM) and ruled lawful in May 2012 by the National Labor Relations Board.[6] Key elements of SHRM's model guidelines include legal and behavioral guidance for employees on posting that complies with the NLRB's enforcement of employee-employer labor relations.

These observations about enterprise policy on cybervetting and Internet collection are meant as a starting point. All businesses, agencies, and organizations should have relevant policies designed to suit their needs. Because work-related postings and other online disclosures relating to the enterprise may include proprietary data, enterprise policy should include guidance on the information assets themselves.

Information Assets Protection

The following chapters specifically outline procedures to be used for Internet searching for intelligence, but it is important to have an ethical strategy based on core tenets. Among core tenets for a business or government enterprise are the following:

- Enterprise information is a key asset to be protected.
- The enterprise will take all reasonable, legal measures to protect its systems, networks, and data to protect its information assets.
- All authorized users will be required to adhere to enterprise information technology (IT) policies and should expect that their systems use will be scrutinized for compliance, data protection, and effectiveness as needed at any time (as expressed in authorized use policies).
- Authorized users of any systems, business or personal, can create Internet records that could have an adverse impact on the enterprise because outsiders, unauthorized users, and adversaries of the enterprise may see Internet postings. Therefore, users should be careful what they post on the Internet. The enterprise may take measures to detect Internet postings that could be of concern and will discipline any authorized user found posting material deemed to be harmful to the enterprise.
- The enterprise respects the individual privacy of its authorized IT systems users and will take steps to ensure the protection of their personally identifying information. While enterprise IT systems are proprietary and exist for business use only, it is understood that users' data will at times share enterprise IT resources. The enterprise reserves the right to review all information residing on its systems at any time, for any purpose, and will take appropriate action if any information found is deemed to be improper or illicit or poses a potential risk for the enterprise.
- The enterprise expects all authorized users to be of assistance in protecting systems, networks, and data, and failure to help protect the enterprise will be subject to discipline.

Full disclosure of these principles will help users to understand the value of IT systems and the need and intent that their employer has to protect itself in the interconnected world of computers. Awareness establishes a legal basis for security measures and admissibility of information found about misuse. Awareness is also a first step in enlisting users as part of the security solution, which depends on all users' cooperation.[7]

Last, it is a necessary legal step in establishing the intent to protect proprietary information as a valuable asset. In an ideal world, the Internet would allow all users to experience the freedom to express whatever they wanted to and to enhance the creativity and productivity of all the businesses and agencies online. In the real world, the Internet has become not only a crucial asset for US users but also a source of significant risks. Prior to the rise of the Internet as a risk, the enterprise could guard its physical files, libraries, and other physical assets. Because computing, networking, and data have become essential to success and efficiency, it is critical to exploit their benefits while guarding against the added risks posed by the virtual world to which we are all connected.

Notes

1. This is based on my discussions with chief privacy officers and chief legal officers at several government agencies and corporations over the past 10 years.
2. Cassell, Kay Ann, and Hiremath, Uma, *Reference and Information Services in the 21st Century, an Introduction*, 2nd edition (New York: Neal-Schuman, 2009), with a description at http://www.neal-schuman.com/reference21st2nd (accessed August 21, 2010).
3. Schlein, Alan M., *Find It Online, the Complete Guide to Online Research*, 2nd edition (Tempe, AZ: Facts on Demand Press, 2001); Sherman, Chris, and Price, Gary, *The Invisible Web, Uncovering Information Sources Search Engines Can't See* (Medford Township, NJ: Information Today, 2001).
4. Hannula, Mikva, and Lönnqvist, Antti, How the Internet Affects Productivity, Tampere University of Technology, Finland, http://www.cluteinstitute.com/ojs/index.Php/IBER/article/view/3896/3940 (2002) (accessed July 17, 2014).
5. eDiscovery, see http://www.uscourts.gov/SearchResults.aspx?IndexCatalogue=AllIndexedContent&SearchQuery=e%20discovery (accessed August 21, 2010).
6. https://www.shrm.org/templatestools/samples/policies/pages/socialmediapolicy.aspx, accessed March 31, 2014.
7. Wilson, Mark, and Hash, Joan, Building an Information Technology Security Awareness and Training Program, Special Publication 800-50, National Institute of Standards and Technology, October 2003, http://csrc.nist.gov/publications/nistpubs/800-50/NIST-SP800-50.pdf (accessed June 1, 2010).

Chapter 13

Tools, Techniques, and Training

Introduction

If your enterprise or unit needs a process for Internet searching, analysis, and reporting, it is important to ensure that those tasked with carrying out the process have adequate training and preparation to do so. Yes, everybody googles. That does not mean that everybody knows what they are doing or can properly assess the results. If investigative and intelligence conclusions are to be reached, strategies evaluated, and decisions made based on Internet data, there are basic attributes that are required for the execution of searches, which could be characterized as "user requirements," like those specified for software systems requirements.[1] The search and analysis processes should deliver results that are, to the greatest extent possible,

- Reasonably complete and comprehensive
- Accurate, with identifiable references properly attributed to the subject
- Useful for the purpose for which the search was conducted
- From sources believed to be reliable
- Verified or verifiable through multiple sources and analysis
- Current and properly dated
- Efficient, that is, accomplished within allocated budget
- Timely, that is, accomplished within established deadlines
- Designed and conducted in a manner that does no harm to searchers or subjects

When my private intelligence practice began, we found that for search terms (people, firms, topics) with many references, it is possible to engage in endless collection and review of links, with the hope that the next click will bring you to the holy grail of the search. After a point, it is like the slots player at the airport in Las Vegas: How often will you win, and how many more times must you drop in a coin and wish? The house has the game stacked against you, and more play simply means more loss—just get on the departing plane. Therefore, it is important to establish at the beginning how much searching, review, and capture of results is enough for a given purpose or at what point the prospect of winning any more diminishes to near zero.

When important decisions are to be made based on results, it becomes all the more important that the completeness of the search is sufficient that no major reference is overlooked; the search engines and sites most likely to be productive have all been queried; and the additional leads found in initial search results have been incorporated into follow-up searches. For fairness in using cybervetting, a similar process must be applied for all candidates (or all candidates in certain categories, such as those seeking high-level clearances), so that there will be no discrimination in who is searched or the reach of the search. Because most of the references will be positive or neutral, the goal of the search is not to find what is derogatory (because that may not exist), but rather to meet the requirements set for a "full search." The full search is to be defined by policy, which should describe the scope of the search as its most important attribute. When I searched Federal Bureau of Investigation (FBI) indices for references to a person of interest, in 28 years, I always found more than one person with the same name. On the Internet, the prospect that you will find only one of a kind, whether it is a person, business, or another search term, is low. Some people's names are also common words (e.g., Baker, Price), so many references found will have nothing to do with the subject. Accuracy is essential because there are not always secondary identifying factors to use in evaluating whether to attribute a reference to the subject of interest, such as with federal court indices, where names alone are used for parties to criminal, civil, and bankruptcy cases. It is possible to report items that may or may not be identifiable with the subject, but doing so may detract from the value of the report and raise questions that need resolution. Factors that can help determine whether a reference is identifiable with a subject (besides having the same name) include geographical location; identifying numbers (e.g., Social Security number); physical description; age/date of birth; education; employment; city or community; activities; hobbies; sports; photos; advocacy (i.e., espousing the same position on topics); family; friends; and associations. The name of the subject can also be important because name variations, nicknames, misspellings, and the like are common. The decision to report a questionable reference should depend on the relevance, and potential seriousness of the behavior or content, if it proves true and attributable to the subject.

In vetting people and firms, it is often possible to find many references attributable to the subject with a relatively high degree of accuracy. However, often the purpose of the search is to determine whether there are any derogatory references (e.g., arrests, civil suits, bankruptcies), and mountains of data that merely confirm what the requester already knows (e.g., address, employment, education) provide no added value. Required report contents should therefore be determined based on the purpose of the search before the search begins. A report can contain a complete profile of the subject, including all known, verified attributes; only specified biographical items; or only derogatory or previously unknown data. How many prior addresses are needed in the report? Establishing the manner in which results will be reported makes the report ideally suited to the purpose for which it was requested and perhaps a much shorter task to accomplish (e.g., report only bad behaviors).

Reliable sources exist on the Internet, but not all sources are equally reliable. Some sources (e.g., media reports) are generally reliable, but we all know of examples when the news media got the story wrong, and there is a reason that nearly every newspaper runs a corrections column. The analyst must assess the nature of the source: Is this a publisher whose purpose is to convey information (e.g., an obituary, list of graduates), to present well-documented events (e.g., a court case), or to argue for a viewpoint (e.g., a blog advocating a side on an issue)? An address directory is likely to be correct in most instances, but a social site posting may be a cruel joke. An Internet intelligence analyst must apply classical library or journalist standards to the evaluation of the reliability of the sources used and the confidence placed in the particular items reported. If appropriate, it will be necessary to find other sources to help verify the item or at least shed light on the authoritativeness of the source.

Verifying information found on the Internet can be tricky. For example, finding a biographical profile of a subject can be helpful, but the first questions are these: Who posted it? Was it fact-checked? Is there independent confirmation of its contents? Many Internet searchers accept the contents of a LinkedIn profile as factual, but forget that the subject himself or herself likely posted it. Likewise, other business, social networking, and job placement sites contain autobiographical curricula vitae (CV). Because a considerable percentage of résumés, job applications, and self-descriptions contain exaggeration and outright untruths, it helps to compare fact-checked biographies with those of the subject. Even then, profiles should not be presumed accurate because a business will ask its executive to provide the biography posted, and there are few sources online that post CVs that are authored by someone independent of the subject. This illustrates the difficulty of verifying what you find online. Among many examples of "facts" I found online in the past 8 years are the following:

- An erroneous police department posting of a "most wanted" person who had already been arrested, tried, convicted, and served time for the offense
- A government database of those sanctioned for misbehavior, accessible on the Internet, that contained no reference to a severe punishment issued to a person who was found listed in the same government agency's online newsletter as having been punished

- A young entertainer whose face appeared in obscene poses as well as "wet T-shirt" photos online, but the obscene pictures were phony, "Photoshopped" frauds
- Four individuals with the same first name, middle initial, and last name, of similar ages, living in a 6-mile radius in a top-10 city suburb, two of whom had similar backgrounds
- Several individuals whose criminal records appeared in online references, but not in court records retrieved by a paid data broker, and several others who had more criminal and civil court records than were found by data brokers

Just because it can be difficult to verify facts found online does not mean that it is a bad idea to collect and analyze online intelligence. Some policy makers currently forbid their staffs any use of the Internet in vetting to avoid the possibility of error. Unfortunately, every database, whether government or privately owned, is apt to contain errors.[2] The key analytical issues to be confronted are whether the purported fact in question is material to decision making; whether the fact has more than one authoritative source, reporting substantially the same thing (and not all coming from the same source); and whether it is necessary to take additional steps prior to using the fact in a judgment. Once the analyst, reporting supervisor, and client settle on a mode of operation for critical fact verification, it is relatively easy to handle issues that arise. For instance, prior to using a finding in an adjudication, an interview with a third party or the subject of the inquiry may be necessary, and often, this step can provide the most fair resolution when the derogatory information should not stay "on the record" if it is not true. The issue of verification illustrates why sound policies are necessary for Internet intelligence, just as they have been for centuries in taking testimony from witnesses or references. Before a judge, the currency of information can make the difference between a law enforcement officer being granted or denied a warrant.[3] The reason is simple: If the information is out of date, it may not justify the warrant. This principle is analogous to the US adjudicative guidelines for determining eligibility for access to classified information, which ask whether the misbehavior found is very old and may represent a lapse that occurred before the individual corrected himself or herself.[4]

On the Internet, finding the "time/date stamp" for references is not always simple. Some postings are undated, some carry an automatically updated current day, some only have a copyright at the bottom of the page, and some relate when the item was originally written and when it was last updated. In looking at a person's or entity's history, it can be important to determine when certain events occurred, so it is important for analysts to record dates where available. Standard references include the reported date of publication and the date that the item was retrieved from the Internet. Because the content of the Internet changes frequently, items found are apt to disappear. Merely reporting the text of a posting with its uniform resource locator (URL, web page address) may not provide a client a view of the web page as posted because the client cannot return to the same source web page if it is removed from the website or altered. A copy of the page should therefore be retained. When historical information is found (e.g., date of graduation, period of employment), it is helpful to include the date posted to judge the accuracy of the content. Like all investigative activities, Internet collection requires attention to dates and times whenever they are available.

Efficiency and timeliness in investigations can become key issues, especially when a deadline is set to complete reporting. In Internet inquiries, it is possible to find a large number of potential references using search engines and databases, but reviewing, analyzing, and reporting the results can be time consuming. When my practice started, our method was to use various search engines and favorite websites from a long list we compiled to find the references to a subject. The list of URLs used grew and grew (with some deletions) as more and more potentially productive websites appeared on the Internet, all offering a portal for finding information. We found that "serial searching" can take days, and it would not be unusual to spend several workdays on one subject. Manually going from link to link is slow. Soon, we found ways using metasearch engines, automated searching, and a refined list of URLs better suited to the subject to reduce the search time required for a subject with many references from up to 40 hours down to about 2 hours. Nevertheless, it is necessary for the analyst to "grind out" the review of each potential reference because available computer software applications have not yet reached the stage at which a program can replace the human analyst.[5]

To ensure that cybervetting input into an investigative report is completed in a timely fashion, using the least possible analyst resources, an enterprise should determine a reasonable scope for each project, allocating the time available to complete the tasks within the deadline. When the analyst finds it impossible to complete all assigned tasks on time or finds additional leads that appear to offer more or potentially better information, the report may still be completed on time, with a notation that some references could not be reviewed and indicating what type of information may still be available. In my experience, examples of difficult searches include common names (many false positives), prolific Internet users (with many references), and subjects who have large numbers of lengthy or complex references to be reviewed. When Internet vetting becomes the norm, it will be necessary for employers to define what constitutes a complete search because there may be data in any inquiry left undiscovered or not reviewed. Because every collection project will vary, it is reasonable to define a standard in terms of the time spent, tools used, references reviewed, skills of the analyst and reviewer, and similar attributes of the effort. By defining the expectations for each type of search or each individual search conducted, the enterprise can ensure that a sound, fair method is applied. Additional experience inevitably makes the process more efficient, and new tools often help make searching more efficient and effective. Because it is not prudent to avoid Internet searching entirely or to conduct incomplete and inept spot searching, a best-effort approach within the available resources and time constraints is productive, cost-effective, and ethically sound.

Training Analysts

The level of training of an analyst conducting Internet intelligence operations has a direct correlation with the level of success achieved. Therefore, in such activities as cybervetting, trained analysts should be used to the maximum extent possible. It is common for business and government employees today to be self-taught in such computing functions as desktop applications (e.g., browsers, word processors, and spreadsheets) and Internet search. There are several cybervetting courses available to law enforcement, private security, and investigators in the private intelligence realm,[6] but they can be costly and should be updated as the ever-changing Internet offers new tools and techniques. Once an analyst has received introductory-level training, the single best way to learn is to conduct research in the sites, search engines, and databases online and topics relating to Internet resources that can improve the analyst's productivity. Collaboration with others similarly employed is helpful. Providing the tools for the analyst to use is crucial, as is tutoring in the use of those tools. Chapter 18 specifically addresses automated search tools. An analyst who will be expected to conduct Internet vetting routinely should be given at least a basic set of automated tools because these help ensure that a large number of potential sources are queried in every search. Not only do more advanced methods and tools assist the analyst in providing more efficient services, but also they help confirm that the process is fair, complete, and effective.

One way to help ensure that proper policies and procedures are applied to Internet searching is to require that analysts log their activities and preserve the results of searches. When search engines and automated searching are used, the analyst can capture and store the list of references found. When Web pages are located containing substantial information that will be included in the report, the analyst should capture images of web pages found (e.g., by printing the pages in PDF form), store the pages, and include copies with the investigative report. When newer analysts are in training, tutors can help them to review the links found, references reviewed, items chosen for reporting, and the recording of URLs and pages chosen. Should a report be disputed or facts called into question, it is then possible to return to the original search material and review it for any normal reporting attribute—completeness, accuracy, verification, and so on.

Because each enterprise may be held responsible for the integrity and methodology used by investigators in producing Internet intelligence, the policies and procedures established to guide the investigators are important. Allowing individuals to determine when and how to search, and how to use results and make decisions based on self-determined criteria, could potentially result in collection and reporting that conflict with enterprise principles or create liability. An organization properly may place no restrictions on individual employees' use of Internet search tools for their own, work-related enlightenment. However, all enterprises should recognize the potential power of adding competent Internet searching to the collection and analysis of the information used in business decision making. In my practice, I have found that when two or more analysts focus on the same topics, the results are often better than when only one person does the task, and a reviewer (supervisor, editor, publisher) can strengthen the results that an individual analyst obtains. Everyone has access to the library, but it takes a librarian-analyst with practice and training to obtain the best results from the great global library of the Internet.

Open-Source Intelligence Process

For those contemplating becoming a professional in open-source intelligence, complete training is recommended. Because organizations are apt to task employees with Internet searching as one of their "other duties as assigned," what follows is a brief summary of how a relative Internet novice can work to high intelligence standards when carrying out Internet intelligence duties. As with all work activities, great improvement comes from better training and more experience.

The purpose of intelligence and investigation is to find facts that allow decision makers to reach conclusions. To do so, open-mindedness, objectivity, a broad scope of general knowledge, curiosity, and determination are helpful to the researcher. Whether the subject is a person, company, organization, or topic, all of the subject's attributes are potentially important and so should be found and considered by the collector and analyst in formulating which attributes are relevant for decisions and appropriate for inclusion in the report. However, the focus of the inquiry may be defined more narrowly by the client.

The client's requirements and the collector's standards control the scope, value, timing, and format of reports. Often, misbehavior plays a powerful role in decisions, and thus finding evidence of delinquency is an object of inquiry. Verification of the truthfulness, trustworthiness, qualifications, and eligibility of individuals, organizations, and groups is also a frequent goal. Some think that the goal of vetting is to find instances of misbehavior, but in reality, the purpose is to find evidence about the subject to enable and support a decision about eligibility, qualifications, and fitness. Sometimes, investigators cut their process short when they find significant indicators of unworthiness, but it is just as important to find mitigating circumstances and verify the occurrence, seriousness, frequency, and impact of alleged wrongdoing within the time available and guidelines for collection. All inquiries seek certainty, but all collectors must exercise a certain degree of healthy skepticism, even if convincing evidence has been found. In the end, the people entrusted to investigate must seek the truth; thus, the process should always include verification if it is available. Clients should be counseled to seek further verification of derogatory information and interview the subject, if appropriate, to ensure that any adverse decision contemplated is based on all the facts. Sound practice may require that the subject be confronted with any allegations so he or she is given the opportunity to refute them. It is then up to the client to make final judgments based on the findings.

The intelligence collection process begins when the collector chooses sources and methods designed to find the facts needed to meet the goals of the case, within the resources and time available, to the client's specifications.[7] Sourcing is critical to success. Where the Internet is concerned, the analyst must begin with the assumption that the Internet may have changed, even in the recent past, and it may be necessary to add, delete, or otherwise change the mix of online sources to be used. Continual monitoring of activities using Internet sources is increasingly important to decision makers in such areas as investments, risk management, brand protection, employee vetting, operational security, and competitive intelligence. It may be worth the extra time to conduct a search for (new) sources prior to researching the topic at hand. Specific Internet sources are listed in later chapters.

Responsible open-source intelligence depends on application of the well-established principles of all research, with added emphasis on assessment. When an authoritative or unique source provides ostensibly factual information, and especially when online sources with no history of reliability are used, due diligence requires asking and answering a set of appropriate questions. A short list of those questions includes the following:

1. How factual is the information? Determining the accuracy of online information may not be easy. The Internet's wide range of sources and purposes includes fantasy, games, social interaction, comedy, deliberately altered content, controversial opinions, argumentation, religious zealotry, scientific controversy, and artistic expression, to name just a few. Media online and various organizations report results of surveys, opinion polls, and statistical trends that seem to change and vary and that have differing credibility. Even data-reporting measurements, time/date, and geospatial data can be skewed, falsified, or superseded by corrections not present in a posting. For example, some satellite map photographs might not provide recent, accurate, up-close, or clear views of the sites depicted. Some Wiki postings are deliberately slanted to manipulate the reader. Reports of events online are a good case in point. Web postings describing events involving civil disorders taking place in China, Iran, Burma, Venezuela, North Korea, and other media-controlled countries may lack the scope, accuracy, and verification expected from countries with a free press. The usual intelligence and news media sourcing are unavailable, so analysts may have to rely on unverified eyewitness reports from Twitter, blogs, e-mails, posted videos, and so on. The inherently risky reporting of events abroad becomes even more problematic when sources cannot be authenticated, facts verified, and potentially explosive content (e.g., bloody police-protester confrontations) put in context in a timely manner. Although the opportunity for almost anyone to post on the World Wide Web from

anywhere has brought the world closer to us all, the need to derive consistent meanings from millions of voices is challenging. To determine the facts from Internet sources, analysts must consider the following related to the sources:

■ Identity
■ Bias
■ History
■ Sponsorship
■ Closeness to the facts/events
■ Expertise
■ Potential to err
■ Accuracy
■ Timeliness

The authoritativeness of the source is no guarantee of the factuality of events, observations, and items reported, but it can help address the accuracy, completeness, honesty, and intent of reports. The next logical test is whether other sources report the same things. Traps in multiple-source verifications include repeated reporting of the same individual source's data, which occurs when source specificity is absent. The media are especially inclined to pick up reporting from other publications and repeat an original report as their own, without verification. Sometimes, mere repetition leads to acceptance of a report as fact. Also, summaries of multiple reports, estimates, surveys, and projections can provide differing impressions, depending on timing and circumstances. Data completeness can clash with deadlines, and conclusions may differ as time goes on. So, while the ideal of multisource verification should be sought, each item should be judged on its own merits.[8]

2. What is the attribution of the posting? Did the subject really make the online "confession," complete with video, for the world to see? Collectors should approach an online posting skeptically, as an artifact that can be analyzed for the likelihood that it is what it appears to be or may not be what it seems. If the posting contains facts, it may be necessary to verify them offline. A post we found had a photo of a wild-looking young man at a New Year's Eve party with a caption something like "Joe on Meth." Perhaps Joe was drunk or even on drugs, but the photo, which was tagged with Joe's true name, apparently was posted by an anonymous "friend." Fortunately, it was possible to identify the friend from his user name, and clearly, interviews would be in order before attributing the use of drugs to Joe. Some clients would prefer not to pursue this kind of posting, but if Joe is addicted to drugs, he may not be a prime candidate for hiring or granting a clearance.

3. How can the online data be verified? This is the classic intelligence dilemma because there may be only one source for an item that could cause an adverse judgment. In processing this type of information, the intelligence collector

must look for separate reports and sources confirming the report and try to find other ways that the item can be verified. Sometimes, the Internet can provide evidence hiding in plain sight, as in the case of a subject with several reported instances of foreign travel to countries hostile to the United States, who had posted numerous photos of herself in various scenes at tourist sites in those countries. In a way, too much has been made about the parts of the Internet that cannot be trusted. Intelligence analysts do not seem to have great difficulties assessing supermarket tabloids as intrinsically different from the mainstream press, and experienced Internet analysts will also be able to weigh the credibility of online sources. As with all intelligence reporting, when an item may not be supported by independent evidence, there is a way to portray that information to the client while cautioning the client that it lacks verification.

Reporting of Internet investigative results should be done to the same standards required of reports from other sources. Topical headings can be used to organize the data into related groups. Each item should have a source citation—the URL from which the item was taken. Where the item may be material to a decision, a copy of the web page should be captured (PDF format preferred) and appended to the report. Examples of reports are included in Chapter 19.

Quality Control

To provide professional results, Internet intelligence collectors should draft reports that are reviewed prior to submission to the client. The reviewer and collector must develop and apply methods to ensure that the report of an Internet search is

- Accurate, that is, the search terms used are correct and the results are captured in a forensically valid manner. In most cases, this means that spelling must be double-checked, and Web pages containing content of search results are captured. Digitally signing findings also ensures that the analyst can verify that the image remains the same when reviewed later. Some utilities (e.g., programs that download web pages) normally date/time stamp the action for later verification. To be accurate, the contents of findings (e.g., names, places, dates, and descriptions) must be verified or at least be consistent with known facts. Items should be labeled or flagged if their content is actionable, comes from a unique source and remains unverified, or if there is doubt about accuracy, particularly if the item is derogatory in nature. The single greatest danger in using Internet intelligence is in accepting findings as fact without verification, which impugns the integrity of the report.
- Thorough, that is, as many logical search engines, sites, and potential sources of data on the topic as possible are queried for references. It is a common

mistake for Internet searches to be conducted quickly and sloppily, omitting logical sources out of ignorance or laziness. Further searching on new terms, based on findings, can result in more and better results. If the search is part of an open-source intelligence collection process, the results will not be professional if the search is not comprehensive. Because Internet collection and analysis can be time consuming, there is an optimal balance in each situation between the time/labor available, research goals, and judging when "enough is enough." But, certainly, Google alone is not enough.

■ Timely, that is, contains up-to-date information, delivered within any required deadlines. Good analysts search, analyze, and report more rapidly than others, but it is hard to say that any research is complete and final because there are so many different sources and, often, so many references to include or discount. A key danger in Internet intelligence searching and analysis is the compulsion to continue searching or stop prematurely. The analyst's sense of when the process is as complete and accurate as possible is the art of the process.

■ Fair, that is, includes references and details that have a high probability of being accurate and complete, without false references, major missing pieces, or subjective input from the analyst (including the analyst's prejudice), and adherence to the standards set for the conduct of the process. People are rightly concerned about their personal privacy in the Internet age. However, individual subjects (and their acquaintances) publicly post a great deal of data of potential relevance to an Internet search for background vetting, due diligence, or the like. To be fair, a search report must not violate the Title VII discrimination standards (e.g., race, religion, national origin) and must respect the rights, including privacy rights, of subjects of inquiry. At this writing, *fear of violating privacy rights or feelings of individuals is the single biggest reason why necessary Internet searching is officially avoided by some government and business employers.*

In the intelligence community in the information age, the Internet provides just another type of open-source information—another INT, if you will (like HUMINT and SIGINT[9]), perhaps WEBINT or CYBINT.[10] Incorporating online findings into all types of intelligence and investigative reporting should not pose difficult challenges and is already being done to a large extent. To the degree that specialization and further automation are required to derive the best possible information from WEBINT, there is progress being made. For background vetting and some types of investigations, additional policies and procedures are required to meet the same level of reliability as that found from other sources. The tools, techniques, and training, along with quality controls used, will determine success in adopting Internet searching as an added resource for collection.

Notes

1. I and my team, doing business as iNameCheck, 2005–present, developed user requirements for Internet searches.
2. Holstege, Sean, Legal-Worker Database Flawed, National Hiring System Shows 4% Error Rate, *The Arizona Republic*, June 30, 2007, http://www.azcentral.com/arizonarepublic/news/articles/0630pilot0630.html?&wired (accessed June 2, 2010). Based on decades of news media reports, this story actually shows a rather good rate of error compared to such notorious records systems as the three major credit bureaus or the Immigration and Naturalization Service.
3. Federal Rules of Criminal Procedure, see http://www.law.cornell.edu/rules/frcrmp/ (accessed August 21, 2010).
4. Adjudicative Guidelines for Eligibility for Access to Classified Information, http://www.gpo.gov/fdsys/granule/CFR-2011-title32-vol1/CFR-2011-title32-vol1-part147/content-detail.html (accessed March 31, 2014).
5. Eight years of reviewing available software for conducting and filtering Internet searches has produced only a few viable systems for small, private investigative agencies.
6. My firm and at least two other businesses offer Internet search methodology training, which can range from 90 minutes to 40 hours, and can be customized for the class.
7. Intelligence cycle as described simply by the Central Intelligence Agency (CIA), https://www.cia.gov/kids-page/6-12th-grade/who-we-are-what-we-do/the-intelligence-cycle.html (accessed April 1, 2014).
8. Pew Research Journalism Project lists ethics codes from authoritative sources, helping to identify attributes of honest, objective reporting; see http://www.journalismethics.ca/online_journalism_ethics/gatekeeping.htm (accessed April 1, 2014).
9. HUMINT is the intelligence community's acronym for human intelligence, and SIGINT for signals intelligence (INT, short for intelligence).
10. WEBINT for Web intelligence, or CYBINT for cyber intelligence.

Chapter 14

Proper Procedures for Internet Searching

Introduction

Proper procedures are needed for Internet searching when an organization establishes a policy for the use of intelligence gleaned from the Internet, such as for background vetting, due diligence, competitive intelligence, and clearances. Practical methodology is covered in Section IV. This chapter is concerned with the strategy adopted by an agency or private entity for formal controls on the collection, analysis, and reporting of information from the Internet in compliance with management policy, including security. Such controls became necessary because of the proliferation of sources of information accessible from the Internet and the wildly varying nature (quality, accuracy) of the data, as well as malware, online. If the Internet is used for collecting certain types of data, such as government records, scientific research citations, press accounts, or product descriptions, there is only limited concern about the attributes of that data (as set out in Chapter 13, such as verification). However, social networking, blogs, chat, and even posted videos and photographs have decidedly less reliability. One way of looking at the nature of data available over the Internet is to examine the disclaimers ever present on websites that essentially exempt the host from the necessity of vouching for the accuracy, completeness, and usability of the data presented. Such disclaimers speak to the expectation that the percentage of data with errors could be relatively high (or perhaps the website hosts do not trust computers).

Criteria

As outlined in previous chapters, application of criteria for assessing the credibility and value of information found on the Internet rests first with the collector and reviewer. When information is collected to support a decision-making process of consequence, the value, accuracy, and reliability of any source used must be considered. This is all the more important with Internet data. Each organization must decide for itself whether to have a policy and set procedural standards for using Internet sources, but among the areas where it is prudent to have such criteria are the following:

- Vetting individuals for hiring, employment decisions, clearances, and due diligence
- Vetting firms as suppliers and partners and for mergers and acquisitions
- Product and brand protection
- Competitive intelligence
- Enterprise security
- Criminal and administrative investigations

A philosophical baseline analogous to the hearsay rule[1] applies to records based on Internet intelligence: If the source is a record created in the normal course of business, with a "business-grade" expectation of accuracy and reliability, then the information would normally be deemed credible. If the source's reliability is unknown, or the content is based on rumor, word of mouth, recollection, or a record created long after the fact, then additional verification will be needed before considering the information credible. The analogy is useful to an enterprise because when information rises to the level of intelligence or evidence (i.e., becomes the basis for a decision), it must meet higher standards. Ultimately, the question is: Will the finding be accepted by a court? Statistics are a good example of the dilemma facing the analyst because the old joke about lies, damn lies, and statistics often applies. The Internet can, for example, be a particularly useful tool to find different sources for statistical information on the same topic, so it stands to reason that a report can include numbers from various sources found on the Internet. The key to ensuring that such reports are reliable is that the data presented are up to the same standard, whether from the Internet or other sources.

Based on the principles presented to this point, the procedures that should be considered for implementation by organizations for the types of Internet intelligence listed include the following:

- Establishing a cadre of trained, skilled Internet investigative analysts as part of the organization's security, research, legal, or personnel departments or as an independent entity, like a library, serving the whole enterprise
- Providing tools, training, policies, and procedures for the Internet analysts and ensuring that they are utilized when the Internet is exploited for decision support

- Subjecting reporting that includes Internet data to periodic ethical and analytical review (i.e., audits) to ensure that the quality and reliability meet organizational norms and comply with laws, regulations, and ethical guidelines

If the organization decides to outsource Internet investigations (alone or as part of its strategy of background vetting, corporate intelligence collection, etc.), the same approach and standards as outlined should be required of the service provider chosen.

At the highest level of performance, it is also possible to set out the key requirements that Internet analysts are expected to meet in their day-to-day functions, which include developing primary and alternative Internet sources along with criteria for credibility thereof; keeping up with Internet changes to add new sources when possible and replace those no longer useful; following the development of tools to make searching more efficient; monitoring legal decisions, statutes, ethical norms, and guidelines for the use of Internet data in specified areas (e.g., vetting); reviewing authorized use and privacy policies of specific source websites, such as social networking sites; and maintaining high ethical work standards. If an organization treats Internet investigative analysts as a specialized group of professionals, their work product will support enterprise decision making. Without this kind of approach, it is possible that costly errors can arise from incomplete or flawed information found by inept googling in the normal course of business, and it is probable that such important decisions as hiring will be subject to charges of discrimination because random and unskilled searching and reporting by untrained individuals will seep into the hiring process and threaten its integrity.

Organizations often avoid taking necessary steps toward progress until they are forced to invest the time and resources by events outside their control, including regulation and competition. In the case of Internet intelligence, a tipping point was reached at least 7 to 10 years ago, when the quantity, quality, and price of data on almost any subject became too great to ignore. The risk of inaccuracy and the skills needed to exploit the Internet efficiently have held back many firms, which often allow staff to use the Internet as they see fit. Professional researchers, including librarians, understand that the Internet is now an essential part of information collection and analysis on any topic. Law enforcement, intelligence analysts, corporate investigators, librarians, and researchers have similarly high standards for the reliability of sources. Provided that they have institutional support, such professionals can be trusted to exploit the Internet for all of their normal tasks. However, without such institutional support, they are left to their own devices and personal discretion in the handling of Internet information. Because of their experience and training, this type of professional analyst should have a role in establishing the procedures, if not also the policies, to be applied by enterprises in utilizing Internet data.

A metaphor used previously for the Internet is a neighborhood where all the doors are screen doors. Because skilled investigators are able to look into the homes, past the screen doors, it is important to include ethics training with the legal training provided for them. Investigators who are active in social and professional networking and in tracking people online will become aware of a great deal of privileged information, including subjects' personally identifying information, provocative and interesting anecdotes, startling and disturbing human behaviors, and facts that may include misbehavior by high-ranking or well-known members of their own enterprise. Because many of today's investigators are part of the very open, highly networked world of Internet information sharing, it is especially important that they understand the discretion and confidentiality with which they are routinely entrusted. Periodically updated reminders of their ethical responsibilities are necessary to ensure that these investigators do not divulge information to which they have become privy in the course of their work, especially online. Further, the ease of collection and reporting of sensitive personal information about subjects and others found online must not lead investigators to be casual in their handling of the data, discriminate against people who live alternate lifestyles, or otherwise act irresponsibly with confidential data.

Because many subjects investigated online are likely to be highly sensitive to the impact on their personal privacy (regardless of the fact that they have posted their information for anyone to see on the Internet), investigators need to take special care to protect the data found. When an investigator finds during cybervetting that a photograph posted publicly shows Phil looking funny in his Speedo, one must resist the impulse to pass the image around.

Based on the legal and policy standards reviewed, it appears that litigation is inevitable if individuals are sanctioned by employers for Internet behavior on or off the job because privacy and the limits of cybervetting have yet to be fully litigated. That probability makes it imperative to have proper policies and procedures for Internet searching for background investigations (just as employers do for other sources used in vetting).

Security

Conducting Internet searching exposes the investigator not only to a multitude of security issues that are of concern to anyone on the Internet but also to additional risks that arise from the nature of searching.[2] It is essential that analysts understand the types of dangers they face online, which, while endemic to Internet users in general, are magnified by the number of searches conducted, particularly with search engines.[3] Significant risks for Internet searchers include the following:

■ Malicious code found on websites, in downloads (e.g., in documents, spreadsheets, images, audio files, browser add-ons, games, programs and HTML [HyperText Markup Language])

- False references, including misidentification (e.g., same and similar names), deceptive postings, "humorous" but untrue texts and images, and nonidentifiable information
- Social site postings that reveal too much about people (e.g., contact information, family and friends, confidential business data, with too few privacy protections)
- Failing to isolate the computer used for searching from that used to transact or store business, banking, or online purchases and for storage of sensitive personal information (because of the risk of infection)
- Assuming that downloaded data are low in risk
- Searching in such a way that it creates a security risk for the client or the subject of the search (e.g., by leaving evidence of a search or "visit" online, retrievable by others)

Numerous government, business, and media reports have documented that there are organized criminal groups, "crackers," and malicious individuals who use the Internet to commit fraud and a variety of crimes, including identity theft and remote takeovers of others' computer systems through implanted programs ("bots") controlled through networks of directed systems ("nets"), comprising "botnets." Controllers of botnets use them to harvest banking, commercial accounts, credit card information, and commercial secrets; launch spam e-mail campaigns and phishing; and conduct distributed denial-of-service attacks and for takeover attempts aimed at penetrating computer systems. Among the botnet masters have been organized criminals from Russia, Eastern Europe, America, China, and others, including intelligence operators supporting nations' Internet warfare methodology. Botnets allow controllers to hide their identities, conduct mass attacks, spread malicious code to more potential victims, and "park" data on unwitting parties' systems without detection. The key factors allowing botnets to control literally millions of computers are zero-day attacks using undiscovered security vulnerabilities, successful social engineering, and users' failure to keep security up to date, allowing implantation of malware without detection. These factors make botnets a major national security issue.[4]

The prevalence of viruses, worms, and other malware is not the only issue Internet intelligence analysts must anticipate. Porn is everywhere online, as are illicit and illegal offers of prescription drugs, software, and gambling, to name a few of the most popular off-color distractions. Porn is a special issue because child pornography is considered intrinsically illegal in the United States: Production, possession, trading in, or sharing child porn is a felony. Many porn sites emphasize youthful images and actions, whether the individuals involved are underage or not. If a search encounters porn, analysts must be careful not to capture images that are child pornography. Because of this, many researchers avoid capturing images and systematically purge content that could remotely contain offensive images.

Because of malware and the possibility of downloading unwanted content during searching, those who intend to spend considerable time conducting Internet intelligence collection and analysis should consider the following approaches:

- Use a separate computer system for Internet searching. This might be a remote system (a "virtual workstation"). The analyst and system administrator should be prepared to rebuild the collection machine, if necessary, if it becomes debilitated by malicious code or content downloaded from searches. If damage occurs to the machine, at least the analyst's and employer's primary systems are not impacted. A corollary is that because e-mail is often used for transmitting malicious code, users should consider separating the system used for e-mail from that used for the most sensitive personal and business data.

- Consider the right choices for browser, data capture, storage, and antivirus scanning. Because Internet Explorer from Microsoft is a prime target of malicious code writers, an alternative browser may reduce the vulnerability of infection. Other options include Firefox, Opera, Chrome, and Safari.

- Consider how to capture content. Because web pages are apt to change and there is no guarantee that a page will be cached or remain available, it is important to save an image of the page, which becomes part of the investigative file and perhaps of the report. Options include copy and save into a document or spreadsheet, save as an HTML copy, capture an image of the screen (e.g., by a snipping tool like that of Microsoft), or print into a PDF document. Some documents or spreadsheets do not actually save "embedded" web content, but rather save a link, so that a document might not be exactly what was composed if the Internet page changes. Using a PDF printed copy of the page does not guarantee an exact duplicate of the page's appearance (because of the different ways that web pages are composed, including dynamic content), but most often, the text is captured accurately and the analyst can be sure that the saved PDF will retain its content indefinitely. In addition, the PDF copy can be digitally signed, providing verification that it is identical to the image originally captured.

- Consider how and where to store content. Files containing the results of Internet searches may contain sensitive and valuable data. Evidence, intelligence, and information of use in decision making should be stored in a secure, reliable manner, like other vital business data. Personally identifying information should be protected against unauthorized access and misuse. Stored data should be indexed to facilitate retrieval, secured to limit access and deny use to unauthorized parties (usually through encryption), auditable, and support chain of custody (should court use become necessary). Besides the potential need for retrieval for further processing, files may contain data of value in subsequent investigations (e.g., a background investigation on an associate of an employee). Generally, investigative records should not be stored on the search machine because accidental infection with malware from searching could result in unwanted changes or unauthorized access to those files.

Standard Methodology

An organization is well advised to incorporate Internet sources into standard operating procedures, including methodology applied to investigations and intelligence collection. Based on the specific attributes of Internet searching as a source of information, especially as facts found online are used in decision making, it is important to have standard procedures in place. These should be consistent with policy and constitute a first line of defense for any allegation of unfairness or lack of professionalism in conducting investigations. A large number of agency heads with whom I have spoken about cybervetting have expressed the belief that their liability for *not* including the Internet in background investigations far outweighs potential liability from what is found. All have expressed confidence in judging facts from fiction in postings. Yet, few have a standard for how to handle the Internet, as opposed to other sources with which their investigators are far more familiar. As with any relatively new venture, Internet investigations benefit from establishment of norms that all can understand, and the standards adopted will help any enterprise in taking advantage of the wealth of data available online.

Notes

1. The hearsay rule in federal and state courts is generally defined as a statement made out of court that is offered as proof in court; see http://legaldictionary.thefreedictionary.com/Heresay+rule (accessed April 1, 2014).
2. Stone, Paul, Internet Presents Web of Security Issues, American Forces Information Service, US Defense Department, http://www.defense.gov/specials/websecurity/ (accessed April 1, 2014). Among the concerns found was "too much information" online about Department of Defense command-level persons.
3. Computer security tips from the US Computer Emergency Readiness Team (CERT), including browsing dangers, can be found at http://www.us-cert.gov/cas/tips/ (accessed April 1, 2014).
4. Comey, James B., FBI director, Statement Before the Senate Committee on Homeland Security and Governmental Affairs, Washington, DC, November 14, 2013, http://www.fbi.gov/news/testimony/homeland-threats-and-the-fbis-response (accessed November 25, 2013). Williams, Paul, Organized Crime and Cybercrime: Implications for Business, CERT Coordination Center, Carnegie Mellon University, 2002; botnet definition, http://searchsecurity.techtarget.com/sDefinition/0,,sid14_gci1030284,00.html (accessed June 2, 2010), also with descriptions of other online security issues.

INTERNET SEARCH METHODOLOGY

This section focuses on how to conduct effective Internet searches for investigative and intelligence purposes on subjects such as people, entities, and other topics. Some search projects may be limited by restrictions imposed by the client's policies or procedures or those of the investigative unit. The aim of the guidance presented here is to provide the best possible search methodology, limited only by the law and ethical practices.

Each subject is different, so each collection task should be approached with a combination of routine steps and steps customized to fit the specific subject. The routine steps should consist of established subtasks (usually the bulk of the work) and may include automated functions that retrieve data from an array of identified search targets. In addition, subtask variations appropriate to the geographical area, government jurisdictions, and biographical details should be added as appropriate. Customized subtasks should include queries of professional and personal reference sources and connections peculiar to the individual subject. It is useful for analysts conducting subtasks to maintain lists of search engines' and websites' uniform resource locator (URL) addresses for ready reference.[1] The search should be designed to survey the Internet, consult key websites, and find references that are responsive to the purpose of the task and, if possible, avoid unnecessary collection. For example, a search on a person or business might normally include looking at white and yellow pages directories to verify or discover addresses, telephones, fax numbers, e-mail addresses, and so on, but if contact information is not needed, that subtask can be disregarded.

Note

1. Berners-Lee, T., Masinter, L., and McCahill, M., Uniform Resource Locators (URL), Network Working Group, December 1994, http://www.ietf.org/rfc/rfc1738.txt (accessed April 28, 2014).

.

Chapter 15

Preparation and Planning

Introduction

Planning is essential to success in all intelligence and investigative collection. Exploitation of the vast quantities of data on the Internet and accessible databases potentially relevant to any topic can be greatly enhanced by preparation. Some preliminary queries may substantially add to the searcher's list of URLs (uniform resource locators) normally used for the type of subject being searched (e.g., people, businesses, brands), and some preparations should be done just before and during searching.[1] First, frame the question: What is known about the person, entity, or topic? Next, the search should be based on the following:

- Nature of the data needed: What is reportable?
- Purpose of the search (including potential uses of results)
- Best sources, including standard search engines and websites
- Geographical location
- Government jurisdiction(s)
- Resources available
- Time available (deadline)

After deciding on an initial search strategy, keyword choices should be made. Keywords should include all logical and likely variations of the name, nicknames, user names, e-mail addresses, and other identifiers that potentially could appear in Internet postings and databases. Reverse directories can be consulted for co-inhabitants, significant others, and relatives. Sometimes, postings by people or entities close to a subject can include items containing important information about the person or entity of interest. It may be desirable to combine keywords and use Boolean operators (and, not, or) to home in on the data specifically sought and perhaps find leads to further information. More about search strategy appears in this chapter, but it is important not to underestimate the value of preplanning.

Databases available via the Internet include both paid and free resources, from both commercial and government sources. An initial consideration includes whether to use a subscription service (e.g., LexisNexis's IRB, TLO, CLEAR) to find a profile of the subject based on such input as utilities, government and court records, real estate records, employment listings, licenses, credit data, and permits. One reason to consider this type of record check first is the rapidity with which it is possible to find a relatively reliable, detailed profile of a person or entity and confirm facts that will facilitate Internet searching, largely by allowing the analyst to eliminate references not identifiable with the subject using geography, age, and similar characteristics.

One aspect of subscription services that should be borne in mind is that their records and source data used for their profiles contain errors, so important details provided should be verified. If a subscription service is not available, it is possible to use a pay-as-you-go online service, such as

Intelius[2]
US Search[3]
InstantCheckMate.com[4]
PublicRecords360.com[5]

Please note that these examples are not being endorsed, and they represent only a few of the seemingly large number of online database service providers that appear to be growing in numbers and service offerings. Most of these data brokers provide reports on a graduated price scale, so that a "complete background" with an arrest check could be $100, but determination or verification of address and telephone number might be $4.50. Understanding the reliability of the underlying source data is important for evaluating any data broker. For example, only 10-finger national checks done by the Federal Bureau of Investigation (FBI) and state police using their fingerprint files (or in some instances, DNA files) can provide relatively certain arrest and conviction checks. Even the best law enforcement and court records, however, contain incomplete, inaccurate, or otherwise unreliable content, largely because the input is missing or flawed because of resource limits.[6]

Depending on the purpose, deadline of the search, and the resources allocated to it, a decision should be made about whether to use a fee-based service at the beginning, or defer that choice until the end of an Internet collection project, if most of the information needed is on hand or if it is expected that the data will be available from free online sources. As with all investigations, identifiers are needed for accurate fee-based searches, such as full name, address, phone, date of birth, or Social Security/tax number. *Comment*: One does not have to be a licensed private investigator to use many fee-based online data providers—one only needs a credit card. Researchers who routinely access data brokers' information as part of a paid service may be required to have private investigator licenses under many state and local laws. Because some data providers listed previously and others do not verify that online customers have licenses or any legitimate reason to collect information on people, it is possible that criminals or those with malicious intentions could amass a dossier on anyone.

Internet vetting of people in support of employment background investigations can be the singular tasking of an analyst, and if so, the analyst should assemble a routine list of planned searches. However, when other types of investigations are conducted, the starting point may not be a detailed application or résumé, but rather a few initial facts that may only include a telephone number, e-mail address, name, or nickname. In these types of cases, the search plan is fundamentally different from repeated production of background facts. The analyst-investigator must use a series of searches to build the person's profile from whatever facts are available, and preparation must include a wide list of potential websites and sources that can help establish the identity of the subject and verify identifying information.

Many people think that by using a major search engine (e.g., Google, Bing, or Ask) and querying a handful of popular websites (e.g., Facebook, Twitter), they will find all the relevant information needed. However, that approach will not provide a thorough search. Most competent Internet investigators have a list of favorite search engines, websites, and databases that they routinely include in collection, and they will recognize leads from references found and frequently find productive sources outside their normal URL list, based on experience and initiative. Because so many social and business networking sites create communities of relatives, friends, fellow employees, association members, and "birds of a feather," it is often possible to find references to and even writings by a subject in postings under the profile of those close to him or her. Therefore, not only before the search begins but also as it is progressing, experienced analysts will find and incorporate new search terms designed to unearth hidden references. Productive searches may be done on a combination of the subject's name and that of an associate, an attribute (e.g. "sales," "poker," "sailing"), an institution, or a profession. For example, one obtains different results by searching my name alone and by adding "FBI."

It is worth mentioning that true integration of Internet searching into the investigative and intelligence processes means that when close associates of a subject are identified, solid leads for whom to interview as developed references will be found. Another important element in planning searches is to list websites where data may reside that have not been indexed by the major search engines and therefore may be part of the "invisible Web."[7] More is presented on that topic further in the chapter. Essentially, there are numerous databases accessible through Internet links that are not indexed by search engines. To find out if there are references to the subject in unindexed data, one needs to use the search interface provided on the host website to find stored information, rather than an Internet search engine. Government, university, library, private business, and media websites (to name just a few) provide access to databases that may contain substantial information about a search topic. For example, the current and archived stories of many news media sites can be searched online. Sometimes, there is a charge for accessing the full story behind a "hit" on the term searched (which may be presented in a brief excerpt). Often, an analyst must take care to conduct keyword searches in accordance with the database search protocol, which may differ from standard Google Boolean protocols. For example, the PACER (Public Access to Court Electronic Records) database of federal court records requires a search in the Last Name, First Name format. Dangers of this type of search include spending money to review and eliminate false positives and failure to find a record identifiable with the term searched. In any case, planning to include unindexed Internet content in searches is a necessary part of professional collection.

Whatever the experience of the analyst, it is possible to start the search plan with a list of websites (URLs) where it is most likely that relevant references will be found. In manual searching, as well as in mapping out potential automated searches, having a list of URLs categorized by content is necessary to carry out comprehensive search plans. A great benefit of major search engines is that they can provide excellent lists of sites on which various types of data should be located. Planning a search should include a quick review of the types of sites where the subject's references will most likely be found. Among the sources and tools available (see Chapters 16 and 17) that may be cataloged for use in a search are the following:

- Directories
- Search engines (including metasearch engines)
- Specialized tools (archives, media, including news, video, audio, photos, music)
- Unindexed sites (e.g., invisible or dark Internet data)
- Private or proprietary sites

In addition, sites containing blogs, social networking, government records, local news, associations, educational institutions, and similar content should be considered. Some of these websites may host substantial quantities of relevant but unindexed data or data indexed by a nickname unknown to the searcher.

Although there is no substitute for training and experience, many people have taught themselves to be relatively competent Internet analysts by conducting many searches. Students often learn approaches to finding data on the web that elude others because of the academic disciplines available on campus and mentors, including librarians, instructors, and fellow students who freely share their methods to help each other succeed.

The Library

Many people may overlook a priceless resource that can save time and add expertise to any Internet search and could be a close ally of professional analysts—the library.[8]

Whether in a university library, company research unit, government library, county facility, or city library, the librarian has been trained to help the user find where to obtain the answers needed. Intelligence researchers often forget that outside the agency or company, almost any librarian is pledged to provide unbiased, confidential assistance to help any client to find what he or she needs. Libraries not only contain volumes of data on any subject, but also today are apt to provide automated indexes of publications, people, entities, and topics that can lead an analyst to the most authoritative and useful content on the topic sought. Because libraries subscribe to fee-based directories, indices, bibliographies, periodicals (including research publications), business profiles, and other sources, they are important sources to consider when planning a project.

The Reference and User Services Association of the American Library Association defines reference transactions as "information consultations in which library staff recommend, interpret, evaluate and/or use information resources to help others meet particular information needs."[9] Today's library is likely to provide a website accessible to anyone on the Internet for general assistance and to library patrons with user credentials for specific services, possibly including access to subscription databases. Certain libraries provide helpful tutorials to assist in finding references on the Internet. For example, the Library of Congress has posted many excellent resources available over the web, such as an extensive list of online research resources at http://www.loc.gov/ (which includes search engines). The University of California at Berkeley posted a search engine tutorial at http://www.lib.berkeley.edu/TeachingLib/Guides/Internet/SearchEngines.html. The three search engines Berkeley profiled are Google, Yahoo (which is another manifestation of Bing), and Exalead. The Humboldt State University Library has posted a tutorial on research strategy by topic at http://www.libguides.humboldt.edu/guides. A tutorial providing frequently updated international search resources by Emeritus Prof. Wayne A. Selcher, PhD, of Elizabethtown College,[10] appears at http://www2.etown.edu/vl/starter.html. These are examples of excellent resources readily available to anyone, including professional Internet researchers.

A few hours' reading of search tips (found by googling "Internet search tips" or similar terms) can provide a good primer for new analysts and can update experienced searchers' skills. Beginners in Internet searching may not be inclined to think of themselves as fledgling librarians, but in fact, they are asked to understand at least where to find the online directories and catalogs they may need to use for any type of search. Having library resources available may save much time and expense. When an investigator is starting the search for a new subject in a new area, the librarian can probably reduce the time needed to plan the collection by suggesting good places to start. Print and electronic copies of such reference works as telephone and crisscross directories, biographies, lists of publications, business profiles, medical resources, journals, legal references, obituaries (often a source for the living as well as the dead), government databases, and scientific resources are available through the library. The trend in publishing reference materials, including encyclopedias and directories of all types, favors electronic databases over printed reference materials. Once a resource proves useful, the analyst should make a note about where to find it again and maintain a list of useful sources.

Scope Notes

The most important lesson I learned from over 8 years of Internet searching is that, based on client directions, time, and resource constraints, some of the most critical references to a subject may not be found, which can lead to the false impression that there are no derogatory references. The vast majority of investigations will show only favorable or neutral information about the subject. However, an inadequate search often misses key references. Examples of poor searching include links not reviewed, dependence on one or a few search engines and websites, failure to use all available keywords (e.g., name variations), and omitting alternative sources, such as looking only in government records when a news media reference may provide facts about arrests, convictions, and judgments.

Constraints imposed on searchers can also have an impact on results, such as when the assignment calls for using only a person's name and work or formal e-mail address or ignoring personal e-mail addresses, nicknames, handles, and similar additional keywords. The client's directives and search unit's policies control the search. Because of lingering uncertainty about the propriety of including off-duty activities in employers' cybervetting, some inquiries are destined to avoid the very references most likely to produce evidence of online misbehavior or other derogatory results.

Another aspect of scope is how much time and effort to spend looking for information using secondary search terms. Besides a person's name, nicknames, other identifiers, addresses, telephone numbers, e-mail addresses, and handles, references may be found by searching on a spouse, significant other, siblings, parents, children, friends, and associates. The analyst must decide how far into the community of online associations to pursue possible references to the subject. Areas that might be overlooked include photographs, videos, and similar media postings that can be tagged (indexed) in the name of the subject or to a person close to him or her.

It is important for the analyst to understand the potential for finding substantive information in seemingly unlikely places. For example, photographs of a foreign trip might raise important issues if a subject is seeking a clearance and has not reported the trip abroad or apparent associations with foreigners depicted, even if the content of the photos themselves seems benign.

Searching images, blogs, and other, more specialized activities may be productive. In planning the scope of a search, aligning the time allocation and search methods with limitations provided by the client can be critical to success. If the client is to be charged a fee for the search, scope is also vital to pricing because analyst time in searching, filtering, capturing, assessing, and reporting findings must be done at a rate that allows the service to stay within budget (and profit margin). Clients charged by the hour versus a firm fixed price make it easier to scope a search, while short deadlines can complicate the process. At this writing, Internet searching is generally a time-consuming business because it is necessary to take the time required to review the references found—something machines alone cannot yet do. Automation can, however, reduce the time spent and expand the scope and accuracy of searching. More on automation appears in the following material.

The starting point for planning the scope of a search is the subject (person, entity, topic) about which information is needed. If the name is all that will be used for searching, the scope will normally be limited to the name and all logical variations. If, in addition, the client's policies and procedures, tasking, and desired results have a broader scope, there are several other search terms and strategies that should be considered, including the following:

- Seek references on all identifiers, including nicknames, user names, e-mail addresses, handles, and so on of not only the subject but also selected family, friends, associates, fellow employees, classmates, and social networking friends.
- Review records available online for spouse, significant other, immediate family, ex-spouses, and so on (which sometimes reveals legal, employment, and behavioral issues that do not appear elsewhere).
- Use crisscross directories, "Whois" lookups (website registration data), and search on telephone numbers, Internet protocol (IP) addresses, websites, blogs, photographic images, video, and game sites where references to the subject or additional searchable identifiers may be found.
- Use cached or archived pages where older references to the subject on defunct web pages or websites no longer in existence are found.
- Use advanced searches and combinations of search terms to find references that otherwise might be in the usual haystack of search results hiding the needles.
- Review search engine results efficiently, such as by scanning thumbnails to find the most relevant quickly, starting with the first and last pages of results, changing the number of results per page (e.g., from the default 10 to 100), and reading the most promising links first, setting aside the others for scanning later.

Besides planning for search engine collection, an analyst should consider the list of more specific and "invisible web" sites where databases may contain references to the subject. Among these are business, college, association, government, volunteer, court, news media, real estate, and licensing databases (to name a few). Depending on the purpose of the search, consider querying lists posted by government and watchdog groups containing people and entities involved in illicit activities, including the Excluded Parties List (government contracting denied), OFAC (Treasury's Office of Foreign Assets Control sanctions), US Customs' online list of adverse rulings, Securities and Exchange Commission's (SEC's) enforcement actions, State Department's list of foreign terrorist organizations, Food and Drug Administration's (FDA's) debarment list, World Bank's list of ineligible contractors, and POGO's list of federal contractor misconduct, to name a few. A list of these types of websites appears in Chapter 17.

In addition to preparation for searching, organizations tasked with substantial quantities of searches of a repetitive nature on short deadlines may consider using specialized analysts, who focus on certain types of online records. For example, an analyst might be expert in government records from federal, state, county, and municipal databases. Another analyst might be accomplished in exploiting social networking, media, metasearch engines, or Internet chat rooms. Because of the need to include a large number of sources and assessments of findings in any search, parallel tasking can reduce the overall time needed to complete the assignment. Some duplication will result. When another specialist ("reports officer") is used to compile the draft investigative report from the input of the team, the resulting work can be more complete, cogent, and fully documented with the content and sources provided by the specialists. Having a routine method for documenting results facilitates the production of the final report, which is after all the aim of the exercise.

Collection and analysis in Internet intelligence go hand in hand, as initial expectations are revised based on findings, and follow-up searches on hunches provide unexpectedly good data or perhaps wash out. The search plan should be revised as the project progresses to ensure inclusion of all logical sources of information within the resource and time constraints available.

Not only is planning essential to achieve efficiency in Internet intelligence production, but also it is critical to lawful, principled, ethical investigation. Having a cogent, consistent approach protects the analyst and the client from possible claims of bias, unfairness, violation of privacy, and unethical conduct. Given the persistent proclivity of some to misbehave, it is likely that they will object and even go to court when their misdeeds are exposed by good online investigations. However, the organized investigator will be able to demonstrate that the search, analysis, and reporting were conducted within all appropriate norms, and the results are a proper depiction of the subject's behavior.

Notes

1. Hetherington, Cynthia, Web 2.0 Investigations that Move Beyond Google, ASIS International Webinar, February 17, 2010; Hock, Randolph, *The Extreme Searcher's Internet Handbook* (Medford, NJ: Cyber Age Books, 2004).
2. http://www.intelius.com/.
3. http://www.ussearch.com.
4. http://www.instantcheckmate.com/.
5. http://www.publicrecords360.com/.

6. Brien, Peter M., Improving Access to and Integrity of Criminal History Records, Bureau of Justice Statistics, US Department of Justice, July 2005, NCJ 200581, http://www.bjs.gov/content/pub/pdf/iaichr.pdf (accessed April 15, 2014). Neighly, Madeline and Emsellem, Maurice, Wanted: Accurate FBI Background Checks for Employment, National Employment Law Project, July 2013, http://www.nelp.org/page/-/SCLP/2013/Report-Wanted-Accurate-FBI-Background-Checks-Employment.pdf?nocdn=1 (accessed April 15, 2014).
7. Sherman, Chris, and Price, Gary, *The Invisible Web, Uncovering Information Sources Search Engines Can't See* (Medford, NJ: Information Today, 2001).
8. Cassell, Kay Ann, and Hiremath, Uma, *Reference and Information Services in the 21st Century, An Introduction*, 2nd edition (New York: Neal-Schuman, 2009).
9. Ibid.
10. Selcher, Dr. Wayne A., professor of international studies emeritus, Department of Political Science, Elizabethtown College, Elizabethtown, PA.

Chapter 16

Search Techniques

Introduction

Professionals looking for intelligence on the Internet find the effort fruitful, if not always easy. The information provided in this and the next two chapters assumes that the reader has some familiarity with personal computers (PCs) and surfing the Internet. This chapter provides pointers from those who rely on the Internet for open-source information on a daily basis. The bibliography contains reference volumes that provide a complete introduction to the Internet and its exploitation.

Internet Content

Well over half of the Internet is in the English language.[1] On the Internet, most web pages appear in HyperText Markup Language (HTML),[2] which allows the creation of, and access to, structured documents (including text, pictures, and other content), but many sites also have scripts and dynamic features in programming languages such as JavaScript[3] and effects provided by Flash Player[4] and other plug-ins. Engineers structure servers to face Internet users and back-end servers to provide access to databases and continually updated content, including advertising, to present what users want and what vendors or hosts choose to present. Thus, appearing on the Internet are text, gateways into databases, and dynamic content pulled into the browser in a combination of static and continuously changing spaces. Websites' displays of stock market updates, news headlines, moving pictures, live videos, and other content are designed to attract and entertain users, call attention to advertising, and communicate in more sophisticated ways than static, two-dimensional documents. The analyst needs to look beyond the flash and find the facts, then capture the web page contents needed (at least the text containing the facts found).

Fortunately for searchers, expertise in the Internet's structural components is not needed for finding intelligence. However, it is important to remember that the programming behind everything we see on the web is responsible for how it is displayed, and we should capture content using appropriate tools to ensure professional information collection and retention. Because the content of web pages can change frequently, it is imperative for an analyst/investigator to capture the reportable content properly at the time of the search.

Every Internet page has a uniform resource locator (URL) address (i.e., what you see in the box at the top of the browser), which is translated by a Domain Name System (DNS) server into the correct Internet protocol (IP) address, to which the browser is directed.[5] Visiting an Internet page allows the browser to pull its content (via a stream of packets) into a computer and onto a screen that the user can peruse. Each link on which the user clicks takes the browser to a new web page. Before clicking on a link, the user must decide whether it is a likely source of useful information. As Internet information collectors become more familiar with sources, they initially assess the potential authority, accuracy, and reliability of references by the URLs of websites found in search tools. Further, it is often necessary to trace the authors and owners of websites to collect and analyze information and find leads on those hosting and posting on the Internet (more on that in Chapter 17). Therefore, it is important to understand the basics of URLs, IP addresses, and their roles.[6]

The many types of Internet content can be daunting to analysts, as it is necessary to find ways to identify, filter, capture, evaluate, and report the text, photos, videos, audio, and other content about a subject of interest. Generally, the content is in digital format, so it can be copied and filed by the investigator and digitally signed if necessary to preserve its integrity as evidence.[7] The systems and tools available provide a solid start, but there is still no substitute for a trained, experienced, knowledgeable, and creative analyst who understands how to look for, find, assess, and report what is needed. Contrary to popular belief, there is no application—not even Google—that can easily find everything you seek.

The Browser

Using a computer's browser,[8] an analyst collects data from resources online and utilizes Google and other search engines to access websites. Professional investigators should become familiar with the functions of their browser when a search is conducted and may wish to experiment with different browsers to select the one most comfortable to use in searching. The popularity of browsers is measured differently by rival market organizations, and changes often, based on features favored by users. Besides Chrome (47% market share in some reckonings), Internet Explorer (25% market share), Firefox (about 20%), Safari, and Opera are popular browsers.[9]

Browser statistics are impacted by marketing claims, different versions of some brands (e.g., Internet Explorer), and built-ins (e.g., adware blockers that have an impact on statistics analysis derived from popular websites). Toolbars for browsers allow rapid access to search engines, providing add-on applications that can facilitate searching. Browsers may store URLs visited and cookies (tiny scripts) reflecting an interaction with a website. Browsers also may store copies of web page content (e.g., text and images), which may reside in temporary computer memory to speed up reloading of a web page. When investigations are sensitive, analysts may wish to consider whether it is prudent to store vestiges of searches on the computer used and therefore may wish to adjust the browser's settings. A user can browse in private mode and delete links, cookies, and temporary files created through the browser.

Depending on the tasks for which a search computer is used, advertising can appear on web pages, based on items purchased, products researched, and content from e-mails parsed by Google, Yahoo, AOL, and other Internet service providers. Scripts call up images and ads from websites and products indicated by the previous browsing and e-mail history of the machine. Therefore, an analyst may wish to be careful to separate browser use for personal purchases and e-mails from investigative searches. When an image of a web page is captured for an investigative report, it may be unwise to have items from the analyst's personal browsing that appear in the copy made and in the computers' caches of browsing history. Because cookies interact with websites visited, the investigator's browser should be free of personal history.

Another key consideration is that a great deal of searching will inevitably produce links to websites with malicious code[10] designed to infect a browser or workstation, often with the purpose of making the target computer a "zombie," stealing financial information, such as credit card or bank account data, or injecting adware into the browser. Even the most careful analyst clicks on links that pose dangerous risks to the investigative workstation because innocent websites may be attacked and infected or DNS servers reprogrammed to divert browsers to fake websites. Therefore, wise investigators deliberately use an "investigative box," that is, a workstation separate from their normal workstation or PC, to avoid the risks of infection and to allow rebuilding of the PC's operating system if it should suffer from a catastrophic attack. Any PC used for intelligence collection should be equipped with antivirus, antimalware, and firewall software, but those are not 100% effective. Because browsing websites is an indispensable part of investigations, care should be taken to limit potential damage.

The Search Engine

The search engine is a highly useful tool for collecting and analyzing information from the Internet, accessed with a browser. In the United States, the following is a recent depiction of the popularity (market share) of search engines:[11]

Google	67.6%
Microsoft	18.3%
Yahoo	10.4%
Ask	2.4%
AOL	1.3%

The reason Google is the tool of choice is that the developers of Google have created systems that provide rank-ordered views of references to the search term in very little time (usually in less than a second), gleaned from a much larger storehouse of data than any other search engine offers.[12] Google's tools (robots or bots, "Googlebots") are constantly crawling the Internet (i.e., surveying and recording or caching pages and links found) and indexing the terms on those pages in a file of over 100 billion gigabytes. Then, Google's algorithms find references to a search term instantly, determine the most likely desired results (a complex calculation, given the ambiguity of language and features like autocompletion, spelling correction, and synonyms used), and deliver search results to users in pages listing two-line summaries of references in PageRank order, a patented popularity ranking calculated using over 200 factors. Clicking on a link returned by a Google search takes the user to the live web page (not the cached version on Google's server). However, one may find that the term searched is no longer there, for example, if the page is inaccessible, changed, or deleted. If so, the posting that Google indexed is in the cached page that accompanies the Google reference. The cached version may even allow access to a page that otherwise would be inaccessible if registration is required for access to the live version. The combination of these and other technologies and services enables Google to offer searches that no other search engine currently can match for quantity, quality, and usefulness.

Although Google provides useful search results, it is an advertising company, earning huge profits from providing users with links to advertisers that may relate to the subject of the search. The excellence of Google as a tool is somewhat mitigated by the intent to optimize the ads that might appeal to the user, rather than the specific purpose of the search. However, the more experience a person has with Google, the less the chance that the ads will interfere with success in research. Another factor to remember is that although it provides access to more Internet references than other search engines, Google provides a snapshot of part of the Internet at a time within 30 days or so of when a page was cached; that is, references may not be current, and searches are not conducted against all Internet content. Another way to measure the ability of Google to present Internet information is to use estimates of the number of pages Google has indexed against the total number of Web pages. Google has not published how many pages it has indexed in several years, but indicated in March 2013 that it holds 30 trillion unique pages (up from 1 trillion pages in 2008).[13] Published estimates say that there are almost a billion websites.[14] If there are 5 to 10 pages per website on average, that means that there are a half trillion to 1 trillion web pages (a conservative estimate). Whatever the accuracy of these estimates, Google's indexed pages represent only a fraction of the total number of pages available on the Internet. Of course, not all pages are suitable for indexing, such as those with dynamic content and those that are gateways to databases that Google cannot access or index.

Inasmuch as Google is the habitual choice of most Internet researchers,[15] it is worthwhile for a user to become familiar with ways to obtain the best results from Google. Google tips and tricks (sometimes referred to as "Google hacks," meaning specific ways to conduct advanced searches) are readily found and easy to understand and use and greatly improve results.[16] It is a good reminder to any researcher or analyst that it can be helpful to look at a search as a process in itself, which can be studied and improved to ensure the best results. A few minutes preparing to do the search in a cogent way pays big dividends in results.

Getting to know the general ways in which search engines operate can be helpful in evaluating the results and in further collection. Not all of a search engine's indexed pages may be presented in search returns because the engine's software may not include pages that are almost never visited. More searching may be required to find items that algorithms rank lower or that are not displayed in results. The subculture of advertising analysts and webmasters, who try to attract potential customers to websites and ads, carefully measures success in terms of the number of "hits" on sites, pages, and terms—page popularity. Search engines like Google, Bing, and Yahoo also measure the popularity of sites, pages, and terms but may elect not to index or present the least popular in search results. The analyst does not care how often a page was visited and is focused on finding all the substantively useful references to the subject. Therefore, the analyst should not assume that the search engine is prioritizing results in the most useful way for intelligence collection and analysis.

Following are additional key attributes of the Google search: The combination of PageRank order of results and Boolean advanced searching with individual or multiple terms allows Google to deliver the most useful references for investigators. Special tools and features allow a focus on images, videos, maps, news, blogs, and so forth, and country-based searching, as well as topical searches (e.g., for businesses in the United States, United Kingdom, or Canada).

Translation of foreign language pages is available, although results are rough (i.e., ungrammatical and inaccurate in interpretation). Tracking and search preferences allow analysts to use Google as an all-around, personalized intelligence collection platform, updating findings periodically. Cached pages allow access even if a page has recently changed. Google's advanced search page allows a user to formulate single or multiterm search attempts without worrying about the precise Boolean query format.

Besides Google, analysts should consider using other search engines to find additional references that are presented in a different order and may not appear in the first several hundred Google results. Google, Yahoo, Bing, and Ask together conduct over 97% of the searches on the Internet, as shown previously. It is useful to know these major engines (by popularity, volume of indexed pages, and potential to assist a searcher):[17]

Yahoo (yahoo.com) is reputed to have several billion pages indexed and currently a 10% share of searches conducted. Because of agreements with Microsoft, it appears that a Yahoo search actually employs the Bing search engine. Yahoo search ranks by keyword density and integrates its directories and other services (which are similar to Google's) well with searching. Boolean search protocols are much like Google's.[18]

Bing, a Microsoft service,[19] has updated its search engine (since June 2009 called a "decision engine") and in midsummer of 2009 agreed to power Yahoo! Search. Bing's market share was recently over 18%. Bing includes semantic technology from Powerset (purchased in 2008), which reportedly allows results to include related searches to help users find information. Images, video, local, news, and product searches supplement web-wide searching, and services such as translation and mapping compete with Google's. Despite back-end updates and integration with social networking sites, Bing has lagged behind Google's market share.[20]

Ask.com, which finds answers to questions by searching its database,[21] was reputed to have over 2 billion pages indexed and conducted just over 3% of searches in March 2010, but currently conducts about 2.4%. Ask reportedly ranked results by ExpertRank, the number of the same subject pages that reference a site. Refinement of search results through filters, suggestions, and editorial comments is its unique feature, including an attempt to allow users to phrase questions in "natural language," as well as keywords.[22]

AOL search (now powered by Google), which owns MapQuest, enhances Google's search engine results with its own additions and conducts only about 1.3% of searches.

Other search engines include AltaVista, which is powered by Yahoo, as is Fast (AlltheWeb.com). Gigablast claims to do "real-time spidering." Netscape search is powered by Google. Snap.com is powered in part by Gigablast, Smarter.com, SimplyHired.com, and X1 Technologies and enhanced by Ask.com.[23] These search engines may not rank highest in number of searches conducted, pages indexed, market share, or elegance of presentation, but all have enjoyed a following because of their success in finding what a large number of people were seeking. At this writing, it is obvious that consolidation has reduced the choices of search engines, legacy offerings are disappearing, and the trend is toward the top four.

The choice of the search engines listed should not be interpreted as a rejection of others, such as Lycos.com, Mama.com, and Exalead.com (and there are others).[24] These other search engines may not provide any more or better results than the largest ones, but on occasion, they manage to find and rank the highest useful references to the subject of a particular search. It is not how many references, but which terms and pages a search engine may have indexed, cached, and presented that will determine its success for an individual search on a specific occasion.

Metasearch Engines

The goal in using multiple search engines is to find data that is more relevant quickly, so each analyst must decide how many search engines to use and how much time should be spent reviewing results. One approach is to use metasearch engines, which use several different search engines simultaneously to gather sets of results from each, and then amalgamate findings into ranked pages of links.[25] The results usually contain fewer of the component engines' results and present them in a different order. Three of the largest and perhaps most successful metasearch engines are

Dogpile.com[26]: combines Google and Yahoo

Clusty.com (Yippy.com): combines results from multiple search engines, including Bing and Ask, as well as blog search engines into folders of related references, reportedly to assist researchers to do more efficient filtering[27]

Mamma.com: uses combinations of sources[28] and offers web, news, images, videos, and local categories of searches

The advantage of using metasearch engines in addition to others is that sometimes an analyst can find key references to the subject more quickly and likely lists of websites to pursue further information collection. A disadvantage is that, depending on the limitations of the metasearch engine's algorithms, fewer results are presented, and some relevant results are missed because many fewer indexed pages are cached.

Companies like Google, Bing, Exalead, and Copernic also provide search software to companies for internal use. Enterprise search engines and Copernic are discussed in Chapter 18.

Finding Search Engines

Among the ways to refresh and validate the tools used in Internet searches is to conduct research periodically into search tools and sources themselves, including Internet search engine sources such as Search Engine Watch (http://searchenginewatch.com/) and Yahoo's catalog of search engines and directories (http://dir.yahoo.com/Computers_and_Internet/Internet/World_Wide_Web/Searching_the_Web/Search_Engines_and_Directories/).

Search Terms

Even the best search engines depend on apt choices of search terms entered in the appropriate manner. The default operation of most search engines is to look for all and each of the words entered in the search box. A search for John Doe in Google produces references to John Doe, John (alone), and Doe (alone). Today's search engines use sophisticated algorithms to interpret a user's request, including correcting spelling, finding similar topics, and incorporating commercials into search results. Although that is useful in many circumstances, results can be inundated with irrelevant references that the search engine's algorithms included based on their own criteria. To search an exact word or phrase, a Boolean expression or advanced search must be used. This is important because searches for John Doe and "John Doe" produce quite different results. For some inquiries, searching both ways is appropriate. Following are some suggestions for search term selection:

Use variations of names to capture all relevant references. For example, John James Doe can also be searched as John J. Doe, John Doe, Jack Doe, JJ Doe, and Doe, John. It can be helpful to include a discriminator (place, employer, school, activity, date) to find the right John Doe and to yield results that are more useful, such as John Doe Dallas, John Doe Texas A&M, John Doe Texas Instruments, or John Doe pilot. Knowing and using such discriminators can be especially helpful when searching a common name and when looking for a particular set of references. If a Boolean operator like AND is the default, as in Google, simply adding the term in the search box works. If not, use the advanced search feature.

Eliminate references not identifiable with the subject of the search. Perhaps John Doe the Cleveland sports star, who is not identifiable with the subject, has dozens of references in the first few pages of results. By using Boolean queries, one could eliminate the Cleveland Doe (e.g., by using the Boolean NOT query, searching John Doe -Cleveland or -Indians in Google). The single biggest problem with the search engines is that they provide many references that are not useful, even though the results literally match the search term. Finding ways to help the search engine focus on the subject of interest will provide better results.

Find Internet sites that may have information about the subject not indexed by search engines. If you find a reference to Texas A&M in your John Doe search, try the Texas A&M site, alumni organizations, professional organizations in the subject's field, and the local or campus newspapers, TV channels, and news publications in College Station, Texas. Such websites may indeed have data on Doe that has not been accessible to search engines' indexing. Such references may reside in databases that can easily be searched by going to the website and using its built-in search engine. Even if that website's internal search engine is Google, the data residing on servers accessible through the site may not be available to the Internet Google servers.

When time available for the search is limited, it is important to view results most efficiently. A normal impulse is to use one search term and view only one or two of the pages of thumbnail results (i.e., 10 to 20 results), which often limits the effectiveness of the search. The two major hurdles all searchers face are the time consumed in executing searches and the time used to review and analyze results for useful data. In truth, people are so used to getting what they need from a quick question to Google that the accuracy, thoroughness, completeness, and timeliness of the process may suffer. Some strategies that may help include increasing the number of results shown on each page from 10 to 20, 30, 50, or 100; changing filtering options to include "explicit images" (e.g., because involvement in porn could be relevant to the purpose of the search); and including language preferences, especially if the subject is foreign or has spent time abroad. In addition, overseas versions of Google and other search engines can help find links to websites abroad. These examples illustrate the advantages of knowing how Google's features work.

Time can be a significant factor in search filtering, such as specifying the year or time frame in conjunction with a search term. Advanced search options allow the user to limit the time frame and thereby eliminate references irrelevant to the purpose of the search. This is one of the drop-down options in Google advanced searching.

Social and Commercial Searching

Today's Internet features all types of sites supported by advertising and sales that aim to attract users not only as one-time buyers but also as continual users. Websites become communities where people carry on a variety of functions, stay logged on, communicate in a variety of modes, and share data in a number of different ways. Certain websites are in such common use that they count visitors per minute, hour, day, and month, as well as the registered members who constitute their customer base. Because some references to these sites (e.g., user true names) are indexed and included in search engine results (e.g., Facebook, LinkedIn, MySpace), it is possible that separate searching is unnecessary. However, the variety of activities online carried out over some of these sites suggests that they should be included in separate searches, especially if the purpose is to find anomalous, illicit, or otherwise derogatory behavior. In addition to those listed in the following discussion, some of the websites in this category are handled in a separate section of Chapter 17.

Social Networking Sites

Some social networking websites have become so large that they must be considered as international communities unto themselves, worth a separate search even though they are indexed by search engines. This is because a thorough search should include even the most recent postings (more recent than 30 days) and because content on these sites can change frequently. Rapid growth continued for almost all social sites in the past 5 years, including adoption of mobile versions for cell phone access. Growth in Internet use into 2014 included nearly universal use and longer times on social networking sites and a shift from MySpace (the previous favorite) to Facebook (now by far the favorite). Recent statistics from a study by Pew[29] showed

- 71% of online adults use Facebook
- 18% of online adults use Twitter
- 17% use Instagram
- 21% use Pinterest
- 22% use LinkedIn

Recent 2014 statistics from eBiz MBA[30] ranked the top 15 social networking sites and users:

1. Facebook, over 900 million
2. Twitter, 310 million
3. LinkedIn, 250 million
4. Pinterest, 150 million
5. Google+, 120 million
6. Tumblr, 110 million
7. Instagram, 85 million
8. VK, 80 million
9. Flickr, 65 million
10. MySpace, 40 million
11. Tagged, 38 million
12. Ask.fm, 37 million
13. Meetup, 35 million
14. MeetMe, 10.5 million
15. ClassMates, 10 million

Users sign in using an e-mail address and password, some pick a nickname, and they have multiple ways to share and post information, varying levels of privacy settings, and a favored group of friends. True name searches can lead to Facebook profiles, whether conducted via Google or the Facebook website (because Facebook makes it easy to find and connect with friends and friends of friends). To see more than the public profile, one must sign in to Facebook (membership is free). Facebook also offers applications and features that facilitate sharing a variety of interests, from short notes to photos to links and other content. Facebook's authorized use policy (AUP)[31] states in part that a user will not employ an automated system to collect other users' information without permission, will not post false personal information or create a false profile, and will obtain consent from users whose information is collected. An investigator can see the parts of a user's Facebook profile that the user has decided will be displayed to the public (i.e., not limited to exposure only within a chosen circle of friends). Whether it might be considered a violation of the Facebook terms for an investigator to collect posted information without the consent of the user remains an unanswered question. A public profile that can be viewed without logging on to Facebook carries no privacy protection, and a profile accessible when signed on may be available to 900 million people (a number almost three times the US population—hardly what could be called "privacy protected").

Professional Internet searching cannot be contemplated today without including social network sites. Some companies offer commercial services providing the content of social networking sites about persons, labeling their service as cybervetting. Publicity about several companies' services suggests that about 35 social networking sites are included in systematic automated collection for these services. Based on research for this book, it appears that a wealth of information may be available about a person from social networking sites. However, there are many other types of websites and databases accessible on the Internet that could also provide valuable information about people and other topics. Restricting cybervetting collection to a limited number of social network sites omits not only those social network sites not chosen but also a vast range of other online data sources.

YouTube (a Google property) hosts videos and currently holds massive numbers of postings, while serving millions of daily users uploading and viewing videos. The size of hosted content can be illustrated by a 2008 court case[32] in which a judge reportedly ordered YouTube to turn over about 12 terabytes of data documenting users' viewing habits to Viacom, which sued YouTube over unauthorized display of copyrighted materials, including 150,000 clips that had been viewed 1.5 billion times. Although videos can be an important source of information and documentation of misbehavior, they are currently searched by keyword, title, or the poster's identity (usually a nickname) and not by matching video content, such as a facial image.

MySpace, formerly the largest social networking site, still hosts about 10 million monthly US visitors.[33] True name searches will find MySpace hits, but most MySpace users' profiles have nicknames. Nicknames can be handy for finding other Internet postings by the same person (i.e., by searching the nickname or e-mail address), but investigators must be careful because there are some popular nicknames used by several or even many people. MySpace links users with friends and their profiles; has blogs, photos, and videos; and specializes in music and entertainment choices. Bands, musicians, and performers have MySpace promotional profiles. MySpace privacy and use policies[34] say that neither members nor visitors may employ users' content without permission, whether posted publicly or for a limited audience through privacy filters. However, free membership, most members' choice to display their content publicly, and indexing through search engines all mean that users should have no reasonable privacy expectations.

Twitter is the largest "microblogging platform," with over 645 million registered and 115 million monthly users (according to some research),[35] with 58 million daily tweets, and reportedly receives 43% of its traffic from phones and 60% from third parties (social networking sites). About 40% of Twitter users look but do not tweet. Despite the limitation of 140 characters of text and public nature of tweets, people share some remarkably personal and revealing postings, including unflattering behaviors and statements. The Library of Congress is reportedly archiving all public tweets. Some advertisers and database services providers track tweets for such information as trends, marketing preferences, and security indicators, and some law enforcement and intelligence agencies analyze tweets for near-real-time threat and intelligence information.

LinkedIn, a business networking site, in March 2014 had about 50 million users,[36] with over 245 million visits and over a billion page views. LinkedIn profiles are written and posted by members (unlike most of those on sites like ZoomInfo.com and Plaxo.com, which harvest links and establish sometimes error-prone profiles using automation as well as subscriber input). LinkedIn provides a number of services to subscribers, such as sharing contact information and photos of members, displaying résumés, finding marketing and business opportunities, and staying in touch with old colleagues. Analysts should carefully verify details of items that users post, but because they are the best source of their own background information and may depend on LinkedIn to find opportunities, there is logical support for the authoritative nature of profiles. LinkedIn profiles can be useful when little is known about a subject and more education and work history are needed as starting points. Like a résumé or application, the LinkedIn profile requires verification.

Professional investigators are well advised to keep up with less-popular social networking sites that may also provide information; this includes those listed in the top 15 social networking sites. The popularity of such sites is apt to evolve as the social networking marketplace changes. One of the trends visible in recent years is the posting of photos, videos, and other content "in the Cloud," accessible to users on multiple devices. Publicly accessible data indexed by search engines may contain valuable cloud-based data for investigators.

A separate category of popular social networking websites concentrates on finding mates, significant others, dates, and sexual partners; some of these sites have millions of subscribers.[37] These include Match.com (35 million estimated monthly users), PlentyofFish (23 million monthly users), Zoosk (11.5 million monthly visitors), OkCupid (10.2 million monthly visitors), and eHarmony (7.1 million monthly visitors). Many different types of dating and friendship websites exist for niche groups, including ones based on religion; sexual orientation; ethnicity; national origin; international affairs ("Russian women," "Asian women"); biracial dating; wealth; and activity preferences. The AshleyMadison.com trademark is "Life is short. Have an affair" and describes a type of activity that has enough of a following online to warrant investigators' interest. Most of these specialized social networking sites charge fees and require registration, and some claim to allow only those approved to become members. Many dating sites appear to cater to those seeking PG-rated social experiences; others offer an X-rated approach. Generally, subjects who subscribe to dating websites do not use their true names, and their user names do not appear in search engine results.

As might be expected on the Internet, which still produces high profits for porn sites, there are quite a few websites that are focused on sex, porn, and "hookups" between people, both straight and gay. Most of these sites require membership and charge fees; many generate spam, display false but enticing offers, include explicit content on their pages and in subscriber communications unsuitable for most workplaces, display online porn offers, and even act as hubs for identity theft and malware distribution.[38] The home page of the adult type of site often contains views of nudity, sex acts, alternative lifestyles (e.g., bondage and discipline, fetishes, group sex), and other potentially controversial content. Display of such images and audio could be considered offensive and create a hostile work environment under Title VII of the Civil Rights Act. Often, porn/adult websites seem to have an uncanny ability to see the browser user's location, as they display come-ons and pop-up ads featuring scantily clad or nude people tagged with a town near the user (matched through the IP address from the browser). Some porn sites generate cookies and open new browser windows with explicit content. Among the porn-social sites are AdultFriendFinder.com, XTube.com, Fling.com, WildMatch.com, even some links found on Craigslist.org, and many more. Some claim to be adult sex classified advertising. Some have been widely criticized (e.g., AdultFriendFinder) for fraudulent postings and links. Analysts need to consider whether to use a proxy server in accessing such sites (to shield the origin of the inquiry and protect the analyst's computer from malicious code and advertising from the porn sites). Registered users on adult sites use nicknames and postings that are not generally indexed by search engines unless they are also listed elsewhere online. Because adult sites may be venues for misbehavior, such as violating a company's authorized computer use policy, an investigator may need to sign up to search for a subject on a particular site.

Another category of website espouses or supports causes, advocacy, protests, and charitable fund-raising online, like Care2.com (which claims over 25.4 million members); Meetup.com (which hosts many different types of sites of affinity groups, causes, and protest groups); and Indymedia.org (which publishes stories and announcements about protesters' causes). Intelligence collectors may need to focus on this type of site if civil disobedience, vandalism, or violence is threatened against a person or entity. Examples of protest groups that have engaged in illicit activities and have been accused of terrorist, animal rights, or eco-terrorist acts, include animal rights groups (e.g., WAROnline.org, SHAC.net, Animal Liberation Front at animalliberationpressoffice.org and animanliberationfront.com, DirectAction.info, People for the Ethical Treatment of Animals at PETA.org and StopAnimalTests.com) and environmental rights (Earth-Liberation-Front.org, OriginalELF.com, Protest.net). Other activism is focused on such causes as peace, antinuclear weapons/energy, anticorporate/World Bank/International Monetary Fund, communist, socialist, Maoist, Islamist, Neo-Nazi, white supremacist, gun rights, militias, and many other groups. Not all such causes, or their websites, espouse illegal activities to achieve their aims. However, planned activities such as demonstrations can include open invitations to individuals or groups that may engage in dangerous and illegal activities threatening business and government.

Some websites belong to organizations advocating for rights, such as privacy advocates like Electronic Frontier Foundation (eff.org), Electronic Privacy Information Center (epic.org), and Center for Democracy and Technology (cdt.org). There are many others, of course, including political parties' websites and their support groups, as well as think tanks, major nonprofits, and other nongovernmental and nonprofit organizations. Although many pages of these sites are indexed, it may be necessary to search them directly to access documents referring to a subject that appear only in unindexed databases on the sites.

E-Commerce Sites

Certain e-commerce (online sales) websites have become so popular that they have captured vast audiences of Internet users from print and broadcast media, catalog/telephone sales, and retail outlets. Of course, the major retailers like Wal-Mart, Sears/Kmart/Land's End, Costco, Target, Macy's, Nordstrom, and so on, all have useful online sales sites. In addition, some major corporations, particularly high-tech firms, have mastered Internet marketing of their products, such as Cisco, Dell, HP, Microsoft, Intuit (QuickBooks and TurboTax), Adobe, and others, many of which conduct the bulk of their sales online. Some pages of commercial websites may be indexed, but in a thorough search, it may be important to include a query on these websites: eBay and its companion site PayPal are the quintessential classified sales and payment processors on the US Internet. Many businesses have been built around their services, which include a measure of anonymity for users. Nicknames of users may be based on e-mail addresses or user names appearing in other places. Finding an eBay account may allow an analyst to detect activities such as selling items deemed inappropriate (e.g., items apparently from work, like the individual we once found who was selling T-shirts and memorabilia from the TV show where he was a technician or the girlfriend of a manufacturing company employee found selling items from her boyfriend's factory that had not yet been placed on sale to the public). Although eBay's AUP does not allow illicit sales, it has powerful legal and security staffs who help law enforcement deal with persistent attempts to sell stolen, contraband, and improperly offered merchandise and sellers who take money without providing products they offer. PayPal has grown to offer commercial and credit card as well as small-scale personal payments. Most PayPal accounts link to a user's credit card or bank account as their foundational funding source. PayPal members can "bill" each other or outsiders with an e-mail that facilitates a transaction over PayPal. Investigators frequently must conduct a transaction to elicit identifying information about an eBay or PayPal user.

Skype, a company founded by Estonian technologists, was bought and subsequently sold off by eBay, acquired by Microsoft in 2011, and is an example of an

Internet service offering communications capabilities to anyone with an Internet connection and host device. Skype is a massive peer-to-peer telecommunications network, offering free software, free computer-to-computer and Internet-to-phone telephone calls, video teleconferencing, instant messaging, and a degree of privacy. The privacy comes from the fact that packets sent from Skype software carrying voice or data travel over the Internet through other Skype users' computers, and the packets themselves are privacy protected. This makes interception of Skype communications through a host's routers difficult, if not impossible, and even if the packet stream is intercepted, it may not be comprehensible. Skype users employ nicknames as well as true names for accounts. Skype also offers low-cost telecommunications services, both nationally and internationally, that connect with wireline and wireless telecommunications carriers. Reverse directories do not usually list the subscribers to Skype telephone numbers. Some spam and automated solicitations slip past Skype's filters. Because the user chooses the area code of a Skype-issued telephone number, it may not be an indication of the subscriber's actual place of residence.

Craigslist is a large, online, localized, free classified advertising service that allows postings in a variety of types of listings clustered in regional geographical areas. Many types of resale personal items, notices, and service offerings appear on craigslist. Like eBay, some illicit activities (such as prostitution and sale of contraband) may be detectable on craigslist. Users communicate through an anonymizing e-mail relay interface or post their own e-mail address or telephone number.

Amazon is a large Internet bookstore that has become a one-stop shopping website for media and all sorts of products, with some social networking features, hosting for client servers, and a commercial networking site. Using their account log-on, patrons can rate a book, publication, or other products, tagging such postings with a true name or nickname. Some users post frequently, providing insight into their views, reading/shopping habits, and personalities. Amazon's Kindle is an example of an electronic reader-turned-tablet computer that has an Internet connection and allows a variety of activities with published materials. Other e-book readers and tablets available from Sony, Apple, Barnes & Noble, and so on enable a variety of reading and computing options and Internet communications, some of which are hosted as well on smart cell phones and larger platforms. Based on the popularity of its iPhone, Apple (and its imitators) offers many types of networking applications on a cell-based Internet platform and on iPads and iPods that lead the way in continued evolution in networking for entertainment and communications, as well as other functions. Among these are geolocation-based services that allow users to connect, communicate, or query based on where they are. Fierce competition is ongoing from many cell phone and device manufacturers. Because multiple types of Internet-based services and social networking are meshed in these platforms, searchers should anticipate that further development of these devices will continue to provide opportunities for intelligence for their users.

Directories

Web directories have provided a vital resource for many years, giving an encyclopedic list of topics in every major category and subcategory area, with links to sources. Open Directory Project, a free service (http://www.dmoz.org/, now in partnership with AOL), is the prime example of a resource where subject matter experts ("volunteer editors") have listed the best places for a user to find information on the chosen topic. Varieties of commercial directories are also available, such as Yahoo. In some cases, the sites listed provide a fee to the website providing the directory. Perusing the catalog of topics can help put a researcher on the right track toward information of a certain type. In addition, looking at a site like Yahoo! Directory can assist the analyst in finding the major sources on a topic because presumably the repositories have been screened for their value and quality.

Many Internet users are accustomed to googling a roughly worded question, almost as an impulse when seeking information. One weakness of this approach is that to increase the speed of the process, the user has not surveyed the topic, formulated the question carefully, or found the primary sources of the type of information sought. The user with blind faith in the search engine's algorithms is willing to accept whatever comes up in the first two pages (10 to 20 results) that Google provides. It is a remarkable tribute to search engines that they so often provide answers "close enough" to what the user needs (or thinks he or she needs). When it is the local bicycle shop, restaurant, or product shopping, these quick searches fit the bill. However, they are decidedly insufficient qualitatively or quantitatively for the serious investigator. The online directory allows a researcher to zoom in on a topic from the atmosphere down to ground level, surveying the landscape from various heights to ensure that key resources will not escape notice. As searchers gain experience and develop rich lists of favorite websites, the directory may no longer be as useful. Yet, it still pays to know the topic, especially if it is unfamiliar to the analyst.

Online versions of free telephone directories are useful for identifying and locating individuals, including WhitePages.com, AnyWho.com, 411.com, PeopleFinders.com, and Zabasearch.com. By getting to know what types of name-based and reverse directory information are provided for free, it is often possible for the analyst to verify contact and basic biographical information about a person or description of an entity. Many online directories also link to fee-based services. In general, fee-based services provide data that are potentially useful but must be verified to avoid errors and could be relatively costly if the analyst escalates the extent of information requested for progressively higher fees. One annoying aspect of some fee-based directories is that they promise to provide data (e.g., identification of the subscriber to a telephone number, profile of a person) by suggesting that the facts "are in our database." When the user requests the data, they may or may not contain the type or extent of detail promised and may be inaccurate or dated. Because of their unreliability and overaggressive marketing (e.g., suggesting that they have data when they do not), their use is generally discouraged.

Blogs

Weblogs or "blogs" have evolved from commercial and personal online publishing and social chat functions. Blog sites (e.g., Huffington Post, BuzzFeed, Blogger, Wordpress) encourage readers to comment on postings, write their own publications, follow topics and writers of choice online, and create new expressions of art, knowledge, guidance, commentary, news, formal and informal communications, and interest group notifications (among others). Blogs are so numerous (over 181 million online in 2012, according to Nielsen)[39] that in almost any specialty area, it is difficult to keep up with their comings and goings and the fora influential on the topics discussed. Those writing blogs (over one-third of whom are housewives, according to Nielsen) and commenting on them often use pseudonyms or nicknames that must be searched to find what is published and must be matched with true identities. Blogs are often offered free hosting and software to help bloggers create essentially their own websites, which are sometimes refereed and sometimes unmonitored. Rants, comments, and postings can at times become crude and controversial. Almost any contentious issue will appear in the blogosphere. Finding postings by a subject can reveal strong personal feelings, demonstrate writing ability, and illustrate a subject's maturity, judgment, and discretion (or lack thereof).

Keyword searching for blog postings is facilitated by websites[40] such as the following:

- BlogSearch.google.com is Google's all-around blog search engine, offering e-mail alerts, a "blog search gadget" for a Google home page, and a blog search feed in Google reader.
- IceRocket at http://www.icerocket.com/ provides blog and web searching and tracking and other tools and includes Twitter and MySpace in its searches.
- Technorati.com provides blog-searching tools and tracks the top 100 bloggers.
- BlogPulse at http://www.blogpulse.com/ was a Nielsen property that allowed blog searches until 2012.

Chat

Online chat rooms are nothing more than websites that allow users to type in text messages, monitor others' exchanges ("lurk"), and follow specific topics, general areas of interest, or whatever users decide to post. Most chat content is not indexed or archived, but users can decide to copy and save dialogues, forward them, and quote them at will. There is no expectation of privacy in chat rooms, but each chat room has its own rules about participation, expected behaviors, and privacy, which are strictest for sites designed for teens and children. Usually, even in the strictest of chat rooms, the only penalty for violating such rules is expulsion. Many chats are monitored (censored), but many are not. Today's chat evolved from Internet Relay Chat (IRC), which developed before the modern Internet as a method for researchers using networked systems to exchange messages and discuss ideas.[41] IRC channels exist among groups of users who consider themselves different from the great mass of Internet users. Among those still using IRC are computer programmers, hackers/crackers, peer-to-peer network relay aficionados, adult/porn sites (e.g., live video with text), gangs and criminal groups, as well as many types of innocent users.

Webcams, cell phones, and other devices allow multiple group connections for chats within simultaneous chats. Some chats include voice exchanges, in either large or small groups. It appears that, generally, legacy forms of chat are giving way to other methods of online brief communications, including instant messaging (which can spontaneously connect two or more participants), conference calling, and Twitter. Investigators may find themselves in chat rooms in such circumstances as monitoring adults seeking to lure children into sexual activities or tracing illicit activities involving hardware, software, movies, videos, and music. In such cases, capturing the content of chat is important, and searching for keywords may not be possible outside the website. Chat room users may choose an identifier unique to the site or use an online ID established already. Examples of popular chat rooms,[42] some free and some fee based, some requiring software for advanced features, are AOL chat, which also offers texting and video calling, Babel.com, Talkcity.com (now part of Delphi Forums at http://www.delphiforums.com/chat. ptt), ICQ (http://www.icq.com/en), PalTalk.com, ShoutMix.com, and TeenChat. com. Many others specialize in dating, flirting, matchmaking, affinity groups, nationalities, and multiple services like those offered by Yahoo and AOL.

Additional search tools and strategies appear in the next chapter.

Notes

1. Internet World Stats, http://www.internetworldstats.com/stats7.htm (accessed April 15, 2014).
2. HTML introduction, http://www.w3schools.com/html/html_intro.asp (accessed April 16, 2014).
3. Oracle, http://www.java.com/en/ (accessed April 15, 2014).
4. Adobe, www.adobe.com/products/flash.html (accessed April 15, 2014).
5. InterNIC Domain Name System tutorial, http://www.internic.net/faqs/authoritative-dns.html (accessed April 15, 2014).
6. IP address tutorial, http://computer.howstuffworks.com/internet/basics/question549.htm (accessed April 15, 2014); network packet structure tutorial, http://computer.howstuffworks.com/question525.htm (accessed April 15, 2014).
7. Digital signature (and digital certificate, public key infrastructure) defined, http://searchsecurity.techtarget.com/definition/digital-signature (accessed April 15, 2014).
8. Browser definition, http://www.webopedia.com/TERM/B/browser.html (accessed April 15, 2014).

9. ZDNet report of NetMarketShare statistics, March 2014, http://www.zdnet.com/browser-trench-warfare-early-2014-report-7000027099/ and http://en.wikipedia.org/wiki/Usage_share_of_web_browsers (accessed April 15, 2014).

10. Malicious code (National Institute of Standards and Technology [NIST] definition), http://csrc.nist.gov/publications/nistir/threats/section3_3.html (accessed April 17, 2014). Help Net Security report on malware on higher educational networks, http://www.net-security.org/secworld.php?id=15802 (accessed April 17, 2014). Security Engineering Research Team Quarterly Threat Intelligence Report, Q4 2013, Solutionary, http://www.solutionary.com/_assets/pdf/research/sert-q4–2013-threat-intelligence.pdf (accessed April 17, 2014).

11. comScore Releases February 2014 US Search Engine Rankings, March 18, 2014, https://www.comscore.com/Insights/Press_Releases/2014/3/comScore_Releases_February_2014_U.S._Search_Engine_Rankings (accessed April 17, 2014).

12. Inside Search, Google, https://www.google.com/insidesearch/howsearchworks/ (accessed April 17, 2014); How Google Works, http://www.googleguide.com/google_works.html (accessed April 17, 2014).

13. Koetsier, John, How Google Searches 30 Trillion Web Pages, 100 Billion Times a Month, March 1, 2013, *VB News*, http://venturebeat.com/2013/03/01/how-google-searches-30-trillion-web-pages-100-billion-times-a-month/ (accessed April 17, 2014).

14. Internet Live Stats, http://www.internetlivestats.com/total-number-of-websites/ (accessed April 17, 2014).

15. comScore Releases February 2014.

16. https://support.google.com/websearch/answer/35890 (accessed April 17, 2014).

17. Harry, David, How Search Engines Rank Web Pages, September 2013, Search Engine Watch, http://searchenginewatch.com/article/2064539/How-Search-Engines-Rank-Web-Pages (accessed April 17, 2014).

18. See https://help.yahoo.com/kb/index?page=answers&startover=y&y=PROD&source=home.landing_search&locale=en_US&question_box=web%20search (accessed April 17, 2014).

19. See http://onlinehelp.microsoft.com/en-us/bing/ff808415.aspx (accessed April 17, 2014).

20. See http://en.wikipedia.org/wiki/Bing_(search_engine) (accessed April 17, 2014).

21. See http://www.ask.com/web?q=how+ask+works&qsrc=364&o=0&l=dir&qo=homepageSearchBox (accessed April 17, 2014).

22. About Ask.com, http://about.ask.com/en/docs/about/index.shtml (accessed August 21, 2010).

23. Descriptions are from the search engines themselves. Prescott, Lee Ann, Social Networking by the Numbers, principal, Research-Write, December 2009, http://www.slideshare.net/laprescott/social-networking-by-the-numbersdecember-2009 (accessed April 10, 2010).

24. See http://www.thesearchenginelist.com/ (accessed April 17, 2014).

25. Sherman, Chris, Metacrawlers and Metasearch Engines, Search Engine Watch, March 23, 2005, http://searchenginewatch.com/2156241 (accessed April 17, 2014); UC Berkeley, Meta Search Engines, http://www.lib.berkeley.edu/TeachingLib/Guides/Internet/MetaSearch.html (accessed April 17, 2014); Wikipedia, http://en.wikipedia.org/wiki/Metasearch_engine (accessed April 17, 2014).

26. http://www.dogpile.com/support/Faqs (accessed April 17, 2014).

27. Boswell, Wendy, Clusty, http://websearch.about.com/od/enginesanddirectories/a/clusty.htm (accessed April 17, 2014).

28. About.com on Mamma, http://websearch.about.com/od/metasearchengines/a/mamma.htm (accessed April 17, 2014).

29. Social Networking Fact Sheet, Pew Internet and American Life Project, September 2013, http://www.pewinternet.org/fact-sheets/social-networking-fact-sheet/ (accessed April 17, 2014).

30. http://www.ebizmba.com/articles/social-networking-websites (accessed April 17, 2014).

31. https://www.facebook.com/legal/terms (accessed April 17, 2014).

32. Helft, Miguel, Google Told to Turn Over User Data of YouTube, *New York Times*, July 4, 2008.

33. Quantcast April 2014 statistics, https://www.quantcast.com/myspace.com (accessed April 17, 2014).

34. MySpace Terms, https://myspace.com/pages/terms (accessed April 17, 2014).

35. Statistic Brain, January 2014, http://www.statisticbrain.com/twitter-statistics/ (accessed April 17, 2014).

36. Quantcast, March 2014, https://www.quantcast.com/linkedin.com?country=US (accessed April 17, 2014).

37. eBiz MBA April 2014, http://www.ebizmba.com/articles/dating-websites (accessed April 17, 2014).

38. Pepitone, Julianne, Porn Dethroned as Top Source of Mobile Malware, *NBC News*, March 2014, http://www.nbcnews.com/tech/security/porn-dethroned-top-source-mobile-malware-n44371 (accessed April 17, 2014).

39. http://www.nielsen.com/us/en/newswire/2012/buzz-in-the-blogosphere-millions-more-bloggers-and-blog-readers.html (accessed April 17, 2014).

40. Descriptions were obtained from the websites themselves.

41. IRC descriptions may be found at http://irchelp.org/ and http://www.livinginternet.com/r/r.htm (accessed April 17, 2014).

42. Ibid.

Chapter 17

Finding Sources

Introduction

Thousands of websites offer access to government records and other types of public information compiled by agencies, nonprofits, news organizations, and commercial enterprises. Investigators should remember that, as with other published materials, verification is necessary before accepting any record as fact and before assuming that when a record is not found in an online database, it does not exist. In all probability, even a thorough search will not include absolutely every database or reference that could contain a reference to the subject. However, by maintaining an up-to-date, complete list of uniform resource locators (URLs) for potential searches, the analyst can credibly assert that a search was as thorough as possible. Not all government and commercial records are offered online, not all online records are offered free, and it is not always possible to obtain identifiable records because many repositories offer only a name to match, without other identifying data to verify that it is the same person as the subject.

It is appropriate to spend a moment on disclaimers, which are found with virtually all databases. Disclaimers generally say that the agency or entity hosting the database is not responsible for any errors, and use of the data found is the responsibility, and at the risk, of the user. Some disclaimers sound like they were written for software (disclaiming liability for any use, any damage, or failure to perform as indicated). If the implicit threats we read in this type of disclaimer were true, then the database might have little value, like software that would not work in your computer. Yet, we should not depend on data that may contain errors (and have little choice but to trust the software, despite disclaimers). The solution is to be careful to verify relevant facts found in records and to understand that even a fairly low percentage of risk in the accuracy of data or functioning of the database must be admitted by hosts that are in business and government and cannot hope to provide 100% irrefutable information online. When data found online may be the basis for action, the analyst should be careful not only to present the data with any caveats deemed necessary under the relevant laws (e.g., Fair Credit Reporting Act), policies, and guidelines, but also to point out that any next steps—especially adverse action—require confirmation of the data. After all is said and done, the vast majority of information available online is reasonably accurate and often provides leads to useful evidence.

The sources cited in this chapter are among those that have proven most productive for my practice.

US Government

US Government information is increasingly available online because of e-government initiatives of the last several administrations, beginning in Clinton's time (i.e., 1993–present). After September 11, 2001, access to some online records was modified to ensure that operational security of the government would not be jeopardized by allowing terrorists to use the records for attacks. Another trend in recent years has been to remove identifiers (date of birth, Social Security number, address) from records made available online in an effort to protect people against identity theft and misuse of personal information. However, there are incredible amounts of data in public records still available online, for free and, in some instances, for a fee. An invaluable resource to find US Government records is USA.gov, through which many different types of databases can be found.

Among the useful US Government sites for finding misbehavior by people and entities are the following:

PACER (Public Access to Court Electronic Records; http://pacer.gov/) provides access to most federal criminal, civil, and bankruptcy court records. Users must register and pay $0.10 per page.

The US Court of Federal Claims is accessible at http://www.uscfc.uscourts.gov/.

US Tax Court dockets can be searched at http://www.ustaxcourt.gov/UstcDockInq/asp/SearchPartyOptions.asp.

The Excluded Parties List System (https://www.sam.gov/portal/public/SAM/#1; click on Search Records, Advanced Search - Exclusion) allows the user to search for those excluded from government contracts and payments.

The Treasury Department's Office of Foreign Assets Control provides the Specially Designated Nationals and Blocked Persons List of those cited for trade sanctions for economic, national security, and foreign policy reasons, which can be found at http://www.treasury.gov/resource-center/sanctions/SDN-List/Pages/default.aspx.

The US Department of Commerce, Bureau of Industry and Security, publishes a Denied Persons List at http://www.bis.doc.gov/index.php/the-denied-persons-list; the list delineates those entities and persons denied authority to export.

The US Customs Rulings Online Search System (CROSS) is available at http://rulings.cbp.gov/index.asp.

The Securities and Exchange Commission (SEC) enforcement actions are available at http://www.sec.gov/divisions/enforce/enforceactions.shtml, and the EDGAR (Electronic Data Gathering, Analysis, and Retrieval) system allows a user to search for company filings with the SEC at http://www.sec.gov/edgar/searchedgar/webusers.htm#.U7DaD_l92GJ.

The Department of Health and Human Services (DHHS) excluded individuals and entities search is available at http://exclusions.oig.hhs.gov/, and fraud enforcement is searchable at http://oig.hhs.gov/fraud.asp; the Federal Drug Administration debarment list can be found at http://www.fda.gov/ICECI/EnforcementActions/FDADebarmentList/default.htm. DHHS also lists names of those who have defaulted on student loans at http://bhpr.hrsa.gov/scholarshipsloans/heal/defaulters/index.html.

The State Department posts lists of foreign terrorist organizations at http://www.state.gov/j/ct/rls/other/des/123085.htm.

The Justice Department posts a searchable, nationwide list of registered sexual offenders that interacts with state and territorial lists; it is available at http://www.nsopw.gov/?AspxAutoDetectCookieSupport=1.

The Bureau of Federal Prisons has an inmate lookup list available at http://www.bop.gov/inmateloc/.

Other agencies offering online postings of enforcement activities include the Occupational Safety and Health Administration (OSHA) and the National Labor Relations Board (NLRB).

The Patent and Trademark Office offers search options on its site at http://www.uspto.gov/patents/process/search/index.jsp, but often search engines will find references to patents and inventors placed online by commercial firms.

State, County, and Local Governments

State, county, and local government information also can be found online, as agencies scan and load records into databases to make operations more efficient and to comply with open-government laws and regulations. It is important to remember that many government agencies (e.g., the 3,069 US counties)[1] struggle with the cost and complexity of compiling and maintaining records, and automation has not gone smoothly at some (witness the debacles in federal and state attempts to automate registration for health care insurance in 2013–2014). Vital records such as births, deaths, marriages, and the like have been transitioned from paper to computers, but many state and county agencies hosting such records have relied on fees to offset the costs of maintenance and staffing. Therefore, it is not unusual for agencies to require registration and charge users a fee for an online search, for records retrieval, and for a certified copy of the record—even though the record must be publicly available by law. Some jurisdictions charge more than others, some require a subscription or account for access, and many opt to provide records through selected contractors or automation providers such as LexisNexis.

Handy websites for locating online government records are provided by BRB Publications at http://www.brbpub.com/default.asp and http://www.publicrecordsources.com/. Professional licenses can be found at http://www.verifyprolicense.com/, from the same publisher. Links help the searcher to find the right county for an address, free online public records, and research companies that will retrieve records from a courthouse or government office for a fee and list publications to help searchers learn about how different types of records are accessed and kept. Each state, county, and municipality may have different standards and access rules, although many states have attempted to allow searches of all county court records through a single state web portal. It is prudent to spend a few minutes determining what types of online records a state or other government entity may offer because the records could include the subject of inquiry, more are available online than ever before, and more come online frequently.

Reference works such as Hetherington and Sankey's *The Manual to Online Public Records*, which provides a state-by-state listing with government records URLs, can be helpful, but no sooner do such books go into print than some of the records offered, or the URLs, change.[2] One can always search the Internet for a current link to a jurisdiction's online records (e.g., "Montgomery County, MD, property records"), but be careful to distinguish the government links from the commercial ones. Among the types of records that may be of use when posted are the following:

- Vital records (birth, death, marriage, divorce)
- Criminal and civil court records (including family and traffic courts)
- Sexual offender registry
- Corporation, company, and commercial entity registrations
- Uniform Commercial Code (UCC) records
- Real estate property, assessment, and tax records
- Worker's compensation records
- Driver records
- Vehicle and vessel ownership and registration
- Accident reports
- Occupational licensing (usually handled by separate boards for each specialty)
- Prison inmates and incarceration records

- Tax delinquencies and auctions
- Voter registration

Sometimes, a local record might surprise you with an unexpected posting. For example, we found a "most wanted" poster displayed online by a small municipal police force, stating that our subject was wanted for fraud. It was interesting to find the posting, and the crime had been committed by the subject. We knew that because months before the online posting, the subject had appeared in court and pled guilty to the fraud charges. In fact, the subject had finished serving his sentence by the time the wanted poster was found online, so he was no longer "wanted." This instance illustrates the fact that an analyst must be careful to weigh all the facts found in postings, and to assess not only their relevance but also their timeliness and reliability, before reporting the instance as found. It is also prudent to include analyst comments when there is doubt, uncertainty, or lack of accuracy in any aspect of the findings reported.

Other Government-Related Sources

Other government-related sources are available:

The World Bank posts a debarment list (disallowed contractors) at http://web. worldbank.org/external/default/main?theSitePK=84266&contentMDK=64 069844&menuPK=116730&pagePK=64148989&piPK=64148984.

The POGO (Project on Government Oversite) website posts a list of federal contractors alleged to have engaged in misconduct at http://www. contractormisconduct.org/. This database contains some well-known, large companies and lists allegations and contract amounts.

Health Guide USA has links to each state's medical license databases to allow verification for physicians' credentials: http://www.healthguideusa.org/ medical_license_lookup.htm.

GuideStar lists nonprofit entities in a searchable database (with registration required for details) at http://www2.guidestar.org/Home.aspx.

A private company, Prime Time Publishing Company, offers to validate Social Security numbers. When a Social Security number is entered at http://www. ssnvalidator.com/, the system verifies that its user is not deceased and provides the approximate date and state of issuance.

Active military and veterans of the armed forces can be found on a variety of websites, including http://www.military.com/buddyfinder/, http://www. military-search.com/, and http://www.searchmil.com/. Some of these sites include ads from fee-based people search services.

A directory of federal agencies at http://www.usa.gov/directory/federal/index. shtml can be used to locate and contact federal employees.

The Council on Licensure, Enforcement and Regulation has a directory of professional regulatory boards and colleges online at http://www.clearhq.org/.

Business-Related Sources

A variety of information sources about businesses provide online access to profiles, including corporate filings in the SEC's EDGAR database at http://www. sec.gov/edgar.shtml. For private lists of profiles, Hoover's at http://www.hoovers. com/, Dun & Bradstreet at https://creditreports.dnb.com/m/home?storeId=11154, and the Better Business Bureau at http://www.bbb.org/search/ are good sources. Other options include the http://biznar.com/biznar/ "deep web business search" (with sometimes bizarre search results), http://us.kompass.com/, which says it lists millions of businesses, and Yahoo business directory (which includes company websites) at http://dir.yahoo.com/business_and_economy/directories/companies/. A manifestation of user-provided information on businesses and people is the website http://www.corporationwiki.com/, and http://www.wikipedia.org/ is also apt to have information posted on many businesses. As telephone books have moved online, several have posted information about businesses in yellow pages-style listings. Caution should be exercised in using a wiki or online yellow pages as a primary source of data because by its nature, a wiki allows collaborative editing and creation of postings by anyone, which can make a wiki's content suspect, and yellow pages may not be reviewed and edited by the owner or someone who can verify the details. The level of review and verification provided for posted materials, including source citations, is primary evidence of credibility.

There are websites devoted to messages and forums for those following corporations' stock value and business development, including the message board hosted by Yahoo at http://finance.yahoo.com/mb/YHOO/. Postings are usually by nickname, preserving the anonymity of the writers, and sometimes feature scathing criticism and even insider revelations (which can bedevil corporations and pose legal risks). Another site with business message boards that can occasionally include vitriolic criticisms of businesses is RagingBull.com, and numerous blogs and chat rooms include business-related commentary. Several websites are like a cross between yellow pages and business profile repositories, hosting data that are created from other websites (often from the businesses' own websites). An example is Manta.com, which claims to list over 22 million US businesses. Details of business profiles that are found through Google searches should be verified because they may come from the business itself or Internet postings from nonauthoritative sources.

Some websites cater to ratings of employers, such as http://www.jobitorial.com/, where employees may praise or pan their workplace, usually using pseudonyms. The

Motley Fool (Fool.com) focuses on stocks and users, like those on Yahoo message boards, entertaining not only straight news items but also commentary (sometimes quite critical and factually questionable) about companies and their leaders.

News

Many current and several-year-old news items are likely to be found by search engines. However, these only scratch the surface of potential news media references to a subject. For many years, news archiving and retrieval services have offered searching by subscription, including Dialog.com, Nexis.com, ThompsonReuters.com, and Factiva.com. Free news references can be found on News.Google.com and News.Yahoo.com. Major newspapers and news websites also offer archival searches, many charging a fee for full texts of stories. Current (e.g., last 2 weeks) stories are usually available for free. Magazines, journals, and other publications increasingly can be retrieved, but possibly through pay-as-you-go sites or by subscription. Some major news sites are searchable by comprehensive, automated search engines like Copernic.com (which now owns Mama.com, a metasearch engine). More on Copernic appears in the next chapter.

A successful strategy for finding references to persons and businesses in smaller communities and suburbs is to search for news media websites in the municipality, county, region, and state where the subject is located and in the subject matter area of the subject's work or hobby. This search should include educational institutions' publications as well as commercial news sites. Events such as newsworthy awards, arrests, achievements, lawsuits, family deaths, graduations, and so on may appear in news media reports and verify or reveal known or new facts about the subject. At http://dir.yahoo.com/news_and_media/ and http://www.dmoz.org/News/, a researcher can find media outlets that should be considered as potential sources of stories that may or may not be indexed by the major search engines.

Web 2.0

The term *Web 2.0* (2004–present)[3] refers to interactive websites and applications that facilitate information sharing, interoperability, user-centered design, and collaboration on the World Wide Web, allowing users to interact and collaborate with each other in a social media dialogue as creators of user-generated content in a virtual community. Examples of Web 2.0 include web-based communities, hosted services, web applications, social networking sites, video-sharing sites, wikis, blogs, mashups, and folksonomies. A Web 2.0 site allows its users to interact with other users or to change website content, in contrast to noninteractive websites where users are limited to the passive viewing of information that is provided to them. Mashups are services that combine data or functionality from two or more services, and "folksonomy is a system of classification derived from the practice and method of collaboratively creating and managing tags to annotate and categorize content."[4]

What makes Web 2.0 useful from the investigator's standpoint is that applications, websites, and interactive communications (including mobile, instant messaging [IM], and mashups) all not only allow extended networking and communications but also enable investigators to track subjects in many new ways. Some of the new websites offering Web 2.0 features also enable a user to track other users (e.g., Friendfeed.com) and to sign on to a social networking site using another site (e.g., Facebook.com). When added to the formidable functionality in Google alerts (Google.com/alerts), it is possible to find information about current activities of someone online, especially when the subject actively posts updates on popular websites and is "tracked" by others. When an individual poses a threat, is investigated for ongoing criminal activities, or (unfortunately) is stalked by a malevolent person, these applications enable a type of surveillance previously unknown. Two aspects of these Web 2.0 features are that the implications of usage are not known to substantial percentages of users (thus creating vulnerabilities they are unaware of), and the average user may be divulging information to the public at large that is neither prudent nor well understood. An example is if someone announces a departure from home on a trip and sends photos of the travels, allowing a burglar with access to these postings to see that the person is away and the home may be unoccupied.

The popularity of Web 2.0 (exemplified by the hundreds of millions of users of Facebook and Twitter, to name just two websites)[5] is a primary reason why personnel security must consider employee and candidate activities online because so many people define themselves by online activities. An intelligence or investigative collector employing Web 2.0 should find out the "handles" used by subjects of interest for their postings and communications. Often, these handles also appear in e-mail addresses, profiles, and frequently in Twitter and similar instant messaging (IM) services. It is not unusual for an individual to use the same handle for multiple Web 2.0 services.

It is also normal for several websites to list the person's true name in conjunction with the handle, especially on social networking sites. A key goal in the initial stages of any Internet investigation is to find all available virtual identities of the subject because of the additional data that could be available and the possibility that the added information may not be available without searching all of the subject's handles. Although some human resources (HR) departments have avoided searching social networking sites on applicants for "ethical reasons" (actually, legal doubt), there is a good reason to search them: They link a true name (which may not appear in their profile but nevertheless leads to their profile) with a user name, nickname, or handle seen elsewhere. This type of handle is a virtual alias on the public Internet and should be treated as such.

Among the more productive postings from today's websites are blogs and mashed up social networking entries. Today, the likelihood that an individual will be documented in illicit, socially unacceptable, or otherwise derogatory behaviors is much higher because of the proliferation of Web 2.0 services because the quantity of casual, unguarded content attributable to individuals has increased considerably (see Chapter 4, Internet Search Studies). On the other hand, the proclivity for users to engage in joking, exaggeration, jargon, and double entendre could easily confuse and mislead an observer. In discussing the value of collaborative tools on the Internet, on March 26, 2010, Navy Department chief information officer (CIO) Rob Carey said in a blog post[6]:

> Of course, with access comes the responsibility to ensure that certain measures are taken to keep our networks and our people safe. To that end, users must protect their information online, be aware of who and what they interact with, and abide by existing regulations on ethics, operational security and privacy.

CIO Carey recognized the value of online collaboration for the Navy, and the US Armed Forces have developed several Web 2.0 applications to enable efficiencies within the services. However, he also recognized that individual users must play a role in the protection of data, secure computing, and privacy protection to ensure that the vulnerabilities do not outweigh the strengths of new collaborative tools.

Web 2.0 has become a rather amorphous term for online services enabled to optimize networking. Naturally, searches have followed the path of those desiring to find and connect with their friends and contacts online. In large part, services and searching have migrated from desktops to laptops to handheld computers and cell phones, many of which are enabled with multiple networks, both wired and wireless; and photo, music, and video streaming capabilities and are connected via literally thousands of intermeshed applications to automate the mobile, ever-connected user. What these functions may mean for users, their employers, and their colleagues is a rapidly evolving series of policy, privacy, and social/behavioral questions.[7] According to Pew,[8] as of January 2014,

> 90% of American adults have a cell phone.
> 58% of American adults have a smartphone.
> 32% of American adults own an e-reader.
> 42% of American adults own a tablet computer.
> 67% of cell phone owners find themselves checking their phone for messages, alerts, or calls—even when they don't notice their phone ringing or vibrating.
> 44% of cell phone owners have slept with their phone next to their bed because they wanted to make sure they didn't miss any calls, text messages, or other updates during the night.
> 29% of cell phone owners describe their cell phone as "something they can't imagine living without."
> As of September 2013, 73% of online adults use social networking sites.

These statistics suggest that the percentage of users previously considered "power users" may have multiplied, from perhaps one-third in 2010 to 80% or more today. Without speculating too much on the accuracy or implications of that idea, one might infer that the proportion of those online who are likely to succumb to an impulse to act out and post unflattering items is nearing 100% of the proportion who would act out in the physical world.

As millions of users flock to the latest online services, they create both intelligence collection opportunities and the reasons for such collection. Two types of search tools have emerged from the evolution onto social networking platforms by Web 2.0 users: "real-time" and archival searchers. The real-time tools allow searches of Twitter and similar systems that are used to post short texts, photos, videos, and other items. The archival searches depend on indexing of materials posted online that takes place over about a 4-week period. Investigators need to know whether a search is likely to produce recent postings, and the only way to be sure is to go on the websites used by a subject and look for recent postings (which may or may not have been indexed yet by search engines). Relying on a search engine for recent postings is risky. Searching on Twitter for tweets provides up-to-date results, while using Yahoo! Search may not. With the jump in Web 2.0 use, several commercial search engines like Trackle, Monittor, Yauba, and others offered near-real-time, social website-inclusive searches, but some quickly failed. Soon, a new group of aggregator websites appeared, offering profiles of persons by fusing data from social sites and other postings, including Friendfeed, Pipl, PeopleSmart, Zabasearch, PeopleFinders, Spokeo, AdvancedBackgroundChecks, Zoominfo, Radaris, MyLife, and others (this list does not constitute a recommendation). An example of the potential value for investigators of correlating social networking postings to identify individuals and discover behaviors is illustrated by a study reported in 2009 by Arvind Narayanan and Dr. Vitaly Shmatikov from the University of Texas at Austin,[9] who developed an algorithm by which they identified the names and addresses of anonymous Twitter, Flickr, and Live Journal users by looking at relationships between all the members of a social network—not just the immediate friends connected with members. They found that one-third of those who are on both Flickr and Twitter can be identified from the completely anonymous Twitter graph, despite the fact that the overlap of members between the two services is thought to be about 15%. The researchers suggested that the more social network sites are used, the more difficult it will become to remain anonymous.[10]

Searching Web 2.0 sites can be useful for finding people[11] and major stolen items, monitoring brands, protecting intellectual property, discovering slanderous or otherwise troublesome postings about a company or brand, and many other similar uses. Some can unearth employees in the act of embezzling, theft, and unauthorized disclosures. Law firms often focus appropriately before and during trial on the evidence to be used and witnesses, oblivious to the fact that witnesses, stakeholders, interested parties, and even jurors, may be using the Internet to post and review both relevant and irrelevant items and both appropriate and inappropriate comments and sometimes posting items that may have a material impact on the trial. Preparation to depose or examine a witness on the stand can be strengthened by reviewing what the witness said about the topic or related issues that may well appear online. Posted materials can help impeach testimony or steer a cross-examination away from an area where the likely answers of the witness might hurt the attorney's case. If one side in a case reviews Internet postings but the other does not, there could be an advantage to the side that does. Public-sector witnesses have been blindsided when defense lawyers' searches have found online materials used to question the objectivity of their testimony.[12] Some lawyers who are Internet savvy scan for postings related to their cases, but this useful practice has yet to catch on with the legal profession as a whole.

Looking Up Subscribers

Often, an investigator will discover a telephone number, address, Internet protocol (IP) address (i.e., the string of numbers identifying a computer), a URL, or other listing information that needs to be identified or connected with the individual or organization of interest. People who post illicit materials online using anonymous virtual identities are pursued by stakeholders, for example, who try to identify them through the IP address, URL, e-mail address, or whatever concrete information is available. A variety of resources and search strategies exist for the investigator. Telephone numbers and addresses can be found in crisscross directories. Some of our favorite resources include the following:

Zabasearch.com provides name and telephone number searching, and free results may include the approximate date of birth and date of data capture.

Whitepages.com provides name, business, address, and telephone number lookups, and sponsors have links offering more data for a fee.

AnyWho.com is AT&T's national white and yellow pages and reverse lookup directory.

Similar services to those listed can be found on 411locate.com, addresses.com, people.yahoo.com, switchboard.com, and ussearch.com (which offers fee-based added information) and other sites.

When using online white and yellow pages, it is important to remember that misspellings, inaccurate (e.g., outdated) references, and other errors appear in free listings. In addition, unlisted telephone numbers (and the proliferation of unlisted cell phones as primary or sole numbers) have made it more difficult to obtain or verify primary contact information for some subjects. Likewise, rural towns where post office boxes are preferred over residential mailboxes may impede finding or verifying a name-address physical combination. When crisscross directories like those suggested fail to provide sufficient information, real estate records may be an alternative. Sites like http://www.netronline.com/ may be helpful in finding free online listings provided by counties, some of which can be searched by address, name, and so on. For example, an investigator starting with a name or an address could find the mailing address, owners' names, property description, and taxes of many homes in the United States.

Websites are frequently a focus of Internet intelligence interest. Unfortunately, because of spam, many website owners hide their contact information through anonymization services provided by website hosts. Large services like GoDaddy. com, ThePlanet.com, 1and1.com, FatCow.com, NetworkSolutions.com, Microsoft, and Yahoo offer a variety of options for website owners, from registration of the domain name to shared or exclusive use of servers, site certificates, sales checkout, credit card merchant services, and so on. Design and maintenance of website content are often done by outsourced contractors, including the host companies. It is important to know how to look up domain name ownership, IP address, and other website attributes so that those active on the web can be profiled accurately. This is generally known by the term *Whois lookup*. Several services offering Whois tracing include the following:

http://www.who.is/whois/

http://www.betterwhois.com/

http://www.domaintools.com/ provides current, deleted, and expired domains and other services, including reverse IP lookup and traceroute

http://www.networksolutions.com/whois/index.jsp offers Whois lookup and multiple services

L-Soft offers a service for lookups for listservs (server-based e-mail broadcast services) across the Internet at http://www.lsoft.com/lists/listref.html

IP2Location offers to provide the geographic location of IP addresses at http://www.ip2location.com/1.2.3.4

The Internet Assigned Numbers Authority (IANA) at http://www.iana.org/ provides coordination of the Domain Name System (DNS) and protocols for routing web traffic to the proper IP address from the URL entered and manages the global DNS root and the pool of IP numbers, allocating them to the regional Internet registries. It may be necessary to look up registries, registrars, domain name holders, and IP addresses using IANA and Internet registry resources. The Internet Corporation for Assigned Names and Numbers (ICANN) at http://www.icann.org/ coordinates IP addressing around the world. The American Registry for Internet Numbers (ARIN) is responsible for North America and the Caribbean and is available at https://www.arin.net/resources/index.html.

The Internet is using IPv4 and IPv6 (a larger number of IP addresses coming online) to route network communications. The main thing for an investigator to understand is that just as the packets (bits of data) flowing to and from a computer "know where to go" using the Internet's protocols, it is possible to find out, at least to a limited extent, who is at the other end of Internet connections by identifying the IP addresses used to route those packets. In the future, IPv6 may allow identification of senders through better authentication built in to the protocol. However, the trend toward protecting users' privacy against spammers harvesting e-mail addresses from the public Internet may offset the investigator's ability to identify users from virtual identities.

E-Mail

E-mail plays a part in many Internet investigations. E-mail addresses can sometimes be found using search engines, and both the user name and the entire address should be searched. E-mail can sometimes be traced on its route from sender to receiver, at least to the extent that the message header is not tampered with, depending on the e-mail service provider. E-mails may be sent from an Internet service provider (ISP) like Yahoo, Microsoft, or AOL or through a web mail service like Google's Gmail. E-mail also may come from a mail server operated by a corporation using its own mail server or an outsourced mail service provider. E-mail addresses may reflect the website of a business owner (e.g., john.doe@company. com) or the e-mail service provider (e.g., jdoe2@verizon.net, bigsam@hotmail.com). Internet investigators will sooner or later confront the need to identify the sender of an e-mail. The prospects of success for identifying "anonymous" e-mailers are not always high, but at least the initial steps are comparatively simple:

1. Obtain the message header. Ask the recipient of the e-mail to capture the message header and send it to you. Merely forwarding the message will not provide you with the original e-mail's message header. To obtain the message header, that is, the routing information about where the e-mail came from, the recipient should view and print it or copy and paste it from the e-mail program used. With Yahoo! mail, click the link "Full Headers" at the bottom of the page. With Outlook, click "Options," and the routing information appears. In Gmail, click on the down arrow next to "Reply" at the top right of the message pane and select "Show Original." In any e-mail program, look in help for "message header" or "full header" for instructions on how to find the routing information.
2. Review and analyze the message header. The header usually displays the sender's e-mail and IP address (which consists of numbers in the format XXX.XXX.XXX.XXX, for example, 123.435.987.654), shown closest to the sender's e-mail address at the bottom of the header. The IP addresses shown between the bottom and the top (where the recipient's e-mail address appears) are the IP addresses of servers through which the message was routed.
3. Use a reverse IP address lookup service to identify the IP address of the sender. This will usually at least provide the user's ISP, allow placement in

a geographical region, and in some cases provide the IP address of the mail server used by the sender. It may not be possible to identify the individual sender from a dynamic IP address unless the mail service provider will agree to determine who used that IP address on a specific date at a specific time (shown on the message—if the time/date stamp is accurate). Most ISPs and mail service providers demand a legal process (subpoena or warrant) for an outside investigator to identify senders by IP address. Law enforcement or court intervention would be needed for that step. With a fixed IP address, the mail host of the sender and possibly the sender himself or herself can be identified. Internal enterprise investigators may be able to use IT records to identify the sender of an e-mail launched within the enterprise.

4. In attempting to identify the sender of an e-mail, do not overlook analysis of the possible suspects' activities at the time that the e-mail was sent and include an analysis of the user name, content, and context of the message itself. These often provide clues to the sender's identity. Although it is possible for someone to create a free e-mail account just to send one e-mail, it is also possible that the sender used the same "anonymous" e-mail address or handle for many other communications, which may be linked with the sender on the Internet. Some e-mail accounts contain public profiles identifying the user. Some are linked with the user's work or true name e-mail addresses on social, business, and other sites.

5. When all else fails, it may be possible to engage the sender of an e-mail in an exchange of messages that could lead to his or her identification. This ploy demands sophisticated manipulation of the communications so the person is not tipped off that someone is trying to identify who he or she is and requires that the person answer the e-mail. If the sender is determined to remain anonymous, he or she may never return to the e-mail account used. However, some people are curious to see if there is a response to their provocation.

Commercial Database Providers

An increasing number of database companies provide registered clients such reports as business credit (e.g., Dun & Bradstreet at dnb.com and Experian at smartbusinessreports.com), employment verification (e.g., TheWorkNumber.com), and education verification (National Student Clearinghouse at StudentClearinghouse.org). As services continue to increase, databases like these should be sought out in periodic updates of resources available to the online investigator. The goal is to utilize a number of different sources, fusing the results into findings needed.

As an analyst becomes more experienced and comfortable with Internet investigations, it is almost inevitable that the analyst will be asked to find out something that simply is not available on the Internet. There are many types of misbehavior, including malicious and destructive communications, hate speech, bullying, stalking, slander against individuals and organizations, and postings corrosive of morale and civil behavior. Hard economic times sometimes bring out the worst in people, as do extreme political, religious, and moral beliefs. Personal disputes and sexual pursuits arise frequently in all groups. Analysts are asked to identify anonymous actors using the Internet to carry out misbehavior. Although every assignment may prove possible to accomplish, the ability of users to hide behind virtual identities can erect an impenetrable barrier. When a high degree of difficulty is found, it is important to enlist the help of others, such as information technology (IT) systems administrators and "white-hat" hackers, who may be able to trace activities using their systems security methods, including system logs, firewalls, user-monitoring tools, and Web-tracing tools. Often, the subject is a person within the organization itself, even if the communications appear to come from outside. The analyst contributes to the identification of the subject and resolution of the case, even if it proves impossible to use conventional Internet investigative methods, because a thorough inquiry explores every possible means (within reason and ethical constraints). Collaboration with others with different skill sets has proven to add value to all types of Internet investigations.

Although it may appear that the URLs of the suggested sources listed make up a long list, they are only a part—examples—of the wide variety of sources available. If an analyst were to use a substantial number of the URLs in manual searches, it could take a long time. Further, searching is step 1; review, filtering, capture, and analysis must still be done. Automating the search process can dramatically improve efficiency, so that is the topic of the next chapter.

Notes

1. http://www.naco.org/Counties/learn/Pages/Overview.aspx (accessed April 21, 2014).
2. Hetherington, Cynthia, and Stankey, Michael L., *The Manual to Online Public Records, The Researcher's Tool to Online Public Records and Public Information*, 6th edition (Tempe, AZ: BRB, 2008).
3. Wikipedia, http://en.wikipedia.org/wiki/Web_2.0 (accessed April 21, 2014).
4. Wikipedia, http://en.wikipedia.org/wiki/Folksonomy and http://en.wikipedia.org/wiki/Mashup_%28web_application_hybrid%29 (accessed April 21, 2014).
5. Social Networking Fact Sheet, Pew Internet and American Life Project, September 2013, http://www.pewinternet.org/fact-sheets/social-networking-fact-sheet/ (accessed April 17, 2014).
6. Carey, Rob, Navy CIO's blog, http://www.doncio.navy.mil/Blog.aspx (accessed June 10, 2010).
7. Smith, Aaron, Mobile Access 2010, Pew Internet and American Life Project, July 7, 2010, http://www.pewinternet.org/~/media//Files/Reports/2010/PIP_Mobile_Access_2010.pdf (accessed August 22, 2010), which illustrated rapid growth in wireless Internet use in all types of devices, including the fact that as of May 2010, 59% of adult Americans go online wirelessly, with increases in both laptop and cell web users.

8. Pew Internet and American Life Project, mobile technology fact sheet, as of January 2014, http://www.pewinternet.org/fact-sheets/mobile-technology-fact-sheet/ and social networking factsheet, as of September 2013, http://www.pewinternet.org/fact-sheets/social-networking-fact-sheet/ (both accessed April 21, 2014).

9. Schneier, Bruce, Schneier on Security: Identifying People Using Anonymous Social Networking Data, April 6, 2009, http://www.schneier.com/blog/archives/2009/04/identifying_peo.html (accessed April 17, 2010), relating the results of a study by Arvind Narayanan and Dr. Vitaly Shmatikov, from the University of Texas at Austin, in De-Anonymizing Social Networks, for IEEE Security and Privacy '09, available at http://randomwalker.info/social-networks/.

10. As the Texas study in Note 9 illustrated, sophisticated computer analysis may be capable of sifting huge quantities of data online to find previously hidden activities of "anonymous" users, meaning that one future possibility includes automated vetting tools that expose prior postings when candidates are cybervetted.

11. Taub, Eric A., Going beyond Google to Find a Lost Friend, *New York Times*, March 25, 2010.

12. For example: Dwyer, Tim, The Officer Who Posted Too Much on MySpace, *New York Times*, March 10, 2009, http://www.nytimes.com/2009/03/11/nyregion/11about.html?_r=2 (accessed April 21, 2014). A man arrested for illegal possession of a gun while on probation, resisting arrest, and using a stolen motorcycle was acquitted of the most serious charges (gun possession) by claiming that the officer's MySpace page, which referred to the film *Training Day* and had other cynical postings, showed that the officer's word could not be trusted, and the defendant's claims of brutality and dishonesty were accepted by the jury.

Chapter 18

Automation of Searching

Introduction

Search engines are amazing in their automation of the search process because they deliver the results of several complex and difficult system functions in less than a second consistently and with high quality. Like the dial tone always present when we pick up the phone, we take it for granted that in mere seconds we can execute a search and dive into results. Search engines like Google combine the spiders that crawl the web, applications that capture text and images, many servers that store billions of pages, indexing that allows instant retrieval, and algorithms to serve up references in the order most probably useful to the user. These are all wondrous functions. However, further automation is required to reduce the time needed for professional analysts to collect and present information quickly and simultaneously from many different search engines and websites where references are most likely to be found. When one looks for an automated Internet search tool, not many choices are found besides Internet search engines and intranet database-searching systems. Although in the broadest sense, Google is a tool, it is really a website offering a search service sponsored by commercials. Unfortunately, few good options for unadulterated desktop search software for the use of an investigator exist.[1]

Two types of software appear to be in relatively common use: enterprise search-database software, sometimes characterized as "middleware," and metasearch tools. The enterprise tools are designed to allow multiple different databases, including the Internet, to be accessed, and output normalized, for many users. They are generally large, expensive systems, demanding separate servers with access to source information, including the Internet. Metasearch tools are relatively simple Internet retrievers, combining multiple search engines into a single browser interface, to allow a user to obtain the output of several search engines simultaneously (as outlined in Chapter 16). Although metasearch engines are free and several types exist, their value is limited, especially because their output is based on that of their constituent search engines. At the end of the day, Google and Bing (Yahoo) are the only major search engines with consistently comprehensive results as of this writing. Because a competent, thorough search needs much more than would be provided by these tools alone, a different approach is required for automated web searching.

Why Automate Searching?

Given the capabilities of Google, is further automation of searching needed? The answer becomes obvious after only a few hours of searching. The list of websites (uniform resource locators, URLs) that must be visited to conduct a complete search on the same subject each time is long because one must visit sites not indexed by search engines and weed through ads. The number of pages returned for the average search is high and contains false positives. The manual, serial searching method is lengthy, repetitious, and exhausting, packed with duplication. The searcher longs for the capabilities of a super-metasearch engine that can deliver the most relevant, deduplicated results in the quickest, most painless manner, without ads. It is difficult to carry out a thorough, accurate Internet search quickly.

Broken down into its core processes, the automated search needs to

- Enter the same search term or terms into the search boxes in a list of URLs (the user enters a term once, and the system enters the same term as many times as needed)
- Conduct a multithreaded search (i.e., simultaneously visit the URLs designated and retrieve search results) in about the time it normally takes one search engine to do one search
- Present the references found to the analyst for review, ideally in rank order
- Eliminate nonrelevant, duplicate, and nonidentifiable references and broken links (e.g., links returning "404" errors—page not available)

Additional capabilities for an automated search system could include downloading and storing chosen web pages, facilitating search of new terms found as searching progresses (e.g., a new user name/e-mail address), and extracting data from search results and placing the data into draft reports and possibly relational databases. Two of the steps outlined are time consuming: executing the searches and reviewing the results. After years of looking for tools (software that is either free or affordable for an individual user), I have found few that are both ideal for the investigator and affordable in cost.

Enterprise Search Middleware

A whole branch of applications has been created for corporate data mining to "know what we know" from massive databases that all large enterprises now have, including those stored "in the cloud." These intranet applications often can extract data from multiple different types of databases through application programming interfaces that convert a query into the right language for each individual database. As "middleware," the applications then retrieve and "normalize" the data found and present them to the user in a way that is simple and usable, such as converting the information's format for use in a desktop program such as a browser, document, or spreadsheet. Besides in-house shared data storage, one of the databases used for inputs into the middleware can be the Internet.[2] However, the unstructured data formatting and searching dynamics of the Internet are formidable challenges for retrieving identifiable information and integrating it into the mix. Often, middleware programs help visualize the data by presenting it in charts, graphs, images, and other renditions that essentially allow the user to look at large amounts of information charted over a timeline, with links, trends, developments, anomalies, and other attributes highlighted, including grouping both identical and similar information. At the high end, the programs optimize a process of decision making, such as pricing new products made from complex components imported from several different places and predicting when price points, new technologies, competition, or timelines require action or change, process management and logistics have improvements, and so on. Several programs facilitate data mining for police and corporate security investigators by processing voluminous information in government databases. Enterprise database software tools such as those described can cost from hundreds of thousands to millions of dollars, including several thousand dollars for each user in software, maintenance, and training. Unless the investigator has access to a large agency's customized systems and budget, such tools probably are unsuitable or unaffordable for Internet searching. Those who do use custom systems inevitably receive information that is more useful from their in-house databases than the Internet because the systems are not optimized for thorough Internet searching. Further, the Internet search input may be no better than the constituent search engine, likely Google.

Investigative analytical and visualization tools are being used by large intelligence and investigative agencies. An example is i2's Analysis Product Line, including Analyst's Notebook,[3] which provides an integrated suite of database software designed for the investigator looking for relationships, patterns, and trends (used, it is claimed, by over 2,000 organizations worldwide, including government agencies).[4] A competing system is Sentinel Visualizer, which claims to provide advanced link analysis, data visualization, geospatial mapping, and social network analysis.[5] Raytheon's Digital Information Gateway (Visual Analytics) and Navagent Surf3D

Pro appear to be used as similar analytical platforms, integrating data from multiple stores and the Internet.[6] These types of systems can cost several thousand dollars per user for software, maintenance, appropriate hardware, and training. Many intelligence and investigative agency analysts use these tools successfully, and data captured from the Internet during investigations can be incorporated into the process. However, these systems are neither designed nor optimized for open-source data integration into the applications because they do not conduct comprehensive Internet searching as an integrated function. One reason is that intelligence and law enforcement agencies do not want to have a system that is integrated with their sensitive and classified internal databases connected directly to the public Internet. Another reason is that the Internet is not just another database, but rather a huge network of disparate types of data sources and program languages.

Essentially, professional analytical software for investigative analysts was not designed for Internet searching and costs too much for most individuals and small agencies. The types of software/middleware designed for law enforcement, court, and jail records management systems allow queries of public records (e.g., driver's licenses, car registrations, telephone directories) and law enforcement databases (e.g., the National Crime Information Center, court and inmate records).[7] Some systems span multiple jurisdictions, merging data from many databases. Unfortunately, these systems are much better at integrating structured data from linked records systems than they are at including Internet data, which are unstructured. Still, continued development of these systems is closing in on the goal of true integration of open-source data into the corporate body of knowledge. Many investigators prefer a personally managed tool singularly focused on open-source information from the Internet.

Some desktop tools have appeared with law enforcement and intelligence agencies as targeted markets, offering analytical software that fuses data from disparate sources, using geographical, descriptive, relations, patterns, connections and trend attributes, and sometimes social network analytics, to visualize or depict threats, risks, relationships, and opportunities. For example, Vere Software's WebCase software[8] is sold as a single-user or corporate edition (about $595–$745 in 2009 dollars) and in 2009 was reviewed favorably.[9] Other examples provided by the International Association of Crime Analysts' Resource Center[10] include software by Palantir,[11] HunchLab,[12] PowerCase,[13] and others. The core functions of this type of software relate to management, analysis, and depiction of data already collected and not full-featured web search.

A class of tools designed to facilitate web crawling and retrieval or "scraping," data mining (like Google, but not nearly as quick or robust), is optimized for marketing intelligence professionals, so it is not reviewed here.[14] Suffice it to say that harvesting e-mail addresses or comparing products, prices, and presentations are not what a professional Internet investigator is seeking.

Best-in-Class Desktop Tool

Currently, an example exists of a commercial off-the-shelf tool well suited for Internet investigators; this tool is known as Copernic Agent Personal (free) and Copernic Agent Professional (licensed) and is made by a Montreal company (Copernic.com) that also owns the classical metasearch engine Mamma.com.[15] Copernic's free desktop Internet search tool is good, but its turbo-charged Copernic Agent Professional version for about $40 is exceptional. At this writing, the free download version of Copernic Agent for personal use appears on the website, but the professional version no longer does, having been discontinued January 31, 2014.[16] The professional version has allowed a user to do customized searching efficiently and facilitated review, filtering, and reporting. In addition, Copernic makes desktop and enterprise search tools that index and search corporate or agency data (again, free for private use, with a modest fee for commercial use). Copernic also makes a tool, Tracker, to follow and update website activities and topics, and another tool, Summarizer, to extract the essence of text found to facilitate the reporting process. While Copernic Agent Professional was not the only tool available, its success among private and corporate investigators, as distinct from law enforcement, qualified it to be the only one mentioned here. Fortunately, Copernic Agent Personal is still available.

Investigative Search Tool Requirements

The ideal automated search tool is able to access chosen websites' search functions in large numbers. Copernic, for example, may query more or less 200 sites and return results in a few seconds. Filtering the results can be more efficient when the application allows the analyst to discard references that are false and select those that need in-depth review quickly and easily. Code that helps identify true references by name resolution (entity resolution) can help the analyst to filter possible references to a subject quickly and home in on those most likely to be identifiable. Much of the postsearch processing still must be the responsibility of the human analyst because computers are unable to make final identity and verification judgments.

Today, massive databases of public and private data are offered for a fee to subscribers of services like those provided by LexisNexis (e.g., Acurint, furnished to private investigators through IRB).[17] Competing large data broker firms, all of which are careful to verify subscribers' lawful purpose for access, include TLO and CLEAR.[18] One of LexisNexis' most successful capabilities in delivering records services is the ability to mine huge databases, reportedly carried out by advanced computer systems developed for the purpose.[19] The systems retrieve references to the subject of a query and pull related information into a cohesive report. As remarkable as the Acurint systems are, it is revealing that similar systems are not available to search for, identify references to, filter for accuracy, and compose a report from information available on the Internet. One reason is the enormous push of advertising and spam that are focused on web search today, which reportedly was one factor in Copernic discontinuing its Agent Professional software: "The information available on the web is growing exponentially and current search engines push a lot of sponsored links which affects greatly the search results quality."[20] Although the data brokers claim to include such Internet-related information as the subject's e-mail addresses and, in some instances, social networking references, their systems are as yet incapable of providing comprehensive search results.

Several government agencies and private companies are trying to develop tools that can deliver comprehensive reports from the Internet. As a nonprogrammer, I find it easiest to explain the current situation by reflecting that in the Federal Bureau of Investigation (FBI), I always found at least two or more people with the same name when searching FBI indices. The world's billions of people are reflected in Internet data, and one can imagine how many people with the same name appear online. Ensuring that the information found relates to the subject of interest and not someone else is still the art of the analyst.

One way to automate searching would be to have a multistep processor, such as one that does the following:

> User enters known data into a database (new file on subject) →
> Autosearch retrieves terms from database, executes Internet searches →
>> Search can include enterprise databases via intranet →
> Autoretrieve captures online pages (text), places results in database →
> Autoanalyze performs name resolution on new database items →
>> Ranks results by likelihood of relevance
>> Selects new search terms from text retrieved
>> Sends new terms through autosearch, which executes new searches
>> Repeats the autoretrieve and analysis process for second-tier results →
> Autoreport presents all results to the user in a draft text report →
> User edits the draft report, selects items for inclusion or deletion →
> User finalizes the report, sends it for review and publication

This process could include artificial intelligence (AI; a complex set of algorithms to allow the computer system to decide the highest-value retrieved data and place them into a draft report according to criteria programmed into the software). One type of AI might filter out false positives from search engines, and another might simply record sources for all confirming facts found (e.g., references that show the subject has the same address and profile already known) and report only conflicting or derogatory findings. AI would allow more processing and less human analysis, but in the end, there is still a need for analysts to make decisions about which references are identifiable with the subject, which are usable based on policy and standards of reporting, and which should be followed up with further investigation to determine the facts and resolve any potential discrepancies. The contribution of automation is that the analyst's time is focused on assessment and reporting of results rather than a manual process of search, review, select, capture, and report. Relieving the analyst of time-consuming, repetitive actions can allow much more efficient exploitation of open-source intelligence and allow processing of more subjects more quickly and with better results.

A Homegrown Solution

To solve the problem of collection online, my company developed our own proprietary tool for analysts to use in conducting searches. It functions much like a group of search engines bound together into a multithreaded search engine. The tool is loaded with URLs that usually produce the best search results (major search engines, alternative search terms such as exact match, and a variety of social networking and selected online search sites). The analyst enters a search term (name, e-mail, IP address, phone, postal address, or up to 10 keywords). The predetermined searches are done simultaneously in a few seconds. The analyst then scans the results from each fruitful search and captures the content from the links. The tool is flexible, allowing the analyst to update the queried URLs as needed to fit the purpose. It allows hour on hour of serial, manual searching to be done in minutes. We are still in the process of building our next-generation search-and-analysis tool, which we hope will reduce the time required to analyze search results by capturing references in a database from which identifiable information can be scanned, reviewed, and accepted or rejected efficiently and reports can be generated automatically.

Reducing Analytical Time Using Automation

As related previously, the analyst oversees a multistep process in providing reports of open-source Internet intelligence on any topic, including the search, filtering, analysis, composition, and reporting. Each of the steps mentioned is actually a serial, multitask process because the initial search is supplemented by searches of new terms found in results. Here is how we have managed to reduce the time needed for an investigator to report results of an Internet search:

- Do as many searches as possible simultaneously, using available automation, then search key URLs from a list manually. For a new practitioner, we recommend using Copernic Agent, search (Google and Bing) and metasearch engines, and URLs mentioned in the previous chapters, including those best suited for the case, to ensure that the search is comprehensive, accurate, and reliable.
- Review and select results for inclusion in reporting, capturing images of Internet pages deemed to contain substantive information.

- Summarize findings and provide links to sources of items used in the report.
- Append images of the web pages used in the report, if appropriate.
- Assemble and retain a file with collected items and the report.
- When using a team to search, furnish a reports officer with the results mentioned for inclusion in a combined report of findings.

For an individual subject, this process can be accomplished in about 2 hours by an experienced analyst or team. However, if the references are extensive and the contents of data found are lengthy, considerable additional time may be required to search, analyze results, choose the most apt items responsive to the assignment, and compose the report language.

The magic of the analyst is exercising the logic and intuition needed to find and report what those requesting the search want to know. Often, the question is whether there is some past behavior by a person or entity that may signal that the subject poses a risk in a future association, such as an employee, contractor, holder of a clearance, witness, suspect, customer, partner, trustee, supplier, or merger acquisition. The successful analyst recognizes and reports precisely the facts that may be of concern for the moment in decision making. This is the essence of value-based intelligence.

Caching and Data Mining

Today's collection tools, database programs, and storage capabilities allow even the small agency to identify, capture, and cache data likely to be of investigative use. For example, if the analyst can identify a series of websites/URLs that contain postings of potential interest to the client, then they can be collected continuously and placed in storage. At first blush, this may seem to be a daunting task for an analyst who is not a programmer of search tools or databases and does not have the information technology (IT) skills to be the architect of an enterprise records management system. However, the tools mentioned in this book can be used to construct a low-cost solution that is capable of collecting valuable data on practically any topic. For example, using free Internet search and tracking tools can allow an analyst to find, copy, and store web pages in HTML (HyperText Markup Language) or Portable Document Format (PDF) in a free MySQL or Excel database or simply in an unstructured folder. For less than $100, the analyst can put the database on a separate hard drive with a terabyte or more of space. Several search utilities, costing from nothing (i.e., part of a personal computer operating system) up to about $50, allow the analyst to mine the database in moments, using word search, to retrieve information on any topic. Now, the analyst has a proprietary solution to data collection and exploitation on a matter of special interest.

With programming help and advanced tools, analysts have used the method outlined to capture information about criminal activities online, copying and storing the computer activities of pirates, fencers, drug dealers, thieves, crackers, credit card fraudsters, and spammers. Once a channel for illicit activities is identified, it can be monitored and recorded for enforcement, intelligence, and security use. This approach could be described as the great equalizer on the largely unpoliced Internet. Of course, the richness of information found online allows marketers, researchers of all kinds, and curious individuals to find intelligence on almost any topic in the same way.

The Human Interface in Internet Investigations

A colleague in law enforcement complained privately that today's crop of incoming investigators is more apt to expect to find all the answers at the computer screen and seems reluctant to use interviews, field investigation, and traditional surveillance techniques to gather information. There may be some truth to this observation, but in reality, human interaction must be used to identify the websites of greatest interest and to find out the methodology and motivation of offenders. With only one or a few undercover operators, perpetrators' Internet communications systems can be identified and monitored by intelligence officers. Coordination among officers is critical to build on both human and cyber intelligence to gain and maintain the best surveillance and witness elicitation possible. Among the sources used for this type of approach are the following:

- Recently captured, arrested, or convicted individuals knowledgeable about online support for the illicit enterprises
- Data retrieved during computer forensic analysis of systems used in crimes and in lawful intercepts
- Confidences shared with trusted inside sources by those involved in the illicit enterprise
- Online infiltration of an illicit enterprise by an investigator
- Witness reports

To collect intelligence needed on people and entities engaged in misbehavior, it is sometimes necessary for an investigator to assume an undercover role. Care should be taken in such undertakings to ensure that the undercover officer does not commit illegal or unlawful acts, which can result in evidence inadmissible in a legal or administrative proceeding. In addition, both ethical and psychological reviews are needed to keep the undercover person on track and avoid the kinds of activities that could be reprehensible. Recent history has taught both law enforcement and private investigators many lessons about how not to carry out undercover activities. Undercover activities fall under the rubric of "Don't try this at home," requiring professional training and experience in investigations.

Closely related to the undercover role is the concept of "pretexting." Neither undercover investigation nor pretexting is illegal or unethical in and of themselves, but if either involves certain types of inducement to commit crimes, illicit deception, or fraud, it can be unlawful. Classical pretexting calls for an operative to ask questions as though he or she were entitled to receive the answers, which may involve misleading or misdirecting the subject. Using a too-broad definition of pretexting unfortunately led private investigators in a notorious case to pretend to be the subjects of their investigations in communications with telephone companies to obtain copies of the subjects' telephone bills. This constituted wire fraud, a federal crime. When an investigator assumes a role that is not fraudulent (e.g., an old classmate, a journalist, or a friend's friend) and asks questions of a subject or associates, a pretext can remain within legal and ethical boundaries. For example, asking a subject or his family about his welfare and inviting him to an upcoming reunion can result in elicitation of substantive data, and the discussion might occur over the Internet. Another example is when an investigator using a pseudonym makes a request to a subject to be included among customers of an illicit enterprise, such as distribution of contraband, like pirated movies, music, and software. When a pretext such as these results in acceptance of the undercover operator, it may be possible to gain access to illegal, ongoing web communications. Such communications can be captured and cached to facilitate collection of evidence, intelligence, and security protection information.

A persistent question about propriety in background vetting online is whether it is ethical to pose as a fellow alumnus or associate or, without identifying oneself as an investigator, to ask a subject to be included as a trusted insider ("to friend" the subject) with access to privacy-protected data on a subject's social networking site. A subject, on learning the friend is an investigator, might consider such a ploy to be a violation of privacy. However, there are two issues to consider. One is the reason that the investigator might want to view the data only shown to the subject's "friends." If there is reason to believe that the data could contain substantive information about misbehavior by the subject, there could be a strong reason to attempt the subterfuge described. Further, if the subject has a wide circle with a large number of friends, the "privacy" protected may be minimal. The investigator, possibly aided by others in the background investigation, should consider other alternatives, such as interviews of the subject's associates (who could be among the social site's listed friends). "Friendship" the subject to access a restricted profile may be deemed ethical and less intrusive than interviews of the subject's associates. However, using such ploys routinely, without a compelling reason, such as a lack of alternative means to resolve questions, would not be considered proper.

Another issue relating to Internet investigative ethics is whether viewing a subject's associates' postings is proper. The subject may have been notified, and consented to cybervetting, but his friends have not. This question concerns the degree to which the privacy of the associates is breached when their publicly visible postings are perused by the investigator. We have found that it is not unusual for a friend or acquaintance to post information of value about a subject, including seriously troubling behaviors. Of course, some postings are humorous or attempts to tease a friend. There are three issues to consider: Is the posting public? Are the data collected about the subject? Can the finding be reported without breaching the associate's privacy? Because the postings are (for the most part) public, there is no legal protection to the information or the identity of the one uploading it, no matter who posted it. Like a newspaper story that names several people, there is no logical or legal basis for contending that the mention of others, including the author, constitutes a reason for declining to read the story about any one of those named. When the information is substantive, it should properly appear in the report (with or without naming the others, as the investigator considers appropriate). When the information is not relevant, identifiable, or useful, it does not appear in the report, so it could be argued that no one's privacy is substantively breached. The inclusion of associates' names and other information about them in a report on the subject could be avoided (to protect their privacy) but might need to be included as a list of potential witnesses to corroborate misbehavior.

Internet intelligence is only one component of a whole picture comprising open-source intelligence that is needed about people, entities, and topics for which strategic and tactical decisions must be made. Even while deeply engaged online, analysts must remember that recognizing the human intelligence opportunities is as important as finding the data targeted. Combining open-source intelligence from the public Internet, deep web, cached data, and recent postings calls on the investigator to keep up to date with what is available online, how to find and exploit new sources, and how to assess findings. Those who do this well can make a significant contribution to the knowledge needed by enterprise decision makers.

Notes

1. Based on my company's review of moderately priced desktop software options for comprehensive Internet searching for investigative purposes, 2005–present, few choices were available at the time this book was written.
2. A good depiction and definition of middleware and its functions can be found at http://www.pcmag.com/encyclopedia_term/0,2542,t=middleware&i=47013,00.asp (accessed April 22, 2014).
3. IBM's i2 is described at http://www-01.ibm.com/software/info/i2software/ (accessed April 22, 2014).
4. Kardell-Lessard, Stacy, and Feneis, Penny, Determining Entity Relationships in Combating Refund Fraud, Minnesota Department of Revenue, i2 Analyst's Notebook, http://www.taxadmin.org/FTA/Meet/07am_data/Papers/Tuesday/Technology/RefundFraud.pdf (accessed April 22, 2014).
5. Sentinel Visualizer is found at http://www.fmsasg.com/ (accessed April 22, 2014).

6. Digital Information Gateway (Visual Analytics), a Raytheon offering, http://www.visualanalytics.com/products/dig/index.cfm (accessed April 22, 2014); Navagent Surf3D Pro, http://www.navagent.com/ (accessed April 22, 2014).

7. International Association of Crime Analysts (IACA) evaluation of crime analysis software, http://www.iaca.net/resources.asp?Cat=Software (accessed April 22, 2014).

8. Vere Software Internet Investigator's Toolkit, http://veresoftware.com/index.php/webcase_overview/downloads (accessed April 22, 2014).

9. Guardian Digital Forensics tool reviews, http://digitalforensictools.blogspot.com/2009/02/webcase-vere-software.html (accessed April 22, 2014).

10. http://www.iaca.net/resources.asp?Cat=Software (accessed April 22, 2014).

11. http://www.palantir.com/ (accessed April 22, 2014).

12. http://www.azavea.com/products/hunchlab (accessed April 22, 2014).

13. http://www.xanalys.com/products/ (accessed April 22, 2014).

14. Many examples are provided on http://www.kdnuggets.com/software/web-content-mining.html (accessed April 22, 2014).

15. Copernic is found at http://www.copernic.com/.

16. http://www.copernic.com/en/products/agent/ (accessed April 22, 2014).

17. LexisNexis is found at http://www.lexisnexis.com/, as is Acurint. IRB is at http://www.irbsearch.com/ (accessed April 22, 2014).

18. TLO, a Trans Union company, http://www.tlo.com/, and CLEAR, by Thomson Reuters, https://clear.thomsonreuters.com/clear_home/index.jsp (accessed April 22, 2014).

19. O'Harrow, Robert, Jr., *No Place to Hide* (New York: Free Press, 2005).

20. http://www.copernic.com/en/products/agent/ (accessed April 22, 2014).

Chapter 19

Internet Intelligence Reporting

Introduction

Based on current legal and policy standards (or lack thereof) about the use of Internet intelligence, it appears that the highest risk is in the reporting and subsequent use of online data. Merely conducting an online search creates a record in the computer used, which might be legally discoverable, even if no report of findings is made. Reports may be oral or written, but it is clear that even when formal reports are not written, the activities of the web searcher are chronicled in one form or another in the computer systems used to access the Internet. Today, many enterprises allow anyone to search any topic, to process any information gained as they wish, and to reach whatever conclusions or decisions they believe are appropriate based on their findings. Major search engines store records of queries not only on the workstation of the researcher, but also on proxies, firewalls, and search engine servers, identifying queries with Internet protocol (IP) addresses. A serial murderer in the Midwest was convicted based in part on evidence of searching and mapping done on his personal computer (PC). Internet search records could be subpoenaed to show bias or unfair treatment. If a pattern of unfair practices were suspected (e.g., bias in hiring), the enterprise's Internet search records could be obtained for civil or criminal proceedings.

Although work-related googling is widely allowed, some agencies and enterprises have adopted policies about cybervetting. Many forbid or discourage cybervetting. A problem created by forbidding cybervetting is that enterprise computers are apt to contain vestiges (evidence) of unauthorized web searching by employees, and decisions or conclusions they reach may not be linked to information they found online. Even though cybervetting guidelines may need to be more complex than simply forbidding the practice, it is better for the enterprise to set conditions for the use of search results, and require documentation, to protect against false charges of discrimination. In-house investigations are not limited by the Fair Credit Reporting Act, but the same set of ethical and legal principles should be applied so that employees' conduct is lawful. The bottom line of cybervetting guidance should be that online investigations must be authorized and properly documented, and actions taken must be based on findings recorded.

Records

The overall positive effects of using the Internet as a quick reference tool far outweigh the risks of second-guessing the decisions made based on such searches. However, when the decisions made could have an impact on people, significant assets, or information, the enterprise policy should be to create and maintain business records of the process. Among the benefits derived from such documentation are protection of process integrity against liability claims for impropriety, a "paper trail" from which processes can be improved, and records that can be consulted for facts in the future. Because substantive Internet intelligence reporting may be provided to several different recipients, combined with results of other investigative steps (e.g., interviews), or may be summarized for executive use, it is important to have coherent reporting and records retention schemes. What follows is a series of recommendations about how open-source intelligence and specifically Internet information should be reported.[1]

Ultimately, the client decides the best, most efficient way that findings should be conveyed. Experience has shown that when a report is complete but simple and straightforward, it has great value. Further, if it is well written, that is, clearly worded, holds the attention of the reader, and is grammatical and well organized, it is most effective in communicating the essential facts that decision makers need.

Content

The first principle of good business and government record keeping is to have a file for each case or project, in which a copy is kept of each document, reference, or link that was used in the matter. If the issue does not rise to the level of a case or project, then it is appropriate to keep a copy of any memo, notes, or correspondence in a file on the general topic, indexed for retrieval, should that be necessary in the future. Records routinely kept in this manner can resolve many potential issues that might arise, including refreshing recollections, documenting actions taken, and being available to support or defend against a legal claim. Internet searches, in both raw and finished form, should be preserved in files when appropriate, such as when an adverse decision is made or when details could be needed in the future. When in doubt, keep a record long enough so that if an issue arises months, or even 3–5 years, from the file's creation, the facts about the file's contents will be known. Files containing personally identifiable information should be retained according to the enterprise's schedule for records disposition and destruction.

Basic principles of business and government reporting should be observed, including recording the dates that items are found, the original dates the items were created and their authors (if available), the precise locations, and any other details that identify and describe the data found, who handled them, and how they were preserved. Investigative agencies routinely record the identities of investigators and analysts, a summary of how information was obtained, and information disposition. Data should be stored in a manner designed to protect their security and integrity. By observing such routines, analysts will ensure that the reliability of the content is as high as possible and may be qualified as evidence in a court.

There are several ways to approach report content, based on client needs. One type of report is the report by exception, in which known facts and items developed that are not expected to have an impact on a decision are omitted from the report. Unreported data are still maintained in the file containing the record of the inquiry in case someone needs to refer to them, but they are not set out in the case report. For example, when the purpose of the report is to ascertain whether there is any information available from an Internet search that could have an impact on a hiring or clearance decision, the investigator could be told to leave out of the report verification of address, employer, telephone number, and so on and even the fact that the subject has a Facebook profile. Names of other people not needed for adjudication could be omitted. Of course, the report should not contain information identifying the subject as a member of a protected class (race, religion, ethnicity, sex, etc.) with few exceptions. However, if the subject's behavior or documents online show that the subject misbehaved (e.g., violated a law, showed bad judgment, mistreated someone, or was dishonest), those items would be placed in a report. If there were no derogatory findings, the subject's name could be placed on a list about whom there was nothing to report, based on the criteria for the Internet search conducted. This approach could be helpful to those enterprises seeking to include cybervetting in personnel screening because, although the collection and analysis of Internet data may be resource intensive in covering a long list of searches, the reporting is simplified for efficiency.

Another type of reporting is to capture and present any and all information found. Information is frequently organized under topical headings like those found in an Outlook address book: name, address, telephone numbers, e-mail addresses, employer, position, and so on. These headings can be expanded or limited based on findings and client requirements and can apply to people, entities, and topics. New headings can be created to suit the case, such as arrests, civil suits, online activities, news media reports, and so on. When a report is lengthy, it is appropriate to include an executive summary at the beginning, briefly presenting all major results. More significant findings, that is, those deemed material to the client, should be prioritized by inclusion as early as possible in a lengthy report.

Analyst's Comments

When reporting items found online that may need explanation, it is appropriate to include an analyst's comments. The comments should be set off from the factual reporting and clearly indicate their origin and purpose. For example:

> [Analyst's note: The author of this posting using a name identical with the subject's does not appear to be identifiable with the subject because his residence is located 354 miles from the subject's residence.]

It is appropriate to include analyst's comments in circumstances such as the following:

- The item reported may not be true, may not be identifiable with the subject, or should be treated skeptically.
- The manner in which the item was found could have a bearing on how it is used.
- Additional information could place the item in a new light.
- Other facts found tend to either confirm or deny the item reported.
- An explanation may be needed for a particular type of Internet activity or language used (e.g., jargon).

In the event that an analyst's experience could contribute to the interpretation of a report but inclusion of opinion in the report itself is inappropriate, a separate report cover page or transmittal communication may be used. This is a tradition in law enforcement and intelligence reporting when commentary or guidance is added to a factual report. In language that clearly separates findings from observations, opinions, and possibly suggested guidance, the analyst can set out helpful comments for the client. A (fictionalized) example might be the following:

> In the attached report, references to "PPXX69's" Facebook and Flickr profiles, with the accompanying photos and text, appear to be a series of spoofs, attempts at humor and teasing (some of which could be viewed as obscene) by more than one person. It was not possible to verify that the subject posted the material or whether the content of the photos and text refer to, portray, or are attributable to the subject. In the view of experienced Internet analysts, these profiles were not intended to be taken seriously. The subject is linked with the items reported by tagging of the subject's name in several of the photos on Flickr and in the Facebook profile and the use of a nickname that appears in other profiles of the subject. To

understand or verify the apparently humorous nature of the postings, the subject's explanation could be sought.

During my career, I have had the privilege of participating in every aspect of intelligence and investigative collection, reporting, high-level executive recommendations, testimony, all-source assessments, critical infrastructure protection, intelligence analytical management, training, and comprehensive project documentation. The most important principle I learned is that decision makers want a report to provide the critical facts as clearly and succinctly as possible. Executives look for a summary at the beginning, substantial evidence presented in clear writing in a well-structured body, and reliable sources for the facts reported. Nonpertinent data may be collected and retained until it is confirmed that they are unneeded but should not be included in a report. Intelligence reporting may need to include items that appear to contradict the central theme or tenor of the evidence because not every situation is black and white, and competing versions of the facts may be found. Internet and open-source data may contain items deliberately posted to deceive, and a key purpose of collection and analysis is to find and weigh the credibility of all evidence. In the early twenty-first century, it has unfortunately become the norm for some advocates to exaggerate, prevaricate, and deceive to convince the public. It is good to remember that, today, the report of open-source intelligence is competing with many types of media catching the client's attention, so the most effective reports are grammatical, succinct, accurate and convincing, and hold the reader's attention.

Organization and Formatting

In some types of intelligence assessment (usually at a higher management level), it is not only the essential facts that are reported but also the framework for the decisions to be made. In this type of document, the report is a summary of all the relevant intelligence reporting, and is structured to convey

- Facts as well as can be known
- Options, with all major choices outlined
- Pros and cons for each option
- Summary of the evidence for the best option
- Recommendation for the option to be chosen

The decision support report type outlined is similar to the transmittal document, in which not only findings but also opinions, assessments, and recommendations are provided. However, it differs in that it includes intelligence summaries with opinions.

The best format for a report is one that will fit the needs of the client and assist the analyst in organizing the contents in a logical, easy-to-understand order. Outlines for two popular types of reports are included to illustrate the types of headings used for a report in which the subject is an individual or a company.

A report on a person may use the following outline (include prior as well as current information if called for):

Executive summary
Name, aliases, and identifying information
Contact information (telephone numbers, addresses, e-mail addresses)
Court records (criminal and civil)
Financial situation, including bankruptcies, liens, and judgments
Other derogatory information (e.g., government sanctions, expelled from school, discharged from employment, accusations, conflicts of interest)
Spouse, significant other, and family
Property ownership
Education
Employment
Profiles and biographies
Online activities
Associates
News media reports
Photographs

A report on a company or entity may use the following outline (include prior as well as current information if called for):

Executive summary
Name, other "doing business as" names, and identifying information
Contact information (telephone numbers, addresses, e-mail addresses, websites)
Court records (criminal and civil)
Bankruptcies and credit problems
Liens and judgments
Other derogatory information (e.g., government sanctions, stockholder issues, accusations, disputes)
Conflicts of interest
Product recalls, consumer complaints, Better Business Bureau report
Entity ownership and control, including Securities and Exchange Commission (SEC) filings
Entity reputation and place in the market
Federal, state, and local charters, licenses, and permits
Property ownership

Business credit report (e.g., Dun & Bradstreet, if not covered previously)
History
News media reports

As mentioned, topical headings can be added or deleted as appropriate. Some individuals and organizations have multiple websites, and online activities may or may not be a large portion of the report, depending on such activities.

Source Citations

There are two widely used methods of source citations in open-source intelligence reports, one in which the sources appear directly beneath the item reported and the other in which footnote- or endnote-style superscript numbers or letters are appended to the item, referring to a citation appearing in a section at the end of each page or, more often, at the end of the report. Normally, citations are not used in the executive summary. Sources should be shown wherever possible in the main body because, by the nature of open-source reporting, it is possible that doubt or a dispute could arise over the accuracy of an item's substance. Open-source reporting is unlike that from covert or clandestine sources. Most of the time, it is not only unnecessary to protect sources and methods in Internet investigative reports but also important for the consumer of the report to be able to see the source to help judge the reliability of each item. Internet citations should include the URL from which the data were collected, allowing the reader to refer to the page. A Portable Document Format (PDF) copy of the web page should be placed in an appendix to the report, or at least maintained in the case file, in case it becomes necessary to review the original source. Because websites may change frequently, the version of the page as found should be preserved.

Attribution

In reporting an item found on the Internet, the analyst should take care to examine the basis for attributing the information to the subject. Matching a name may not be a strong identification by itself. If attribution is crucial to the value of the report, the analyst should not assume that the reader has the same level of conviction that the data are identifiable with the subject. It may be desirable to spell out the factors that led to the identification, especially if they are not readily visible in the text. If the client is familiar with Internet reports and likely to reach the same conclusions based on the information presented, the facts found can be laid out without comments. However, if the report may be reviewed by others (e.g., an executive concerned with a no-hire decision or withholding of a security clearance, a decision against a merger or pursuing an intellectual property theft case against a competitor), it may be prudent to point out the basis of the item's attribution. Following is a fictionalized example from an actual case:

> Cornelius McCarthy, using the name Markus Smith, addressed a group of teammates in an Internet presentation preserved in an audio recording and posted online as part of his activities as a leader in the Hundred Years War massively multiplayer online fantasy game. In the audio recording (transcript attached), McCarthy used obscenities, racial epithets, and insults for team members as part of his role as an army leader. He also urged the team to spend all day and all night, as he does, in pursuing online game objectives.
>
> Source: http://www.hundredyearswar.com/audio/839021hfnaso_4f
>
> [Analyst's note: The subject was identified by the tag "Pillager" on the audio file at the above URL, which is a user name the subject also employed on his MySpace and Facebook profiles, as well as revealed in a *Variety* interview of April 1, 2014, in which he asserted that his leadership role in the online game enhances his managerial credentials at XWR Systems, where he is employed as a software security programmer. His true name, user name, and online fantasy war pseudonym are recorded together on all of the above profiles found, as well as in the *Variety* story.]

The analyst should carefully note and record (if not report) all of the indicators used to attribute a finding on the Internet to a particular person or entity. This is a good practice even if there is no question asked or denial on the part of a subject that it is a valid attribution. The analyst will find that there are many ways to link an individual or entity with behavior, and often, it only takes an alert observation to record ample evidence of the connection. Note that it is possible for a hacker to impersonate someone else online and post items that seem attributable, but are not. Ultimately, attribution should be verified if adverse action is contemplated.

Verification

Attributing a particular behavior or posting to a subject may reflect a single instance or may be part of a pattern of behavior. Although it appears that many Internet users have multiple virtual identities (user names, nicknames, handles), it is not unusual for a person to

- List all or many of his or her different nicknames in a Facebook or other profile
- Reveal and publish his or her true name and nickname in a single communication
- Use Twitter or e-mail to update a group with a link to a true name and nickname together

Finding the virtual identities used by a subject assists the Internet investigator to find all or many of the instances where online behavior is observable and attributable to the subject. It is also an excellent way to add to evidence that the attribution is correct and to verify that the same individual is involved. Verification in this sense includes instances such as

- An individual with the same true name and nickname(s) is involved in the same types of activities, involving the same group(s) of people, over a period of time in the same place.
- An individual habitually and repeatedly uses the same websites, has the same friends, and uses similar language to describe interests, actions, and choices on different occasions.
- An individual makes multiple references to the same activity or behavior on different occasions, in different places, and in different contexts.
- A friend or acquaintance of the subject records or makes references to acts of the subject.
- An individual maintains different profiles over time that refer to other profiles of the same individual, in which identical or similar postings appear.

Verification may sometimes involve a high degree of certainty that the behavior is attributable to the subject, based on multiple references to the same user (based on name, location, and habits) and repeated instances over time. However, verification may be much less certain when there is little to prove or indicate that the same individual is responsible or is portrayed in the references found. When the investigator finds that the available data offer little or no support to verify that the postings are attributable to the subject, such as name only, that fact should be reported. Not every substantive report can be verified. For example, a PACER (Public Access to Court Electronic Records) online federal court record of a subject's bankruptcy, based on name-only references, could be verified by an Acurint report from LexisNexis. However, if the Acurint report did not show a bankruptcy, perhaps the only way to verify the reference would be to conduct a physical court records review. As with many open-source intelligence endeavors (including human source reporting), the results may contain strong evidence, compelling and verified references, probably attributable behaviors, and possibly identifiable items or may raise questions (or generate leads) that need to be resolved through additional investigation.

Verification of Internet intelligence reports ultimately may depend on the subject. There are various ways to use information or an admission from the subject to verify misbehavior or otherwise important issues raised by open-source intelligence collection. Before a "confrontational interview" of the subject (i.e., an interview in which a subject is asked about a possibly troubling or derogatory reference), it may be possible to elicit from the subject sufficient information to confirm or deny the reference in question. Among the methods that could be considered are the following:

- Asking the subject, prior to a confrontational interview, to provide written or oral information likely to include the topical area where the question arose. For example, asking the subject to list all of the social networking and photo-posting sites he or she utilizes online could reveal that the posting in question is one listed or is omitted. Because the requested list may be part of the application process, for which deception constitutes grounds for denial of employment, the answers given would be helpful in any decision.
- "Friending" the subject on a social networking site or activity website where the behavior in question might be a logical topic of discussion. Some believe that this tactic can be unethical, especially if the subject is duped into believing that he or she is dealing with a real friend. Impersonation may be in conflict with of state or local laws, especially if something of value is sought and obtained from deception. However, if the investigator pretends to be a fellow alumnus or other "friendly stranger" and is accepted by the subject, then any admission made by the subject could be considered freely made. This type of elicitation should be done by those trained in the art and supervised to prevent crossing an ethical line. Assuming an undercover role on the Internet, as in any instance, should not be done in such a way that it encourages illegal or illicit activity by anyone, but can ethically be done to elicit information from a subject willing to enter a discussion.
- Interviewing an associate or contact of the subject who (based on investigation) appears to be able to shed light on the issue and who may be in a position to elicit further data from the subject, if that is appropriate in the investigation.

When the subject is interviewed on an issue that arose because of the results of an Internet investigation, it is important to have ready a document with those results to support the interview. The use of the term *confrontational interview* (twice previously and here) is not to suggest that the interview is hostile or aggravated in any way. Rather, it is designed to allow the interviewer to attempt to elicit from the subject the facts and circumstances surrounding the items found during the Internet investigation.

Experience has shown that, at first, subjects tend to omit listing potentially embarrassing websites used and postings that they would rather a potential employer did not see. When given the opportunity—because they are confronted with apparent knowledge on the part of the interviewer—most people will admit and explain the potentially troubling behavior found. If the subject continues to deny any involvement with a derogatory posting, the report can be shown to the subject with a request for an explanation. At this point, as with the entire interview, the subject can elect to tell the truth, deny the truth, or explain why the reported information is not what it seems. In any case, the results should be sufficient to verify or rule out use of the findings in the report or in adjudication.

The Internet is a new frontier to many tens of millions, who have made it a new playground, as well as a place where business and government conduct much of their operations. As users cope with the fact that the Internet does not offer an opportunity to avoid responsibility for behavior that is otherwise illegal, illicit, unethical, or socially unacceptable, employers and investigators will also cope with large-scale fantasy, humor, and pranks online. Verifying findings in open-source intelligence will be a challenge no matter what the medium of communications. Recent studies showed that around 40% of employers are finding disqualifying information about candidates online.[2] The opportunities presented by the Internet for discovering and addressing computer-based behaviors potentially destructive to the enterprise should be exploited to ensure that business and government take logical, measured steps to hold authorized users—those given the privilege of being hired into a job with computer access—to a high standard.

Notes

1. Reporting guidelines provided in this chapter are based on my more than 45 years of report writing of all types, including news media, investigative and intelligence reporting, analysis, predictions, executive recommendations, and strategic risk/threat analyses.
2. Lorenz, Mary, Two in Five Employers Use Social Media to Screen Candidates, July 1, 2013, Survey Results, Talent Factor, http://thehiringsite.careerbuilder.com/2013/07/01/two-in-five-employers-use-social-media-to-screen-candidates/ (accessed April 23, 2014).

Chapter 20

Illicit Websites and Illegal Behavior Online

Introduction

Internet investigations frequently focus on individuals or organizations to determine the nature of their behaviors online. Increasingly, investigations of terrorism, organized crime, fraud, economic espionage, smuggling, and other serious crimes find websites used in criminal enterprises. As the growth of e-commerce reflects (estimated at $263.3 billion annually, an increase of 16.9% [±4.9%] from 2012 in the United States, according to the Census Bureau),[1] the Internet is a good venue to advertise, attract customers, direct prospects to sales sites, proselytize, collaborate online, plan and coordinate activities, order goods, and keep track of enterprises. Digital goods are especially easy to sell online. Unfortunately, digital goods might also include pirated films, videos, music, software, and the like.

Cybercrime

Child pornography, unauthorized use of computer systems, and contraband digital assets are three examples of crimes that have moved aggressively online. It is worth taking a moment, because of the frequency that such cybercrimes are found, to outline the difficulties they pose for enterprises, investigators, and the Internet as a venue.

Child Pornography and Internet Porn

Child pornography laws in the United States and most of the world generally define depiction and possession of images of underage sexual activity as illegal.[2] In the United States, federal criminal law in Title 18 US Code Sections 2251–2260 forbids production of child pornography (15- to 30-year sentence); selling or buying children for sexual exploitation (30 years to life); possession, distribution, and receipt of child pornography (5- to 20-year sentence); and importation of child pornography (10-year sentence). The severity of the sentences alone testifies to the seriousness with which the federal criminal justice system treats child pornography. Yet, it is all too easy to encounter what appears to be "kiddie porn" online. One of the reasons was articulated by the Department of Justice: "Unfortunately, the child pornography market exploded in the advent of the Internet and advanced digital technology. The Internet provides ground for individuals to create, access, and share child sexual abuse images worldwide at the click of a button."[3] Approaches to child porn and its relationship with child sexual abuse challenge all levels of law enforcement and have inspired collaboration for decades.[4]

The distribution of child pornography anonymously, worldwide via the web, has allowed a formerly well-controlled crime to explode from the mid-1980s to the present. Ironically, the digital nature of the images has allowed law enforcement to discover and verify possession of known illegal porn in the computers and media of suspects, facilitating enforcement. However, the wide proliferation of images and mingling with other adult materials has created a large burden for the criminal justice system. As much as half of federal, state, and local law enforcement computer forensic examinations have involved kiddie porn. Child pornography involves explicit photos and videos that can be found in many places, including foreign websites offering downloads of images that are illegal to view, possess, or convey in America. From the titles and cover photos, even hotel adult videos available on demand on room TVs seem to involve underage performers, although technically they may be of legal age. Complicating enforcement is the cultivation of adult male taste for "young" females engaging in explicit sexual acts, as illustrated by frequent use of such terms as *coed, schoolgirl, teen,* and *young amateur girls* in porn titles. Appearance and dress or undress can make it virtually impossible to ascertain the age of the participants to a casual viewer, but seeking youth in porn sites online is apt to result in finding illegal materials.

Because the statutes forbid mere possession of child pornography, Internet users must be careful to avoid youthful images. However, the same caution applies to investigators, who can inadvertently download child pornography in the course of a routine investigation. The National Center for Missing and Exploited Children, by an act of Congress, handles reports of child exploitation, including child pornography. Further information is available on their website (http://www.missingkids.com/home), and specific child exploitation guidance can be found at http://www.missingkids.com/Report.

Pornography is a big business on the Internet and can constitute a problem in and of itself for employers and investigators, such as by consuming systems/network bandwidth, employee diversion, creating a hostile workplace environment, and malware downloads. This has prompted human resource departments to confront all types of Internet employee diversions in the workplace, not the least of which is an estimated one in five employees accessing Internet porn on their work computer.[5] Some porn websites are run by organized criminals who offer other services as well, such as prostitution; commit other crimes, such as credit card fraud; and harvest identity information online for spammers and crackers. The relatively large content and programs associated with photos and videos allow crackers to induce porn users to download malware, including bots that can make a user's computer into a "zombie." Botnets of zombie computers are used in a number of cybercrimes, including distributed denial-of-service attacks, spam and phishing (fraudulent spam directing users to fake financial websites), and harvesting of financial information from individuals and enterprises. Banks and credit card companies devote a significant number of resources to securing users' identities and transactions against criminals whose advantage stems from the popularity of online pornography. But, employers potentially face the most serious risks from online porn, among which are inappropriate and offensive materials displayed on workplace screens; illegal materials, including child pornography captured by and stored on enterprise systems; significant diversion from work time and attention by access to online porn; and malware imported into enterprise systems from porn websites. Such malware might be used to access and copy high-value intellectual property (IP) from the enterprise.

Unauthorized Use of Computer Systems

Federal and state laws forbid unauthorized access to and use of computer systems, which can include acquiring, altering, or deleting proprietary data and misusing or disabling proprietary systems. There is a subculture of Internet users who believe that it is their right, if not legal and ethical, to log on to any system that allows them access (even if they must deceive or dissemble to do so) and to acquire and use as they see fit any information that they find. Title 18, US Code, Sections 1029 and 1030 forbid unauthorized access to or misuse of systems or data. These statutes were enacted at least in part because someone can steal data and computer/network services from another merely because he or she can cause the targeted system to let him or her in. Early hackers—intruders—learned that social manipulation and "dumpster diving" were even more successful than clever computer programming in gaining unauthorized access to systems by finding out users' passwords through deception and in the trash. Today's headlines about Chinese, Russian, and organized crime "hacking" (actually, cracking or black-hat hacking) reflect the fact that computer systems or their users can still be induced to allow intruders inside, and nation-states, as well as criminals, have reasons to penetrate enterprise systems. At risk for business and government are invaluable IP, secrets, and personally identifying information, as well as significant amounts of cash losses.[6]

As indicated in the studies endnoted previously and numerous media stories, large numbers of computer system penetrations have resulted in recent years in the theft of millions of users' identities,[7] financial information, and sensitive personal data, as well as money. Many large, market-leading companies have lost computer-hosted hardware, software, research, and development data worth hundreds of billions of dollars. Although the loss and recovery costs are high for personal data, they are almost incalculable for data that could lead to the failure of an enterprise because of theft of its most valuable technology. In some IP cases of which I am aware, market leaders became also-rans in less than a year or two, and the losses in jobs, corporate value, and national economic strength totaled many tens of billions of dollars. Competition in the world economy depends on our ability to protect the private enterprise's and government agency's knowledge, skills, and automated operations. Some believe that economic warfare is under way between nations willing to support cyber war against competitors and against nations like the United States, which are as yet incapable of protecting the automated enterprises of the nation and its businesses. In truth, any enterprise or agency depends for its success on the ability to resist internal and external cyber attacks and to ascertain how best to control its own cyberspace. Because the insiders of each enterprise profoundly contribute to or detract from its cyber security, their role is crucial to protection.

International organized criminals use cyberspace to target individuals and US infrastructure, using an endless variety of schemes to steal hundreds of millions of dollars from consumers and the US economy. These schemes also jeopardize the security of personal information, the stability of business and government infrastructures, and the security and solvency of financial investment markets.[8]

Among the vital lessons that an Internet intelligence investigator-analyst must remember is the likelihood that malicious code will be encountered in all probability after a certain amount of searching. Further, the role of the analyst might be interesting to a cybercriminal for many reasons, not least of which is if he or she is under investigation. The data in the analyst's possession might be sensitive and could even relate to the cybercriminal. While Internet information is being collected, it is possible for a sophisticated person or group to detect the collection and target the analyst. Among the measures to be considered, therefore, are the use of proxies and separate computer workstations for online searching, strong antivirus and antimalware, and constant vigilance to detect attacks on the analyst's systems. Some types of investigation could use undercover roles (e.g., virtual identities such as e-mail services, social website personae, and masked Internet protocol addresses) to help avoid detection by subjects of investigation or others who could pose a threat to the analyst. A concerted attack using high-end software designed for penetrating computer systems (e.g., password cracker or malware payloads in ostensibly innocent e-mail) could pose a threat to most computer systems.[9] It is up to the analyst and his or her team to assess the nature of the subject they are investigating and to take adequate measures for self-protection if there is a likelihood that the case could involve black-hat hacking.

Contraband Digital Assets

Besides child pornography, there are several other kinds of digital property that may be illegal to access, take without permission, possess, sell, alter, or delete. Examples include pirated (illegally copied) films, videos, music, video games, and software. The Motion Picture Association of America and its think tanks estimated that losses to Internet piracy by the film industry are $6.1 billion annually, and the US economy loses $20.5 billion annually in 2013 numbers.[10] The Directors Guild of America estimated 2010 economic losses of $25 billion.[11] A 2007 study by the Institute for Policy Innovation estimated that, each year, copyright piracy from motion pictures, sound recordings, business and entertainment software, and video games costs the US economy $58 billion in total output, 373,375 American jobs, and $16.3 billion in earnings, and costs federal, state, and local governments $2.6 billion in tax revenue.[12] The estimated ad revenue of pirate websites in 2013 was $227 million.[13] Even if these estimates are high or lack a firm statistical foundation, they illustrate the significant damage caused by cybercrime.

Copyright piracy losses pale in comparison with the damages from annual thefts of manufacturers' IP, including research and development of new products: "The scale of international theft of American intellectual property (IP) is unprecedented—hundreds of billions of dollars per year, on the order of the size of US exports to Asia." This was over $300 billion according to a report in May 2013 by the Commission on the Theft of American Intellectual Property.[14] Various estimates in the past several years also suggested that US losses of IP totaled hundreds of billions of dollars annually, and congressional testimony about Chinese cyber espionage against the United States, based on US intelligence community stats, estimated annual losses of $338 billion (not only by China).[15] Significant portions of data breach losses come from personally identifying information lost, including fraud, from the Internet, from hacking, from stolen laptops, and from stolen computers.[16]

Because there are too many intangibles to place much weight on these statistics, precise quantification of the issue of IP loss is not possible. However, the important lesson is that IP theft is a growing crime with much greater impact than others, benefitting perpetrating countries and companies at the expense of victims and resulting in devastating damage to victim companies and their national economies that lose their market to a competitor. Prolonged and deep losses of IP can mean the end of industries and of a national economy itself, and the 10 million or so Americans who have their identities stolen yearly suffer both financially and in terms of faith in the Internet as a safe medium. Internet investigations are crucial to brand and IP protection. Early appearances of new products and services based on stolen IP can allow a firm or agency to detect the loss and begin addressing recovery. Today, it may take only weeks for a competitor to integrate designs acquired through corporate espionage into a new product, and the reverse-engineering process has been mastered in parts of the world with weak policing of IP (e.g., China, Southeast Asia, parts of the former Soviet Union, Eastern Europe, and Latin America). Although civil and criminal law may help protect US corporations from competing products based on stolen IP within North America, investigation and recovery in the rest of the world can be challenging.

Among the many examples[17] of significant losses caused by IP economic espionage are the following:

■ Major cell phones and personal digital assistants
■ Personal computers
■ Software, including games
■ Electronics manufacturing and testing equipment
■ Automobiles and auto parts
■ Purses and leather goods
■ Golf clubs, tennis rackets, sporting equipment
■ Electronics manufacturing, control, and testing equipment
■ Aeronautics control systems and software, hardware, and parts
■ Biotechnology research, including pharmaceuticals
■ Night vision and distance imaging
■ Designer clothing

Periodic reports about knockoffs of high-end watches sold on street corners in major cities and on the Internet illustrate the issue. Whether or not a $39 to $99 "Rolex" is considered the real thing by a buyer, knockoffs do their damage to brands and the sales of legitimate products. Resilient markets for contraband goods allow stolen, counterfeit, and diverted products to be sold through both physical and online outlets. Perhaps the most insidious of these is the Internet market for pharmaceuticals. Hundreds of websites offer prescription drugs online, including major drugstore chains, mail-order pharmacies, and health insurance plan–associated drug providers.[18] Illicit online pharmacies have proliferated in the past dozen years, offering generic and discount drugs, with and without a prescription, and often pretending to be Canadian pharmacies. American consumers who seek discount drugs online can easily be confused about the illicit online pharmacies because they look and behave much like legitimate mail-order drugstores. Often, the online pharmacies are not in Canada, and drugs they sell are shipped from abroad to US customers. Among many examples encountered over the past few years are the following:

- Large (multihundreds of millions of dollars annually) Indian and Chinese pharmaceutical manufacturers offering discount brand-name prescription drugs through distributors online that pretend to be Canadian pharmacies. Often, these websites show photos of brand-name prescription drugs but sell Asian-made generic drugs instead.
- Russian online pharmacies offering drugs without prescriptions, claiming locations and licenses in North America but in fact located abroad, often providing substandard, generic products.
- Drug distributors online located in Canada, England, the Seychelles Islands, and Asia specializing in Viagra, Levitra, Cialis, and other sex-enhancement drugs but offering a wide variety of brand and generic medicines ordered via the Internet and mailed to the customer. Some demand prescriptions and some offer a free prescription from a staff physician, who issues a script from an online form without ever seeing the patient.

The most dangerous aspect of the online pharmacies (besides loss of money by customers) is that the actual composition of the drugs received in the mail may be counterfeit (including inactive and even dangerous ingredients), substrength, or generic products that may not medicate the patient as intended. Some customers of Internet pharmacies take harmful knockoff medicines, over- or undermedicating themselves, all because they tried to lower the costs of their prescriptions. Drug companies lose billions of dollars annually from illegal online sales. Investigative efforts by the companies, Food and Drug Administration (FDA), Federal Bureau of Investigation (FBI), and US Customs and Border Protection (to name a few agencies) continually find high-volume illegal activities and overseas operations that are apt to be up and running again quickly when they are shut down by enforcement, either physically or online. The volume of imports makes it difficult to intercept all but a handful of medicines that arrive in overseas mail. The cumulative costs of lost sales, investigations, and brand protection, meanwhile, are passed along to all customers. Internet investigators may be asked to contribute to efforts against online illegal activities of all kinds. Among the steps to be included are the following:

- Identify the owners and operators of the websites, where possible. Even though they are anonymized, websites can still be traced to the host network.
- Trace the corporate structure and financing of businesses associated with the website. Often, the owner, administrator, and technical and billing contacts are part of the illegal operation. Sometimes, the website is maintained by a commercial host that is not involved in illegal acts and would cooperate rather than be implicated.
- Find associated websites, communications channels, and points of contact online. Because of the proliferation of organized criminal enterprises such as those mentioned, Internet investigations have become an important part of prevention and response for both law enforcement and private security. Some illicit websites are clustered in shared hosting servers.

Information (Cyber) Warfare

> There is also that National Strategy to Secure Cyberspace dating back to 2003; but there is no publicly available cyber war strategy.
>
> **—Richard A. Clarke**
> *Cyber War: The Next Threat to National Security*
> *and What to Do About It*
> (New York: Harper Collins, 2010)

Information warfare is an old practice, dating back centuries, involving misinformation, misdirection, injection of fear and doubt into the enemy's military and population, cutting off communications, denying and falsifying intelligence, and related operations. Cyber warfare takes old infowar concepts and brings them online. Among the nuances of cyber warfare are the ability to control, damage, or destroy Internet-based weaponry, communications, utilities, and services (including critical infrastructures); rapid proliferation of misinformation, utilizing social media and the web for proselytizing and recruiting; and gathering intelligence on the enemy or potential enemy (among many others). Necessities for cyber warriors include high-level computer programming and engineering, mapping and controlling cyberspace, and mastering cryptography as used online.

> Although any person or organization can engage in offensive information warfare, many of the operations that take place in practice are attributed to a few general classes. These include insiders, hackers, criminals, corporations, governments and terrorists.
>
> **—Dorothy E. Denning**
> *Information Warfare and Security*
> (New York: ACM Press, 1999)

As mentioned, because computer networks are a part of the US critical infrastructure and because (as Chinese Army officers have been saying since 1995 and Al Qaeda leaders since about the same time) the vulnerability of the US information infrastructure (including the Internet) constitutes a "great equalizer" between asymmetric armed forces, cyber warfare has increased as a threat.[19] Chinese military doctrine suggests that information operations are appropriate even when war is not under way.[20] Open discussions in Chinese military and media publications make it clear that cyber warfare is already under way between the Chinese and any potential adversary, including the United States.[21]

In the past 20 years, many major cyber attacks have illustrated the cyber warfare threat, including intrusions by both state and nonstate actors on Estonia, Korea, Israel, Syria, Iran, the Ukraine, the United States, and many large companies like

Google. Some of these attacks were suspected or known to have come from (or been allowed by) the authorities in nations hostile to the targets. Besides disruption or destruction, cyber warfare aims include espionage, tracking dissidents, preventing demonstrations and coups, facilitating military takeovers, and exerting control over information available to populations, including shutting down Internet access.

A key area of concern to Internet investigators is attribution: Who conducted an online attack, a cyber intrusion, or posted online? Information warfare activities consist of casing or scouting targets, infiltration, preparation for attack (which might include planting code on computers for use in a later attack), and small-scale attacks to test defenses, detection, tracing, and monitoring reactions of the target. These acts may leave evidence in server logs and files. Such evidence must be traced to identify a perpetrator, which inevitably involves Internet searching. The difficult job of proving who conducted a cyber attack, or preparations for one, is a study in digital and network forensics. Internet analysts will engage in inquiries that may involve state actors (e.g., intelligence and military units of foreign nations), terrorists, crackers, and organized criminals, as well as ordinary hackers.

Experienced investigators may be able to intuit from experience the nature of the attack and the probable intent—even identity—of the perpetrator when it is not possible to pinpoint the actor with certainty. Piercing the veil of anonymity is a vital task, whether the misbehavior is a teenage prank or a serious criminal act. Proxies and intermediate network hops help in concealment but may provide clues to the actors.

Press accounts and literature—both fiction and nonfiction—for over 20 years have profiled "hackers" who are devoted to understanding how computers, networks, and applications work and how to manipulate them for any purpose. Defeating systems' defenses is a particular specialty of hackers. Today's tool kit includes a substantial amount of software created to help information technology (IT) systems managers with security and testing and applications designed to do such esoteric tasks as breaking encryption, creating and finding steganography (images with hidden, embedded data), and guessing passwords.[22] Journeymen cyber warriors no longer need to program to achieve their goals because plenty of software is available for their use online. Skilled hackers possess certain attributes, such as persistence, deep knowledge of computer functions, and insatiable curiosity, as well as varying ethical and legal standards. However, the hacker of 2014 wants to distinguish himself or herself from crackers (black-hat hackers), who apparently live to break into systems owned by others and are considered cybercriminals. Like many who have been involved with computer experts, programmers, cryptographers, computer forensic analysts, information assurance specialists, and other expert users, I believe that there are "white-hat hackers," who are highly ethical and apt to assist law enforcement and national security practitioners, and "black-hat hackers," who are apt to commit crimes with computer systems. Internet investigators will inevitably run into both types of individuals and should remember that skilled hackers are capable of avoiding detection, impersonating others online, and mastering many networked systems. It is also worth noting that anyone who spends a great deal of time in an activity such as using computers is inevitably going to make mistakes and leave clues and evidence of their activities.

What is similar about the average amateur subject of Internet investigations and the professional cyber warrior is their humanity. Humans are error and accident prone. Investigators focused on the most professional and determined adversaries such as organized criminals, terrorists, and cyber warriors should not assume that the investigation is impossible or too difficult to accomplish. In over 45 years of experience, it has never ceased to amaze me how frequently intelligence officers forget or neglect to follow procedures and, by doing so, allow counterintelligence to discover their activities and minimize their effectiveness. Anyone can make a mistake. A subject may have an overt profile online and undercover activities that are linked. It is the Internet analyst's job to find the mistakes and links and see how they fit into the subject's portrait.

The most serious threats to business and government computer systems include talented and determined individuals, cyber warriors, who will be among those investigated online. The Internet analyst should remember that any subject of investigation could be one of them and be prepared to find his or her tracks online.

Notes

1. Census Bureau 2013 fourth quarter e-commerce report, http://www.census.gov/retail/mrts/www/data/pdf/ec_current.pdf (accessed April 23, 2014).
2. Child Exploitation and Obscenity Section, US Department of Justice, http://www.justice.gov/criminal/ceos/ (accessed April 24, 2014).
3. Ibid.
4. Wortley, Richard, and Smallbone, Stephen, Child Pornography on the Internet, Guide No. 41, Community Oriented Policing Services, US Department of Justice, 2010, http://www.cops.usdoj.gov/Publications/e04062000.pdf (accessed April 24, 2014).
5. Patrick, Erin, Employee Internet Management: Now an HR Issue, *Society for Human Resource Management Magazine*, http://www.shrm.org/Publications/hrmagazine/EditorialContent/Pages/CMS_006514.aspx (accessed April 25, 2014).
6. PriceWaterhouseCoopers (PWC), Key findings from the 2013 US State of Cybercrime Survey, cosponsored by the Software Engineering Institute CERT Program at Carnegie Mellon University, *CSO Magazine*, and United States Secret Service, June 2013, https://www.pwc.com/en_US/us/increasing-it-effectiveness/publications/assets/us-state-of-cybercrime.pdf; Fortinet 2013 Cybercrime Report, http://www.fortinet.com/resource_center/whitepapers/cybercrime_report_on_botnets_network_security_strategies.html; Comprehensive Study on Cybercrime, United Nations Office on Drugs and Crime, http://www.unodc.org/documents/organized-crime/UNODC_CCPCJ_EG.4_2013/CYBERCRIME_STUDY_210213.pdf (all accessed April 24, 2014).
7. The Open Security Foundation's DataLossDB gathers information about events involving the loss, theft, or exposure of personally identifiable information (PII). See http://datalossdb.org/statistics (accessed April 24, 2014). Identity theft resources and information: http://www.ftc.gov/bcp/edu/microsites/idtheft/ (accessed April 24, 2014).

8. Op. cit.
9. Hacking tools—notice they are also security tools—are described in http://sectools. org/ (accessed April 24, 2014).
10. Bialik, Carl, Putting a Price Tag on Film Piracy, *Wall Street Journal*, April 5, 2013, http://blogs.wsj.com/numbersguy/putting-a-price-tag-on-film-piracy-1228/ (accessed April 24, 2014).
11. Directors Guild of America, spring 2010, http://www.dga.org/craft/dgaq/all-articles/1001-spring-2010/internet-issues-piracy-statistics.aspx (accessed April 24, 2014).
12. Siwek, Stephen E., The True Cost of Copyright Industry Piracy to the US Economy, Institute for Policy Innovation, IPI Center for Technology Freedom, October 2007.
13. Moses, Lucia, New Report Says How Much Advertising Is Going to Piracy Sites $227 million in 2013, *Ad Week*, http://www.adweek.com/news/advertising-branding/new-report-says-how-much-advertising-going-piracy-sites-155770 (accessed April 24, 2014).
14. Report of the Commission on the Theft of American Intellectual Property, May 2013, National Bureau of Asian Research, including remarks by Dennis C. Blair and Jon M. Huntsman, Jr., http://www.ipcommission.org/report/IP_Commission_Report_052213.pdf (accessed April 25, 2014).
15. Testimony of Larry M. Wortzel before the House of Representatives, Committee on Energy and Commerce Subcommittee on Oversight and Investigations, July 9, 2013, http://docs.house.gov/meetings/IF/IF02/20130709/101104/HHRG-113-IF02-Wstate-WortzelL-20130709-U1.pdf (accessed April 25, 2014).
16. Almeling, David, Snyder, Darin, Sapoznikow, Michael, McCollum, Whitney, and Weader, Jill, United States: A Statistical Analysis of Trade Secret Litigation in Federal Courts, *Gonzaga Law Review*, March 2010, http://www.mondaq.com/unitedstates/article.asp?articleid=97150 (accessed May 5, 2010); Yager, Loren, director of international affairs and trade, GAO, Intellectual Property, Risk and Enforcement Challenges, testimony before the House Judiciary Subcommittee on Courts, the Internet, and Intellectual Property, October 18, 2007, http://www.gao.gov/new.items/d08177t.pdf (accessed June 1, 2010).
17. Products identified as involved in IP theft are from cases known to me.
18. I have tracked Internet pharmacies offering drugs to US customers illegally. FBI's online pharmacy advice is available at http://www.fbi.gov/page2/march09/pharmacy_030309.html (accessed April 25, 2014).
19. Markoff, John, and Barboza, David, Academic Paper in China Sets Off Alarms in US, *New York Times*, March 10, 2010 (accessed April 25, 2014).
20. Chinese Academics' Paper on Cyberwar Sets Off Alarms in US, *New York Times*, March 21, 2010, http://www.nytimes.com/2010/03/21/world/asia/21grid.html?pagewanted=all (accessed April 25, 2014).
21. Liang, Qiao, and Xiangsui, Wang, *Unrestricted Warfare, Senior Colonels, Chinese Peoples Liberation Army* (Beijing: PLA Literature and Arts Publishing House, 1999). The book asserts that warfare is no longer strictly a military operation, that the battlefield no longer has boundaries, and information warfare provides asymmetric advantages to China; Ventre, Daniel, Chinese Information and Cyber Warfare, April 13, 2010, http://www.e-r.info/?p=3845 (accessed April 25, 2014), which noted: "In 1995 the General Wang Pufeng, considered as the 'father' of Chinese doctrine of Information Warfare, said that The goal of Information Warfare is no longer the conquest of territories or the destruction of enemy troops, but the destruction of the enemy's will to resist.

Information Warfare is a war in which the ability to see, to know and to strike more accurately and before the adversary, is as important as firepower. In 1997, Colonel Baocun Wang added that
- Information Warfare can be conducted in times of peace, crisis and war;
- Information Warfare consists of offensive and defensive operations;
- The main components of Information Warfare are C2 (Command and Control), Intelligence, Electronic Warfare, Psychological Warfare, Hackers Warfare and Economic warfare."

Wortzel, Larry M., commissioner, U.S.-China Economic and Security Review Commission, China's Approach to Cyber Operations: Implications for the United States, testimony before the Committee on Foreign Affairs, US House of Representatives Hearing on "The Google Predicament: Transforming U.S. Cyberspace Policy to Advance Democracy, Security, and Trade," March 10, 2010: Lieutenant General Liu Jixian, of the PLA Academy of Military Science, writes that the PLA must develop asymmetrical capabilities including space-based information support, and networked-focused "soft attack," against potential enemies. Xu Rongsheng, chief scientist at the Cyber Security Lab of the Institute for High Energy Physics of the Chinese Academy of Sciences, told a Chinese news reporter that: "Cyber warfare may be carried out in two ways. In wartimes, disrupt and damage the networks of infrastructure facilities, such as power systems, telecommunications systems, and education systems, in a country; or in military engagements, the cyber technology of the military forces can be turned into combat capabilities." Liu Jixian, Innovation and Development in the Research of Basic Issues of Joint Operations, China Military Science, March 2009, in Open Source Center CPP20090928563001; Dongfang Zaobao, July 10, 2009, in Open Source Center CPP20090710045002; see http://www.internationalrelations.house.gov/111/wor031010.pdf (accessed May 8, 2010).

22. One site offering both security and hacking tools is http://sectools.org/ (accessed April 25, 2014).

Chapter 21

Model Cybervetting Investigative Guidelines

Introduction

Internet investigations are not limited to background investigations on applicants for jobs or clearances, but the issues surrounding cybervetting of individuals are significant and deserve specific attention. The principles for cybervetting may apply to other types of Internet inquiries. What follows are generic model guidelines designed as a starting point for a government agency or business entity and adaptable for the use of any enterprise. Because national, state, and local laws, regulations, and ethics vary as far as the Internet and privacy are concerned, these guidelines and the standards on which they are based are intended to comply with most current laws in North America and Europe, but not necessarily all of them. For example, some legislation forbids using certain types of Internet content, in certain ways, in screening job applicants. Legal review and customization should be a part of adapting the strategy, policy, and procedures modeled here.[1]

Enterprise Strategy

Prior to adoption of standards for Internet use in investigations, including cybervetting, an enterprise should have an established policy (see Chapters 10 and 22). A good place to start is with the enterprise's authorized use policy (AUP), which provides direction to those with authorized access to enterprise computer systems. The norms for protecting IT systems, as expressed in the AUP, should be consistent with those for Internet searching. Today, many businesses and government agencies have a de facto policy of allowing any employee to use Internet searching as they see fit in their roles and to judge a person who is the subject of a search based on information obtained online in making decisions for any purpose. Unfortunately, there are several reasons why this unrestrictive approach can be a bad idea, including that employees may

- Choose to conduct Internet searches on some persons and not others, raising issues of discrimination, fairness, and equal treatment
- Conduct Internet searches in a casual, incomplete, and unskilled manner or vary search methods/protocols for different subjects, thus raising the same issues as mentioned and possibly missing critical information readily available to a competent searcher
- Judge Internet search results in a subjective way, overlooking some issues, focusing on postings that may not relate to the subject, and reaching invalid conclusions about findings without proper attribution or without verifying findings with other investigation
- Act on Internet findings without adequate documentation of the basis for a decision, thus leaving the enterprise without a defense in case of a complaint or lawsuit

In both government and private-sector discussions of cybervetting, it is not unusual to find misunderstanding of the key reasons for Internet searching of persons, which include seeking indications of prior (un)trustworthiness in computer use (a job- and AUP-related factor for most employers and employees); ascertaining behaviors from Internet postings that relate to an individual's eligibility and qualifications for employment, including good judgment (i.e., finding facts online that prior to the Internet were found offline); and finding facts, intelligence, leads, and background information relevant to, and therefore that assist, a background investigation. It seems that the freedom for employers to use the Internet as they wish is somehow limited in some people's minds (including some state legislatures), restricting the right of an employer to use the Internet to learn what might be revealed about a person. Provided that logical and legal approaches are taken by both employee and employer, there is no reason that both cannot be free to use the Internet as they wish. The existence and use of the Internet do not entitle anyone to act in an illicit or antisocial manner or display misbehavior online.

It is useful to reiterate the reason for cybervetting, even if an applicant has logged on and shown a prospective employer the contents of websites, social networking profiles, and other online sites (as some law enforcement and intelligence agencies require). How else will an agency verify that the applicant has displayed all the sites, all the content, and all the past postings that may be relevant to an offer of employment? When an agency decides to ask a candidate to display his or her postings, it is an acknowledgment that review of the data is important, yet it is equally important to verify the applicant's honesty and candor and see if there is more online (including items posted by others relevant to the subject).

Model Internet Search Guidelines

These Internet search guidelines shall be applied when an Internet search is conducted for an investigative purpose, including searches for gathering background information to support hiring, promotion, and access to protected data; conducting investigations for due diligence; to protect or resolve security issues with information systems; to gather evidence of illegal activities; and for investigations and intelligence operations conducted at the direction of the legal, human resources, information technology (IT), and security departments.

- Internet searches will be conducted in a thorough, professional manner to achieve optimal results either in-house or through an authorized vendor to ensure that they are conducted
  - By trained and experienced personnel using approved systems
  - In substantially the same manner for all individuals of the same type or category
- In accordance with legal, ethical, and enterprise requirements

Internet searches will be conducted, to the extent possible,

- Efficiently, within the time, information systems, client requirements, and up-to-date methodology available
- Thoroughly, accessing and retrieving data from as comprehensive an array of resources as possible
- Accurately, using precise search terms, logical variations, and sound methods to find and attribute information correctly
- To meet the stated needs of the client within enterprise policy

Results of Internet searches will be analyzed and reported in accordance with the following criteria:

- Attribution of information to individual(s) will be supported with evidence, including images of web pages found and summaries of references, with specifics that verify attribution, along with any indication of limitations or conflicts with items attributed to the subject.
- Information that could tend to mitigate, refute, or shed doubt on behavior attributed to an individual will be reported along with that which is attributed.
- Information verifying the subject's background or activities will be reported, along with substantive information that conflicts with details provided by the

subject, and any information that could be described as derogatory in nature, new information about the subject, or might lead to an adverse decision concerning the subject.

▪ Sources (links, uniform resource locators [URLs]) and images of pages (captured in Portable Document Format [PDF], image or HyperText Markup Language [HTML] format) with full dates of each item will be reported as appropriate, and collected data will be maintained as long as the report is retained.

▪ Ultimately, verification of data found online may depend on information received from other sources and directly from the subject, who may be asked to explain findings and to whom results of investigation may be shown in accordance with regulations and policies.

▪ Findings not included in the report (e.g., items deemed not identifiable with the subject) will be retained in a file on the search conducted.

▪ Reports will be formatted to meet the requirements of the investigation, as appropriate, such as the following formats:
  - Either include all items found on the subject or only those items that are needed for a specific purpose, "reporting by exception" (such as including only derogatory or complimentary items and omitting known or routine data that do not have a bearing on the outcome of the process)
  - Combine Internet findings with other findings or report Internet findings separately

Analysts tasked with reporting the results of Internet searches must be careful to assess whether findings include false references (e.g., same name, another person); false information (posted in error or on purpose as an attack, teasing, or as a "joke"); or a disclosure of information about a protected class (e.g., race, religion) or about a highly sensitive and potentially embarrassing situation not meant for disclosure. In some instances, an investigator may gain the impression from postings relating to a subject's circle of acquaintances that items about the subject are hazing or harassment or possibly untrue and would require verification and explanation for a full understanding of their meaning. In some instances, findings could include attributes and activities that may not, under Equal Employment Opportunity law or regulation, be considered for employment.[2] Reports must properly include facts and findings relevant to the investigation and not those considered irrelevant or prohibited under the law. Internet searches conducted as part of a background investigation for employment, promotion, or access to protected information are to verify that the person is eligible and qualified for the job and he or she provided true information about his or her background and to discover any information that appears to call candidacy into question. All misbehavior should be reported. Minor incidents of juvenile misbehavior online will not be grounds for adverse action, provided that the individual demonstrates the intent to meet enterprise standards.

Prior to final adjudication of a candidacy with substantial Internet search results that could cause an adverse finding, findings should be reviewed by a designated management unit, and subjects should be provided an opportunity to address the issues raised; verify, explain, or deny the items reported; and furnish facts or mitigation. In appropriate instances, a person should be given the opportunity to express an intent to adhere to all applicable requirements. This process will be followed when a group of candidates deemed otherwise equally qualified for a position includes one or more with derogatory Internet search findings. The process will be carried out by trained staff and address issues raised to determine the

Facts and circumstances (mitigating or otherwise)
Seriousness of and culpability for any misbehavior
Dates of occurrence
Likelihood of recurrence
Subject's determination to avoid similar misbehavior in the future

A decision should be made on the subject's competitive position as a candidate based on the findings from the review.

All personally identifying information involved in an Internet search, reporting, and review should be considered confidential and properly secured against unauthorized disclosure, using approved enterprise processes. When the Internet search and personally identifying materials are no longer needed, they should be destroyed and destruction documented in accordance with enterprise process.

Authorized Internet Search (Cybervetting) Personnel

Those conducting Internet searches (cybervetting) under the guidelines must be trained; must demonstrate capability with the proper systems, methods, and judgment needed; and should be experienced in Internet investigation. If in-house, the unit should be trained, equipped, and audited to ensure fairness and efficiency. If Internet searching is outsourced, the provider should be contracted to meet enterprise standards, and the provider's reports and methods should be reviewed periodically for accuracy, timeliness, and adherence to requirements.

Among the attributes necessary for Internet analysts are strong ethics; an understanding of the types of information found online, major search engines, tools and techniques, the legal and regulatory issues that might arise from certain findings, report writing, and investigative documentation; discretion; and familiarity with security principles. Analysts should be trained in using automated search tools. Less-experienced analysts should be supervised and mentored to ensure that their results meet guidelines. Reports on Internet searches should be approved by supervisors prior to presentation to the client. Because reliability, credibility, attribution, and verification are particularly important in Internet investigations, analysts and supervisors of reporting should pay particular attention to

- Data apparently attributable to the subject without verification
- Comparison of data attributed to the subject with known facts
- The nature of sources linking subject with derogatory information
- The certainty that derogatory information refers to subject and not someone else
- The credibility of the websites and postings involved
- Potential sources of verification of information derived from postings
- Indicators of accuracy or inaccuracy in postings
- Mitigating circumstances relevant to analysis of findings

During a review of adverse findings based on Internet search results, it may be appropriate to consider alternatives to actions, such as discharge, denial of an employment opportunity, or denial of a clearance in favor of rehabilitation, probation, monitoring, and training, particularly when the individual is new or unfamiliar with AUP standards and the behavior found is unacceptable in the workplace but relatively commonplace on the Internet. The purpose of the process is to assess whether the subject's documented past behavior indicates that future behavior can reasonably be expected to be of a similar, unacceptable nature or will meet employer standards with appropriate guidance.

Definitions to Consider

The following definitions should be considered when establishing policy, procedures, and guidelines for Internet searching (cybervetting):

Consent is an individual's documented acknowledgment or acceptance of specified conditions.

The Internet is a worldwide network of interconnected computers.

Internet posting is placing information online to make it accessible over the Internet.

Internet searching is a process of locating and retrieving data available on the Internet.

Notice is documented communication to individual(s) of specified conditions.

Verification is the process of confirming facts and evidence, such as obtaining corroboration from different sources or determining direct authorship of a posting.

Vetting is collection, examination, and evaluation of information for acceptance, such as a background investigation on an individual who is a candidate for hire, promotion, or granting or maintaining a security clearance.

Enterprise policies and guidelines for Internet investigations benefit when knowledgeable and experienced personnel participate in their formulation, just as the inquiries themselves are more effective and efficient when carried out by a group that has specialized in them.

Notes

1. Precursors to the Internet investigative standards and guidelines presented here were developed in my research studies as a first draft of potential guidelines for use by the US Department of Defense, working through the Defense Personnel Security Research Center (PERSEREC) under a Northrop Grumman contract. These were refined by a 1-year study in which I participated with the International Association of Chiefs of Police (IACP) and PERSEREC, resulting in publication of Developing a Cybervetting Strategy for Law Enforcement, accessible from the IACP at http://www.iacpsocialmedia.org/Portals/1/documents/CybervettingReport.pdf. Additional legal views may be found from Jodka, Sara H., The Dos and Don'ts of Conducting a Legal, Yet Helpful, Social Media Background Screen, *American Bar Association's Law Practice Today*, September 2013, http://www.americanbar.org/content/newsletter/publications/law_practice_today_home/lpt-archives/september13/the-dos-and-donts-of-conducting-a-legal-yet-helpful-social-media-background-screen.html (accessed April 25, 2014). The suggested guidelines presented here reflect my views alone.
2. Federal job discrimination laws summary, http://www.eeoc.gov/facts/qanda.html (accessed April 25, 2014).

Chapter 22

A Model Internet Investigation Policy

Introduction

A business or government agency must confront the risks and opportunities presented by the Internet. Significant security and personnel suitability issues are created when individuals engage in illegal, illicit, and unethical behaviors online. Such behaviors include

- Unauthorized release of sensitive, proprietary information, either inadvertently or maliciously
- Prohibited acts on work or personal computer systems that have an impact on the enterprise, including criminal and antisocial behavior
- Time and attention-intensive personal pursuits that substantially distract individuals from their duties, may expose systems to malicious code, and may usurp information technology (IT) resources, including computer cycles and network bandwidth using the enterprise network

In addition, large quantities of data posted on the Internet may contain references to applicants, employees, contractors, partners, customers, a merger/acquisition entity, or other individuals who have a relationship with the enterprise. Such references may include information with a material bearing on decision making or that may have a negative impact, such as unauthorized disclosure of proprietary information. The enterprise therefore should create a policy for dealing with Internet investigations by which results must meet all applicable laws and regulations and withstand possible outside scrutiny.[1] These standards do not preclude accessing open-source information, including Internet searching, for authorized purposes other than investigations.

Following is a generic enterprise policy for Internet searches:

> Enterprise Internet search standards and guidelines shall be followed when Internet searches are conducted on an individual or entity for an investigative purpose, such as part of a background investigation ("cybervetting") on any candidate for employment, promotion, or access to valuable assets, including information systems. Enterprise Internet search guidelines prescribe authorized searchers, procedures, and adjudication protocols. Executive approval and documentation are required for any exceptions to this policy, which will be in effect until changed in writing.

Key Considerations

Following are key considerations for every enterprise regarding the inclusion of Internet searching in investigations:

- Some individuals may not realize that material posted online may be available publicly.
- Internet activities include fantasy, games, humor, exaggeration, lies, and other content that could create a misimpression of a person's behavior, character, or intent.
- Some postings may be intended for private use only and not for broader access.
- Some information may concern an individual's protected class, including race, sex, national origin, or ethnicity, which is not to be considered in employment actions under Title VII of the Equal Opportunity Employment Act and related laws.[2]
- More than one individual may use the same e-mail address or user ID online, thus complicating the identification of the person who posted specific materials.
- Although a person is accountable for his or her misbehavior, mitigating factors regarding Internet postings should be evaluated (e.g., humorous items).

Higher-Risk Candidates

Certain categories of individuals may be considered to represent a higher likelihood of having relevant Internet materials that could have an impact on enterprise decisions or justify cybervetting because they will occupy a more sensitive position, including

- IT professionals and systems administrators
- Website designers, software authors, and programmers

- Persons with access to the highest levels of sensitive data, including executives and managers and those in a position to compromise devices or networks, funds, proprietary data or competitive trade secrets, based on their assignments
- Sworn personnel of law enforcement, intelligence, military, security, executive, and similarly demanding positions
- Those with a prior history of extensive computer/Internet use
- Those with a prior history of computer systems abuse or online misbehavior
- Anyone about whom indications of improper Internet use arise from disclosures during application processing or from investigation

Application Procedures and Forms

Internet investigations for background vetting (cybervetting) should be supported by application procedures and forms that strengthen and document the notice-and-consent process for candidates, elicit information to be used in Internet searches, and protect the privacy of individual applicants by limiting the data required (e.g., no log-on passwords for websites or systems should be requested). An employer may wish to include a policy statement about cybervetting, such as that a hiring decision about an applicant's Internet references will not be taken prior to an interview concerning any questionable items. The forms (integrated into those used already for applicants) should include

- Notice that the background investigation will include cybervetting
- A signed consent form acknowledging the above
- Internet-related questions as part of the application form, which should ask for
  - E-mail addresses, user names, and nicknames used online
  - Websites, blogs, online communities, and profiles used frequently, including social networking sites
  - Existing or past postings that might be considered offensive or illicit
  - Instances of disciplinary action or sanctions for misuse of an information system
  - Other questions deemed appropriate for the computing environment of the enterprise

The current state of the law at all levels makes the issue of prior notice and consent for cybervetting debatable. Currently used notice and consent forms authorizing a background investigation may be sufficient for many enterprises. Most application forms ask for all the names used by the applicant, but often employers do not require a listing of all of the candidate's e-mail addresses and user names, which in fact are virtual identities and aliases online. Explicit prior notice of cybervetting is preferable to its inclusion without notice, but many attorneys believe that the current process can include cybervetting at the discretion of the employer.

They argue that when the applicant understands that prior employers, references, associates, and records will be consulted to verify his or her qualifications and eligibility for the position, addition of public Internet records is no more intrusive than the rest of the background investigation. Those arguing against searching without notice point out that some of the posted materials were not intended for viewing by prospective employers. No case law appears to back up this argument to date.

Legal Issues

In the absence of legislation, litigation, and a history of cybervetting, every enterprise properly should consider measures to handle those relatively few instances (6% to 30% of those cybervetted, in our experience) for which derogatory information from Internet investigation could result in an adverse finding. Despite the percentages, even one or a few individuals can represent a significant risk of large-scale loss. Background investigations, including cybervetting, are often conducted only after a conditional offer of employment. In such instances, an adverse decision must be documented, and the candidate may be legally entitled to an explanation under the Fair Credit Reporting Act and related federal laws and regulations if the cybervetting is conducted by a third party.

The subject is the person in the best position to verify findings, including attribution of postings, and explain the behaviors involved. An interview is most often appropriate for this purpose and should be a part of enterprise procedures. Interviews conducted during the background investigation process are a part of the investigation, especially when they concern verification and clarification of information discovered online or by other investigation. The honesty of a candidate in providing information to an employer is critical. However, for those heavily involved in Internet use, including e-mail, instant messaging, websites, profiles, social networking, and so on, it may be difficult to remember all the details of activities over the past 7 years or more. For example, e-mail addresses no longer used by an individual may be forgotten, and failure to list a forgotten e-mail address on an application form may not be dishonest (any more than forgetting a street address). One reason for an interview about Internet activities might be to refresh a candidate's recollection about dated postings, virtual identities, or online activities not included on a form but found during an Internet search.

When an Internet investigation and subject interview leave an enterprise with unresolved issues, there are options short of rejection of a candidacy that may be appropriate. Some government agencies have asked a candidate for a high-level clearance or law enforcement position to demonstrate on his or her personal computer the nature and extent of online activities. In the case of a Bozeman, Montana, city requirement for applicants to provide passwords for access to their online accounts, a firestorm erupted in June 2009 at this intrusion into private activities.³ However, if illegal or prohibited activities or derogatory postings are suspected, the best option for the candidate and the employer may be to have the candidate show the investigator the postings in question. Several chiefs of police have stated that Internet data are too important in judging the trustworthiness of candidate police officers not to require them all to log in and show an investigator their online profiles. This approach avoids violation of user agreements that prohibit sharing passwords to accounts, while allowing the candidate to provide a guided tour that demonstrates and explains postings.

Illegal activities may be detected by Internet searching. A common crime is copyright violation by collecting films, music, and software via file-sharing groups online rather than authorized retailers. It is important for an employer to consider questions concerning such activities prior to adjudicating a candidacy because common misdemeanors and misbehavior are likely to be encountered, and some standard is better than none. Examples include

- Frequent, high-volume, illicit file sharing in which a candidate engaged
- Underage drinking and illicit drug use
- Inflated claims of education and prior employment experience (possible fraud)
- Use of work resources (e.g., computers, time, and materials) for personal rather than professional purposes (possible theft of services)
- Unauthorized access to, taking, disclosure, alteration, or deletion of proprietary data

Confidentiality

It is important to the integrity of the Internet investigative process that the confidentiality of the inquiry and any data with personally identifying information be maintained. Security measures should be carried out, documented, and audited periodically in conjunction with related enterprise systems. When no longer needed, confidential, personally identifying data should be permanently deleted.

Ethics in Investigations

It is important to set limits on methods used during cybervetting to avoid those that could be considered unethical or illegal. Examples of ethical principles include the following:

- Search methods must not violate laws or regulations.
- Internet investigators must not impersonate a subject of inquiry.
- Internet investigators should abide by authorized use policies (AUPs) of websites to the extent possible.

Disciplinary Action

Employers should include provisions in enterprise disciplinary policy relating to use of the Internet in violation of the employee handbook, ethical standards, industry standards of behavior, and government regulations. The employer's AUP should reflect the same provisions. Because of the commonality of activities online that could be viewed as illicit or potentially damaging to an enterprise, employers should consider establishing programs to orient, train, supervise, and monitor authorized users who have a history of Internet behaviors that are not allowed at work. Examples include such activities as using file-sharing software for film and music sharing, connecting unauthorized external modems or devices to the workplace network, participation in massively multiplayer online fantasy games or other online games at work, accessing and using pornographic materials or other data unsuitable for the workplace, sharing passwords for access to sensitive data or systems, making unauthorized copies of employer data, and storing large personal files improperly (especially illicit copyrighted materials) on workplace servers. The seriousness, frequency, and likelihood of recurrence of such misbehavior should be considered in disciplinary or rehabilitative measures taken under enterprise policy.

Model Forms for Candidates

Following are model forms or instructions incorporating the elements needed for cybervetting that can be used in addition to traditional (existing) forms to integrate Internet searches into applicant processing.

> **Notice**
>
> Information systems are critical to the success of the enterprise and misuse of enterprise systems, networks, and data is regarded as serious and costly misbehavior. Employees must adhere to enterprise AUPs, which state that information systems are for business use only, and online misbehavior that may cause harm to the enterprise is prohibited on any computer system. Therefore, enterprise background investigations include an Internet search (cybervetting), that is, a review of information online that may relate to a candidate's eligibility and qualifications. Information from cybervetting that could by itself lead to an adverse decision will be reviewed by the enterprise with the candidate, who will be given an opportunity to explain or comment on the information before a final decision is made. As a part of cybervetting, candidates will be asked to provide information about their use of computer systems and the Internet. Failure to provide complete and accurate information could be grounds for denial of the position or dismissal.

Consent

I authorize the inclusion of cybervetting in a background investigation to determine or verify eligibility and qualifications for the position sought.

_____

(Signature)

Questionnaire

Candidates should provide answers to the following questions:

List all online communities in which you are an active member.

List any e-mail addresses that you have used in the past 7 years. Remember to include college, military, and Internet service provider (ISP) e-mail addresses. Include all personal, work, school, organizational, military, cell phone, and instant messaging e-mail addresses. List the type and whether it is current or shared by another user.

List any screen names, handles, or nicknames used online not listed above.

List your own websites, blogs, or other personal profiles that are online (e.g., Facebook, MySpace, www.yourname.com).

List anyone who shared the use of an e-mail address, or access to the same computer with you, including your spouse or significant other(s), family, roommates, and so on. Explain.

Have you ever been disciplined or penalized by an ISP or information systems owner for failure to abide by an AUP? If so, explain.

Have you ever been denied Internet or other information systems services? If so, explain.

Have you ever knowingly violated laws, regulations, or the rules or AUPs of an information system provider, including work or home Internet service?

Have you created computer programs, configured or managed information systems, or otherwise participated in computer systems administration? If so, briefly describe.

Have you ever been accused of or been responsible for an information systems outage, failure, intrusion, or security incident? If so, describe.

Have you ever participated in unauthorized file sharing, unauthorized access to digital content (e.g., software, music, movies, files), or similar unauthorized systems activities? If so, explain.

Have you ever connected unauthorized devices (including memory media, modems, personal digital assistants, wireless Internet, cell phones, music pods, tablets, etc.) to an information system belonging to an employer or someone else? If so, explain.

Please make any comment or statement you would like to add about your history of computer systems and Internet use.

These suggested forms are not intended to provide all-inclusive, legally vetted wording for all businesses and government agencies, but they are a starting point from which policies and procedures can be created.

Notes

1. The Internet investigation policy presented here was developed in the course of my consulting for business, government, and academic clients over the past 8 years.
2. Federal job discrimination laws summary, http://www.eeoc.gov/facts/qanda.html (accessed April 25, 2014).
3. McCullagh, Declan, Want a Job? Give Bozeman your Facebook, Google Passwords, *CNET News*, June 18, 2009, http://www.cnet.com/news/want-a-job-give-bozeman-your-facebook-google-passwords/ (accessed April 25, 2014).

Chapter 23

A Model Internet Posting Policy

Government agencies, businesses, and other organizations should consider adding instructions on Internet posting to their authorized use policy, employee handbook, confidentiality agreements, and disciplinary procedures. Employees, contractors, and other authorized users can post to the Internet from work and from home, and items online can be destructive to the enterprise if they are untrue, unauthorized, or illicit. Anonymous slander of businesses and agencies is relatively common online, posing challenges, including identification of the perpetrator and a response to contain the potential damage. The following is a succinct statement of a model posting policy[1]:

> The Internet is important to us as individuals and to our enterprise because so many people communicate and rely on information they find online. False, inaccurate, slanderous, or illicit postings can be damaging to the enterprise, our suppliers, partners, and our customers. We depend on our communications, marketing, and human resources departments to post enterprise messages online, including on our website and on other websites. Because of the risk of mixed messages, miscommunication, and unlawful and damaging data online, all employees and contractors are required to adhere to the following:
>
> - Enterprise e-mail addresses and official titles are not to be used in Internet postings or communications except as part of approved business functions.
> - Internet postings and communications should not include references to the enterprise without prior coordination with and approval from the appropriate department and your manager.

- Employees and contractors shall not post items on the Internet that depict in text, photos, videos, and so on enterprise functions, data, uniforms, events, or plans unless they are approved in advance by the appropriate manager.
- Employees and contractors shall not engage in activities or post items on the Internet that are illegal, illicit, antisocial, or offensive or could discredit or reflect badly on the enterprise.
- Employees and contractors who find Internet postings believed to discredit the enterprise should bring them to the attention of management and the security department.
- In the event that an employee or contractor is found responsible for a posting or communication that is at odds with enterprise policy or is damaging to the interests of the enterprise, appropriate disciplinary action will be taken, up to and including dismissal.

Besides a stated policy, organizations should consider additional awareness and training measures to deal with the fact that large numbers of employees and contractors are active online, with social networking and other profiles and activities. It is impossible and counterproductive to prevent employees and contractors from posting their employment details online. Recruiting, marketing, and a host of other business functions benefit from the public face of the enterprise on the Internet. However, it is important to have the support of all insiders in protecting the organization from negative postings. Therefore, an enterprise-approved approach to postings on such sites as LinkedIn, Facebook, and photo- and video-sharing services should be communicated to authorized users so that they will have guidance and can more easily comply.

A common problem for employers is employee postings that are considered illicit or antisocial. Such postings can reflect badly on an enterprise, damaging its reputation, when it is apparent from postings that the misbehaving individual is an employee or contractor. Even when there is no direct liability or attribution to the enterprise, the disrepute caused can extend beyond the poster to the employer. Proper Internet posting etiquette should be promoted in training and briefings.

Contractual obligations with suppliers, customers, partners, and others can be impacted by postings of employees, contractors, and their associates, especially when they refer to inside information or reveal proprietary materials. Enterprise reputation and security could be at stake. Insider trading and confidentiality rules by the Securities and Exchange Commission (SEC) and other regulators could be violated by rogue postings. Awareness and training for employees and contractors should include reminders to protect proprietary data belonging to the enterprise and all of its contractor/partner organizations.

Among the considerations to be included when addressing Internet activities are the confidentiality agreement used by many businesses and government agencies and the approach to employees who are undergoing disciplinary procedures or punishments, considered for layoff, in a dispute, or pending dismissal. Disgruntled employees may vent online in their own name, in another person's name, or anonymously. The personnel and security departments should formulate an approach that anticipates and mitigates the risk that a disgruntled employee could use the Internet to attack the enterprise. Case law supports the enforcement of confidentiality agreements in such cases.

Employees and contractors have a First Amendment right to express themselves as they wish, and experience has shown that references to employers online are overwhelmingly positive. Authorized Internet postings should be encouraged, including those on professional business websites likely to cast the enterprise and the employee in a positive light. Nevertheless, there should be sufficient direction in behavioral standards and guidelines to discourage improper and unlawful Internet postings.

Note

1. The Internet posting policy presented here was developed in the course of my consulting for business, government, and academic clients over the past 8 years.

Chapter 24

Internet Intelligence Issues

Introduction

This book does not pretend to solve all the issues surrounding Internet investigations, cybervetting, and intelligence, but it will allow any practitioner or organization to establish the foundation for sound methodology, policies, and procedures. The urgency of the need to address Internet behaviors and data available online is illustrated in this book, but perhaps a bit more discussion would be useful for both cyber investigations and ethics.

Privacy

Discussing Internet searching with an executive officer of a law enforcement, intelligence, or security function elicits the view that their agencies are free to use the Internet to collect public information about an individual or entity without question. The same discussion with corporate clients and attorneys, and some government attorneys, for the past 8 years has elicited different views, as have the relatively few published court and academic legal opinions. Uncertainty over what privacy means on the Internet has paralyzed individuals and organizations, who understand the issue of web postings' potential threat to an enterprise's well-being, and that paralysis means that there are no Internet search standards. Despite the favorable view in the courts (see Chapter 8) that public postings are not protected, doubt persists. Internet searching as an area of professional practice has probably suffered because of this uncertainty.

The International Association of Chiefs of Police (IACP), in conjunction with the Department of Defense Personnel Security Research Center (PERSEREC), conducted a study to determine appropriate guidelines for developing cybervetting and Internet posting policies for law enforcement and the intelligence community (IC). The IC guidelines remain unpublished, but their contents are essentially the same as the December 2010 publication, "Developing a Cybervetting Strategy for Law Enforcement," available from IACP.[1] Because the study carefully involved legal, privacy, human resources, law enforcement, and intelligence experts and aimed for a balanced approach acceptable to a consensus of sometimes-opposing views, the guidelines represent the best effort of all stakeholders and authorities. They remain, so far, unique in available guidance for any organization.

The Privacy Act of 1974 as amended (5 U.S.C. 552a) does not contain a definition of privacy, and the act itself restricts federal government maintenance and disclosure of information about individuals and permits people to access and correct records about themselves. Generally, federal and state laws, and decisions upholding privacy rights, recognize a "right to be left alone" and to have a "reasonable expectation of privacy" in one's home and certain other nonpublic places.[2] Computers, networks, and the Internet create additional venues where it is necessary to gauge the extent to which an individual has a reasonable expectation of privacy.

A working definition of *Internet privacy* is the ability to control the information revealed about oneself on the Internet, which implies that a person has the right to post items in a restricted manner without fear that those items will be used in a way that the person did not intend.

This concept, however, confronts the physical world's legal standard of "plain view" because anyone, including government authorities, have a right to collect and act on what can be seen in plain view. In fact, law enforcement is sworn to act on unlawful behavior, contraband, and other illicit observations in plain view—ignoring criminal behavior is not an option. Regardless of the intentions of the individual uploading content to the Internet, if the posting is placed in plain view, there is no reasonable expectation of privacy. At least two layers of plain view exist, in my opinion: items that a poster intends for a number of other persons to see and items that are protected from display to all but a very few persons (or only their proprietor). In either case, when privacy is invoked by the requirement to use authentication for access (e.g., a user name and password), then there is an expectation of some degree of privacy. One could argue that on Facebook, for instance, there is no expectation of privacy on a public profile—it is in plain view. On a profile visible to all 1 billion-plus Facebook users, again, there is no reasonable expectation of privacy. On a profile visible to a large number of "friends" (e.g., 30 or more people), it would be difficult to argue that the poster has effectively kept the materials to himself or herself. Only if the posted items are restricted to a small group could the poster expect that they are private, although anyone of the group viewing the items could theoretically reveal them to others, for example, by copying and posting them in a public forum. For all such postings, the objective test of privacy is whether the public or other people have free access to them. Although the intent of the poster is important, if the materials are visible to others, they are not private. They are in plain view.

The plain view description provided is complicated by the unintended consequences of posting on a site where programs may make items visible, or actively disseminate them, to other viewers. For instance, Facebook has introduced several privacy settings changes (and rescinded some under user pressure) that caused a person's postings to appear on his or her friends' profiles. Another example is LinkedIn updates on contacts, which create thumbnail entries in a user's home page whenever a contact does certain things, such as update his or her photo or profile. The attempt to market through social and business networking sites also makes users' data available to businesses affiliated with them. All of these fly in the face of privacy and the user's ability to control the dissemination of the data posted.

It is useful to consider the mechanisms used to protect the privacy of the information stored on a website in assessing whether it is in plain view. When a posted item is indexed by a search engine and displayed in search results to all users, it is clearly in plain view. Because the same method (user name and password) is employed to protect one's banking and credit transactions, society has come to accept this form of authentication as a protective barrier, behind which data remain private. You log on to the bank website. You log on to Facebook, MySpace, or whatever social site. However, there are at least two modes of protection when log-on credentials are needed: information exposed to all or a substantial number of members who can also log on and that body of postings to which access is supposed to be denied except by express permission of the user. Just because the authentication is similar, that does not mean that Facebook data enjoy the same privacy protection as online banking. Clearly, items posted on social sites do not enjoy protection from those with authorized access, in the inner circle of the individual's profile, and from any programming designed to share data by pushing it to others online. It is the nature of the exposure allowed by the poster, within the access allowed by the website, that determines the degree of privacy reasonably expected for data placed online.

For investigators, the plain view approach to privacy is both ethical and fair. If a user is naïve or unlucky or ignorant enough to broadcast—actually publish—data that are of use to an inquiry, then it is appropriate for the investigator to find and collect them. Users overwhelmingly choose little or no protections for postings[3] and therefore have no claim to privacy of their published data in plain view—although recent surveys show that while teens are more apt to post many personal details, adults increasingly desire to protect their information online, realizing that many personal details about them are available on the public Internet.

Smoking Guns

Some agencies and companies have made an effort to discover the types of materials posted that could pose a danger or problem for them as an employer. In every instance, it has been possible to find publicly visible, outrageous behavior online. Examples of the kinds of problems that arise were provided previously and include illegal and illicit activities by public servants and senior employees, outrageous postings that defame the employer, law enforcement officer misbehavior that impairs criminal justice and court functions, treasonous leaks by intelligence personnel, and insider revelations that violate intellectual property protection and stock trading laws.

In guidance for cybervetting provided in an American Bar Association publication,[4] a CareerBuilder study was quoted that demonstrates the utility of Internet searches, listing the top reasons from findings online that caused no-hire decisions:

- 50%—Posting provocative/inappropriate photos or information;
- 48%—Posting about drinking or using drugs;
- 33%—Bad-mouthing a prior employer;
- 30%—Bad communication skills;
- 28%—Making discriminatory comments related to race, gender, religion, and the like;
- 24%—Lying about qualifications.

Employers are already dealing with complaints about, and accidental discovery of, individuals' misbehavior online, including facts found on the Internet that would have resulted in no-hire or termination decisions had they been known. Based on my firm's experience, many highly responsible positions are filled without cybervetting, costing corporations considerable sums when disqualifying facts are learned—too late. The cost of cybervetting may be a factor in the decision not to engage in cybervetting. However, the price of even a few wrong hires outweighs that of cybervetting, especially with regard to the key positions with the highest risk of loss if the person selected is a bad choice.

Most serious online misbehavior detected results in administrative sanctions against employees (e.g., firing or discipline), so most cases of this type do not appear in public. For medium-to-large enterprises, Internet issues are a daily or at least weekly occurrence. The Internet and people's uses of it are evolving much faster than are organizations' measures to address emerging online security problems.

Completeness of Internet Searching

The vastness of the Internet and wide variety of activities raise a question about what constitutes a thorough search. Some personnel departments during background investigations arbitrarily combine a Google search with queries of Facebook, MySpace, Twitter, and other popular social networking sites, ignoring hundreds or thousands of other types of online data. Each enterprise should define what constitutes sufficiency of Internet searching for its purposes, based on a risk assessment and cost-benefit analysis of vetting requirements and methods. Complicating this calculation is the fact that there are thousands of websites that promote and host illicit activities, from extramarital affairs, to exchange of copyrighted works without permission, to sale and purchase of stolen property. Most illicit sites are part of the "dark Web," that is, they are not indexed by Google and will not appear in casual Internet search results. Many users of the illicit websites will engage in illegal activities without ever being brought to justice. Frequently, the pseudonyms (handles) used in illegal transactions are also found in postings that allow identification of the individuals using them. By correlating the results of astute searches with identifying information on hand, analysts can identify those involved in online misbehavior, especially if they are sloppy and prolific posters.

In addressing the issue of what would constitute a comprehensive view of the Internet, an enterprise may wish to consider which illicit websites may pose a threat. Habitual users of such websites would probably represent an unacceptable risk. For example, an individual in the habit of sharing digital films or music outside copyright restrictions would be a high-risk hire for a movie or recording studio. An animal rights protester would be a risky new employee at a pharmaceutical research firm engaged in animal testing. A bank would not want to hire someone who bought and sold stolen credit card information online. As part of its own security protection, an employer may wish to analyze those websites posing the greatest threat and document, to the extent possible, those individuals known to use the sites. There are Internet intelligence firms that offer the capability of searching the virtual identities of candidates against data captured from the deep web. Intelligence of this type can be crucial in background vetting.

As Internet investigations mature, there are at least several types of due diligence that will be added to those routinely conducted today:

■ A thorough, automated search of Internet-accessible sites and databases for references to a subject's true name, virtual identities, activities, and associates.
■ A search of captured data from illicit websites continuously maintained by Internet intelligence service providers (probably private, not government).
■ A defensive scan of Internet activities by employers (or their outsourced service providers) to find postings potentially dangerous to the enterprise. This is done today for such purposes as brand protection, market assessment, and stock monitoring.

It is likely that services such as those described will be provided by the same large data vendors that today furnish government and business with intelligence from large files on people and businesses. Small service providers will include private investigators and researchers.

Adjudication

All investigative and intelligence work requires a customized, actionable product, presented in a timely fashion to a decision maker. The Internet age has made the intelligence process easier, yet complicated the process with a glut of data, some of which is decidedly less trustworthy than traditional sources. When I was privileged in the 1980s to take a course at the Defense Intelligence College in the literature of intelligence from the great Walter Pforzheimer, the first legislative counsel for the Central Intelligence Agency,[5] I was struck by his insight into the difference between published accounts of spy stories and the cases themselves (as they appear in government files and the recollections of working officers). Having participated with another great man, Tom Troy, in researching the history of the Federal Bureau of Investigation (FBI) and CIA (for his authoritative books on Bill Donovan and the CIA),[6] I had learned that historical fact and fiction are often intertwined in publications. These lessons had been learned as well in seeing the difference between news accounts of FBI cases that I investigated, supervised, and managed and what J. Edgar Hoover was apt to call "true facts." What other kind of facts are there? Apparently, Internet facts. It takes more than a healthy dose of skepticism to judge the results of Internet investigations and to make the resulting intelligence trustworthy.

Making fair and factually supported decisions about people and organizations requires cogent review of all the relevant information available, assessing accurately that which is most reliable. The Internet is full of plausible but untrue data, yet the quantity of factual information far outweighs the falsehoods. Careful evaluation can and does produce a worthwhile product. The investigator, supervisor, and adjudicator must understand how to make valid judgments based on Internet data that are integrated with all other source information. In addition, a process for balance in weighing the value of the information found is available in the guidelines used for adjudicating eligibility for access to classified information. Its principled approach allows the kind of judgments that will withstand scrutiny and tests of fairness. In my experience, routinely discussing findings with a subject and using a team of senior managers to make decisions that can be adverse are necessities in today's litigious society. Enterprises need people—all of us flawed—who can be oriented, trained, and mentored to succeed. When a relatively minor past mistake is found, that should not be the only reason for an adverse decision. In the national security arena, it is vital that trustworthy people be hired and granted clearances. In law enforcement, only the most reliable should be issued a badge and a gun. In granting access to computer systems as a trusted user, especially in the nation's critical infrastructures—largely private enterprises—only those worthy should be selected.

Conclusion

Internet searching and cybervetting have become a vital part of the investigative and intelligence processes. Increasingly, background investigations depend on it. Despite the gaps that exist in current law and the hesitation of some, Internet-sourced information should become an integrated part of findings for government, the private sector, and anyone involved in the information business. The notion that privacy and morale are impediments seem laughable at this time in history. Applicants and even students who are preparing to be candidates for business and government positions expect that their postings will be found and reviewed as part of the vetting process.[7] The public would be horrified to think that someone could engage in notorious behavior blatantly posted online that is ignored by an employer. Litigation may be brought by some who will be punished for their blatant Internet misbehavior, but there is no basis in law for their claims. Fair and ethical vetting will produce much better background investigations, and people have already learned that what one puts online can get a person in trouble.

During 8 years of learning how to conduct Internet intelligence collection and reporting, I have been indebted to my son Edward J. Appel, Jr., Elizabeth Renzette, Tiffany King, Tracey Kropff, and Dr. Roberta Griffith, as well as my friend Jim Emerson, for what our team has been able to do. They taught me that there is a professional, right, and ethical way to do what is described in this book, and the quality of the intelligence results from thousands of cases reflects the quality of these exceptional people.

Notes

1. Available at http://www.iacpsocialmedia.org/Portals/1/documents/CybervettingReport.pdf (accessed April 26, 2014); I conducted and co-wrote this material.
2. Privacy Act of 1974, as amended, http://www.justice.gov/opcl/privstat.htm (accessed April 26, 2014). In *Griswold v. Connecticut* (381 U.S. 479), the Supreme Court overturned convictions of the director of Planned Parenthood and a doctor at Yale Medical School for dispersing contraceptive-related information, instruction, and medical advice to married persons, asserting the right to protect one's individual interest in independence in making certain important and personal decisions about one's family, life, and lifestyle. Case law continues to uphold individual privacy.
3. According to Pew Internet and American Life, the trend among older teens is to share more online: see Teens, Social Media and Privacy, http://www.pewinternet.org/Reports/2013/Teens-Social-Media-And-Privacy/Main-Report/Part-2.aspx (accessed January 21, 2014); also, Anonymity, Privacy and Security Online, September 2013, suggesting that there is growing adult concern about protection of privacy and personal information online, although details are available about most, see http://www.pewinternet.org/2013/09/05/anonymity-privacy-and-security-online/ (accessed April 26, 2014).
4. Jodka, Sara, The Dos and Don'ts of Conducting a Legal, Yet Helpful, Social Media Background Screen, Law Practice Today, American Bar Association, September 2013, http://www.americanbar.org/content/newsletter/publications/law_practice_today_home/lpt-archives/september13/the-dos-and-donts-of-conducting-a-legal-yet-helpful-social-media-background-screen.html (accessed April 26, 2014).
5. Walter Pforzheimer died at age 88 in 2003.

6. Troy, Thomas F., *Donovan and the CIA: A History of the Establishment of the Central Intelligence Agency* (Frederick, MD: University Publications of America, 1981).
7. Pew Internet and American Life, Anonymity, Privacy and Security Online, September 2013, and other Pew studies, see http://www.pewinternet.org/2013/09/05/anonymity-privacy-and-security-online/ (accessed April 26, 2014).

Index

A

Abuse online, *see* Crime and misbehavior
    online
Activism, 201
AdvancedBackgroundChecks, 218
Adventure junkie, 33
Aggregator websites (Web 2.0), 218
AI, *see* Artificial intelligence
AltaVista, 194
Amazon, 53, 203
Americans with Disabilities Act, 88
America Online (AOL), 10, 27, 75, 104
    chat, 206
    e-mail, 28, 137
Analyst's Notebook, 227
Anonymous identity, 106
AnyWho.com, 219
AOL, *see* America Online
Artificial intelligence (AI), 230
ASIS standards, 128–131
    background checking, 128
    CareerBuilder study, 129
    government records, 130
    identification and attribution, 131
    job requirements, 128
    risk to privacy, 129
    unlawful discrimination in hiring, 128
Ask.com, 10, 194
Association of Internet Researchers, 132–135
    assumptions, 133
    ethical pluralism approach, 132
    fair game, 134
    guidelines, 132–133
    legal requirements, 133
    public forum participants, 134
    questions of disclosure, 132
    utilitarian, 134

    valuable concepts, 133
    virtual worlds, 132
AT&T, national white and yellow pages, 219
AUP, *see* Authorized use policy
Authorized use policy (AUP), 3
    constitutional rights, 84
    enterprise strategy, 261
    Facebook, 198
    liability for service providers, 76
Automated searching, 225–236
    best-in-class desktop tool, 229
    caching and data mining, 232–233
        daunting task, 232
        great equalizer, 233
        HyperText Markup Language, 232
        search utilities, 232
    enterprise search middleware, 227–228
        analytical and visualization tools, 227
        data mining, 227
        enterprise database software tools, 227
        intranet applications, 227
        targeted markets, 228
        web crawling, 228
    homegrown solution, 231
    human interface in Internet investigations,
        233–235
        collection of intelligence, 233
        ethics, 234
        lessons learned, 233
        open-source intelligence, 235
        pretexting, 234
        privacy, 234
        undercover operators, 233
    investigative search tool requirements,
        229–231
        artificial intelligence, 230
        databases, 229

government agencies, 230
LexisNexis, 229
true references, identification of, 229
metasearch tools, 225
middleware, 225
purpose, 226
  capabilities, 226
  core processes, 226
  list of websites, 226
reducing analytical time using automation,
  231–232
  logic and intuition needed, 232
  multitask process, 231
  new practitioner, 231
software types, 225

B

Babel.com, 206
Behavior online, 25–38
connections and disconnecting, 34–36
  attempt to expunge revealing references,
    36
  business and government leaders, 36
  cottage industry, 35
  "eighty best friends," 34
  removal of embarrassing materials from
    websites, 35
evolution of Internet uses, 29–34
  adventure junkie, 33
  BYOD, 32
  demographic data, 30
  handheld devices, 31
  highest percentages of Internet use 30
  increased bandwidth, 29
  mobile tools, 31
  online role-playing game, 33
Internet use growth, 25–29
  blocking of employee Internet surfing, 29
  core vulnerability, 28
  derogatory information, 26
  destructive increase, 25
  e-mail providers, 28
  most popular websites in the United
    States, 28
  personal online activities at work, 27
  phenomenon, 25
  social engineering, 27
  social networking sites, 26
  user passwords, 28
  wireless telephone networks, 27
physical world, virtual activities, 34

Behavior and technology, 1–2
  changes in Internet use, 1
  employees, 1
  implications of illicit behavior, 1
Best practices, 49
Better Business Bureau, 214
Bing, 10, 27, 194
  intentions driving, 71
  search software provided by, 205
Black-hat hackers, 44, 251, 257
Blogs, 205
Botnets, 173, 251
Brain trust, exodus of, 81
Brick-and-mortar business, 72
Bring your own device (BYOD), 32, 121
Business-related sources, 214–215
BYOD, *see* Bring your own device

C

Cached pages, 193
Caching, data mining and, 232–233
CAGR, *see* Compound annual growth rate
California Database Protection Act (CDPA), 89
CareerBuilder study, 129, 284
CDPA, *see* California Database Protection Act
Central Intelligence Agency (CIA), 86, 286
Children's Online Privacy Protection Act
  (COPPA), 88
CIA, *see* Central Intelligence Agency
City of San Diego v. Roe, 99
Civil litigation, 154
Civil Rights Act of 1964, 78, 88
Clinton, William, 118
Cloud
  services, 4
  stolen document stored in, 68
Clusty.com, 195
Commercial searching, *see* Search techniques
Compound annual growth rate (CAGR), 4
Computer Fraud and Abuse Act, 44, 87, 110
Computer Security Act of 1987, 88
Confrontational interview, 245, 246
Consumer Privacy Bill of Rights, 118
Copernic, 215
  Agent Personal, 229
  Agent Professional, 229
  search software provided by, 205
COPPA, *see* Children's Online Privacy
  Protection Act
Copyrighted works, exchange of, 45
Corporate contraband, 77

Corporate data mining, 227
Cracker method for intrusions, 144
Craigslist, 203
Crime and misbehavior online, 39–47
    by the numbers, 40–41
        "bottomless pit" of relentless crimes, 41
        criminal conspiracies, 40
        reporting of Internet crime, 41
        types of criminal investigations, 40
    digital delinquency, 42
    electronic evidence linked with Internet
        protocol connectivity, 39
    FBI computer forensic laboratories, 39
    "free" intellectual property, 42–44
        anti-cybercrime enforcers, 43
        black-hat hacker, 44
        digital records, 44
        digital rights management, 43
        gray-hat hacker, 44
        law enforcement, struggle of, 43
        prosecutorial choices, 43
        white-hat hacker, 44
    insider, 44–45
        copyrighted works, exchange of, 45
        digital evidence, 45
        Internet advertising, 45
        privileged access, 44
        risk of loss from insiders, 44
        trend toward indiscreet behavior, 45
    Internet Crime Complaint Center, 40
    Internet of things, 39
    misbehavior online, 46
    online venues, 41–42
        criminal enterprises, facilitation of, 42
        employer responsibilities, 41
        Internet Relay Chat, 41
        organized Internet crime, 42
    threats, 39
Cromer v. Lexington-Fayette Urban County
    Government, 108
Customized subtasks, 177
Cyber bullying case (first US), 110
Cybercrime, 249–255
    botnets, 251
    child pornography and Internet porn,
        250–251
    contraband digital assets, 253–255
    dumpster diving, 251
    examples, 249
    international organized criminals, 252
    knockoff watches, 254
    malicious code, 252

    unauthorized use of computer systems,
        251–253
    zombie, 251

D

Dark Web, 285
Data mining, 14, 227, 232–233
Davis v. Gracey, 102
Decision engine, 194
Deep web business search, 214
Demographic data, 30
Dialog.com, 215
Digital forensic evidence, 62
Digital rights management (DRM), 43, 65
DNS, *see* Domain Name System
Doe v. 2TheMart.com, 105
Dogpile.com, 195
Domain Name System (DNS), 190
Domestic principles, *see* International and
    domestic principles
Driver's Privacy Protection Act, 88
DRM, *see* Digital rights management
Dumpster diving, 251
Dun & Bradstreet, 222

E

EarthLink, 104
Economic espionage, 141
ECPA, *see* Electronic Communications Privacy
    Act of 1986
Electronically stored information (ESI), 111
Electronic Communications Privacy Act of
    1986 (ECPA), 87
E-mail providers, 28
Employee Polygraph Protection Act, 88
Employees
    accountability for, 79–81
    administrative sanctions against, 284
    blocking of Internet surfing by, 29
    compromise of insider account, 28
    dismissal, 106
    employer liability and, 61
    employer monitoring of online misbehavior,
        60
    felony crime committed by, 80
    illicit behavior on the Internet by, 1
    irresponsible, 137
    millennial, 137
Endicott Interconnect Technologies Inc. v.
    National Labor Relations Board, 106

Enterprise, *see* Implications for the enterprise
Equal Employment Act, 60
Equal Employment Opportunity Commission, 88
Equal Opportunity Employment Act, 270
ESI, *see* Electronically stored information
Espionage cases, 79
EU Data Privacy Protection Act, 93
Exalead, search software provided by, 205
Excel database, 232
ExpertRank, 194

F

Facebook, 53, 282
    authorized use policy, 198
    quantity of data uploaded, 13
"Face time" video telephone calls, 75
Factiva.com, 215
Fair Credit Reporting Act (FCRA), 15, 60, 86, 110, 128, 238, 272
False social networking profiles, 18
Family Educational Rights and Privacy Act, 88
FatCow.com, options for website owners, 220
FBI, *see* Federal Bureau of Investigation
FCRA, *see* Fair Credit Reporting Act
FDA, *see* Food and Drug Administration
Federal Bankruptcy Act, 88
Federal Bureau of Investigation (FBI), 255
    agents, arrest of, 80
    collection of information by, 125
    computer forensic laboratories, 39
    Director, 39
Federal Information Security Management Act (FISMA), 87
Federal Rules of Evidence and computer records, 91–93
    admissibility and authenticity of evidence, 91
    authentication and veracity, 93
    case law, 93
    hearsay rule, exception to, 92
First Amendment right, 279
FISMA, *see* Federal Information Security Management Act
Flash Player, 189
Flickr, 52, 218
Food and Drug Administration (FDA), 186, 255
Friendfeed, 218

G

Garcetti v. Ceballos, 99, 106
Geolocation-based services, 203
Gigablast, 194
GoDaddy.com, options for website owners, 220
Google, 27, 53
    e-mail, 28, 137, 221
    hacks, 193
    intentions driving, 71
    search software provided by, 205
Government sources, *see* Sources (finding)
Gramm-Leach-Bliley Act of 1999, 15, 86
Gray-hat hacker, 44
Griffin v. State of Maryland, 99
Guidelines, *see* Model cybervetting investigative guidelines
GuideStar, 213

H

Handheld devices, 31
Hanssen, Robert, 67, 80, 143
Health Guide USA, 213
Health Insurance Portability and Accountability Act of 1996 (HIPAA), 15, 86
Hearsay rule, exception to, 92
HIPAA, *see* Health Insurance Portability and Accountability Act of 1996
Hiring
    gold standard for, 60
    unlawful discrimination in, 128
Homeland Security Act of 2002, 87
Hoover, J, Edgar, 150, 286
Hotmail, 28
HTML, *see* HyperText Markup Language
HyperText Markup Language (HTML), 189, 232, 264

I

IACP, *see* International Association of Chiefs of Police
ICQ, 206
Illicit websites and illegal behavior online, 249–260
    cybercrime, 249–255
        botnets, 251
        child pornography and Internet porn, 250–251

contraband digital assets, 253–255
  dumpster diving, 251
  examples, 249
  international organized criminals, 252
  knockoff watches, 254
  malicious code, 252
  unauthorized use of computer systems,
    251–253
  zombie, 251
information (cyber) warfare, 256–258
  attribution, 257
  background of, 256
  great equalizer, 256
  humanity, 258
  journeymen cyber warriors, 257
  major attacks, 256
pirated goods, 249
Implications for the enterprise, 59–70
  employer liability, 61–62
    attribution of documentation, 62
    deep pockets, 61
    digital forensic evidence, 62
    illicit employee behavior, 61
    potential cost in lost bandwidth, 62
    technospeak, 62
  evolving personnel security model, 65–69
    admitting prior misbehavior, 67
    candidate trustworthiness, 66
    computer misuse at home, 67
    digital rights management, 65
    insider as traitor, 67
    post-September 11 (2001) impetus, 65
    scrutiny, 65
    sociological trends, 66
  new user (trust), 60–61
    cell phones, 60
    employer issues, 61
    gold standard for hiring, 60
    recent trends, 60
    value of enterprise data, 61
  social media vetting, studies of, 59
  surveys, 59
  vetting, monitoring, and accountability,
    62–64
    attribution for online misbehavior
      controversy, 62
    cynics, 63
    privacy, 63
    social contract, 63
    user accountability policy, 64
IM services, *see* Instant messaging services

iNameCheck cybervetting case study, 54–57
  Adjudicative Guidelines, 54
  derogatory findings, 54, 55
  implications of review, 56
  important observations, 56
  serious risk, 56
Information (cyber) warfare, 256–258
  attribution, 257
  background of, 256
  great equalizer, 256
  journeymen cyber warriors, 257
  major attacks, 256
Insider threat, 141–145
  agency leaders, 142
  benevolent big brother, 143–144
    cracker method for intrusions, 144
    inevitable balance, 144
    insider threat solution, 143
    need for good behavior online, 144
    social engineering, 144
  economic espionage, comparison to, 141
  "friending" applicants, 142
  narrow thinking, 142
Instant messaging (IM) services, 216
Intelligence issues, *see* Internet intelligence
    issues
Intelligence reporting, *see* Internet intelligence
    reporting
International Association of Chiefs of Police
    (IACP), 281
International and domestic principles, 117–126
  government standards, 122–125
    candidate disclosure, 124
    clearance standards, 123
    Executive Orders, 123
    explicit authority, 125
    Joint Security Commission, 124
    personnel security measures, 124
    Public Internet postings, 124
  parallel guidance (Internet research ethics),
    125
  US and international privacy principles,
    117–122
    BYOD, 121
    collection and use of information,
      principles of, 117
    communications, 122
    Consumer Privacy Bill of Rights, 118
    executive order, 118
    mitigating factors, 119
    mobile devices, proliferation of, 120

reliability factor, 118
socially irresponsible behavior online, 119
U.S. Government information system, conditions of, 121
whole person concept, 118
Internet advertising, 45
Internet Crime Complaint Center, 40
Internet intelligence issues, 281–288
adjudication, 285–286
lessons learned, 286
true facts, 286
completeness of Internet searching, 284–285
dark Web, 285
due diligence, 285
illicit websites, threat of, 285
privacy, 281–283
Facebook, 282
intelligence community, 282
Internet privacy, working definition of, 282
plain view description, 283
public postings, 281
smoking guns, 283–284
administrative sanctions against employees, 284
CareerBuilder study, 284
cost of cybervetting, 284
outrageous behavior online, 283
Internet intelligence reporting, 237–247
analyst's comments, 240–241
circumstances, 240
critical facts, 241
example, 240
inappropriate opinion, 240
attribution, 243–244
bottom line of cybervetting guidance, 238
content, 238–240
information capture, 239
principles of reporting, 239
records keeping, 238
ways to approach, 239
organization and formatting, 241–243
decision support report type, 241–242
report on a company, 242
report on a person, 242
structure, 241
topical headings, 243
paper trail, 238
records, 238
serial murderer, 237

source citations, 243
verification, 244–247
confrontational interview, 245, 246
friending the subject, 246
friendly stranger, 246
inability to verify report, 245
open-source intelligence, 247
virtual identities, 244
work-related googling, 237
Internet privacy, working definition of, 282
Internet Relay Chat (IRC), 41, 16, 206
Internet searching, framework for, 147
Internet search methodology, 177
Internet service provider (ISP), 71, 87, 221
Internet's potential for investigators and intelligence officers, 3–23
authorized use policy, 3
finding the needles, 19
growth of Internet use, 4–12
cloud services, 4
compound annual growth rate, 4, 6
demographics of Internet users, 7
digital evidence, 9–10
diversity of Internet use, 4
googling applicants, 10
implications, 9
new neighborhood, 11
nonbusiness activities, 8
objection to cybervetting, 11
record of past behavior, 11
role-playing games, 9
search engines, evolution of, 10
social networking, 12
Internet posts and the people they profile, 16–18
false social networking profiles, 18
Internet Relay Chat, 16
personal profiles, 17
third-party postings, example of, 18
need for speed, 19–20
counterproductive investigative methods, 19
phenomenon, 20
search and analysis tools, 19
practitioner's perspective, 12–13
dossier, 13
marketing and sales, 13
open-source information, 12
professionals, 13
profiling, 12
public availability, 3

search, 13–16
  casual searching, 16
  Facebook, quantity of data uploaded, 13
  global data created and replicated, 13
  haunting conclusion, 14
  number of queries made, 14
  personal approach to searching, 15
  telephone directory, Internet as, 16
  sufficiency of searches, 20
Internet of things, 39
Invasion of privacy torts, 107
Invisible Web, 181, 185
IRC, *see* Internet Relay Chat
ISP, *see* Internet service provider

J

JavaScript, 189
Joint Security Commission, 124
Journeymen cyber warriors, 257

K

Kindle (Amazon), 203
Knockoff watches, 254
Konop v. Hawaiian Airlines, 102

L

Laws, 83–96
  Americans with Disabilities Act, 88
  California Database Protection Act, 89
  Children's Online Privacy Protection Act,
    88
  Civil Rights Act of 1964, 78, 88
  Computer Fraud and Abuse Act, 44, 87
  Computer Security Act of 1987, 88
  constitutional rights, 83–85
    authorized use policy, 84
    illegal collection of information, 84
    litigation, 84
  Driver's Privacy Protection Act, 88
  Electronic Communications Privacy Act of
    1986, 87
  Employee Polygraph Protection Act, 88
  Equal Employment Act, 60
  Equal Opportunity Employment Act, 270
  Fair Credit Reporting Act, 15, 60, 86, 128,
    238, 272
  Family Educational Rights and Privacy
    Act, 88
  Federal Bankruptcy Act, 88

Federal Information Security Management
    Act, 87
Federal Rules of Evidence and computer
    records, 91–93
  admissibility and authenticity of
    evidence, 91
  authentication and veracity, 93
  case law, 93
  hearsay rule, exception to, 92
Gramm-Leach-Bliley Act of 1999, 15, 86
Health Insurance Portability and
    Accountability Act of 1996, 15, 86
Homeland Security Act of 2002, 87
international treaties and standards, 93–94
  Canadian Personal Information
    Protection and Electronic
    Documents Act, 93
  Council of Europe Convention on
    Cybercrime, 93
  EU Data Privacy Protection Act, 93
  existing laws, summary of, 94
National Labor Relations Act, 88
Privacy Act, 15, 85, 282
Privacy Protection Act, 102
Public Information Act (Freedom of
    Information Act), 86
Sarbanes-Oxley Act, 15
statutes, 85–91
  criminal infringement, 88
  federal background screening laws, 88
  federal statutes, 85–89
  Oklahoma Social Networking and Social
    Media Policy and Standards, 90
  state statutes, 89–91
Title VII of the Civil Rights Act 1996, 88,
    130
Uruguay Round Agreements Act, 88
USA Patriot Act, 86
Legal and policy context, 71–73
  brick-and-mortar business, 72
  collection of user data, 72
  free services, 171
  Google, 72
  intentions driving search engine providers, 71
  Internet service providers, 71
  US Congress, 171
Legislation, *see* Laws
LexisNexis, 212, 229
Liability, privacy, and management issues, 75–82
  accountability for employees, 79–81
    arrest of FBI agents, 80
    brain trust, exodus of, 81

espionage cases, 79
felony crime, 80
personnel management, 80
liability for employers, 77–79
applicant background investigations, 78
areas of concern, 78
avoiding serious liability, 78
questioning of candidates, 79
virtual identities, 79
liability for service providers, 75–77
authorized use policy, 76
corporate contraband, 77
courts, 76
"face time" video telephone calls, 75
government agencies, 75
"one-stop shopping" firms, 75
role of commercial Internet portal, 75
telecommunications networks, 76
LinkedIn, 53, 200
Litigation, 97–116
admissibility of electronically generated and
stored evidence, 111–112
electronically stored information, 111
memo's guidance, 111
anonymity, 99–100
City of San Diego v. Roe, 99
*Cromer v. Lexington-Fayette Urban County
Government*, 108
Davis v. Gracey, 102
Doe v. 2TheMart.com, 105
due process, 103–105
analysis, 103
authentication of online information,
105
central issues, 103
comment, 103
court ruling, 104–105
*Endicott Interconnect Technologies Inc. v.
National Labor Relations Board*, 106
expectation of privacy, 100–103
court's two-part test, 100
lower court decisions, 100
Supreme Court, 101
US Court of Appeals for the Armed
Forces, 101
Garcetti v. Ceballos, 99, 106
Griffin v. State of Maryland, 99
Internet privacy for the twenty-first century,
108–110
conflict, 109
"false" pseudonym, 110

first US cyber bullying case, 110
relevant issues, 109
Internet search litigation, 97–99
cases, 98–99
decisions against employers, 98
employee claim, 97
US Government employee, 97
invasion of privacy torts, 107
Konop v. Hawaiian Airlines, 102
libel/defamation, 105–106
anonymous identity, 106
comment, 106
court criteria, 105
employee dismissal, 106
Lorraine v. Markel American Insurance Co.,
111
Oja v. US Army Corps of Engineers, 107
Omnibus Crime Control and Safe Streets
Act, 100
Pietrylo et al. v. Hillstone Restaurant Group,
98
Raytheon Company v. John Does 1–21, 104
sanctions for public postings, 107–108
Stacy Snyder v. Millersville University, 108
trends and legal challenges to investigative
searching, 112
United States v. Charbonneau, 102
United States v. Ziegler, 102
Live Journal, 218
Lorraine v. Markel American Insurance Co., 111

M

Malware, 174
Mama.com, 215
Mamma.com, 205
Management issues, *see* Liability, privacy, and
management issues
MapQuest, 194
Meetup.com, 201
Metasearch engines, advantage of using, 195
Microsoft
Bing, 10, 194
e-mail, 137
options for website owners, 220
Middleware, 225, 227–228
Mobile devices, proliferation of, 120
Mobile tools, 31
Model cybervetting investigative guidelines,
261–267
authorized Internet search (cybervetting)
personnel, 265–266

adverse findings, 266
ethics, 265
important elements, 266
definitions to consider, 266
enterprise strategy, 261–263
authorized use policy, 261
norms, 261
reason for cybervetting, reiteration of, 262
unrestrictive approach, 262
model Internet search guidelines, 263–265
conducting of Internet searches, 263
decision making, 265
Equal Employment Opportunity law, 264
guidelines, 263
results of Internet searches, 263
Model Internet investigation policy, 269–276
application procedures and forms, 271–272
argument, 272
attorney belief, 271
privacy, 271
recommended information, 271
confidentiality, 273
disciplinary action, 274
Equal Opportunity Employment Act, 270
ethics in investigations, 273
higher-risk candidates, 270–271
key considerations, 270
legal issues, 272–273
conditional offer of employment, 272
Fair Credit Reporting Act, 272
honesty of candidate, 272
illegal activities detected, 273
options, 272
model forms for candidates, 274–275
consent, 275
notice, 274
questionnaire, 275
personal pursuits, 269
references, 269
Model Internet posting policy, 277–279
anonymous slander, 277
awareness and training measures, 278
contractual obligations, 278
enterprise reputation, 278
First Amendment right, 279
statement, 277–278
Monittor, 218
"Most wanted" poster, 213
MyLife, 218
MySpace, 53, 136, 199

N

National Association of Professional
Background Screeners, 131–132
competition, 132
FCRA standards, 132
purpose, 131
standards, 131
National Institute of Standards and Technology (NIST), 88
National Labor Relations Act (NLRA), 88
National Labor Relations Board (NLRB), 106
National Security Agency (NSA), 86
National Student Clearinghouse, 222
NetworkSolutions.com, options for website owners, 220
News media, 150
Nexis.com, 215
NIST, *see* National Institute of Standards and Technology
NLRA, *see* National Labor Relations Act
NLRB, *see* National Labor Relations Board
NSA, *see* National Security Agency

O

Obama, Barack, 124
Oja v. US Army Corps of Engineers, 107
Oklahoma Social Networking and Social Media Policy and Standards, 90
Omnibus Crime Control and Safe Streets Act, 100
"One-stop shopping" firms, 75
Online role-playing games, 33, 127
Open-source intelligence policy, Internet vetting and, 149–156
abuse, 149
information assets protection, 155–156
authorized users, 155
core tenets, 155
individual privacy, 155
legal step, 156
legal and ethical limitations, 150–152
anonymity of users, 151
categories of stored information, 152
entertainment and social networking sites, 151
ethical standards, 152
internal applications, 150
Internet hosts, 150
Internet retailers, 151

news media, 150
true facts, 150
need for policy, 149
policy, 153–155
best-available intelligence assessments,
153
civil litigation, 154
false positives, 154
googling restriction, 153
indiscretion in Internet postings, 154
legal departments, 153
principles, 153
Society for Human Resource
Management, 154
Open-source intelligence process, 163–166
accuracy of information, 164
attribution of posting, 165
authoritativeness of the source, 165
client's requirements, 163
eyewitness reports, 164
misbehavior, 163
principles of research, 164
reporting of results, 166
verification of online data, 165
Organized Internet crime, 42

P

Page, Larry, 10
PalTalk.com, 206
Paper trail, 238
Pay-as-you-go online service, 180
PDF, *see* Portable Document Format
PeopleFinders, 218
PeopleSmart, 218
Photobucket, 52
Pietrylo et al. v. Hillstone Restaurant Group, 98
Pinterest, 53
Pipl, 218
Pirated goods, 249
Planning, *see* Preparation and planning
POGO (Project on Government Oversite)
website, 213
Policy, *see* Model Internet investigation policy;
Model Internet posting policy
Porn-social sites, 201
Portable Document Format (PDF), 232, 264
Posting policy, *see* Model Internet posting policy
PPA, *see* Privacy Protection Act
Preparation and planning, 179–187
fee-based service, 180
incomplete search, 181

invisible Web, 181
keywords, 179
library, 182–184
confidentiality, 183
reference transactions, definition of,
183
search tips, 183
today's library, 183
pay-as-you-go online service, 180
reverse directories, 179
scope notes, 184–186
constraints imposed on searchers, 184
invisible Web, 185
planning, 186
search strategies, 185
specialized activities, 184
starting point, 185
time and effort, 184
Pretexting, 234
Prime Time Publishing Company, 213
Privacy Act, 15, 85, 282
Privacy issues, *see* Liability, privacy, and
management issues
Privacy Protection Act (PPA), 102
Procedures for internet searching, 169–175
criteria, 170–172
analogy, 170
ethical responsibilities, 172
inept googling, 171
metaphor, 171
philosophical baseline, 170
reliability of sources, standards for, 171
tipping point, 171
types of intelligence, 170
nature of data, 169
necessary controls, 169
security, 172–175
botnets, 173
browser choices, 174
chain of custody, 174
malicious code, 172
malware, 174
organized criminal groups, 173
porn, 173
social engineering, 173
viruses, prevalence of, 173
standard methodology, 175
Professional standards and the Internet,
127–139
ASIS standards, 128–131
background checking, 128
CareerBuilder study, 129

government records, 130
identification and attribution, 131
job requirements, 128
risk to privacy, 129
unlawful discrimination in hiring, 128
Association of Internet Researchers,
132–135
assumptions, 133
ethical pluralism approach, 132
fair game, 134
guidelines, 132–133
legal requirements, 133
public forum participants, 134
questions of disclosure, 132
utilitarian, 134
valuable concepts, 133
virtual worlds, 132
bottom line, 138
guidance, 127
inside and outside the workplace, 136–137
example, 136
fundamental mistake, 136
millennial employees, 137
monitoring, 136
librarians, 135–136
approach, 135
indexing, 135
pathway to publications, 136
National Association of Professional
Background Screeners, 131–132
competition, 132
FCRA standards, 132
purpose, 131
standards, 131
online role-playing games, 127
reputational risk, public affairs, 137
"anonymous" identities, 137
false reports, 137
irresponsible employees, 137
SEC regulations, 137
trade media, 137
Programming languages, 189
Prosecutorial choices, 43
Protest groups, 201
Public Information Act (Freedom of
Information Act), 86

Q

Quality control, 166–167
accuracy, 166
common mistake, 166–167
contents of findings, 166
fairness, 167
timeliness, 167

R

Radaris, 218
Raytheon Company v. John Does 1–21, 104
Raytheon Digital Information Gateway, 227
Real-time spidering, 194
Reference transactions, definition of, 183
Reverse directories, 179
Reverse IP address lookup service, 221
Role-playing games, 9

S

Sarbanes-Oxley Act, 15
Search techniques, 189–208
browser, 190–191
popularity of browsers, 190
URL storage, 191
zombie, 191
finding search engines, 195
Internet content, 189–190
Domain Name System, 190
HyperText Markup Language, 189
programming languages, 189
stock market updates, 189
types, 190
metasearch engines, 195
advantage of using, 195
disadvantage, 195
search engine, 191–195
AltaVista, 194
Ask.com, 194
Bing, 194
cached pages, 193
decision engine, 194
Gigablast, 194
Google hacks, 193
real-time spidering, 194
refinement of search results, 194
SimplyHired.com, 194
search terms, 196–197
algorithms, 196
information not indexed by search
engines, 196
normal impulse, 197
references not identifiable, 196
time factor, 197
variations of names, 196

social and commercial searching, 197–206
   activism, 201
   AOL chat, 206
   blogs, 205
   chat, 205–206
   competition, 203
   contentious issues, 205
   Craigslist, 203
   directories, 204
   e-commerce sites, 202–203
   Facebook's authorized use policy, 198
   Geolocation-based services, 203
   googling a roughly worded question,
      204
   IRC users, 206
   LinkedIn, 200
   MySpace, 199
   porn-social sites, 201
   protest groups, 201
   publicity, 199
   search software providers, 205
   social networking sites, 197–202
   true name searches, 199
   webcams, 206
   YouTube, 199
SEC, *see* Securities and Exchange Commission
Securities and Exchange Commission (SEC)
   filings, 144
   regulations, 137
ShoutMix.com, 206
SHRM, *see* Society for Human Resource
         Management
SimplyHired.com, 194
Slander, anonymous, 277
Snap.com, 194
Snowden, Edward, 68, 80, 86, 143
Social contract, 63
Social engineering, 27, 173
Social media vetting, studies of, 59
Social searching, *see* Search techniques
Society for Human Resource Management
         (SHRM), 154
Sources (finding), 209–224
   business-related sources, 214–215
      Better Business Bureau, 214
      caution, 214
      deep web business search, 214
      Yahoo business directory, 214
   commercial database providers, 222–223
      hard economic times, 223
      manual searches, 223
      misbehavior, types of, 222

      personal disputes, 223
      registered clients, 222
   database, 209–210
   disclaimers, 209
   e-mail, 221–222
      analysis, 222
      identifying "anonymous" e-mailers, 221
      message forwarding, 221
      message header, 221
      ploy, 222
      reverse IP address lookup service, 221
   looking up subscribers, 219–221
      AnyWho.com, 219
      options for website owners, 220
      Whitepages.com, 219
      Zabasearch.com, 219
   news, 215
      searching by subscription, 215
      strategy, 215
   other government-related sources, 213–214
      GuideStar, 213
      Health Guide USA, 213
      POGO website, 213
      Prime Time Publishing Company, 213
      World Bank, 213
   state, county, and local governments,
         211–213
      fees, 212
      LexisNexis, 212
      local record, 213
      "most wanted" poster, 213
      reference works, 212
      types of records, 212
      vital records, 211
   US government, 210–211
      post-September 11 (2001) online access,
         210
      sites for finding misbehavior, 210
   Web 2.0, 215–219
      aggregator websites, 218
      archival searches, 218
      commercial search engines, 218
      examples, 215
      instant messaging services, 216
      popularity, 216
      proclivity of users, 217
      real-time tools, 218
      search engines, 218
      value of online collaboration, 217
      web-based communities, 215
Spokeo, 218
Stacy Snyder v. Millersville University, 108

Standards, *see* Professional standards and the
 Internet
Studies (Internet search), 49–57
 academic study, 50–53
 derogatory findings, 51–52
 guidelines, 50
 lack of candor, 53
 most frequented websites, 53
 participant information, 51
 study summary, 51–53
 white paper, 52
 best practices, 49
 iNameCheck cybervetting case study, 54–57
 Adjudicative Guidelines, 54
 derogatory findings, 54, 55
 implications of review, 56
 important observations, 56
 serious risk, 56
 questions, 49–50
StumbleUpon, 53

T

Talkcity.com, 206
Techniques, *see* Search techniques; Tools,
 techniques, and training
Technospeak, 62
TeenChat.com, 206
Telephone directory, Internet as, 16
ThePlanet.com, options for website owners, 220
Third-party postings, example of, 18
ThompsonReuters.com, 215
Time/date stamp, 160
Title VII of the Civil Rights Act 1996, 88, 130
Tools, techniques, and training, 157–168
 analytical issues, 160
 "facts" found online, 159
 important decisions, 158
 key issues in investigations, 161
 open-source intelligence process, 163–166
 accuracy of information, 164
 attribution of posting, 165
 authoritativeness of the source, 165
 client's requirements, 163
 eyewitness reports, 164
 misbehavior, 163
 principles of research, 164
 reporting of results, 166
 verification of online data, 165
 quality control, 166–167
 accuracy, 166
 common mistake, 166–167

contents of findings, 166
 fairness, 167
 timeliness, 167
 reliable sources found on Internet, 159
 results, 157
 time/date stamp, 160
 training analysts, 162–163
 library, 163
 logging of activities, 162
 policies established, 162
 training, 162
 user requirements, 157
 verifying information found on Internet,
 159
Trackle, 218
Trade media, 137
Training, *see* Tools, techniques, and training
Traitor, insider as, 67
True facts, 150, 286
Tumblr, 53
Twitter, 27, 53, 218

U

Uniform resource locator (URL), 160, 182, 223
United States v. Charbonneau, 102
United States v. Ziegler, 102
URL, *see* Uniform resource locator
Uruguay Round Agreements Act, 88
USA Patriot Act, 86
US Comptroller of the Currency, 89
US Customs and Border Protection, 255
User accountability policy, 64
User passwords, 28
US Federal Rules of Civil Procedure, 154
U.S. Government information system,
 conditions of, 121
US legislative proposals, 94

V

Virtual identities, 79, 244
Viruses
 prevalence of, 173
 prevention of, 62–63
Vital records, 211

W

Web 2.0, 215–219
 aggregator websites, 218
 archival searches, 218

commercial search engines, 218
  examples, 215
  instant messaging services, 216
  popularity, 216
  proclivity of users, 217
  real-time tools, 218
  search engines, 218
  value of online collaboration, 217
  web-based communities, 215
Webcams, 206
Web crawling, 228
White-hat hackers, 44, 257
Whitepages.com, 219
Whole person concept, 118
Wiki, caution in using, 214
Windows Live, 27
Wireless telephone networks, 27
Work-related googling, 237
World Bank, 213
Worms, prevalence of, 173

Y

Yahoo, 10, 27, 53, 104
  agreement with Microsoft, 194
  business directory, 214
  catalog of search engines and directories,
    195
  e-mail, 28, 137, 221
  intentions driving, 71
  options for website owners, 220
  "term-and-conditions" agreement, 104
Yauba, 218
Yippy.com, 195
YouTube, 52, 53, 199

Z

Zabasearch, 218, 219
Zombie, 191, 251
Zoominfo, 218

T - #0111 - 101024 - C0 - 234/156/17 [19] - CB - 9781482238853 - Gloss Lamination